THE LANGUAGES OF SEXUALITY

Words, Freud once wrote, are magic. Nowhere have words been more magical than in the writing of sexuality. Through words and concepts we learn what is good or bad, pleasurable or painful, significant or insignificant. The terms we use about sexuality do not simply describe something out there – they help shape what sexuality is.

The Languages of Sexuality offers concise and incisive essays on key words and concepts which have played a significant role in shaping our understanding of contemporary sexualities and intimacies. Nearly a hundred essays illuminate the terms related to sexuality in fresh and often unexpected ways, with entries ranging from 'abjection' and 'abortion' to 'transgender' and 'Viagra'. Written with clarity, insight and passion by an internationally renowned theorist of sexuality, this book is not only an invaluable handbook, but also a personal exploration of the fluid, shifting, ever-evolving meanings of sexual life as reflected and refracted through words and concepts.

This book is an invaluable reference for both students and researchers with interests relating to sexuality and intimate life, gender studies, cultural studies, history and sociology. It will also appeal to a wider audience interested in critical debates about the nature and meanings of contemporary sexualities.

Jeffrey Weeks is Emeritus Professor of Sociology at London South Bank University, having previously held senior management posts there as Executive Dean, (Arts and Human Sciences), and University Director of Research. His publications have been chiefly concerned with the history and sociology of sexuality and intimate life, and he is the author of more than a hundred articles and over twenty books. Recent publications include *The World We Have Won* (2007) and *Sexuality, third edition* (2009).

THE LANGUAGES
OF SEXUALITY

Jeffrey Weeks

Routledge
Taylor & Francis Group

LONDON AND NEW YORK

First published 2011
by Routledge
2 Park Square, Milton Park, Abingdon, Oxon, OX14 4RN

Simultaneously published in the USA and Canada
by Routledge
711 Third Avenue, NY 10017

Routledge is an imprint of the Taylor & Francis Group, an informa business

British Library Cataloguing in Publication Data
A catalogue record for this book is available from the British Library

Library of Congress Cataloging in Publication Data
Weeks, Jeffrey, 1945–
The languages of sexuality / by Jeffrey Weeks.
p. cm.
Includes bibliographical references.
1. Sex. 2. Heterosexuality. 3. Homosexuality. 4. Gender identity.
5. Sex—Religious aspects. I. Title.
HQ21.W44 2011
306.7703—dc22   2010043369

ISBN: 978–0–415–37572–6 (hbk)
ISBN: 978–0–415–37573–3 (pbk)
ISBN: 978–0–203–93032–8 (ebk)

Typeset in Times New Roman
by Keystroke, Station Road, Codsall

FOR MARK

CONTENTS

CONTENTS

INTRODUCTION

I first thought of doing this book many years ago. I have written it in a shorter, more intense period, over the past couple of years. Given what it is, and sets out to do, it inevitably draws on my earlier writings, though much has changed, even between first conception and delivery of this particular book. Sexuality as a theme, a set of pleasurable and sometimes painful practices, a theoretical space, and a site of political passion, ethical debate and social mobilization, is a focus of ever-growing ideas, debate, conflict and creativity. This is not the book I would have written when I first dreamt of it. It is not even quite the book I first proposed to my ever-patient publisher. It is, however, the book I needed to write today, to reflect the richness of current preoccupations and thinking about the sexual. My fond hope is that it will help the reader to understand why sexuality is such a global issue. My aim is not to try to claim the final or definitive word on the concepts it describes, but to further discussion and debate on them.

I have been writing about the history, theory and social organization of sexuality and intimate life for a long time now, since the early 1970s. Then, to plunge into this subject area was a bit like jumping blindfold into a deep, dark pool of murky water. It was only when bobbing up for air for what might have been the final time that I realized what the core issues were. But writing about sexuality remained a hazardous career choice. As late as the 1980s I was warned by an extremely emi-nent sociologist that my career would benefit from writing about something different. I persisted, for good or ill, in researching, thinking and writing about the sexual. The subject could not let me go, or I could not let the subject go. Whatever, I have since written a great deal about the topic: about homosexuality, and heterosexuality and what used to be designated the perversions; about identities and non-identities, and social movements; about sexology and psychoanalysis, sexual research, and sexual theories; about changing patterns of gender, intimacy, families and friendship; about post- or late-modernity, globalization, the Web revolution and millennium blues; about sex-related diseases and the tragedy of HIV/AIDS; and about love and loss, and the importance of relationships. Sexuality is about all these and much more.

What I realized when catching my breath after my first immersion in the topic was that writing about sex involved more than simply talking about orifices, desire, behaviours and pleasures, important as they were. It was also, and above all, about the history, society, cultures and languages which gave meaning to acts, provided the context for the emergence of subjectivities, identities and beliefs, and made the erotic significant in human terms. Sexuality may be about bodies, but it is also about society. It is the social and cultural invention and construction of sexuality that has above all interested me. That is why this book is not so much about sexual activities as about ideas and concepts concerning sexuality. It is only through the languages of sexuality that we can fully understand its changing meanings and significance.

The inspirations for this book are many and varied, but two works sparked off the trajectory I followed. The first was the famous and influential book by Raymond Williams, *Keywords: A Vocabulary of Culture and Society*, first published in 1976. That book, Williams wrote,

> is not a dictionary or glossary of a particular academic subject. It is not a series of footnotes to dictionary histories or definitions of a number of words. It is, rather, the record of an enquiry into a *vocabulary*. . . . Every word which I have included has at some time, in the course of some argument, virtually forced itself on my attention because the problems of its meanings seemed to me inextricably bound up with the problems it was being used to discuss.
>
> (Williams 1976: 13)

In the same way I would say this is not a glossary of terms about sexuality – excellent examples of these can be found elsewhere (see, for example, Eadie 2004) – nor is it a dictionary, attempting precise definitions. It is a series of short essays on key concepts which have played a significant role in defining our understanding of human sexuality.

The second important influence was Jean Laplanche and J.-B. Pontalis's book *The Language of Psychoanalysis*, first published in French in 1967, and in English translation in 1973. The book is concerned with the concepts and language that Freud and subsequent analysts had to forge in order to grasp the complexities of the unconscious. In a similar way, *The Languages of Sexuality* offers insights into the ways in which theorists of sexuality have attempted, determinedly since the late nineteenth century, to find the words and vocabulary to talk about the erotic. Many of the terms used, of course, had a much older etymology, and where appropriate that information has been added in the entries here. But the core of each short essay is an elaboration of the changing meanings and interpretive significance of each concept. The ultimate aim, as was Laplanche and Pontalis's, is to provide a work-tool for researchers and students, as well as for the general reader, to understand not psychoanalysis in this case (though you will find an entry on psychoanalysis in this book) but sexuality.

But having claimed a lineage, I must also add that in the end this is my interpretation of the ideas discussed here. I am deeply indebted to many other writers, inevitably, and some of the key texts I have used can be found in the References at the end of this volume, though this is inevitably selective. Full references can be found in my other books, while those who have given me direct help are named in the Acknowledgements, with overwhelming thanks. But I have to make the usual disclaimer: the interpretations found here are mine alone, and I take full responsibility for them. Sexuality is a fiercely contested field. I am not a neutral observer. I was there for many of the critical debates. My own writings have contributed to the meanings I hope to explicate. At the same time I try to be fair even to opinions I abhor, and to concepts I have disagreed with.

The Languages of Sexuality is organized alphabetically. Each short essay (ranging in length from 800 to 2,000 words, but most around 1,000 words), describes the evolution of the term, and discusses its contemporary meanings and deployment. Cross references to related concepts are indicated in bold in the text. I have not attempted to provide an entry for every possible term. I have preferred to discuss some concepts within a wider framework where its development makes more sense. So, for example, you will not find a separate entry for Michel Foucault's concept of 'discourse', though sexual discourses are referred to in a number of entries. Judith Butler's concept of 'performativity' is not separately listed; it is discussed under **Gender**, **Queer** and elsewhere. 'Race', a crucial element in theorizing contemporary sexuality, is examined under **Intersectionality**, **Mixedness**, and in other places. 'Heteronormativity' is similarly discussed under **Heterosexuality** because that seemed to me an appropriate place to discuss the development of ideas of heterosexuality as a social institution as well as a sexual preference. On the other hand, you will find a separate entry for **Sexuality**, even though the whole book is about that topic. This is because I wanted to show the complexity and evolution of the term. The Index will help the reader to negotiate these cross-references.

This is an appropriate place to add a note on terminology. This can be a potentiality fraught area. Consider the evolution of the word **Queer**. Regularly used by homosexuals themselves in the 1950s and 1960s, it was pretty much tabooed in the 1970s and 1980s as an offensive term of abuse, before making an unlikely comeback in the 1990s as a description both of new forms of militancy *and* of a complex shift in sexual theory, which flourished mightily in the academy and journals, perhaps less so on the streets. **Gay** had a related evolution, from a grassroots euphemism for homosexual, through becoming a mark of liberationist militancy, to normalized descriptor of same-sex lives. It was the very ordinariness of the term, interpreted as a mark of assimilation into heteronormativity, that gave push to the re-adoption of queer. Use of the terms in my own comments therefore needs some sensitivity to context and time. I have tried to dodge some of the hazards by using a relatively new term LGBT – Lesbian, Gay, Bisexual, Transgender. The collective term has the advantage of being all-embracing in a way that gay no longer is. But even here the ground is treacherous. This is often extended by adding a Q – standing for both Queer and Queerying; an I – for intersexed; and even H – for heterosexual. I have decided for brevity to stick to the shorter form, whilst being sharply aware that this might rapidly prove anachronistic. Another term that carries problems is 'postmodern', with its related forms of 'postmodernity' and 'postmodernism'. There has been a lively debate about their meanings, and about their relationship to sexuality (see Simon 2003). I have decided in this book to use a more neutral term that acknowledges both periodization and a wider social and cultural context for shifts in the forms of sexuality, but avoids some of the controversies – 'late-modernity'. Again I am aware that in avoiding one set of debates, I am entering another, perhaps just as controversial. The dilemma is in the end unresolvable. All I can do is acknowledge that my own selection of language positions me very precisely within a specific set of assumptions, theories and political affiliations that I have tried to be open and honest about. It is for you, reader, to make up your own mind about my intentions and interpretations.

No book of this sort can hope to be exhaustive, and I would certainly not wantto claim that. It focuses largely on historical, sociological and cultural interpretations rather than biological or psychological meanings. I am a historically-minded sociologist, or a sociologically-minded historian, by training and expertise, with a long interest also in political and cultural theory. That intellectual bias has no doubt inflected my selection of concepts and my exegeses of them. But as I have emphasized already, it is history, culture and society that gives prominence and meaning to sexuality in the modern world. This book offers a mosaic of ideas about the sexual which I hope will help clarify the issues and controversies that surround it. My hope is that you will find it enjoyable as well as enlightening.

Jeffrey Weeks

ACKNOWLEDGEMENTS

This book may have been written in the recent past but it draws on research and writing I have been involved in since the 1970s. It draws on a much vaster body of work by others, some of whom I have worked directly with, others I have only briefly met at seminars or conferences or socially, and yet others I have encountered only in their writings. My debts to all of them are enormous. It is impossible to list everyone who has influenced or helped me in so many different ways, but I want to thank particularly the following for their help and support, intellectual, moral, professional, economic, technical, and emotional: Peter Aggleton, Richard Allen, Dennis Altman, Maks Banens, Meg Barker, Henning Bech, Gerry Bernbaum, Chetan Bhatt, Sue Bruley, Claire Callender, Bob Cant, Eric Chaline, Tom Claes, Raewyn Connell, Matt Cook, Andrew Cooper, Emmanuel Cooper, Gill Davies, Philip Derbyshire, Catherine Donovan, Rosalind Edwards, Anna Einarsdottir, Richard Ekins, Debbie Epstein, Mary Evans, Clare Farquhar, Liz Fidlon, Jane Franklin, Anthony Giddens, Val Gillies, Harry Goulbourne, Beverley Goring, Leslie Hall, Jane Harmer, Brian Heaphy, Gert Hekma, Janet Holland, Deian Hopkin, Kate Hudson, Jackie Jones, Jonathan Ned Katz, Dave King, Don Kulick, Jane Lewis, Karin Lutzen, Stina Lyon, Derek McGhee, Mary McIntosh, Anamika Majumdar, Theo van der Meer, Rommel Mendes-Leite, Martin Mitchell, Mike Molan, Henrietta Moore, Gareth Owen, David Paternotte, Ken Plummer, Kevin Porter, Paula Reavey, Paul Reynolds, Robert Reynolds, Tracey Reynolds, Diane Richardson, Philippe Rougier, Sheila Rowbotham, Gayle Rubin, Lynne Segal, Steven Seidman, Carol Smart, Donna Thomson, Rachel Thomson, Randolph Trumbach, Matthew Waites, Simon Watney, Elizabeth Wilson, Tamsin Wilton.

For enduring kindness over many years now I want to thank the McNestry family: Ann and Joe; Tim, Pauline and Christopher; and Marie and Richard, Manny, Frank and Hannah Prime. I owe who and what I am to my own family, the Weeks clan: Dennis, Siân, Craig and Chloe; Karen, Paul and Lauren (Jones); Robert, Paula, Kier, Geraint and Rhys; Margaret and Robert (Howe) and boys; and above all my dear mother, without whom nothing would have been possible.

Angus Suttie lived with much of my early writings, and was an invaluable comfort and loyal supporter until his premature death in 1993. I honour his memory. My friend Micky Burbidge has been a continuous thread in my life since my student days. His ill-health in recent years reminds me of the importance of resilience, stoicism and courage in the face of adversity.

As ever I must thank above all my life-partner Mark McNestry without whose constant love, encouragement, care and support nothing at all could be written. Words are too feeble to express my gratitude to him. In the past year we have had a new addition to our lives, Ziggy. He has proved both a constant distraction and a permanent delight. This book was written while struggling to cope with his every need, total devotion, and occasional barks. I wouldn't have had it any other way.

Several of the entries in this book were published in substantially different forms elsewhere: 'heterosexuality', 'homophobia' and 'homosexuality' in Elizabeth Wright (ed.) *Feminism and Psychoanalysis: A Critical Dictionary*, Oxford: Blackwell, 1992; 'fetish', 'gay and lesbian', 'pornography' and 'sexuality' in Tony Bennett, Lawrence Grossberg and Meaghan Morris (eds) *New Keywords: A Revised Vocabulary of Culture and Society*, Oxford: Blackwell, 2005. I am grateful to the publishers for permission to use these here. Other concepts were first elaborated in some of my earlier books and articles, and I here express my deep gratitude for the support I have received from editors and publishers throughout my writing career.

A

ABJECTION

The formal definition of abject and abjection refers to the state of being cast out, rejected, degraded, abandoned, humiliated, and has been used in English since the mid-seventeenth century. It has gained a particular meaning in cultural criticism and sexual theory largely since the publication of the French theorist Julia Kristeva's *Powers of Horror: An Essay on Abjection* (Kristeva 1982; first French publication 1980), though it has a longer pre-history in French literature.

For Kristeva, abjection is a universal psychosexual process which the child goes through in breaking away from the primary relation with the mother, and establishing the boundaries of self and others in the mirror stage. Human development requires the casting out of the potentially pleasurable messiness, disorder and chaos of biological essences, such as excrement, blood, mucous. It is necessary to put these aside as the human infant enters the symbolic order, the order of language and the law. But these elements are so much part of us, they cannot easily be obliterated, and their return has to be constantly guarded against, policed by feelings of revulsion, disgust, horror and fear of bodily decay. The abject represents a threat to meaning, identity and order, but it evokes a constant and disturbing attraction and even pleasure. Repulsion at and fascination with the corpse is a characteristic note. It also feeds into a sense of horror and the uncanny which underpins our fascination with the horror genre. By extension these feelings can move beyond the individual to wider cultural contexts, so abjection as a concept has been used to theorize the casting out, and execration of, marginalized and feared groups, whether women, racial minorities, the diseased, or the sexually despised, such as homosexuals, at various points of history, as unclean, dirty, defiling and contaminating, and their own feelings of degradation and humiliation. But the abject also offers a space for recuperating what has been rejected. It has been particularly influential in the development of French **Feminism**, offering a site of female sexuality that is outside the Phallic order. Kristeva's approach has, however, been criticized like so much other psychoanalytically inflected theory for its universalism. Stallybrass and White (1986: 200–1), rather than seeing this as a universal phenomenon, explicitly relate the concept to the effects of the modern shaping and regulation of sexuality.

1

Though framed in psychoanalytical terms by Kristeva, the concept does not appear directly in Freud and only in passing in Lacan (Halperin 2007: 69, and 144, note 117), though it has been used widely by psychoanalytically inclined **Queer** theorists in relation to the peculiar horror that homosexuality seems to evoke in some groups, and the self-hatred and shame manifest amongst many gay people themselves (Bersani and Phillips 2008). It has found a particular intellectual purchase in attempts to explain the extreme emotions generated by the HIV/**AIDS** crisis from the early 1980s, particularly in the fear and loathing directed against gay men in the USA and other ostensibly advanced liberal societies, who are seen as precisely polluting. The reluctance of many gay men to engage in safer-sex activities, and especially the vogue for **Barebacking** (unprotected anal intercourse between men) has been explained in terms of the death drive propelling them to self-annihilation, the psychic effects of oppression and shame (Dean 2000).

The most passionate and sustained effort from within queer theory to challenge both psychoanalytic and psychological (that is, as he sees it, individualizing) explanations for gay abjection has come from Halperin (2007). He seeks to recover the concept as a social and cultural trope, which recognizes both the massive personal and collective impact of rejection and exclusion, and of the possibilities of resistance, survival and transformation which is characteristic generally of the history of same-sex activity and in particular of the response to the HIV/AIDS epidemic. The novels of Jean Genet ('Saint Genet' in Jean-Paul Sartre's evocative phrase) are the *loci classici*. Genet's degradation and abandonment as a thief, a prostitute, a passive homosexual are transfigured in his writings, especially *A Thief's Journal*, into a form of salvation ('sainthood') and exaltation, 'discovering in the very act of surrender and abasement the erotic and spiritual means of your own transformation and transfiguration' (Halperin 2007: 76). In the same way, Halperin suggests, the experience of abjection amongst gay men overwhelmed by the loss and fear of the epidemic, is not the symptom of an unconscious drive to self-destruction but is a strategic response to a collective not individual problem: how to survive a torrent of hate directed at those threatened by a syndrome of diseases deeply implicated with sexual activities, and how to maintain a culture of resistance, sexual inventiveness and solidarity in the face of horror. Abjection in this reading now becomes one avenue towards understanding gay subjectivity as a social and cultural configuration.

This is a very particular if potent interpretation. Abjection no longer makes any claim to be a scientific concept as interpreted by psychology or psychoanalysis. Instead it becomes a metaphor which helps to illuminate very specific historical experiences.

ABORTION

Abortion, the termination of a woman's pregnancy by conscious intervention, has a fraught history. All cultures and religious faiths have sought to find ways of responding to it, in a variety of different ways, while in recent years it has become a moral and political battlefield, especially in the USA, but increasingly globally. Today about a third of women still live in jurisdictions where abortion is illegal, and in other countries where it is legal decisions about it are usually surrounded by limits and restrictions, concerning the period during which termination is allowed, the conditions under which a decision to abort may be made, and who can make a decision to proceed. At the same time abortion is widely resorted to, whether it is legal or illegal, the result of conscious choice or enforced by cultural norms, or violence. Abortion as an issue remains at the heart of debates on sexuality, because it is widespread – over 40 million women worldwide are estimated to have abortions every year – and because it raises critical issues about the control of female sexuality. At the heart of the prolonged and often anguished debates about abortion are two apparently simple but actually highly complex questions: 'When does life begin?' and 'Who has the right to decide about whether or not to proceed with a pregnancy?'

Until the advent of effective contraception, abortion was probably the most common form of birth control, and the only one that lay effectively within the domain of women. All the great religious traditions – Buddhism, Hinduism, Judaism, Sikhism, Islam and Christianity – wrestled with how to control it, though only the mainstream Catholic and Orthodox traditions have remained firmly opposed in all normal circumstances. But it has become central to religious and moral concerns only in modern times, in response to the industrial and urban revolutions and the population explosions that followed them. If anything, Roman Catholic strictures against abortion have become more and more explicit since the nineteenth century, and are probably more firmly expressed now in the twenty-first century – equated by one leading spokesman for the Church as equivalent to terrorism against the unborn child – than ever before. This has been in large part a response both to its huge prevalence and to the growth through the past century of campaigns to legalize and legitimize it. In reaction to attempts in Weimar Germany to decriminalize abortion, and to modest Anglican attempts towards accepting forms of artificial birth control, Pope Pius XI issued the encyclical *Casti Connubii* in 1930, on Christian marriage, denouncing abortion alongside all other forms of artificial birth control. Pope Paul VI's encyclical *Humanae Vitae* in 1967, despite widespread hopes of liberalization of attitudes towards birth control, reaffirmed the Catholic position, seeing artificial birth control and abortion as an assault on human life, and this has become a bedrock article of faith. As a more recent Pope, Benedict, has affirmed 'what was true yesterday is true also today'. Opposition to abortion is an absolute.

The problem for the Church is that in the rapidly changing world of women since the nineteenth century, such truths have rarely if ever been self-evident. As the British sexologist Havelock Ellis observed in the early twentieth century, abortion 'scarcely appears to excite profound repulsion in a large proportion of the population of civilized countries' (Weeks 1981: 71), and he particularly mentioned its wide incidence amongst poor and working-class women. This was despite the

3

illegality and often draconian penalties against abortion, and the high incidence of fatalities that followed the use of illegal means. In the mid-1930s there were reported to be two million abortions in the USA, with 15,000 deaths of women: a fifth of all pregnancies ending in abortion. In England during the same period, abortion-related deaths amounted to 20 per cent of all maternal deaths. In the USSR, on the other hand, in the period following the Russian Revolution, Moscow had 80,000 abortions a year, with no related fatalities (McLaren 1999: 75). The difference being that abortion was, for the time being, legal. Abortions under conditions of illegality were highly dangerous, especially for working-class women. Wealthier women were always more likely to find a supporting medical practitioner. Most women resorted to more traditional remedies, or to what became known in Britain as 'back-street abortionists', usually women in the local female networks who became known for helping out, but usually in medically risky circumstances.

As Havelock Ellis hinted, amongst most women there was an acceptance of abortion as a legitimate form of controlling fertility, not so much as an expression of individual female autonomy as an essential aspect of protecting and maintaining their families by limiting its size. There was a widespread popular acceptance that life did not begin in the womb till 'quickening', estimated to be at eighty to a hundred days after conception, and the language used by women to describe abortion – 'bringing on a period' or 'making yourself regular' in Britain, 'faire passer' or 'faire descendre' in France – pointed to a highly pragmatic rather than a guilt-ridden attitude. This was confirmed by the widespread availability of quack remedies or abortifacients, often marketed openly in the press as 'female pills' and remedies. The laws against abortion were usually highly unpopular, making prosecuting authorities reluctant to use them.

From the early part of the twentieth century reformers in many European countries and the USA campaigned to liberalize the laws on abortion, though without much initial success. While some countries, like Sweden, decriminalized abortion in the late 1930s, Stalin outlawed abortion once again in the USSR in 1936, in response to fears of population decline. Such fears, whether in the form of openly fascist policies as in Italy and Germany after 1933, or in the more muted form of pro-natalist and eugenics policies elsewhere, militated against reform. Even birth control pioneers such as Marie Stopes in Britain and Margaret Sanger in the USA distanced themselves from any hint of support for abortion reform. Most East European countries legalized abortion in the 1950s under pressure from Moscow, but it was not until the 1960s and 1970s that most Western countries liberalized the laws – the 1967 Abortion Act in Britain was followed by similar reforms in most Western European countries in the next twenty years. In most jurisdictions there was no 'abortion on demand', as many feminists had argued for. On the contrary, abortion was usually deemed to be a health issue, requiring the approval of doctors before the termination could go ahead. But the immediate effect was to end the shame and illegality associated with abortion, and to end backstreet abortions.

The USA took a different route: abortion was legalized by the Supreme Court in the famous *Roe v. Wade* decision in 1973, less on the merits of abortion itself than on the grounds of a right to privacy, which overrode states' efforts to outlaw abortion. The decision has remained the fulcrum of the 'culture wars' ever since, as the debate became re-framed as a battle between two notions of rights: the right to choose, endorsed passionately by second-wave **Feminism**, and the right of the unborn child. The Women's Liberation Movement (WLM) from the late 1960s had put the old feminist claim of the right of women to control their own bodies at the heart of the new politics, with access to abortion the key demand. But *Roe v. Wade* was never accepted as legitimate by opponents, who have attempted ever since by legislation and Presidential attempts to change the composition of the Supreme Court to reverse the decision. The decision itself was a key factor in the rise of a moral Right, bringing together for the first time Catholic and evangelical Christians in a crusade not only against abortion but also in defence of the family and against homosexuality and sex education. The resulting controversy engendered a new climate of violence against pro-choice advocates. The twenty-fifth anniversary of *Roe v. Wade* was marked by a bomb attack on an Alabama abortion clinic, resulting in one death. Other attacks followed. Abortion had become a catalyst for moral and political divides unprecedented in the modern era.

The International Conference on Population and Development in Cairo in 1994 demonstrated that the right to choose in general, and abortion in particular, was inextricably tangled with wider questions of development and underdevelopment, poverty and the power of capital, as well as the role of **Religion** and who had the right to exercise control over women's bodies (Weeks 1995: 61). In a world where the use of abortion was part of a compulsory policy of one-child families, as in China, or a popular means of ensuring the birth of male children through female foeticide, as in parts of India, the right to choose necessarily also involved the right to refuse. **Choice** is never free, but is always shaped and delimited by economic, social and cultural contexts, by the individual circumstances in which a choice has to be made, and by the burden and responsibilities imposed on the chooser. Even when a choice is readily possible, abortion remains a dilemma for women. Pioneers of abortion reform in the twentieth century saw abortion as the lesser of evils in a world which imposed huge burdens on women and little choice. They looked forward to a world of effective contraception, and conditions where women were free to decide what was best for them and their families. Much has changed for the better on a global scale, and the number of abortions is declining as effective contraception becomes ever more available, but abortion continues to crystallize the uneven pace of change, and the moral and cultural divides that shape and limit sexual choice.

AGENCY

Agency is about the capacity of individuals to act in the world as free and self-determining actors, and as such has been a central, if highly debated, concept for both sociology and philosophy. Inevitably questions of agency also raise questions about limitations, and constraints, and in sociology the structure/agency debate has been a long-standing one. Do individuals exist prior to society? Does the social shape and determine subjectivity and identity? What is the balance between individual actions and social determination? How you see agency depends on where you position yourself on such questions.

Sexual agency raises such questions in an acute form. The debate within **Sexology** was for a long time about the degree to which individuals can exercise a degree of **Choice** around their sexuality within what were regarded as limits dictated by nature, especially along the two binaries of male/female, and **Heterosexuality/Homosexuality**. Nature offered the fundamental structure, and ultimate determination. As contemporary explorations of sexuality have rejected **Essentialism**, and followed more historical and sociological paths, and as issues of **Gender**, **Sexuality** and **Bodies** have become highly politicized, especially through **Feminism** and **Gay liberation**, so more sophisticated theories of the limits of agency have developed.

Sexual autonomy may be violated by the unwanted and unlimited exercise of another person's agency (as in rape). One's own agency may be restricted through material inequalities that inhibit opportunity, aspiration or hope, or in the everyday bonds that tie and restrict. The very idea of unencumbered agency is, for some theorists influenced by **Psychoanalysis**, undermined by the unconscious forces that destabilize the fixity of the self. The structures that inhibit sexual autonomy are shaped by the interlocking of a range of social and psychic forces, to the extent that agency is heavily classed, racialized and gendered (McNay 2000) – see **Intersectionality**. Agency is also deeply embodied. Bodies are objects of social practice, in the sense that they are acted upon, and inscribed with meaning; and agents in social practice. Connell (2009: 67) describes this process as body-reflexive practice, that is human conduct in which individual bodies are both subject and object. Gender and sexuality are particular, powerful forms of embodied practice, realized in different ways through particular configurations of power, and they powerfully delimit the possibilities of agency (McNay 2008: 195).

The limits to agency are strong, but so are the possibilities. Power may be omnipresent and inescapable, as Foucault (1979) suggested, but he also argues that where there is power there is resistance. The history of sexuality is more than a depressing catalogue of fruitless efforts by individuals to express their sexual needs and desires against the power of patriarchy, poverty, prejudice, religion, or whatever. Through all cultures and histories there is plentiful evidence of individuals exercising agency and resistance, within the limits of what is possible at any particular time, but also bending, twisting and expanding the possibilities of their societies. A few examples at random, evidenced across many different cultures, make the point: of women escaping oppressive relationships with men despite the weight of patriarchal tradition; of women creating cultures of knowledge about abortion and birth control despite heavy social restraints; of men and women ignoring taboos against homosexuality; of individuals and social groups that cross-dressed and carved out social roles. The temptation for some theorists is to see such examples as yet more evidence of the functional subtlety of power, creating deviant roles to keep the majority population in line, or allowing spaces for limited freedom to relieve intolerable social pressures. Resistance in such examples is little more than a gesture. But rather than focus on abstract notions of power/resistance, it is rather more productive to see these examples of resistant and oppositional practices as exemplars of the ways in which sexual agency slips through the gaps in power relations and social structures to create potential practices of autonomy and freedom, especially to the extent that they embody collective activity.

Increasingly in the contemporary world sexuality has become the focus of collective agency. The rise of the new social movements since the 1960s has provided an opportunity for a number of sexual subjects – women, lesbians and gays, bisexuals, transgendered people, sado-masochists, sex workers and so on – to present themselves on the stage of history, and make claims to rights and justice; see **Sexual diversity**. As Melucci (1989: 6) has argued, social movements are normally invisible networks of small groups submerged in everyday life. They tend to be preoccupied with individual needs and collective identity, and constitute laboratories where new experiences are invented and tested, and participants can develop alternative patterns of personal relationships. They rarely develop system-atic political programmes, though specific campaigns against forms of discrimi-nation or to change the law frequently appear. Motives for involvement are typically a mixture of practical objectives and moral and ethical stances: a feeling of insult, of subtle or not so subtle injury, of pain at suffering, or of outrage at prejudice and discrimination, and above all participants get involved because of the yawning gap between what current circumstances and values dictate and what participants want to become and do. The long-term effect of social movements tends to be to offer a symbolic challenge to the status quo, and to shape a new grammar of everyday life (Weeks 1995: 104). The sexual-social movements have been crucial in generating new voices and **Sexual stories** in recent generations, reshaping sexual ideologies, practices and possibilities.

The critical factor is that a sense of collective identity around sexuality empowers individuals to explore sexual needs and desires in new ways – see **Sexual identity**. Dissident sexual identities have been major vehicles for the exercise of agency. **Lesbian** and **Gay** identities, for example, have since the 1970s allowed millions of people to refashion their sense of self and to engage with the public world in new ways. Through interaction with and **Recognition** by others, people give meaning to their lives, achieve self-realization and self-fulfilment, and develop a sense of authenticity. Critics (McNay 2008: 164–5) have been sharply critical of the over-identification of identity politics and agency. They point to the voluntarism inherent in the emphasis on self-fashioning, and to the danger of naturalizing and essentializing identities, pointing out that identities can be imposed as well as freely chosen. This seems to miss the point, however. The sexual identities that have blossomed since may be culturally contingent and historically constructed but they have been realized and performed as meaningful, and have offered a powerful support for action in the world.

The networks, friendships and social worlds that have developed since the 1960s, especially around non-normative sexualities, have provided the context for a form of grassroots agency which sustains a push for change. A good example of this is provided by the emergence of **Same-sex marriage** as a key issue in LGBT politics. This was never an objective of early lesbian and gay politics, which was largely hostile to traditional marriage. The felt need for the legitimation of same-sex relationships came from the ground up, in response to a dual crisis: the problems encountered by same-sex parents, and the caring issue generated in the **AIDS** crisis. This led to a reorientation of LGBT demands towards relational issues.

This is only one example of a wider phenomenon. Since the 1950s in late-modern societies there has been a transformation of sexual and intimate life that to an extraordinary extent is the result of piecemeal, unplanned, pragmatic but profound shifts in the practices of everyday life, a **Great transition**. People in their millions have engaged in life experiments (Giddens 1992), exercising grassroots agency, not in circumstances necessarily of their choosing, nor always with great success, but in ways which have remade what it means to be sexual.

AIDS

AIDS (acquired immune deficiency syndrome) dramatically emerged in the early 1980s as a dangerous spectrum of opportunistic diseases, caused by HIV (the human immunodeficiency virus). Its first identification in the American gay community in 1980 heralded the beginning of a worldwide health pandemic. It also immediately became the focus of a social and cultural panic, an 'epidemic of signification', of fraught and painful meanings. It was an overwhelming tragedy for the communities most affected, and the individuals who lived and died with the virus. At the same time, HIV/AIDS threw a piercing light on many dark corners of contemporary sexual culture, condensing a number of social stresses and anxieties into a recognizable symbolic target (Weeks 1985). Above all it spoke to deep uncertainties about all the changes that had taken place in sexual behaviours and values over the previous decades. As the epidemic raged worldwide in the decades that followed, taking millions of people to a premature grave, and even threatening a fundamental breakdown in economic life in some parts of the world, the dangerous connection of sexuality, disease and death fed into an unprecedented sense of crisis.

One of the most striking features of the HIV/AIDS crisis at the start of the epidemic was that, unlike most illnesses, the people who were mainly affected by it, and lived and died with it, were chiefly blamed for causing the syndrome, whether because of their social attitudes or sexual practices. And as most people living with HIV/AIDS at the beginning of the epidemic in Western countries were gay men, this was highly revealing about current attitudes and feelings towards unorthodox sexualities. From the earliest identification of the disease in America, AIDS was addressed as if it were a peculiarly homosexual affliction, and the term 'gay plague' became the common description of it. Even the first official designation, GRID (Gay-related immune deficiency) marked out its presumed and charged boundaries. For conservative moralists this was 'Nature's revenge' on the supposed sexual excesses of gay men. Such attitudes provided an excuse for governments to ignore the crisis until it was almost out of control.

From the beginning, however, it was apparent that other groups of people were susceptible to the syndrome: at first Haitians (in the USA), intravenous drug users, and people with haemophilia, because of their dependence on donated blood; but soon many others. In large parts of sub-Saharan Africa, where the virus probably originally leapt the species barrier from animals to humans, and where it seemed to be endemic, it was the heterosexually active population that was chiefly affected, and it was therefore clearly transmittable through heterosexual intercourse. But it was the apparent connection between unorthodox sexual activity and the disease that largely fuelled the major elements of **Moral panic** in the industrialized West, and for a long time coloured responses across the globe.

AIDS was a genuinely appalling disease, which devastated the lives of many people, for which there was no cure, and which at first seemed unstoppable in its rate of spread. By mid-1985 it had become the largest single cause of adult male deaths in New York City and was widespread elsewhere. Anxiety was legitimate. However, the form that the anxiety took was a search for scapegoats, and here gay men were peculiarly vulnerable. Certain sexual practices (for example anal intercourse) and social habits (multiple partners), generally (though often misleadingly) associated with male homosexuals, were given a prime role in the spread of the disease, and it became easy to attribute blame to people with AIDS. From this a slippage readily took place: between the idea that homosexuals *caused* 'the plague' (without any backing in evidence), to the idea that homosexuality itself was a plague. Manifestations of what Susan Sontag called 'practices of decontamination' against the vulnerable soon appeared (Sontag 1989): restaurants refused to serve gay customers, gay waiters were sacked, dentists refused to examine the teeth of homosexuals, rubbish collectors wore masks when collecting garbage from suspected victims, prison officers refused to move prisoners, backstage staff in theatres refused to work with gay actors, distinguished pathologists refused to examine the bodies of AIDS patients, and undertakers refused to bury them. This reflected widespread fear and ignorance. Yet more significant was the toll of illness and death. The epidemic was a disaster for the gay community, above all in the USA. The hopes invested in the new sexual freedoms that developed in the 1970s were devastated by the immensity of loss and mourning, while the lack of basic rights for gay people was dramatized by the ways in which both people with HIV/AIDS and survivors were frequently marginalized, discriminated against and shamed. For a time it seemed likely that all the gains of the previous decades would be lost.

The scientific evidence already by the mid-1980s was clear (though 'denialists' continued to resist into the 2000s, and gained powerful supporters, such as President Mbeki of South Africa). AIDS was carried by HIV, which was not in itself exceptionally infectious. It was only possible to catch it through intimate sexual contact or interchange of blood and bodily fluids. It was not a peculiarly homosexual disease, and most people in the world with the disease were hetero-sexually infected. Its spread could be hindered by relatively small changes in lifestyle (though the changes proved often culturally difficult to embed). All this pointed to the need for public health campaigns which allayed fears, taught about prevention and promoted an awareness of **Safer sex**. At first morally conservative governments, especially in the USA and the UK, were reluctant to intervene. Eventually, across the rich and highly developed world, new health policies kicked in. But not before fear and ignorance produced a host of punitive responses. And as the pandemic spread inexorably across the globe, the pattern of fear, blame, wilful neglect, inconsistent response followed – with a vital difference. Whereas in the richer parts of the world, safer-sex practices and public health and prevention policies stemmed the spread of HIV, and expensive cocktails of drugs from the mid-1990s proved effective in slowing down the impact of multiple illnesses, in the majority of the world the epidemic was inextricably linked with poverty and a web of other diseases.

Just as in the West the reaction to the HIV/AIDS epidemic shone an illuminating light on deep-rooted anxieties and a prevailing climate of uncertainty, so in the rest of the world, the epidemic revealed structural inequalities, exploitation and the hazards of unprecedented sexual change. Vast disruptions of population in response to rapid industrialization, moves from country to city, migrations across borders, flight in the wake of war, eased the spread of sexual and blood-borne infections. Ignorance (for example, the apparent widespread belief in southern Africa that sex with a virgin would cure sexual infections) or prejudice (against condoms, for example, on the grounds that they were unmanly, or in the case of Roman Catholic countries, that they were also contraceptive devices) helped rapid transmission. Transnational travel carried the epidemic from continent to continent. The communications revolution and processes of **Globalization** brought knowledge of it to every corner of the globe.

By 2008 more than 25 million people had died of AIDS-related illnesses. Over 33 million people in the world were living with HIV and AIDS, half of whom were women. Two million were children. The majority of three million new infections and two million deaths were in sub-Saharan Africa. From South America to Southeast Asia, from Eastern Europe to China and India, new epidemics threatened, presaging economic and social collapse, population decline and ever greater numbers of orphaned children.

Science made many breakthroughs, from the discovery of the virus in the mid-1980s through to new drug therapies barely a decade later – but there was no 'magic bullet' in prevention or cure. Bio-medical efforts to prevent transmission had limited effectiveness, though by the end of the first decade of the new century there were signs of a slowing down of the spread of the virus, and the improvement of health education in the Global South. There was, moreover, a huge grassroots mobilization in the fight against AIDS (Altman 1994). Starting in the gay communities of Western cities, but spreading throughout the globe, there was an unprecedented development of community-based responses to HIV and AIDS, ranging from self-instruction in safer sex to advocacy, campaigning and treatment activism. Those most affected often took the lead in combating the epidemic, and in engaging with the medical and scientific establishments in a battle for credibility about who should be able to define the disease and the crisis (Epstein 1996). The gay community, ironically, eventually achieved a new legitimacy as it led the fight against AIDS. The international mobilization against HIV and AIDS, whether through official bodies like UNAIDS or in proliferating non-governmental organizations (NGOs), helped to develop an international discourse around sexual risk and sexual health – though frequently against the backdrop of state ignorance and neglect. Haphazardly and hesitantly at first, Western expertise and drugs began to alleviate some of the worst suffering. By 2008 some three million people were receiving anti-viral treatment in low- and middle-income countries. And sexual practices and identities that had been hidden in shame began to find their voice, and open themselves to history, and therefore change. HIV/AIDS, an unprecedented crisis in sexual behaviour, had an uncanny way of revealing the risks, contradictions, confusions, ambiguities and cruelties in our relationship to the sexual. It is perhaps not surprising that the initial reaction was fear and panic. But in the struggles against HIV/AIDS new possibilities and resources for hope opened up. Amid the tragedies, people survived and showed in many, often unexpected and creative ways, the possibilities of living life well.

B

BAREBACKING

Although originally referring to unprotected heterosexual sex ('riding a horse without a saddle') barebacking has come to refer almost exclusively in public controversy and popular usage to unprotected anal sex between gay men, often in group sex situations, and deliberately pursued as a conscious rejection of sexual health regimes. It is an international phenomenon (Carballo-Dieguez and Bauermeister 2004), but has a particular resonance where the **AIDS** epidemic has bitten hard and deep, and cannot be properly interpreted without an understanding of the impact of HIV/AIDS on gay male communities across the globe.

As a self-conscious social practice, as opposed to individual acts, barebacking has to be understood as a revolt by some gay men against the risk-averse prevention culture that had developed as the HIV/AIDS epidemic exploded. The widespread adoption of regimes of **Safer sex** in gay communities from the mid-1980s reinforced the message that, in the absence of magic bullet vaccines or 'cures', the only effective way of preventing the spread of HIV was through avoiding the interchange of bodily fluids, with condom-protected intercourse the safest bet. At the height of early community-based prevention campaigns about two-thirds of gay men regularly engaged in protected sex, but that still left about a third at high risk. As more effective treatments developed from the mid-1990s many survivors of the early epidemic, and new entrants to the gay scene, began to reject what they saw as the rigidities of safe-sex messages and practice. Barebacking emerged as a sexual-cultural phenomenon in this context, acted out in sex clubs and parties and no doubt bedrooms, sustained by numerous magazine contact ads, websites and porno-films, and the subject of heated polemic, pro and anti, in the 1990s and 2000s.

The most controversial aspect of barebacking was the perception that it not only risked transmission of HIV but actively pursued it. The desire to be penetrated by the virus – 'bugchasing' – or to offer the virus up to HIV negative people – 'gift-giving' – suggested that barebacking was no longer simply a high-risk activity. It had created its own norms and values, its specific experience of **Abjection**, in a distinctive social world of its own.

12

For morally conservative opponents of LGBT claims to equality it offered confirmation that gay men were as sexually promiscuous, predatory and irresponsible as has always been claimed. Even the gay world was passionately divided. For more conservative gays it represented a threat to the new respectability that many anxiously sought. Even radical **Queer** critics have seen in the wilful transcendence of risk by barebackers, in the words of Bersani, a 'literal enactment of the death drive' that apparently fully justifies the revulsion of heterosexuals and homosexuals alike (Bersani and Phillips 2008: 45).

For many gay men, however, barebacking was more than a dicing with death. It had a deep symbolic significance. As sexual pleasure and experimentation had come to define gay men's identity and sense of community it was difficult for some gay men to hold on to that belonging without full sexual freedom, as they saw it – including the freedom to risk infection and death (Yep *et al.* 2002: 1–14). Unprotected sex gave some a transgressive thrill. For others it offered a sense of intimacy that no other sexual practice could offer. A vast range of other explanations have been drawn on to account for barebacking, from condom fatigue, anger, fear of rejection, assertion of masculinity, to power play and the attainment of spiritual ascesis (Ridge 2004). Barebacking had multiple possible meanings. It is important, however, to see it as more than simply a sexual free-for-all. It developed its own codes and rituals. In part at least it had developed, in a distorted form, out of notions of negotiated safety that had become central to safer-sex practice: serosorting (the seeking out of sexual partners with the same HIV status) and seroconcordant sex (only having sex with same-status partners) suggest that it is men's own meanings and the circumstances of sex encounters themselves that determine the degree of unsafe sex.

BISEXUALITY

The concept of bisexuality is simultaneously one of the foundational ideas of sexuality, and one of the most ambiguous, challenged and challenging. It has been a familiar idea at least since the Ancient Greeks, referring to the idea that men and women had constitutional characteristics of the other, that indeed men and women formed but one sex (Laqueur 1990). Its English usage reflects this. 'Bisexed' from the seventeenth century meant having elements of both sexes, and 'bisexual', first recorded in 1829, meant having both sexes in the same individual – what later would be described as 'bi-gender'. From the late nineteenth century, with the rise of **Sexology**, meanings extended not only to refer to the constitutional make-up of an individual and the nature of the embryo, but also to a person's object-choice and sexual practices. In time this morphed readily into a description also of sexual orientation and identity. Four overlapping but separate uses are apparent in discussions of bisexuality over the past century or so: referring to biology, behaviour, and social being, and looking towards a sexuality beyond binarism.

For many sexologists in the late nineteenth century bisexuality was the root of human sexuality. Charles Darwin seems to have been the first to use the term scientifically, in *The Variations of Animals and Plants under Domestication* (1868), when he suggested bisexuality alone could account for hereditary traits. Latent characteristics of the opposite sex, he argued, could be transmitted to future generations in both fauna and flora. Sexologists found the concept useful in attempting to describe the origins of **Homosexuality**, less so of **Heterosexuality**, usually taken for granted as the given of final sexual destination. They usually differed on the biological significance of bisexuality and the links with hermaphrodism and androgyny. There was widespread recognition of the undifferentiated nature of the embryo, and advances in endocrinology – especially the discovery of the role of the sex glands and hormones – made it possible to theorize both a continuum and an imbalance in normal development. Otto Weininger's *Sex and Character* (1906), reflecting 'absolute distinctions between all men on the one side and all women on the other', and suggesting that 'There exists all sorts of intermediate conditions between male and female – sexual transitional forms' (Weininger 1906: 3, 7), gave the idea a strong resonance amongst intellectual circles in Europe, despite his otherwise unsavoury intellectual outlook, including a rabid anti-semitism. But it was Freud who provided the strongest impetus to theorizing bisexuality as a key constituent of sexuality.

Freud was influenced in recognizing the significance of bisexuality by his original collaborator and mentor, Wilhelm Fleiss, whom he saw (rather than Weininger) as the true theorist of the idea. Fliess saw bisexuality as a universal biological phenomenon, which is not restricted to sexualities that could be regarded as pathological, such as homosexuality, and it has important psychological consequences (Laplanche and Pontalis 1980: 53). Freud was more sceptical of the biology; for his theory, bisexuality was primarily a psychological rather than a biological phenomenon. Freud postulated an original psychic indeterminacy in object choice (that is the young child could relate and identify emotionally without distinction to both the mother and father) alongside a polymorphously perverse sexuality. It was only through the psychic traumas represented by the Oedipus Complex and subsequent developments that this potential openness on both choice of love object (male or female) and sexual aim (oral, anal, genital) were shaped into normal, healthy adult (hetero)sexuality, or into perverse sexualities. That both bisexuality and the perversions continue to exist, of course, demonstrated that this psychic process was not inevitably successful – its failure was manifest in unconscious manifestations such as dreams, neuroses and jokes, as well as in the lived realities of many sexually unorthodox lives. But it remained, for Freud, culturally necessary, fundamental to the demands of civilization – see **Psychoanalysis**.

Bisexuality for these early theorists was caught within a double binarism: of masculinity and femininity, and of heterosexuality and homosexuality. The concept could potentially disrupt any notion of a fixed distinction between men and women, yet in practice it became a definition of an indeterminate gender identity. Freud above all recognized the ambiguities of such labels but was unable to free his

14

psychic theories from their inevitability. In the same way, though the idea of bisexuality pointed to the arbitrariness of the heterosexual/homosexual binary, which was consolidating at the same time as the concept of bisexuality, it was often theorized as a failed heterosexual identity, or a halfway house to a homosexual identification. Bisexuality was in danger of being a limbo category.

Yet in terms of behaviour, of bisexuality as a sexual practice, that is emotional and erotic attraction to, or sexual involvement with, both men and women, bisexuality was common on a global scale. Social anthropologists had long recognized this, though most examples were of various patterns of highly gendered behaviour, apparently more likely among men than women. Acceptance of same-sex activity amongst heterosexually married men in South America or the Mediterranean littoral was heavily dependent on their always adopting an active role, while passive partners were despised as not real men. Similarly, puberty rites involving boys ingesting semen of older men, as in New Guinea, were transitional stages of male development, not otherwise disrupting the gender order. Alfred Kinsey and his colleagues (1948, 1953) famously found, though they scarcely used the term, that bisexual behaviour was no less common in the ostensibly more moral and certainly moralistic West. His finding that 37 per cent of his male sample had had same-sex activity to the point of orgasm, while the numbers of self-defined homosexuals, and the incidence of exclusive homosexuality, was very much lower gave the lie to those that suggested that homosexual practices were rare, especially amongst those who continued to identify as 'normal'. The idea of a sexual spectrum, with exclusive homosexuality at one end of a seven-point scale, and heterosexuality at the other, underlined a practical bisexuality in the American population. Later studies, such as Laud Humphreys's investigation of *Tearoom Trade* (1970), sexual activity between men in public restrooms in America, confirmed that beneath the patina of heterosexual conventionality, there was huge incidence of bisexual activity that scarcely recognized the name. This was further underlined dramatically some years later as the evidence of transmission of HIV in the **AIDS** crisis suggested a large amount of bisexual activity beneath the surface of ostensible heterosexuality. Bisexuality became categorized as one of 'the vectors of disease' by moral conservatives and many in the bio-medical establishment, to no good cause. An entirely new sexual category, 'men who had sex with men' was invented to describe the phenomenon, though it was a label that was rarely recognized by those it sought to define. More mundanely, it suggests that even in sophisticated Western societies, now willing to recognize a proliferation of sexual lifestyles, there remained a yawning gap between behaviour and **Sexual identity**.

This rapidly changed in the 1970s with the emergence of sexual liberation movements, where new identities began to proliferate. Now bisexual became a self-proclaimed identity in its own right. Bisexuals constructed their own communities and social worlds, with campaigning groups, social facilities, newsletters, books and, later, websites and chatrooms, and all the paraphernalia of a distinctive social group and sexual category. Bisexuality emerged as a separable **Sexual orientation**, with its own form of hostility and prejudice – bi-phobia. Bisexuality had come out as a fully formed way of being. Sociologists now began to document the similarities and differences of bisexuality in women (Blumstein and Schwartz 1974) and men (Blumstein and Schwartz 1977), to document the relationship with conventional notions of femininity and masculinity, and the overlap with changing lesbian and gay identities. For many in the **Gay liberation** movement of the early 1970s bisexuality was seen as a cop-out, a failure to face the full consequences of coming out. For many women involved in second-wave **Feminism** bisexuality offered a transition to lesbianism, or an exploration of a fuller female sexuality. But for many self-declared bisexuals their identity was as valid, and clear-cut, as more firmly established lesbian or gay identities, an essential aspect of the challenge to discrimination and prejudice. This has been reflected in the political labelling that developed in the 1990s, notably 'lesbigay' and LGBTQ, where bi or bisexual is firmly wedded to a broad front of sexual activists.

Such an alliance or common identification is not without its contradictions. For some theorists, bisexuality profoundly disrupts all fixed categories, so it is perhaps a little strange that many want to fit it into a categorical schema. Garber (1995) has sought to recover the radical implications of Freudian thought by arguing that society has depended on the repression of bisexuality – its **Abjection** – for its very definition of civilization. The subversive return of the repressed through the celebration of bisexual desire can queer the settled order and conventional sexual categories, and open up new possibilities for pleasure, without the fixity of identity. Many bisexual activists, for example, felt that the rise of **Same-sex marriage** as a key lesbian and gay issue undermined sexual radicalism and any challenge to heteronormative values – for example through **Polyamory** – and threatened to consolidate an ethnic-type lesbian and gay identity (Klesse 2006). This suggests that the idea of a distinctive bisexual identity is an unstable one, still uneasily coexisting with the binarisms of heterosexuality and homosexuality, and readily marginalized even within queer discourse (Hemmings 2007). It may also, as sympathetic critics have suggested, lead to the **Commodification** of bisexual desires in a fashion 'ideally suited to, and thoroughly complicit with, the post-modern ethos of consumer capitalism' – though in this it is no different from other forms of sexuality (Storr 2003: 159).

There is no reason to think that the practice of bisexuality in and of itself, is any more transgressive than any other sexual practice. Context is all. At the same time, it is important to recognize that the concept of bisexuality has always had within it the ability to disrupt dichotomous ideas of sexuality, to undermine fixed categories, to go beyond binarisms and to suggest the multiple possibilities of sexual desire. The history of the concept displays the uncertainties at the heart of sexual theories, and the complexities and multiplicities of sexual lives.

BLACKMAIL

Blackmail is widely seen as the most heinous of crimes. It embodies betrayal. It threatens to make starkly public what was hidden, secret. It offers embarrassment or shame in place of discretion. It relies on the fear that exposure will undermine reputation. It is dependent on an accepted notion of what constitutes respectability – and on an awareness of the chasm that opens up if the norms of respectability are jettisoned.

To an extraordinary degree secrecy, embarrassment and shame, discretion, reputation and respectability have been bound up with sexuality, and sexual blackmail has an especially insidious history, as its historian Angus McLaren (2002) has shown. A person's character has been inextricably linked to sexual behaviour in the modern period. If, as Michel Foucault (1979) suggested, sex has come to be seen as the truth of one's being, then when the 'truth' is too difficult to reveal, we have to create a whirlwind of secrets and lies to protect ourselves. But the trouble with secrets is they only exist if someone else knows of them, and if the lies can be revealed. And knowledge is power, a power that blackmailers have been only too willing to use.

The history of the rise and (relative) fall of sexual blackmail shows how the shifting modes of sexual **Regulation** made possible changing forms of blackmail; and it demonstrates the ways in which a history of blackmail can cast a sharp new light on the history of sexuality. Sexual blackmail is part of the power struggles that always play around the erotic. Class, race and gender structure the forms of blackmail that prevail at any particular time (and also shape the differences between the American and British experiences of sexual blackmail). And they mould and limit the stories that can be told, by the victims and perpetrators, by the law and the press. As ever in the history of sexuality, there is no single logic at work, and the unintended consequences can be as important as the intended. The languages of sexuality were as varied two hundred years ago as they are now – though bearing different accents. At times, the courts were willing to turn a blind eye to the major crime alleged (often sodomy) in order to deal with the lower class blackmailer who was threatening the social hierarchy. At other times, the courts and the press were happy to excoriate the victim (especially a woman) if the boundaries of respectable gender behaviour were breached. Sexual blackmail itself became a means of policing the boundaries of sexual behaviour, and therefore one of the means by which sexuality was shaped and reshaped from the eighteenth century onwards.

Sexual blackmailers had a way of always fixing on what was the major contra- diction in the regulation of sexuality. From the eighteenth century, as emerging norms of respectable masculinity demanded the exclusion of **Homosexuality**, sodomy became the focus of the blackmailer's art. Sodomy, it must be remem- bered, still carried the death penalty in England and Wales, notionally at least, till 1861, but social death was almost as threatening for many men as homosexuality became increasingly defined as the characteristic of a certain type of degenerate or diseased (and certainly unrespectable) personality. The Labouchère Amendment, which in 1885 effectively made all forms of male homosexuality, whether in private or public, illegal in England and Wales, and in many other parts of the world under British jurisdiction, famously became known as the 'blackmailer's charter'. Homosexuality (usually male, but occasionally from the late nineteenth century female) was the most tempting occasion for sexual extortion. But blackmail also guarded the fences of female sexual respectability. The vulnerability of women to the double standard of morality in the nineteenth century created many opportunities for the blackmailer. Strangely, these opportunities seemed to increase in the 1920s as some of the conventional constraints around female sexuality appeared to relax. The 'fast woman', the 'gold digger', became new types of perpetrators as well as victims. Racial transgression added a tasty new element. Lord Louis Mountbatten's wife, Edwina, went to court to defend herself against accusations of an affair with the black singer Paul Robeson. (Lord Louis, however, seems to have escaped blackmail for his alleged homosexual liaisons).

Sexual blackmail thrived in an age when conservative sexual norms defined who was respectable or unrespectable, acceptable or unacceptable. Blackmail played on the contradictions between what people presented themselves as being, and what they really were, between what they said they did and what they actually did. It tore apart the veils of discretion that allowed people to live private lives at odds with what society said at any particular time. The threat of public disclosure hence served to terrorize the private – but also helped to ensure that it conformed to what was socially acceptable. This was the social function of the narratives of sexual blackmail that structured the response to sexual blackmail, and inevitably perpetuated the blackmailers' trade.

Sexual blackmail is less potent in a world of greater sexual honesty and openness. Since the 1960s, the coming out of lesbians and gay men has drastically reduced the opportunities for blackmail. In a social climate where premarital sex, cohabitation, divorce, abortion and single parenthood are commonplace, blackmail loses its purchase on female respectability. Of course, as sexual blackmail in the old sense declines, so new patterns of anxiety or threat arise. 'Outing' of **Closet** homosexuals still plays on the survival of hypocrisy. Accusations of sexual harassment or date rape still have to work through our contradictory attitudes towards male and female sexuality. Tabloids and the Web are happy to expose the famous, infamous and not so famous for their sexual peccadilloes. The cocaine-snorting, adulterous alpha male is now more likely to be exposed in the press than privately blackmailed. Financial payments are now made for disclosure rather than to prevent it.

But few would want to go back to the age of sexual blackmail. People doubly suffer when their consensual, private erotic needs are denied or distorted by a hypocritical culture: first by being forced to hide or deny their desires; second by being exposed to the insidious forms of sexual blackmail. Both are effects of a world where moral codes diverge hugely from the ways people live.

BODIES

Bodies, the fleshy, messy, pulsating, highly differentiated assemblages of skin and bones, muscles and blood, DNA and brain cells, reproductive and defecatory organs, are the common-sense loci of sexual instincts and desires. Bodies live and breathe, flourish and decay. Women's bodies menstruate, give birth, lactate and nourish. The differences between female bodies and male have been the foundation for a myriad of gendered distinctions and for massive edifices of social difference, and inequalities. But bodies are never just bodies. Bodies exist in cultures, and have acquired highly differentiated historical meanings. Many cultures across the globe celebrated the pleasures of the body in a variety of different ways. The Christian tradition, on the other hand, took for granted the centrality of bodily impulses, but saw them negatively: for centuries it was preoccupied with the sins of the flesh and the temptations and corruptions which wracked the body, for which the only solution was celibacy or marriage – better to marry than to burn. From the eighteenth century Western cultures abandoned the ancient Greek model of a single sex, and developed elaborate theories of two, distinct but complementary bodies, one potentially open to discipline by reason and society (the male), the other (the female) inevitably belonging to Nature (Laqueur 1990). Sometimes the female body was seen as threatening and engulfing, posing the perpetual danger of over-whelming men; at other times it was seen simply as the vehicle for reproduction and maternity, and otherwise as essentially passive, aroused, 'kissed into life', only by the initiative of a man. The emergence of **Sexology**, the would-be science of desire, and categorizer of bodies and their normal and perverse desires, struggled to marry the insights of the new post-Darwinian biology with the complex realities of differently lived embodied lives, but on the whole reaffirmed the determining power of bodily differences – see **Essentialism**. The founding fathers of sociology – Marx, Durkheim, Weber, Simmel – did little better: they had implicit accounts of the body, but it was not the focus of their work, which was rather class conflict, social order, meaning and social interaction (Shilling 2007). The body remained largely unsocialized. Freud (see **Psychoanalysis**) attempted to go beyond the givenness or naturalness of the biological body, seeing it as overlain by psychical or social significance. He had an acute awareness of the problematic nature of masculinity and femininity, amongst the most difficult concepts known to science, he believed, but in the end he affirmed their necessity: anatomy, perhaps, really was destiny.

Since the 1960s, however, there has been an explosion of interest in the social meanings of and investments in the body. The idea of women's right to control their own bodies, so central to second-wave **Feminism**, indicated the politically and culturally charged significance of bodies. The erasure of female sexuality in 'male-stream' theory was seen as a major factor in limiting female autonomy and self-expression, and the elaboration of concepts of sexism, patriarchy, 'complusory **Heterosexuality**' and 'female corporeality' (Grosz 1994, 1995) demonstrated the ways in which diverse forms of power marked and determined bodily meanings, and gave rise to resistances and subversion. **Social constructionism** emphasized the ways in which social categorizations and regulation shaped gender and sexuality profoundly. Michel Foucault (1979), most strikingly, saw the production of the body as the key to the shift in modes of regulation and governance in modern societies. Technologies of power pressed the flesh into the service of social organization through the disciplining effects of discourse. The 'docile body' was the focus for the production and regulation of human individuals and the control of populations, producing social beings who were simultaneously subjects and subjected. This opened the way not only to seeing sexuality as a mode of social organization, but also showed the way to historicizing other categories, for example gender, race, age, disability. Individual bodies were habituated into particular ways of being by specific regimes of power. The body could no longer be taken for granted: it was a focal point of power relations, and not a fixed point of meaning. It could be, and was being, transformed.

Bodies have always been shaped and reshaped: think of the disciplining of the body required for military service, for agricultural or industrial labour, or the moulding of female bodies into figures of desire. Modern technologies have now ensured that bodies can be constantly engineered and re-engineered in a multiplicity of ways. To conform to market needs they are organized through consumption – of food, drinks, drugs etc –, and by the allure of advertising, by costume, uniform, cosmetics and cosmetic surgery. They are reorganized through discourses of physical beauty, health and fitness. Modern skills have revolutionalized **Reproductive technologies**, ensuring that giving birth is no longer a fate, opening up the possibilities of non-bodily births and countering sexual inadequacies – see **Viagra**. Medicine can prolong life, and give hope to damaged or ageing bodies. Science even offers the possibility of indefinitely delaying the effects of ageing, endlessly prolonging the survival of the body beyond its (presumed) biological term. Are we perhaps cyborgs, half human and half machine, that can tempt us away from the attractions of biology and essentialisms to recognize the human construction of our bodies and our identities (Haraway 1991)?

There are positives and negatives in all of these possibilities. They have enhanced the opportunities for a better, more fulfilling life for millions of people. But in some cases they have also been drawn into the maws of regulations and governance, tying the individual ever more tightly to the demands of power. Ideals of the body healthy and beautiful can be liberating; they can also imprison people in unattainable hopes and dreams.

Many sceptical critics have emphasized the dangers of bodily transformations, tools in the hands of power, and it is important to take note of these critiques. But it is also vital to remember that the body is the site of quite conscious resistances to power. Many body transformations, such as tattooing and piercing, may be expressions of individuality and personal empowerment. Forms of sexual expression which play with the pleasures and pains of the body – such as **Sado-masochism** – or seek to expand beyond genital expressions of the erotic, broaden the possibilities of fulfilled desire. Forms of surgical intervention to 'change sex' have been vital for many individuals in achieving a sense of harmony between body and gender identity – see **Transgender**. Even anorexia nervosa, largely experienced by women (though increasing numbers of men suffer from it) can be read as a struggle over contradictory pulls on a woman and her body, partially if temporarily resolved by a transformation of the body. Bodies are inescapable presences to be worked on, the site of complex human practices. Bodies matter.

The body has never been less docile, Anthony Giddens (1991) has suggested. It has become an inextricable part of the reflexive project of the self in late-modernity. The body may have been seen as a given in the past but it is now the site of constant social interaction, appropriation and re-appropriation. Body self-awareness is a crucial aspect of how we see and define ourselves, how we perform and present ourselves, of who and what we are. It is not an inert feature subject passively to **Commodification** or discipline. It has its own **Agency**.

Early social constructionist analyses had a tendency to obscure how historical categories and cultural variations worked on and shaped identities and desires (Vance 1989). There was always a danger of seeing the human subject as a blank sheet of paper or vacant screen on which the social inscribed its signs. But the body is more than a mere means, conduit or effect (Latimer 2009): 'bodies are addressed by social process and drawn into history, without ceasing to be bodies' (Connell 2005: 64). Embodiment describes an active process in which the body is shaped and changed by human practice. Through body-reflexive practices masculinities and femininities, sexual desires and sexual identities are shaped, drawing on the multiple possibilities of the body but transforming them into active elements of individual lives and social worlds. Human beings are not slaves of the flesh, nor passive recipients of social messages. Through human practice they are active agents in making their lives and transforming their bodies.

C

CHILDHOOD SEXUALITY

Concern about child sex abuse and the early **Sexualization** of young people has focused attention as rarely before in most Western countries on the nature of childhood sexuality. Hovering over the whole issue has been the spectre of predatory **Paedophilia**, sexually exploiting children for adult ends, and even worse involving possible abduction and murder. On a global scale, the exploitation of young people through human **Trafficking** has aroused particular anxiety, and produced significant international mobilization against it. Perhaps not surprisingly, issues around childhood sexuality have been an especially fertile cause of **Moral panic**, and have universally given rise amongst public moralists and politicians to calls for preserving childhood sexual innocence (though, it has to be said, with little material effect). The major paradox of such concerns is that as young people in highly developed countries do indeed sexually mature earlier than ever before, as a result of better health and nutrition, and are exposed to an ever-increasing array of sexually explicit images and speech, so assertions of their sexual innocence and need for protection get stronger. As children have become the focus of meaning in family life, and as the dependence of young people on their parents has increased in many ways through prolonged education and youth unemployment, so concerns about the differences between adults and children have become more acute. The sexuality of the young has become a fraught site of social anxiety.

In a sense there is little that is new about this preoccupation with childhood sexuality. It is a late-modern nuancing of well-entrenched concerns. The draconian injunctions against **Masturbation** from the eighteenth century into the twentieth century were in part about fear of the boundless and anarchic power of the sexual, especially amongst the young. Emerging discourses focused on young peoples' sexuality. Foucault (1979) saw what he called 'the pedagogization' of childhood sexuality in the nineteenth century as one of the four strategic unities that discursively shaped modern sexuality as a site of power, regulation and surveillance. The simultaneous production and protection of childhood innocence was a key element in the new forms of bio-power, linked to the future of marriage and of the race, and the protection against sexual perversity. Protecting the young against premature sexual exposure has been an abiding preoccupation of church and state and myriad civil society campaigns around social purity and social hygiene since the nineteenth century. There have been efforts over the past century in most Western countries to protect young people (especially young girls) from being drawn into prostitution, to raise the age of marriage, to enforce 'ages of **Consent**' to sexual activity, though this has varied substantially across even European countries, and to inhibit homosexuality.

These endeavours have marched ambivalently with a closely related but often deliberately obfuscated question, about the existence of an autonomous childhood sexuality itself. The societal preoccupation with masturbation from the eighteenth century and with sexualization of the young from the nineteenth century hinted that as well as external stimuli there might be a potential sexual subjectivity in those innocent young bodies, but this was barely acknowledged as a respectable possibility. It took the pioneering **Sexology** at the end of the nineteenth century to attempt to put the issue onto a more scientific and empirical basis, though even here clinical evidence was often tempered by professional caution. Richard von Krafft-Ebing, the founding father of sexology, observed that every physician was aware that 'manifestations of the sexual instinct may occur in very young children' (Egan and Hawkes 2010: 79), though few physicians openly acknowledged this. The British pioneer, Havelock Ellis, introduced the term 'autoerotism' to refer to the spontaneous sexual emotion generated within a person's body in the absence of external stimuli, starting in childhood. Masturbation was but one manifestation of this. Spontaneous nocturnal emissions, an especial preoccupation of Ellis's, was another example. All suggested the significance of the sexual impulse throughout a person's life. For Ellis this was a biological fact, not a moral problem. Freud adopted the term autoerotism in his *Three Essays* in 1905 to refer more specifically to infantile sexuality, when sexuality was not organized around a fixed object (that is a man or a woman or some sort of transitional object). He subsequently subtly modified this account, but the point is that here was a clear notion of a fundamental childhood sexuality. This remained a key element in the future development of Freud's elaboration of **Psychoanalysis**. It is central to Freud's development of the Oedipus drama, subsequent sublimation and latency, and the eventual emergence of gendered and sexualized identities in adolescence and adulthood (Laplanche and Pontalis 1980: 45–6).

Freud became universally known as the theorist of childhood sexuality, and this added to the initial scandal around his theories – though recent scholarship has suggested that both Ellis and Albert Moll had fuller theories (Egan and Hawkes 2010: 94). All three problematized to some degree the idea of an automatic progression to conventional adult (hetero)sexuality, and opened the way for theorizations of perversity as rooted, like 'normal' sexuality, in childhood. This did not always prove appealing to later theorists or to the new breed of child therapists and child care specialists who emerged in the 1930s and 1940s. They were concerned to regulate and channel early sexual manifestations to ensure a healthy progress to adulthood, rather than celebrate the sexual instinct and its

23

variations. This has been a continuing note in professional approaches to childhood sexuality ever since.

Recognizing the fact of childhood sexuality does not of course necessarily involve the advocacy of sexual expression by the child, let alone justify adult–child sexual relationships. The acknowledgement of childhood sexuality is, however, a necessary first step in recognizing the developing subjectivity of the young person, not as a prematurely and artificially sexualized proto-adult, but as a person in his or her own right, with a developing sense of sexual self and growing **Agency**. Rachel Thomson's (2004) research in Britain suggests that sexual agency is seen by young people as a private realm, in which they do not expect the state or parents to intervene. Legitimacy for sexual activity comes not from the law or an age of consent, but from a sense that it should happen only when the young individual is ready, that it is a product of agency, choice and control mediated by time. This is likely to offer a better model for adult–child relations than over-protection based on an anachronistic notion of childhood innocence and on endemic fears about premature sexualization of the young.

CHOICE

Choice is a concept that is attractive across the ideological spectrum. For free-marketeers and supporters of **Neoliberalism** choice is the hallmark of a dynamic consumerist society, enthroning the sovereignty of the individual, primarily in economic terms but by extension (an extension not always made by moral conservatives) to all aspects of social and personal life, including sexuality. Choice has also been a central theme of sexual progressivism and especially of second-wave **Feminism** since the 1960s – 'a woman's right to choose' enshrined the key demand for control of one's body that was at the heart of Women's Liberation. 'Pro-choice' has become a powerful signifier of those who support the right of women to access **Abortion**, especially in the USA, where conflicting claims of rights – the right to choose versus the rights of the unborn child – have become the fraught focus of the so-called 'culture wars'.

For most late-modern societies there is, in principle, greater freedom of choice than ever before in relation to sexuality: what we do, whom we do it with, how often, in what sort of relationship. The growing acceptance of **Sexual diversity** as the reality of contemporary culture in effect mandates choice as the ruling norm. The undermining of traditional patterns of relationships and the decline of the master discourses of morality which dominated cultural life until the **Great transition** between the 1950s and the early 2000s, and which stridently demarcated right from wrong, have weakened the hierarchy of sexual behaviours, and increasingly thrown moral responsibility back on individuals: what Bauman (1992: xxii) calls the loneliness of moral choice. In the conditions of late-modernity, Giddens (1992) has argued, we have no choice but to choose. And the choices appear infinite. New forms of **Agency**, such as feminism and **Gay liberation** have opened up opportunities for sexual expression, pleasure and identity for many hitherto marginalized by sexual traditionalism. Gender no longer seems a fixed point around which sexuality revolves, but contingent, open to modification and remaking – see **Transgender**. **Perversion** has morphed into a spectrum of poly-morphous pleasures. Sexuality has been warmly embraced by consumerism, offering a hypermarket of erotic possibilities, as well as the danger of **Commodification** of the body. Science and technology, with all their protean potentialities, have opened the gates to personal transformations – through the surgeon's knife, the therapist's talk, the power of drugs, or the immense seductions of **Cybersex**. There is a universe of choice, for those who have power to choose.

There, of course, is the rub. For not everyone has the same freedom to choose. Despite the temptations and allure, freedom of choice is often extremely difficult in sexual matters, where **Desire**, emotions and social norms are inextricably tangled with relationships of power. A battered wife or an abused child do not choose the circumstances in which they live, in which they are subject to abuse. Children have limited opportunities to choose against adult power. The abused woman may have immense difficulty, tied to emotion as well as economics, in breaking with the abusive husband. Loyalties, commitments, dependency and fear all block the free play of choice, especially for women. On a global scale women's choices are often limited by the knot of development and underdevelopment, exploitation and poverty, the power of capital and the demands of religion and tradition, and who has the right to exercise control over a woman's body. Abortion may have become the symbol of women's freedom of choice in Western countries, but in other parts of the world it might be the stark reminder of (male) traditions of authority. Forced termination of pregnancy – because a woman may give birth to a child of the 'wrong' gender (that is, a girl child), or may exceed the allowed number of children – is the antithesis of choice. Choices are always made in specific economic, social, cultural and political contexts. Choices may seem free, but for those who are subordinate in society real choice may be an illusion, forcing a responsibility on the individual without real freedom. There are strong limits to choice.

Nor are choices always clear-cut. The issue of Muslim women and the veil illustrates this acutely. The secular republic of France has decided in effect that women who desire to cover their bodies in public do not have the right to choose this, because it would be an acceptance of subordination to what is clearly regarded as a patriarchal and religious tradition (Scott 2007). The issue was hotly debated in other West European countries, and the veil was banned in Belgium, for example, as part of the reaction against **Multiculturalism**. On the other hand, defenders of women's right to wear the veil have deployed a feminist argument about individual autonomy and choice, allowing Muslim women to carve out a space protected from the male gaze (Weeks 2007: 114–15). This reminds us that choice is often a contested dream.

Choices may appear to be individual, but individuals are influenced by social context, and choices have social consequences. The choice agenda is more than an empty consumerist hope extended to the body. It is important to recognize the *significance* of choice. Choices can be painful and involve considerable social struggle. A good example of this is provided by the question of coming out as lesbian or gay. This has never been an easy lifestyle choice. Historically leaving the **Closet** has involved a painful individual struggle, and despite widespread liberalization in the West, can still have disastrous consequences in many parts of the world. So to argue that being lesbian or gay is just one lifestyle choice amongst others, no more important than the colour of one's hair, is to downgrade the importance of declaring one's sexuality in often hostile circumstances. Many LGBT people have reacted against this easy relativism by arguing that **Sexual orientation** and identity is not a choice at all, but an essential aspect of the personality, and have shown great hostility to those who have argued for a contingent and historically shaped relationship between desire, sexual practice and identity. For such people, ironically, choice in effect is seen not as an aspect of greater freedom, but a threat to it (Weeks 1995: 62–3).

In the end the discourse of choice has importance only because some choices are more difficult and some are more meaningful than others. An acceptance of sexual diversity and choice does not rule out judgements of relative worth. On the contrary it often requires them. The concept of choice has relevance because it forces us to think about what is truly significant, not just for individuals but for the wider culture.

CLOSET

'Out of the closets into the streets' was the resounding slogan of the **Gay liberation** movement of the 1970s. It addressed a culture where **Homosexuality** was still lived in secrecy and shadows and where internalized feelings of guilt distorted millions of lives. The closet was thus a framework of oppression, and a prison-house of the self. Dictionary definition of a closet in the conventional sense – a cupboard, wardrobe, secret place, even the lair of a wild beast and a sewer – underlines the deep undesirability of the space, but also points to the protections it might provide: dangers and privacy. 'Coming out' (of the closet) as gay was to take the risk of rejecting both dangers and privacy by wearing your homosexuality with pride, abandoning guilt and confronting the wider forces of sexual oppression. Staying in the closet seemed to many the denial of your sexuality, and hence of the ultimate truth about yourself. It was a continuation of the old self-oppression. In the early 1990s, in the wake of the **AIDS** crisis, deliberate 'outing' of closet homosexuals was a tactic adopted by some queer activists (Signorile 1993). In some ways this was a parody of the old tactic of homophobes to control the sexually marginal by exposing their secrets. Outing set out to expose the hypocrisy of people who asserted their heterosexuality, acted publicly in a homophobic fashion, and yet were secretly gay themselves. Behind it was the assumption that the real shame was not homosexuality but the concealment of your true sexuality.

The difficulty with such a position was that it assumed a simple relationship between revelation and truth, between sexual behaviour and **Sexual identity**. History suggested that the organization of sexuality was much more complex, and that sexuality was not so much suppressed or denied as trapped within a binary organization of sexuality that was a major structuring element of Western thought and practice. For queer theorists, the closet was a central mechanism in sustaining the heterosexual/homosexual divide as a relationship of dominance and subordination. In her landmark study, *Epistemology of the Closet*, Eve Kosofsky Sedgwick wrote that 'the closet is the defining structure for gay oppression in this [that is, the twentieth] century' (Sedgwick 1990: 71). The secrecy surrounding homosexuality was not so much a denial of it but a confirmation of its overwhelming presence in giving meaning and definition to the dominance of heterosexuality.

If the heterosexual/homosexual binary is so crucial to Western cultural dynamics as queer theorists argue, the immediate question that comes to mind is to what extent liberalizing tendencies in recent years in most Western countries have worked to undermine it. Seidman (2002) has written of the gradual ending of the closet in America during the 1990s, and it is important to understand what he means by this. The concept of the closet, he argues, had unique socio-historical conditions: the prioritizing of sexual identity and a systematic mobilization of social and cultural forces to enforce the heterosexual norm. This reached its peak not in the nineteenth century but in the 1950s. In the other words the articulation of the closet as a space of privatization and protection took place alongside the tightening of the screw on many homosexual people. Central to it is the idea of a double life and strategies of everyday management that sustain that. The aim is to create a protected space which allows individuals to fashion a gay life and the creation of gay social worlds. The closet, from this point of view, is a strategy of accommodation and resistance which simultaneously reproduces the binary divide between homosexuality and heterosexuality and contests it. From this perspective the development of the post 1970s lesbian and gay world was a contradictory movement, both deploring the closet, but also strengthening it in some ways through the development of distinctive identities, communities and ways of life. The question that Seidman stimulates, for Britain as much as the United States, is the degree to which this comfortable 'ghettoization' of homosexuality is dissolving. For some the very idea of the homosexual is dissolving as formal equality erases the distinctiveness of the gay world (Bech 1999; see also Reynolds 1999). It is undoubtedly the case that in many countries lesbians and gays are increasingly 'normalizing' and 'routinizing' their homosexuality, so that a double life is less and less a defining aspect of their lives, with sexuality one part rather than the core of their identities. This seems to be particularly the case amongst younger people, where gayness is increasingly one personal sexualized identity amongst many, rather than the basis of collective political action.

The closet is a powerful metaphor that dramatizes the secrets and lies that have structured non-heterosexual and queer life. Its gradual erosion in liberal societies is in large part a result of the movement and campaigns built around the notion of disclosure, coming out. The light brought to bear on heterosexuality's denied other by its public performance dramatically revealed its transgressive possibilities and its sheer ordinariness. The irony is that the advances thus achieved also generated new waves of **Homophobia**, discrimination and prejudice in various parts of the world. The closet was both a prison and a home. Openness brings its own dangers as well as new freedoms and opportunities.

COMMODIFICATION

Commodification is a key concept of Marxist theory, closely associated with the idea of the **Fetish**. Under capitalism the worship of the object, the commodity, offers the illusion of freedom but obscures the reality of exploitation. Capitalism distorts and damages human potential, including sexuality, through commodifying it, turning it into something that can be bought and sold, allowing the most personal aspects of the self to be manipulated by market forces. The idea of the manipulated self is traceable through German theorists of the early twentieth century such as Simmel, and is developed and carried through by the Frankfurt school in the inter-war and post-war years, achieving a wider a currency through the work of Herbert Marcuse and his emphasis on repressive desublimation. Individuals may believe they have full freedom of **Choice**, including around sexuality, but are really under 'tutelage', colonized by consumer capitalism and the associated bureaucratization of everyday life. A key feature of the twentieth century, Hawkes (2004: 147) argued, has been a 'commodification of sex and its pleasures in ways that connected the spheres of profitability and self identity'.

In the conditions of late-modernity, propelled by turbo-charged capitalist expansion (at least until the financial crash of 2008) such arguments have been given a new edge, and are clearly articulated in the critique of **Neoliberalism**. What was once seen as special and mystical, even, has become mundane as the commercialization of sex has sucked it dry of any threatening or disruptive characteristics, establishing a series of playgrounds within which to simulate freedom. The contemporary management of sexuality, it has been suggested, constitutes an example of a managerial colonization of everyday life, signifying not only an intensification of 'Fordist sexuality' and a 'Taylorization of sex', but also an escalating threat to imagination and ingenuity (Tyler 2004: 82). Eros is harnessed to the performance principle, and capitalist values have penetrated deep into intimate life, colonizing inter-subjective processes and thus reshaping the sexual world. **Prostitution**, **Pornography** and other forms of sex work are the more obvious markers of commercialized sex, but all aspects of life offer examples, from the invasion of a contract culture in everyday life (pre-nuptial and co-habitation agreements) to the selling of the sexed self via dating agencies and the Web, which can be seen as the marketization of relational values. Hochschild (2003) famously sees this process as commercializing all intimate life, stalling the hopes of early feminists

28

for a more equal society, and corrupting ideals of care and altruism. And there seems little in contemporary society able to challenge these tendencies. Even the counterculture of the 1960s, which heavily influenced the birth of second-wave **Feminism** and **Gay liberation**, has been seen as fully complicit with consumer capitalism.

The **Individualization** associated with this rampant consumerism, it is suggested, dissolves human relationships, leading to the replacement of authentic, reflective subjectivities with narcissistic, hedonistic values (Elliott and Lemert 2006: 60). In *The Minimal Self*, Christopher Lasch (1985) argues that the pluralist concept of freedom represents a surrender to consumerist values, and the celebration of a protean sense of self which accepts oxymorons like 'open marriage' and 'non-binding commitments'. Bauman (2005) echoes this. There are no longer any fixed bonds that link people together as there were in old kinship patterns. People have to make bonds for themselves, but they are dependent now on their own skills, and none are guaranteed to last. In the modern world, 'loyalty is a cause of shame, not pride' (Bauman 2005: 9). He conjures up a picture of our contemporaries abandoned to their own wits, and feeling easily disposable, yearning for togetherness and a helping hand, desperate to relate, yet afraid of being related. Sennett (1992) famously lamented 'the fall of public man', and the dominance of notions of self fulfilment at the expense of social bonds. Lasch's 'minimal self' focuses on survival, one day at a time. Bauman (2005) sees the invasions and colonization of 'communitas', the site of the moral economy, by market forces as constituting the most awesome of the dangers facing our human togetherness. Heath and Potter (2005), like Hochschild, see a 'cultural cooling' manifested in cool emotional strategies, such as those deployed in popular television series like *Sex and the City* and in the lifestyles of the new urban demographic, the 'metrosexual'. Cool is the new hot, and the passions of the 1970s social movements are displaced into the intricacies of private life. Private life is a source of comfort and pleasures. It is also a site of emotional isolation, where possessions are substituted for emotional links, and individuals compensate for their loneliness by 'maniacally' searching for illusory substitutes in consumerism to fill the gaps in their lives.

Such arguments are not a million miles from the idea that we are all suffering from false consciousness, trapped in our hopeless pleasures, imprisoned by ideological blinkers in a system that manipulates, isolates and privatizes, making impossible the most important and precious human bonds. Such arguments have many difficulties, but not the least of them is that they all tend to assume that some people are better placed than others to see through the murky clouds of ideology and false consciousness in order to glimpse the truth of our real nature.

There are problems both with this idea of truth, and with the notion of a pure uncorrupted nature, especially our sexual nature. Sexuality has never existed outside the shaping influence of culture; there has never been a pure undefiled eros uncorrupted by capitalism. To that extent, it is scarcely surprising that contemporary sexuality, as an aspect of a highly commercialized culture, will be shaped by commodification. Whether it tells us the full story of contemporary sexuality is another matter.

COMMUNITY

'Community', Raymond Williams (1976: 66) remarked, is one of the few words which never has negative connotations. It attempts both to express social realities and to offer an aspiration towards something better, more inclusive and intangible. The idea of community, in contrast to social atomization, suggests that men and women should be members and not strangers. As such it has become a key idea in the debate on the late-modern world, coming, Zygmunt Bauman (1989) has suggested, to replace reason and universal truth in post-modern philosophy. There are no values or ethics that are not community based, it has been argued, for communities embody certain traditions: arguments, conversations and involvements sustained over time. Communities, it follows, are not fixed once and for all. They change as the arguments over time continue, and as other communities exercise their gravitational pull. But at the same time, the social relations of a community are repositories of meaning for its members, not sets of mechanical linkages between isolated individuals. A community offers a 'vocabulary of values' through which individuals construct their understanding of the social world, and of their sense of identity and belonging (Cohen 1985). Communities offer embeddedness in a world which seems constantly on the verge of fragmentation, and are particularly significant for those who feel they are marginalized or their very existence is at stake. There is, however, an obvious danger in communities. Social pluralism and the proliferation of associations do not necessarily mean variety for men and women personally: embeddedness means people can get stuck. The challenge for modern advocates of community, therefore, is to imagine community without either neo-tribalism or self-immolation.

Michel Foucault distinguishes between three concepts of community: a *given community*, based on identification; a *tacit community*, the materially rooted system of thought that makes something a possible object of identification; and a *critical community,* which recognizes the contingency of identification, and starts to refuse its power (Rajchman 1991: 102). In the contemporary world given or traditional communities, based on geography or class, for example, are losing their moral density as old values crumble and uncertainty rules. The latent sense of community that can be detected under the procedural republic of liberalism may provide the necessary support for a wider sense of solidarity, but in it lurks the danger that the communal values that are discernible will be conservative and exclusive. A critical community, on the other hand, results from a problematization of a given or latent identity. It is open to new experiences and ways of being, which make new subjectivities possible. The idea of a sexual community as it is evoked in contemporary sexual political discourse embraces this notion of a critical community.

People speak easily of lesbian and gay, bisexual, transgender, sm, polyamorist, same-sex parenting, AIDS and many other sexuality-linked communities, though not, generally, the heterosexual community. Precisely because heterosexuality is hegemonic in our general culture, a general heterosexual community does not exist in most people's minds, though of course there are specific heterosexual communities. It is because sexual and gender dissidence is not the norm, is stigmatized, that a sense of community transcending specific differences has emerged. It exists because participants in it feel it does and should exist.

There are, of course, many problems with this usage. It presupposes a natural unity which is not necessarily there. There is no reason to think that people who share one characteristic necessarily share others. A sexual community is not necessarily geographically fixed; it exists as much in the mind as in a neighbourhood. It is often criss-crossed by many divisions. Others prefer related terms to describe the obvious links that connect marginalized peoples. Plummer (1999), for example, uses the term 'social worlds' very effectively. Others use the term network to describe the loose ties, often transnational, that link people together, especially now through cyber-space. But such sociological terms lack the resonance of 'community'. It may be a myth or a fiction, but it has real effects in evoking a common perception of stigma, prejudice, oppression, and of resistance, struggle and new possibilities.

Four key elements are contained in the idea of a sexual community: community as a focus of identity; community as ethos or repository of values; community as social capital; and community as politics (Weeks 2000b).

As identity: The key assumption is that it is through social involvement and collective action that individuality can be realized and **Sexual identity** affirmed. Identities and belongings are being constructed in the very process of organization itself. Sexual movements are effective in so far as they can speak a language which brings people into the activities, alignments and subjectivities being shaped, and the most effective language available is the language of community. A community must be constantly re-imagined, sustained over time by common practices and symbolic re-enactments which reaffirm both identity and difference. Sexual identity and community are expressed through annual events such as Pride celebrations, or by candlelit vigils for those who have been lost through AIDS, or in support of the victims of persecution. Community stands here for some notion of solidarity, a solidarity which empowers and enables, and makes individual and social action possible.

As ethos and repository of values: Blasius (1994) has argued that the lesbian and gay struggle has produced a sense of community and identity which provides the context for moral agency, and hence for the emergence of a lesbian and gay ethos enacted in everyday life. The lesbian and gay ethos involves the construction of an erotica that displaces traditional hierarchical patterns of the sexual in favour of plural forms; and the emergence of a 'new ethic' is built around not so much an orientation, preference or lifestyle as a sense of self-identified and collectively invented community. Lesbian and gays are pioneering, Blasius concludes, an art of living through one's erotic relations, and thereby introducing something new onto the historical landscape. At one level it offers a highly sexualized sense of common interest – a 'community of the night'. On another, it provides the opportunity for the elaboration of new forms of **Intimacy**.

As social capital: These developments occurred, it can be argued, because of the **Social capital**, the network of values, hopes, resources and social support accumulated by hitherto marginalized communities. This was manifest above all in the community-based response to HIV/**AIDS** in the 1980s and 1990s. But more than that: it provides a clear challenge to those social critics who lament the decline of social capital as a modern ill.

As politics: Politically, radical sexual communities and their associated movements point in two different directions at once, or at least embrace two distinct political moments: a 'moment of transgression', and a 'moment of citizenship' (Weeks 1995). One is the moment of challenge to the traditional or received order of sexual life: the assertion of different identities, different lifestyles, and the building of oppositional communities. In the 1990s this gave rise to **Queer** politics, which sought to break with what was perceived as the caution of contemporary gay politics with its integrationist approaches. The other is precisely this movement towards inclusion, towards redefining the polity to incorporate fully those who have felt excluded. Its characteristic emphasis has been on the claiming of civil rights, formal equality – in other words **Sexual citizenship**. All of these terms are highly contested, but there can be little doubt of their ability to mobilize political energies.

In the contemporary world, with its wide sense of uncertainty around values, the idea of a sexual community has developed because of a deep conviction that it is only through the enhancement of a collective identity that individual autonomy can be realized. The idea of a sexual community, it appears, remains both a necessary and an inevitable one.

CONSENT

Consent is one of the most important words in the vocabulary of sexuality. It carries with it the assumption that sexual activities should be based on the free will of autonomous agents able to decide for themselves whether, or not, to engage in that particular practice. As such it is embodied in international conventions, national laws and is the centre of notions of **Sexual citizenship**. No sexual action can be acceptable unless it is the subject of freely given, informed consent (Archard 1998).

That at least is the conventional understanding. The historical and even contemporary practice is more confused and contested. The notion is deeply embedded in Enlightenment assumptions about the ability to reason and capacity to decide, in the absence of constraints, of self-determining persons. This immediately implies that other persons are not able to display reason and therefore exercise consent (Waites 2005). Overwhelmingly, in the eighteenth century, it was men who were seen as embodying the capacity to reason, while women, children, the mentally incapable and diverse frequently racialized others (especially slaves) were deemed incapable of reason. They were ruled by the passions and the wiles of the body, unable to exercise moral agency. The reasoning, autonomous self inhabited, and was capable of control of, a male body. The sexual contract, as Pateman (1988) has argued, was based on a fraternal pact that excluded the feminine and subordinated the other. These founding assumptions had a long echo. In English law, women could not refuse consent to sexual intercourse with their husbands until 1954, while rape within marriage was not recognized until 1991. It was taken for granted that the marriage contract permitted the free exercise of male power. Similarly in the southern states of the USA, during and after slavery, the sexual availability of black women was a taken-for-granted of white male privilege. Freely given consent was not necessary because the other actors were not regarded as fully human and therefore capable of consent.

The social transformations of the twentieth century have to a major extent reshaped sexual relations between men and women, and between black and white, but the legacy of male (white) power continues in the subtle coercions of everyday life. Relations between men and women, and amongst women and amongst men, are shaped by complex and conflicting emotions and desire, and freely given consent is often limited by disparities of power, physical force, psychological pressures, social and financial inequalities, differing household responsibilities, as well as the complex interplay of lust and fear. Consent is also delimited by what is regarded as sexually appropriate behaviour. Women who have been raped continue to have to prove in court that there was no implied consent given to the alleged rapist – especially if they are deemed to have acted provocatively. At the other extreme, there are certain categories of action where consent is deemed impossible. In countries where homosexuality is illegal mutual consent by partners is not a defence – as was the case in England and Wales until 1967. Similarly, as the notorious 'Operation Spanner' case concerning men involved in consensual sado-masochistic practices in 1990 illustrated, there are limits in the English jurisdiction on people's ability to consent to practices that lead to the infliction of injury on another person – however clearly consent has been signalled (Weeks 1995: 127–9) – see **Sado-masochism**. The regulation of **Pornography**, or sexually explicit music, or sites on the Web, again assumes that there are areas where although consent is technically possible, the 'public good' may override autonomous choices – though in the infinity of cyber-space this becomes increasingly difficult. There are legitimate areas for debate about where the boundaries around consent must be drawn, and increasingly these tend to revolve around 'extreme' activities. Should one, for example, be free to consent to self-mutilation or mutual murder? All societies find it necessary to limit **Choice**. Regulatory forces do this because they assume that their duty to protect people, to limit risk and prevent harm, overrides choice and consent. During the twentieth century moral enthusiasm has been increasingly backed up by developments in biomedicine and psychology which have taken it upon themselves to define what constitutes risk and harm.

The limit case for ideas of consent comes when children are concerned. Globally, most societies deem it necessary to have an 'age of consent' of some form or other for young people, marking an age below which sexual activity is not permitted, though this varies enormously. Even within single countries such as Australia or the USA ages of consent have differed within the constituent states – in the case of the latter from 12/13 in southern states to 18 in California. The range internationally is from 12 in Malta to 20 in Chile, though Shi'ite Iran deems it unnecessary to have an age of consent on the grounds that under sharia law only sex in marriage is permitted anyway. Some of these laws regulate not only sexual activity per se, but different sexual practices – with different minimum ages for genital, oral and anal intercourse, or for sex with young people involving seduction or power relations. The Philippines has an age of 12 but this goes up to 18 when financial transactions are involved. Similarly, Thailand in 1987 introduced a minimum age of 13–15, which goes up to 18 for prostitution. Others differentiate between heterosexual and homosexual ages of consent, with countries in Europe following the Napoleonic Code tending to have the same age, because homosexuality was decriminalized early (though for practical rather than humanitarian reasons), while countries in the Anglo-Saxon tradition tended until recently to have differential ages – higher for homosexuals – once homosexuality was decriminalized. Within Europe the development of the European Union and the influence of the European Court have propelled moves to greater equity, but it is interesting that former British colonies in both Africa and the Caribbean stick to the more punitive Anglo tradition about homosexuality – usually, paradoxically, claiming it as an upholding of a (mythologized) pre-colonial opposition to homosexuality. Here consent remains impossible.

The origins of the age of consent are, in Waites's phrase (2005: 62), 'thoroughly patriarchal', above all being concerned with protecting girls from male lust. From the Middle Ages the English minimum age was essentially concerned with protecting girls as male property. By the late nineteenth century, when the age of consent for girls was successively raised from 12 to 13 to 16, the rationale was different, under the impact of social purity campaigns, but the result was similar. Girls needed protection from male sexuality, based on the assumption that men initiated sexual activity and women did not. There was no concept of autonomous female sexual agency. No minimum age was necessary for men, on the other hand, precisely because they were the doers. Protection was not necessary, at least for heterosexual sex. Protection of boys from the sexual advances of predatory older men has, however, been central to the evolution of an age of consent for (male) homosexuals since the partial decriminalization of male homosexuality in 1967.

The age of consent raises central issues: about the meanings of childhood, the appropriate age for sexual activity, the balance between protection and autonomy, the responsibility of adults in general and those in positions of power and responsibility in particular. These issues dramatize the difficulties in determining the free play of consent, and why it remains a contested concept.

COSMOPOLITANISM

A fundamental question posed by the various forces shaping a globalizing, complex, diverse world is how to find agreed common standards by which to measure individual and particularist needs, and how to construct viable ways of living harmoniously with difference. **Multiculturalism** is one, highly contested possible response. Cosmopolitanism is another. It is based on the belief that despite a multiplicity of possible allegiances, human groups have a shared humanity, with a potential shared set of values, and that different peoples can find mutual respect and ways of working together despite myriad differences. For the sociologist Ulrich Beck the cosmopolitan perspective goes beyond the constricting limits of the nation, and offers 'an imagination of alternative ways of life and rationality, which includes the otherness of the other' (Beck 2002: 18; see also Beck 2006). This requires a rejection of attempts to freeze and reify different cultures, identities and ways of being, and a welcoming of the pleasures and conviviality of intermingling. Unlike those multiculturalists who hold firm to their particularist identities, the potential cosmopolitan citizen is someone who is capable of working across different national traditions, communities of fate and alternative ways of life, and of engaging in dialogue with the discourses of others in order to shape a more global possibility of social practice and belonging (Held 2000: 425).

Such aspirations have a long history, rooted in the Stoical philosophy and the universalistic ambitions of the Roman Empire. Universalistic ambitions have been a recurrent note in Western philosophy. Cosmopolitanism was a key concept of Kantian and Enlightenment ethics, and is traceable in contemporary ethical systems which emphasize our obligation to respond to the vulnerability of the other. It has been strengthened by a growing sense of transnational and international belonging, sustained by emerging concepts of human rights, the common experience of the threats to our common global home posed by potential nuclear disaster, the perils of global warming and international terror, and the interlocking of human possibilities, hopes and fears generated by **Globalization**. Cosmopolitanism points to a global consciousness based on openness to the other, and as such has become a critical term in contemporary social theorizing (Appiah 2006).

What is new in contemporary cosmopolitanism is a shifting perception of the meanings of this common humanity: now less a given of nature that can be taken for granted in ethical endeavour, and more a project for conscious construction, to be elaborated in the process of engagement and dialogue with others. It differentiates itself from traditionalist universalism by its respect for diversity and its refusal to proclaim an a priori set of values, which can all too readily be seen as another way of imposing Western norms. Contemporary cosmopolitanism does not assume a universal right or wrong. Such concepts can only emergence through conversations across cultures. But these near utopian hopes of dialogue have to confront the harsh realities of continuing and in some contexts accentuating disparities of power between peoples, and the difficulties of living cosmopolitan values amidst complex multicultural and multi-faith societies. Cosmopolitanism assumes an ability to take a critical distance from one's own habits and milieu. But globalization can as readily accentuate local rootedness, embattlement and separation as encourage a sense of universal belonging. There is a danger that cosmopolitanism becomes the idealism of the frequent-flyer elite rather than the lived reality of the majority, grounded in the routine complexities of everyday life.

On the other hand, sociologists have seen signs of a vernacular cosmopolitanism (Holton 2009), a bottom-up response to new opportunities of linkages across cultures, not least through the Web. Turner (2009: 752) has identified a 'pop cosmopolitanism', which can occur at the level of fantasy and imagination, and allows an escape from the narrowness of the local. Cosmopolitan citizenship has also had its pioneers in the new sexual subjects that have moved onto the stage of history since the 1970s. Amongst these the 'global gay' (Altman 2001) shows the potential and the difficulties, the challenge and the opportunities. He or she can potentially feel at home in all parts of the worlds where a similar repertoire of cafés, bars, clubs, saunas, cruising areas, local neighbourhoods, styles of dress, modes of behaviour and values systems provide the material base for a 'queer cosmopolitanism' (Binnie 2004: 126ff.), an ability and willingness to engage with others and to develop a sense of common being in a 'queer diaspora' (Patton and Sánchez Eppler 2000). But at the same time local regimes of power continue to promote institutional **Homophobia** and individual persecutions, delimiting full engagement. Cosmopolitan aspirations constantly have to confront the checks and balances of the particular.

Globalization has produced the opportunity for recognition across distance, and for the development of elements of a common life and common cause that provide the case for cosmopolitanism. But it has also exposed the particularities that shape the local identifications and barriers to universal belonging. Cosmopolitanism cannot escape the necessity to engage with the often grubby complexities of diverse cultures.

CYBERSEX

Cybersex, virtual erotic encounters mediated through the Internet, provides multiple forms of erotic excitement, enticement and entanglement at the click of a button or touch of a screen. Commentators, racing to catch up with explosive innovation, have identified cybersex, cyber-stalking, cyber-rape, cyber-victims, cyber-voyeurism, Porn2.0, compu-sex, sex chat rooms, sex news groups, sex bulletin boards, camcorder sex, Skype-sex, cyborgs, sex with avatars, blogs, vlogs, tweeting, sexual games, online prostitution, new forms of pornography and so on. The list is potentially limitless as the power and use of the Internet expands and our erotic imagination finds new virtual nooks and crannies (Plummer 2003: 9–12). The Internet is a site for sexual pickup, courtship, chat, confession, self-affirmation, experiment, fantasy, sexual blogging, fiction and biography/autobiography, friendship, love, multiple relationships, social networking, virtual community, campaigning, **Masturbation** (the ultimate, if not inevitable, sexual release of virtual sex) – and, on the downside, for potential **Sex addiction**, exploitation, violence, threat and fear.

Most optimistically, the Internet is where people create virtual realities in the hope of transforming inherited assumptions about sexuality, identities, relationships and intimacy. As such it is a site of heterosexual and queer spaces and possibilities, of feminist and sex radical explorations as well as a space for their conservative and fundamentalist opponents. Even the most humdrum life can be transformed as you remake yourself and explore your wildest fantasies and desires in the anonymity of the chat room or the pickup site.

The Internet provides a new form of intimacy where anything seems possible, with fewer of the risks than traditional forms of contact. In theory you can pick and choose and still have the semblance of control. It permits twenty-first century forms of connection as traditional locations of interactivity, courtship and mating have weakened – such as the church, the extended family, the local community, the factory floor or the office, the ball or the dance hall or party circuit. Websites offer pragmatic and highly efficient alternatives (though the viral connections of the net might also super-charge many of these older forms). Electronic intimacy offers an apparent degree of freedom and autonomy that people no longer expect to get from face-to-face encounters. It also allows you to maintain relations at a distance. Online contacts offer privacy, you can do it from home, you don't need to dress up for it, you don't have to go through a middleman, and you can see a picture of the contacts and converse with them via email or voice-mail or webcams or video links before you risk a meeting. You do not even have to meet them if an intense online emotional relationship or casual erotic adventure is what you want.

Casually started, passionately pursued, instantly ended. The Internet by the early twenty-first century had become the prime site for gay male cruising as websites like Gaydar became the focus of gay pickups. Business in gay bars and clubs was reportedly well down, and emphasis was shifting away from the site of casual encounters towards either social arenas or explicitly sexual action places. Heterosexual dating sites proliferated exponentially. At the same time sites were exploding for every conceivable taste. On the specialist **Sado-masochism**/BDSM (B&D: bondage and discipline; D/s: dominance and submission; and S&M: sadism and masochism), sites you can specify down to the smallest detail your particular tastes for pain and pleasure. Paedophile sites have expanded dramatically, despite sustained police attempts worldwide to hunt down the users. Websites providing information on 'dogging', heterosexual open-air public sex usually conducted in secluded places, have promoted it exponentially (Bell 2006). The most esoteric desires can be catered for, even down to sexualized cannibalism. Notoriously, a German man, Armin Meiwes, murdered a man he met through the Internet and ate his sexual organs, with apparently the victim's free **Consent**. On his appeal against conviction Meiwes argued that 'I don't need to do it anymore – but I do believe everyone should be able to decide what he wants to do with his own body' (Boyes 2006: 3). Here we have notions of sexual autonomy and self-determination taken to the point of madness.

Historically sexuality, produced by regulation and resistance, has been organized around a dichotomy between reality (the world of scarcity and sexual limits) and fantasy (the world of boundless desires). Cybersex ostensibly dissolves the boundaries, offering a world of infinite, protean possibilities. Its potentialities and powers are already vast, but it seems we are only at the beginning. Already court-ship, friendship, love and sexuality unmediated by the Web seems faintly old-fashioned. What its impact on the messy, imperfect old body and its pleasures and pains will be only time, and the hyper-inventiveness of producers and users of cybersex, will tell.

D

DESIRE

Desire is a term that lies at the heart of sexuality. It suggests a longing for the other that demands satisfaction, and perhaps can never fully be satisfied. It unsettles, destabilizes, overwhelms, dominates, is wilful, playful, pleasurable, painful and always falls short of fulfilment. It is constantly repressed, indeed for **Psycho-analysis** is the result of repression, but is seemingly irrepressible.

Traditionally sexual desire is insistently heterosexual, and phallocratic: it is the male model of desire for the female other that has dominated the imagery. For a conservative philosopher such as Scruton (2001) there is a fundamental difference between male and female desire. The unbridled ambitions of the phallus are balanced by the female desire to pacify what is most vagrant. There is a fragile complementarity between the sexes. A broader view might suggest that desire is polymorphous and polyvocal, female as well as male, homosexual as well as heterosexual, perverse as well as 'normal'. The problem lies not in desire but in the structures (psychic and social) and cultural context in which it plays. Not surprisingly, desire has long been a problem for philosophers of West and East. Desire sets itself against reason and order, and undermines stable relationships and happiness at the same time as it seems essential to making them possible. In Buddhist thought the craving that underpins it is the very source of unhappiness; only its elimination can open the way to Nirvana. In the West, on the other hand, the manufacture of desire has become one of the essential activities of capitalist expansion, and apparently helps to make the world go round.

Current theories of desire owe much to psychoanalysis. Desire is sharply distinguished from need. A need arises from internal tension and can be satisfied through a specific action. Hunger can be satisfied through access to food. For Freud, wishes or desires are linked to memory traces of previous satisfactions and are fulfilled through hallucinatory reproductions of the perceptions, which become signs of the satisfaction. The search for the object of desire is not governed therefore by physiological need, but by the relationship to signs or representation. Desire cannot be a relationship to a real object, but is a relationship to a fantasy. It is nonetheless all the more potent for being imagined. For Freud psychic repression is particularly directed against the incestuous and unattainable desire for the mother and father, and it is this that accounts for the formative role of sexuality in psychic conflicts. It suggests that desire is both insistent and unattainable.

It is this aspect of desire that is at the heart of Jacques Lacan's version of psychoanalysis, which has also been influential amongst feminist theorists – see **Feminism**. For Lacan, subjectivity is formed as individuals become aware of their alienation from themselves, in the pre-Oedipal imaginary realm which always remains with them; and then as through the Oedipal process individuals become aware of the structures of human sexuality which they acquire through the acquisition of language. What this implies in regard to sexuality is that there is no insistent sexual desire which pre-exists the entry into the structures of language and culture, the Symbolic order. 'Desire' is constituted in the very process of that induction, predicated upon absence or lack. Desire by definition cannot ever be fulfilled (Laplanche and Pontalis 1980).

For radical critics such as Gilles Deleuze and Felix Guattari (1977), it is the Symbolic order itself that is an imposition. Leaving the world of flux that preceded 'Oedipalization' and acculturation is the real human tragedy, for in that flux desire is polymorphous and hence 'revolutionary'. Drawing on a range of writers and movements from Hegel and Nietzsche, to Dadaism and Sartre – but above all Nietzsche – their productive theory of desire rebelled against a linked set of targets: left puritanism as much as right-wing authoritarianism, the 'fascism of the mind' as much as of the streets. Now society itself is condemned, along with Lacan's phallocentrism, the family, the 'Oedipalization of society' – and psychoanalysis itself, which is seen as the agent for the imposition of Oedipus and the control of desire. Any acceptance of Oedipus implies an artificial restriction on the unconscious, where everything is potentially infinitely open. There is in this flux no given self, only the cacophony of 'desiring machines', desiring production. For Deleuze and Guattari, desire is not a striving for the lost unity of the womb, but a state of constant productive flux. But this flux is too much for capitalist society to endure, for it simultaneously encourages and abhors this chaos, and cannot live with the infinite variety of potential interconnections and relationships. So the Oedipus complex, instead of being, as in Lacan, a necessary state of the development of a human individual, is seen by Deleuze and Guattari as the only effective means of controlling the libido in capitalist societies (Weeks 2009b). And Freudianism plays a key role under capitalism: it is both the discoverer of the mechanisms of desire and the organizer of its control. Guy Hocquenghem, in *Homosexual Desire* (1978), applies this approach more specifically to homosexuality. Capitalist society manufactures homosexuals just as it manufactures proletarians by imposing a psychologically repressive category, that of homosexuality, on the polyvocal nature of desire. Psychiatry has classified what is marginal, and in doing so placed it in a central position, and has given it social salience. Yet simultaneously it reveals the arbitrariness of social classifications and the power of desire, which cannot so easily be restricted.

Desire therefore is either a perpetual marker for loss and the impossibility of fulfilment (in psychoanalysis), or a revolutionary potentiality crushed by capitalism and the phallocratic order (for radical critics of psychoanalysis and theorists of productive desire). In either case desire outstrips the possibility of immediate satisfaction. Whether it is the wish for love, erotic satisfaction, or the more amorphous but eternal hope for happiness, desire appears to be the eternal itch that marks our humanity, and its limits.

DISABILITY

Since the 1970s there has been a growing awareness, led by the disability rights movement, that people are disabled by society, not by their **Bodies**. A critical distinction is made by theorists of disability between *impairment*, essentially a medically defined set of conditions embracing physical and developmental issues, and disability, which is a profoundly social experience, and is defined by social structures, ideologies and prejudices. This echoes the distinction made by feminist theorists between sex and **Gender** (Shakespeare 2003: 143). Just as in wider sexual theory the medical model of sexual difference has been displaced by **Social constructionism**, and **Queer** theory, so increasingly a social model of disability has developed side by side with new forms of **Agency** by disabled people themselves.

A traditional model remains influential, however, in relation to the sexual needs and desires of disabled people (Shakespeare *et al.* 1996). Their sexuality continues to be seen as a problem rather than an opportunity for a rich and fulfilling life. Gerschick (2007: 256–9) has outlined five challenges that particularly face disabled people in relation to sexuality. The first is the pervasiveness of medicalization, which works to reinforce deeply embedded assumptions and give them the credence of scientific expertise. As Shakespeare (2003: 144–5) has argued popular notions of disabled masculinity focus on perceived impotence and lack of manhood. On the other hand female sexual needs tend to be ignored, or seen in relationship to assumed heterosexual coupledom. Physical impairments in many cases will affect the possibilities or pleasures in sexual interaction, but these still tend to dominate professional responses to sexual desires at the expense of the possibilities of sexual agency.

The second challenge emerges from the entrenched stereotypes and prejudices that shadow disability and sexuality. Non-normative behaviour and/or bodies – based on impairment, size, age, colour, or other visible differences – are ready targets for humour, discrimination, stigma and abuse, and are denied social recognition and validation, which in turn inhibit the development of sexual relationships. The premium given to conventional notions of the body beautiful in Western sexual cultures – and especially in subcultures like the gay male world – work to exclude those who are obviously unconventional. Third, these experiences may in turn be internalized, giving rise to a deep sense of inadequacy, and lack of self-esteem, especially in intimate relationships. A disabled woman, Nancy Mairs, has written: 'my wheelchair seals my chastity. . . . To be truthful, I have so internalized the social proscription of libido in my kind that if a man did come on to me, I'd probably distrust him as at least a little peculiar in his erotic tastes' (quoted in Gerschick 2007: 258).

Fourth, disabled people may readily be objectified in sexual interactions, especially by able-bodied people. Disabled people are subject to all the complexities and **Intersectionality** of diverse disparities of power, race, class and material inequalities, and these may readily accentuate asymmetrical relationships between vulnerable women and able-bodied men, or between men and men, and women and women. Finally, disabled people are vulnerable to physical and sexual abuse in a variety of situations. Researchers have suggested that children with disabilities in the USA are 70 per cent more likely to be physically or sexually abused than their able-bodied counterparts. Such abuse is more likely to be chronic than episodic, and is likely to be perpetrated by someone well known to the person abused. Women are more likely to be sexually abused than men, who are more likely to be physically abused (Gerschick 2007: 259). Experiences of abuse in turn can accentuate feelings of vulnerability and inhibit the development of close relationships.

None of this, however, should be taken to mean that disabled people are passive victims, either of their physical or mental impairments, or of societal oppression. A sense of exclusion has given rise within the disability movement to demands for proper access to social facilities and public space, and this has been applied to sexual issues: 'access to avenues of sexual expression and sexual negotiation', as a critical element in the achievement of agency (Shuttleworth 2007: 179). For Shakespeare (2003: 148), any account of disability in the contemporary world needs to be alive to the fact of people's resistance and agency. Many disabled people are having positive sexual experiences, developing strong relationships and having families. The disability movement itself has provided a sense of common struggle and empowerment (though it has historically not tended to stress sexual issues). Others have found positive benefits in disabled sexuality, especially in the opportunities for rejecting conventional notions of masculinity or femininity, or in exploring non-penetrative or non-genital sexual practices. Like the widespread adoption of **Safer-sex** practices by gay men following the **AIDS** crisis, disabled people have been able to find in their situation opportunities for exploring the erotic in diverse and creative ways. As disabled interviewee, Penny, put it to Shakespeare and his colleagues (Shakespeare 2003: 148), 'For me, sex is about pleasure, humour and respect. It is with these factors in mind that I approach any seeming "difficulty" my impairments present me. . . . My open attitude to my sexuality, arising because I am a disabled person, often defines sex for me as a much more celebratory and explorative experience than for many non-disabled people.'

The sexual practices of disabled people are varied and diverse. In that they are no different from the vast variety of sexual actors that make up the sexual spectrum. Nevertheless disabled sexuality has been problematized, denied or ignored. What the agency of disabled people themselves has increasingly underlined is that it is societal attitudes that constitute the problem, not the sexual pleasures and potentialities of disabled people themselves.

E

ESSENTIALISM

Essentialism refers to determinist forms of thinking that assume that all forms of human behaviour can be explained by reference to an assumed human essence, an inner being that exists prior to the social, and is constitutive of human experience. The term has been used to explain a wide range of social phenomena, including nationalism, race and ethnicity and **Gender**. Essentialism became a key term in debates about the history and cultural meaning of **Sexuality**, and especially **Homo-sexuality**, in the 1970s and 1980s, and despite often heated controversy remains a vital feature of thinking about the body, gender and the erotic. In practice, essentialist forms of thinking usually rely on the assumption that the sexual can be explained by biology in one form or another, and even forms of essentialism that are dressed in the language of psychology, or in some cases religious or cultural positions, tend to fall back on ideas of the natural that in the end are traceable to a biological substratum. The term 'naturalism' has sometimes been suggested as a synonym for essentialism.

Essentialist assumptions are central to traditional ways of thinking about sexuality, both in common-sense knowledge and in theory. Until relatively recently most writers on sex saw it as an irresistible natural energy barely held in check by a thin crust of civilization. This was foundational for the pioneers of **Sexology**. Richard von Krafft-Ebing at the end of the nineteenth century saw sexuality as an all-powerful instinct which demands fulfilment against the claims of morals, belief and social order. Such views assume a pressure-cooker view of sexuality, with sex providing a basic 'biological mandate' which presses against and must be restrained by the cultural matrix (Gagnon and Simon 1974). It takes many forms. For many, sexuality represented threat and fear. 'Sex', as the anthropologist Malinowski put it, 'really is dangerous', the source of most human trouble from Adam and Eve onwards (Malinowski 1963: 120, 127). Liberatory theorists such as Wilhelm Reich and Herbert Marcuse tended to see sex as a beneficent force which was repressed by a corrupt civilization. Sociobiologists or evolutionary psychologists see all social forms as rooted in our evolutionary origins, encoded in the DNA (Weeks 2009a: 20). The basic mechanism, in the words of Richard Dawkins (1978: 7), was 'the fundamental law of gene selfishness'.

43

Essentialist views of sexuality have been inextricably linked with assumptions about gender. The genital and reproductive distinctions between biological men and biological women have been read not only as necessary but also as sufficient explanation for different sexual needs and desires. They appear as the most basic distinctions between peoples. The very definition of the sexual instinct was essentially one derived from male practices and fantasies: overpowering forces, engulfing drives, gushing streams, uncontrollable spasms – such metaphors have dominated the Western discourse on sex. Early sexologists drew on this imagery even as they attempted to put it on a more scientific basis. So sex was defined as a 'physiological law', 'a force generated by powerful ferments', a drive 'which cannot be set aside for any sort of social convention', and most graphically of all, 'a volcano that burns down and lays waste all around it; . . . an abyss that devours all honour, substance and health' (cited in Weeks 1985: 80–1).

The implications of such imagery are deeply conservative, explaining the intractability to change of social institutions, and the inevitability of certain givens (such as male/female differences). More progressive approaches have, on the other hand, found similar justification in biological explanations, to argue, for example, for equal but different roles for men and women, and greater freedom for gays on the grounds of their biological functionality (Wilson and Rahman 2005). Sociobiologists and evolutionary psychologists have seen key social institutions like marriage, parenting and social bonding as 'adaptive', a critical term of evolutionary theory, products not of history or social development but of 'evolutionary necessity'. So, certain aspects of human sexual behaviour, such as male philandering and female coyness, the argument goes, are biological adaptations selected in the infancy of the human race, 100,000 to 600,000 years ago, and have become universal features of human nature, ensuring the propagation of our ancestors' genes. Similarly, rape can be seen as an adaptive strategy, by which otherwise sexually-unsuccessful men propagate their genes by mating with fertile women who might otherwise reject them; or parental love can be reduced to a means of successfully ensuring gene survival.

There is clearly a great intellectual attraction, as well as demotic appeal, in such evolutionary explanations: they provide clarity where social scientists may see complexity, certainty where others recognize only contingency. There is also a certain political logic in the vogue for evolutionary and other biological theories: they provide an explanation for certain apparently intractable social problems, for example, why men are so reluctant to change, why women continue to assume most caring roles, why male homosexuals are apparently more promiscuous than lesbians. Such theories also – and this is a prize attribute – seem to speak to widespread, common-sense beliefs about the naturalness of sexual divisions. They go with, rather than against, the grain of popular prejudice. But if they can claim to explain some things, they cannot generally or convincingly explain others (why there are variations between different cultures, for example, or why history frequently undergoes rapid social change, with new attitudes towards gender and sexuality emerging).

Against all these arguments **Social constructionism** has stressed that sexuality is subject to socio-cultural moulding to an extraordinary degree. Far from being the most natural element in social life, it is perhaps one of the most susceptible to cultural organization. Moreover, the forces that shape and mould the erotic possibilities of the body vary from society to society. This puts the emphasis firmly where it should belong, on society and social relations rather than on nature. This is not to deny the importance of biology. The physiology and morphology of the body provides the preconditions for human sexuality. Biology conditions and limits what is possible (Fausto-Sterling 2000). But it does not cause the patterns of sexual life. We cannot reduce human behaviour to the mysterious workings of the DNA, the eternal gene, or 'the dance of the chromosomes'. Rather we can see in biology a set of potentialities, which are transformed and given meaning only in social relationships.

Such an approach has been especially central to rethinking the meanings of homosexuality since the 1970s. The so-called constructionist-essentialist controversy (Stein 1992) was particularly focused on the historicity of sexual categories and identities, and whether these could be attributed to an essential distinction between homosexuality and heterosexuality, or whether these very categories were historically specific. Though the debate eventually collapsed through sheer exhaustion the consensus amongst historians and sociologists by the early 2000s was clearly in favour of the latter position. Essentialist arguments continued to flourish, however, amongst more traditionalist sexologists and enthusiastic researchers for genetic explanations of every sexual phenomenon. In a world of constant change many perhaps find a comfort in relying on the solidities of biology, and the belief that at the core of our fragile humanity is some basic, essential bodily truth.

F

FAMILIES

The family has a resounding presence in late-modern societies. Conservative commentators lament its decline. Liberals seek ways of strengthening it. Radicals seek alternative models of it, if no longer seeking alternatives to it. In the regularly circulated truism, it is seen as the most basic unit of society. But for something so basic, the family as concept has had a varied history. Who we decide are kin and what we describe as 'the family' are clearly dependent on a range of historical and cultural factors. Historically and cross-culturally 'family' has embraced wide kin groups, households (often including servants) and tight nuclear groupings. Today, there are many different family forms especially within highly industrialized, Western societies, coexisting more or less harmoniously – shaped by class, geography, and different religious, cultural, racial and ethnic communities, and by **Choice**. Many people now speak of their 'families of choice', based on friendship networks and chosen kin. There are 'non-heterosexual families' as well as traditional heterosexual families residing next to each other, more or less in harmony (Weeks *et al.* 2001).

Family patterns are shaped and reshaped by economic and social factors, by faiths, by rules of inheritance, by state interventions to regulate marriage and divorce, or to support the family by social welfare or taxation policies. At various times pro-family policies have become a major theme in various national politics: to boost the birth rate, provide an alternative to social care, build **Social capital**, or to maintain social order and discipline the young. Anti-family policies have had a weaker resonance, though feminist critics in the 1970s sought to critique the family as the factory of gender inequality, and proposed alternatives to it. All these interventions affect the likely patterns of sexual life: by encouraging or discouraging the rate of marriage, age of marriage, incidence of reproduction, attitudes to non-procreative or non-heterosexual sex, acceptance of cohabitation, or single parenthood, the relative power of men over women, and the significance of the binary divide between **Heterosexuality** and **Homosexuality**.

Despite jeremiads about the breakdown of family, trust and social capital (Fukuyama 1995, 1999), contemporary researchers consistently find that family-type relationships are alive and well, and being lived in many different shapes, sizes and forms across late-modern societies (Stacey 1996, 2010). There are big families and small families, with children, and without, reconstituted families and step-families, long-distance families and LAT (living alone together) families, lone-parent families and polyamorist families, traditional families and **Queer** families. Which is why it is safer and wiser now to talk about *families* rather than *the* family. Families may be plural and varied, but remain extremely important for those involved. Family is the arena in which most people, certainly in Western cultures, gain some sense of their social belonging, relate to others across generations, learn about **Gender**, work out individual identities and, if we follow **Psychoanalysis**, it is where our desires are organized from a very early stage. Family bonds continue to generate emotional and social capital across class, regional and ethnic differences (Edwards 2004).

Some family relationships go disastrously awry, with appalling effects on its members, especially the young. Yet despite lamentations on the decline of parenting researchers have found that most parents work conscientiously within their own moral rationalities, which lay down the balance of mothering and fathering activities, attitudes to work and so on, and these tend to reflect various class and ethnic differences, but common efforts to do the right thing (Duncan and Edwards 1999). Young people, often portrayed as the victims of a collapse of the family and social capital, on the contrary show the strength of their ties with others, especially in sibling relationships. Sibling ties are widely viewed as a source of protection, support, obligation and company (Edwards *et al.* 2006). Far from seeing a collapse of values in this changed world, the social worlds of young people are intensely moral worlds (Smart 2006). Many family types, especially in minority communities (the African-American family in the USA, the African-Caribbean family in the UK) have been seen as dysfunctional but again there is now plentiful evidence of the ways in which they can respond to children's needs and provide mutual support (Reynolds 2005). Similarly, there is overwhelming evidence for the effectiveness of same-sex families in bringing up children (Weeks *et al.* 2001). Despite the pessimists, there is clear evidence for the strength and resilience of norms of reciprocity and care across a wide range of social worlds and family forms – see **Relationality**.

Same-sex families offer a powerful case study of what is happening. Everyone, an American gay writer has argued, has the right to shape family forms that fit his or her needs (Goss 1997: 19), and this is like a leitmotif for the emergence of 'new families'. The language of 'family' used by many LGBT people can be seen as both a challenge to conventional definitions, and an attempt to broaden these; as a hankering for legitimacy and an attempt to build something new; as an identification with existing patterns, and a more or less conscious effort to subvert them. For some these new elective relations serve to queer the family. Others are not so certain that this is not a surrender to heteronormativity (Roseneil and Budgeon 2004). But there is a wider point. If there are indeed so many types of family, why should same-sex families be ignored (Stacey 1996: 15)? Non-heterosexual relationships and families of choice are part of a wider struggle over meaning, both participating in and reflecting a wider transformation of family relationships. If the future of marriage is a critical ground of contestation in the wider world, it is hardly surprising that lesbians and gays should focus their demands on it. If parenting is perceived as in major need of rethinking, then why should non-heterosexuals be excluded from the debate? If families get ever more complex as a result of divorce, remarriage, recombination, step-parenting, surrogacy, etc., why should the chosen families of lesbians and gays, including with increasing frequency children, be denied a voice (Weeks *et al.* 2001)?

Rather than attempting to find an essence for this ever more complex reality, it is more useful to see family in the late-modern world in terms of a set of social practices rather than a fixed institution to which we may or may not belong. From this perspective: 'family' can be seen as less of a noun and more as an adjective or a verb. '"Family" represents a constructed quality of human interaction or an active process rather than a thing-like object of social investigation', writes David H. J. Morgan (1999: 16). This approach displaces the idea that the family is a fixed and timeless entity, which one is either a member of, or excluded from. We can view it instead as a series of practical everyday activities which we do and live: through activities such as mutual care, the division of labour in the home, looking after dependents and significant others. 'Family' from this point of view is about particular sorts of relational interactions rather than simply private activities in a privileged sphere. Instead of being an objective phenomenon, 'family' can be interpreted as a subjective set of practices, whose meanings are made by those who participate in them. Family practices focus on everyday interactions with close and loved ones, rather than the fixed boundaries of co-residence, marriage, ethnicity, obligation and privacy that defined the traditional male-dominated family. Such a perspective recognizes the ways in which our networks of care and affection are not simply given by virtue of blood and marriage, but are negotiated and shaped by us (Williams 2004: 17). It is less important whether we are *in* a family than whether we *do* family-type things. Family practices are 'performative', with families constructed through their constant interactive enactment (Butler 1990). We live and perform family rather than dwell within it. Family life is a historically specific, contextualized set of activities, intimately linked with other social practices. If this is increasingly the case, there is no theoretical reason to exclude non-heterosexual everyday practices – or anyone else's – from the pantheon of family and kin.

FATEFUL MOMENTS

This is a concept developed by the sociologist Anthony Giddens as a key aspect of his account of the 'reflexive project of the self' in late-modern societies – see **Reflexivity**. In the complex process of constructing a viable narrative to make sense of one's life in late-modern society, individuals experience fateful moments, 'times when events come together in such a way that an individual stands . . . at a cross-roads in his (*sic*) existence; or where a person learns of information with fateful consequences' (Giddens 1991: 113). It is a period of disruption, reassessment and transition, and can result in a reordering of one's life trajectory.

It is akin to other concepts used amongst social theorists to understand crucial, reorienting events in personal narratives, such as 'epiphanies', which crystallize key experiences, or more mundanely, 'turning points', at which lives are challenged and change. It also has similarities with the concept of liminality, as developed by Arnold van Gennep and Victor Turner, where it is linked with ritual. A liminal period is characterized by indeterminacy and ambiguity as old values, identities, even class structures and status positions are put into question and new possibilities open up, such as at rites of passage, or at carnivalesque moments, where the world is turned upside down, usually to be rapidly restored. Closer to Gidden's original formulation, a descriptive concept of 'critical moments' has been used in accounts of young people's transition to adulthood, with the stress on events that have a crucial impact on their lives and identities (Thomson *et al.* 2002). All recognize the transformative possibilities of key moments in individual lives where often dramatic change becomes possible.

For Giddens, the fateful moment disrupts the painfully acquired stability of the self and forces the individual to reassess their choices and the **Risk** attached to particular actions. People seek advice, draw on expertise and above all reconsider what the fateful moment says about their sense of being, identity and ways of life. Fateful moments may be threatening but they can also be empowering. They disrupt conventional narratives, and force us to rethink the stories of our lives. They shake the kaleidoscope, so that new patterns emerge.

The concept has obvious value in relation to the development of sexual subjectivity and identity. Marriage and divorce may be life-transforming moments which force a reconsideration of a personal trajectory, and reorder life patterns in new, and often strange, ways. But the concept is more widely applicable. We can see the significance of first sexual experience, first love, loss of love, and loss of loved ones and other transitional moments through which life has to be reassessed and remade. The concept has an especial resonance for those whom society has traditionally marginalized, such as lesbian, gay, bisexual or transgender people. Here fateful moments such as perception of difference, coming out, gender transition, or first real encounter with **Homophobia** all force a reassessment of who and what you are, and what you want to do. More recent developments, such as the advent of **Same-sex marriage**, has been described as having an impact equivalent to a 'second coming out' on individual lives, as people contemplate for the first time public recognition of their life choices. As the fateful moment fades, and the kaleidoscope settles into a new pattern, identities are confirmed or radically transformed, the loose ends are tied into place and the rewritten life story can proceed.

The concept is usually deployed in accounts of individual life stories, but also has a wider relevance in social analysis. There are fateful moments in the history of collectives as well as in the lives of individuals. 'They are phases at which things are wrenched out of joint, where a given state of affairs is suddenly altered by a few key events' (Giddens 1991: 113). These new patterns are, of course, heavily overdetermined, in the sense that they embody a variety of forces at play in any given situation, rather than a single causation. Their outcome is never pre-set, or even predictable. And yet they can deflect or re-shape what seems to be a determining pattern deeply embedded in historical processes.

Obvious key moments which have dramatically changed the broad narrative of sexuality would include the emergence of second-wave **Feminism** and **Gay liberation** in the late 1960s which rewrote the story of many people's lives and made possible new **Sexual identities**. The early **AIDS** crisis in the 1980s had a similar impact on the gay community, forcing a reassessment of risk, the contingency of life, the impact of epidemic and the meanings of relationships. Other examples readily come to mind: the impact of war on opening new sexual possibilities; the cultural impact of the 1960s on everything from rock music to clothes and lifestyles; the role of the civil rights movement and Black Power in challenging entrenched injustices in the USA. Such examples did not affect everyone in the same way, or at all. Some people were pushed by these changes into radical new directions; others reacted, sometimes violently, against them. The significant point is that in the context of such collective fateful moments, old stories no longer tell the full truth about individual or collective lives; new stories are told which circulate in communities of meaning and begin to make sense of changed realities. Out of the collective uncertainties new narratives emerge which help to remake the sexual world.

FEMININITY

What do women want? Sigmund Freud anxiously queried. For Freud, femininity, the condition of being a woman, was a perpetual enigma, a puzzle to be solved but perhaps a question that was irresolvable. In one sense this was a profoundly radical question. Conventionally, there was little doubt about what femininity was and what women were. Women were defined by their biological capacities to reproduce, and the nurturance and caring capacities associated with that. This appeared as a universal constant.

Myths about mother figures appear in all the great religious and cultural systems, and are reiterated effortlessly in evocations of Mother Nature and earth mothers. Since the Western conceptual revolution of the eighteenth century, which displaced the idea that men and women constituted but one sex, with women an inverted and subordinate version of the male, theory has battled with the idea of two distinctive, and complementary, genders, but this has heightened rather than undermined the urge to define femininity in relation to masculinity (Laqueur 1990). Modern theories of **Gender** see femininity and masculinity as relational terms, each gaining meaning only through the existence of the other. But the temptation is always to see each category as having distinct essences, giving meaning to each.

Post-Darwinian biology and early **Sexology** strenuously attempted to define more precisely and explain the difference of women from men, and the fundamental qualities of each. Perhaps femaleness was the result of the earlier arrest in women of evolution, necessitated by the reservation of vital powers to meet the cost of reproduction. Or maybe it was based on fundamental differences in cell metabolism, which dictated that women's destiny was to conserve energy. Whatever, there was a general consensus that, as one commentator put it in the early twentieth century, 'the female mind is specifically adapted to her more protracted part in the perpetuation of the species' (quoted in Weeks 1981: 146). A liberal sexologist and reformer like Havelock Ellis saw a 'cosmic conservatism' at work, a perfect harmony between women and men which meant that 'Woman breeds and tends; man provides', and that was the law of Nature. Even as sexologists recognized the variety and legitimacy of female sexual needs, female sexuality was seen as essentially responsive to men's, and deeply rooted in her reproductive capacity. Women remained *the* sex, and femininity was ultimately defined by the nature of female sexuality (Weeks 1981: 146–7). Though much has changed, similar assumptions, suitably modified in language and detail, constantly recur both in popular literature – where men are from Mars and women from Venus – and in the new sciences of sociobiology and evolutionary psychology to this day. They provide the basis of contemporary **Essentialism**.

Freud's work is of continuing interest, especially to feminist theorists, because it was precisely at this moment when traditional views of women's sexuality were being solidified into scientific dogma that Freud sought to problematize femininity. He found the ideas of femininity and masculinity among the most difficult known to science, and that entry into adult gender identities was a prolonged and hazard-strewn journey. He opened up the question of whether women were born or made. Yet at the same time he continued to remain trapped in the binary structures of gender that he sought to question – see **Psychoanalysis**. His model of psychological development was that of the man. In infancy there was state of indeterminacy, a common bisexuality and polymorphous perversity for both the boy and girl child. But whereas the boy negotiated the Oedipal crisis with relative ease to achieve the culturally and psychologically necessary identification with the father, the girl's path to femininity was more difficult. She had to surmount two major difficulties: a change in erogenous zone from the clitoris to the vagina, and a change in love object from the mother to the father. This is precipitated by her growing awareness of her lack of a penis. Every woman was at first a little man, and the difficult entry into femininity was shaped by her castration.

Freud thus placed himself within an impasse, where he acknowledged that femininity was not a given but the result of a complex and painful process, whose ultimate achievement was far from guaranteed; but at the same time he reasserted a male norm of development which inevitably confirmed femininity as a response to masculinity. From the 1920s a lively controversy erupted within psychoanalysis about the meanings of femininity, which has continued to the present, and which has especially engaged feminism. Since the 1970s feminist theorists have found in psychoanalysis an approach that could simultaneously explain the tenacity of female subordination and sexual differences, and be used to challenge the certainties of dominant conceptions of gender relations. They have, however, often found themselves trapped within the same dilemmas that Freud himself struggled with. They could, for instance, find, in Jacques Lacan's recovery of Freud, a theory which broke with the lingering biologism of early psychoanalysis, and emphasized the structures of language and meaning as critical to the construction of sexual difference, and of the feminine (Mitchell 1974). On the other hand, it was difficult to escape the phallocentrism that was central to Lacan and his school, for whom the female sex has 'the character of an absence, a void, a hole' (Segal 1999: 180). Attempts within French feminism, by those heavily influenced by Lacan, to break with him over this, by positing a separate female sexuality and jouissance (intense pleasure) outside the phallic order, had the effect of reproducing the fundamental difference between men and women that Freud had found so problematic to begin with. Luce Irigaray identified a potential femininity, with a language, religion and economy of its own that represented a fundamental break with the phallic order. Julia Kristeva explored the pre-Oedipal semiotic space of mother–child relations. Both rejected an equal rights feminism in favour of a feminism of difference, going beyond any principle of identity between men and women, or any notion of simple difference (women as not men) towards thinking of femininity in a positive way, as a site of female forms of jouissance.

A similar concern with highlighting the specific qualities of femininity can be found in Rich's (1980) concept of a **Lesbian** continuum, and in the development of a feminism which sought to stress the creation of a distinctly female and separatist culture that rejected any contamination with the violence and aggression of masculinity and male sexuality. The dilemma and the danger was that in critiquing the continuing domination of male models, women were at risk of reproducing the fundamental divisions between masculinity and femininity that were inherent in the hegemonic culture. As Segal (1999: 183) points out, feminists have always had to live with a central paradox: to hold on to the category of 'woman' as the basis for challenging the social denigration of the feminine, whilst seeking to critique those notions of femininity that trap women in subordination. Many of the radical interrogations of femininity, however, from Freud on, have ended up locked within the binarisms they seek to escape.

For a further discussion of femininity in relation to masculinity see **Gender**.

FEMINISM

The term feminism came into use in the mid-nineteenth century, meaning the advocacy and support of the rights of women. As a political and cultural practice it has since embraced a host of meanings, from support for full civil rights and political equality with men, campaigns against the 'double standard' of morality, through advocacy of labour and employment rights, to the full emancipatory claims that were always a key aspect of feminist thinking but came to full fruition with the emergence of the Women's Liberation Movement (WLM) from the late 1960s. Since the nineteenth century, but with greater clarity from the 1960s, feminism has been linked with a variety of political affiliations, and specific emphases: liberal feminism, socialist feminism, radical and revolutionary feminism, lesbian feminism, cultural feminism. Attitudes towards sexuality have varied within and across these divides.

Broadly, historians have posited the existence of three 'waves' of feminism: the first wave, roughly from the mid-nineteenth century to the 1920s; the second wave, associated with the WLM, from the 1960s to late 1980s; and the third wave from then to the present. Sexuality had been a key issue in each wave, but its meanings and implications have shifted significantly. There has never been a single feminist attitude towards the sexual.

The roots of modern feminism lay in the gap between the egalitarian and democratic aspirations (for men) unleashed by the late eighteenth-century revolutions and Enlightenment thought, and the continued reality of women's subordination. Pioneer feminist writers in the late eighteenth century, such as Mary Wollstonecraft in Britain and Olympe de Gouges in France, followed the logic of Enlightenment reason to identify this yawning gap, and to argue for the rights of women. It was not until the middle of the following century, however, that the first real stirrings of a feminist movement can be observed. In both Britain and the USA, some of the earliest key players were women of a deeply Christian background, closely linked with evangelicalism in Britain, and with the Quakers in the USA. Many of the American pioneers had honed their campaigning skills in the battle against slavery, just as British evangelicalism had been associated with struggles against the slave trade, and was subsequently strongly associated with campaigns around the sexual exploitation of women through prostitution and the 'white slave trade' (what we would now know as **Trafficking**). This high moral energy fed into outrage at the double-standard of morality which allowed men to be sexually lax but severely restricted women's autonomy. **Prostitution** was the most obvious symbol of this, and a major focus of feminist campaigning in Britain, especially in the 1880s, was on the repeal of the notorious Contagious Diseases Acts, which required compulsory examination of women suspected of being prostitutes in certain garrison towns. However respectable the cause, and however moral the campaigners, such as Josephine Butler, this association with sexual issues caused a schism in the emergent women's movement. The mainstream movement, increasingly concerned with achieving equal suffrage rights with men, were alarmed by the distraction to their cause and distanced themselves, as they did from pioneering **Sexology**, and sex reformers such as Havelock Ellis. Those who focused primarily on sexual campaigns, on the other hand, found their most fervent supporters in the developing social purity movement focusing primarily on vice, and not always easy partners for feminist campaigners. The focus on the perils of uncontrolled male lust pointed to a politics of protection for women and children that often was at odds with the complexities of working-class life, or with claims for female autonomy. Other sex-related issues, such as birth control, were similarly treated gingerly, again because of the enormous controversy they aroused, as Margaret Sanger in the USA and Marie Stopes in Britain subsequently discovered.

A large part of the marginalization of sexual issues by leading feminists was pragmatic. The leading suffragists shared a moral horror at the double-standard, and the widespread nature of prostitution. Underlying the shading of emphases, moreover, was a fundamental agreement on the nature of female and male sexuality: following the work of people like Havelock Ellis, influential as much with Sanger in the USA as with radicals in Britain, it was seen as essentially reactive, 'kissed into life' by the male. Male sexuality was potentially violent and uncontrolled, needing to be domesticated by respectability and a single standard of morality. Issues such as lesbianism, despite the intense friendships generated within the women's movement, and controversies over marriage and 'free love' were treated with high caution when they were dealt with at all. The challenge to male sexual excess was an important challenge to the double-standard but it was framed within a traditional concept of gender differences. This first wave of feminism essentially looked to improvements within the limits of biologically given differences rather than offering a critique or challenge to them.

The intellectual mother of second-wave feminism, Simone de Beauvoir (1972), put the matter rather differently when she argued in *The Second Sex* (originally published in 1948) that one was not born a woman but became one. The idea of becoming a woman, of not so much revealing a hidden self but of making oneself anew, was to be a vital, though contested, strand in the new women's movement from the late 1960s, and especially with regard to sexuality. As with the earlier wave the fundamental stimulus for the emergence of the movement was the ever-widening gap between the language of equality and democracy and the reality of women's lives; what was described by Betty Friedan in *The Feminine Mystique* (1992, first published 1966) as the problem without a name. The issue now, however, was not so much the absence of women's rights, but the failure of the gains of the previous half-century – suffrage rights, improved educational opportunities, involvement of women in the workforce, better access to contraception, greater recognition of female sexuality – to change fundamentally women's sense of being trapped within domesticity, and second-class citizenship. This was compounded for many women of the baby-boom generation, those born in the immediate aftermath of World War II, by a growing gap between their political radicalization, inspired in the USA by the civil rights movement and Black Power, and the antiwar movement, and the reality of their relationship with their fellow male radicals, which revealed starkly that women were still seen as bed-mates and coffee makers rather than fully equal partners with men. There was a form of sexual liberation, but it was defined by men.

Sexuality was now at the heart of a politics that emphasized women's right to choose, and to control their own bodies. The advent of the contraceptive pill had already opened the way to more effective birth control, but **Abortion** proved more controversial. Most Western countries in these years decriminalized abortion, usually for medical reasons, but the issue continued to be fiercely fought over, notably in the USA. Lesbianism at first was similarly controversial. Following the pattern of the first wave, the more respectable part of the American movement, the liberal feminist National Organization of Women, felt it necessary to sharply differentiate itself from what it chose to see as the Lavender Menace. At the opposite extreme some feminists saw lesbianism as essentially co-terminus with feminist sexuality. The lesbian continuum (see **Lesbian**) as defined by Rich (1980) was seen as binding all women together, and the essential basis of opposition to 'compulsory **Heterosexuality**'. Unlike in the first wave, heterosexuality itself was increasingly problematized, theorized as a social institution, a product of history rather than biology (Jackson 2000) – see **Social constructionism**. Radical and revolutionary feminists especially focused increasingly on the **Violence** of male sexuality, and saw it as constitutive of patriarchy. For Andrea Dworkin (1989) heterosexual intercourse in itself was oppressive of women (though she later denied that she saw it as equivalent to rape), and this fed into a long campaign against **Pornography**, seen not just as representing or depicting hostility towards women but as itself violence against women.

Subsequently, international campaigns against the sex trade and child sex abuse were built around similar themes. Sexuality in such depictions was a perpetual threat, with women as inevitable victims. These arguments in turn produced vigorous counter-arguments from other feminists, in the so-called 'sex wars' of the early 1980s, emphasizing the pleasures as well as dangers of female sexuality, and the possibilities of heterosexual as well as lesbian pleasures (Vance 1984). In French feminism, heavily influenced by Lacanian **Psychoanalysis**, even as feminists battled with its own phallocratic tendencies, attempts were made to elaborate a distinctive female eroticism – see **Femininity**. Figures such as Helene Cixous, Luce Irigaray and Julia Kristeva subsequently became influential in the development of feminist post-structuralism, and film and literary theory, and also opening the way to a feminism concerned with difference as opposed to a unitary feminism that was fast disappearing (Evans 2005).

A crucial aspect of the development of a feminism that was coming to terms with diversity was the forceful emergence of a black feminist critique of mainstream white feminism, which foregrounded racism – see **Intersectionality**. This fed into the emergence of a strong Third World and post-colonial feminism. These shifts were central to what became known as third-wave feminism. At the heart of this was a fading away of the WLM as a mass movement, faced both by what Susan Faludi (1992) called a 'backlash' against the achievements and ambitions of the earlier period, and the fragmentation of the movement itself, especially as a result of divisions over sexuality and race. From another direction, the influence of post-structuralist thought and of **Queer** theory further undermined the unitary subject of feminism. If there was no fundamental essence to womanhood, if there was no natural coherence to femininity, only the constant reiteration of socially inscribed gender differences (Butler 1990), what could the focus of feminist mobilization be? There was no longer, if there had ever been, a single feminism; there were many different, often conflicting feminisms (Segal 1999).

Feminism by the 1990s was in a curious situation. It had gone global, most notably through international networks around violence, trafficking, reproductive rights and increasingly **Human sexual rights**, and a series of international conferences – the world population conference in Cairo in 1994, and the Beijing women's conference in 1995 were especially important – where world leaders had paid obeisance to women's equality, whilst baulking at the endorsement of abortion or lesbianism. It had become so absorbed into Western cultures that commentators were briskly discussing a post-feminist world. Female sexual emancipation was no longer seen as a collective endeavour against sexism, patriarchy or hetero-normativity, but an act of individual self-assertion, 'girl power'. And yet despite the enormous gains for women since the late 1960s, by the second decade of the new millennium it was clear that there was still a long way to go before women could achieve full equality, whether in political representation, equal pay, freedom from sexual violence, or freedom of sexual choice. On a global scale, the very gains achieved by women in the West was a factor in the rise of **Fundamentalism**, committed to the reaffirmation of the natural order, while vast numbers of women continued to live in poverty, and were subject to sexual exploitation. How to balance these elements?

It is tempting to emphasize the continuities of women's oppression, the devious ways in which power always recuperates what has been seemingly undermined. Yet a historical perspective must also recognize how much has changed since the late eighteenth century, especially with regard to female sexuality. It is no longer the enigma that Freud identified in the early twentieth century. It has become a key marker of female autonomy. This is only one example of a much greater shift. One of the most significant achievements of feminism over a long and hard-fought history is to change the terms of the debate. Across most of the world women no longer have to make a moral case for equality. Opponents have to make a case against it. The wrongs of women are still manifest across the globe. But, however difficult their full achievement might appear, the rights of women are now at the heart of public discourse everywhere.

FETISH

Fetish is a word that has resonances in two major theoretical traditions, Freudian **Psychoanalysis**, and Marxism. Both borrowed the term from early colonial and subsequent anthropological usage. Its origins lie in the name given to the objects or charms used by Africans of the Guinea and neighbouring coast that were believed by the local peoples to embody magical or supernatural properties. It came to mean any object that was worshipped in its own right by native peoples on account of its inherent magical qualities. It was a simple step from this to understanding a fetish as something that embodied irrational beliefs. Already by the 1860s worship of the constitutional monarchy in Britain was denounced as a fetish.

It is striking that both psychoanalysis and Marxism found this concept useful at roughly the same time, though the concept of the fetish clearly operates somewhat differently in each tradition. For psychoanalysis the key relationship is with the Oedipus complex, the central mechanism in the acquisition of gendered identity. For Marxism, the link is with the congealing of labour power and **Commodification**. But what is apparent is that fetishization is a key to the understanding of the main objects of concern in both theories: the dynamic unconscious, and the dynamics of capitalist accumulation. In both cases the fetish masks the underlying, and painful reality.

Freud first uses the concept in the *Three Essays* (1905), and is building on the perceptions contained in the writings of the pioneers of **Sexology**. There was plentiful evidence in their work that many individuals obtained sexual excitation from ostensibly non-sexual objects, whether inanimate or other parts of the body: feet, hands, fur, shoes, etc. This was the fetish, which stood in for the genital organ in Freud's theory. In a later essay, 'Fetishism' (1927), Freud underlined that this was an exclusively masculine perversion, with the fetish standing in for the absent ('castrated') female organs. The fetish is a compromise between the boy's horrified recognition of castration, and his disavowal of it. It allows him the fantasy of a female phallus, whilst accepting its absence. The fetish, and the process of fetishization, are thus absolutely key to some of the most contested of Freud's theories – the Oedipus complex, female castration, male castration anxiety – and hence to Freud's whole understanding of the ways in which the undifferentiated blobs of humanity that are infants acquire the rules of gender, sexuality, hetero-sexuality and homosexuality.

Of course, the idea of the sexual fetish does not have to carry this theoretical baggage, and its common usage barely refers to it. Conventionally, the term usually refers to any object which has a sexual significance, that is it is applied simply to the substitution and masking rather than the underlying structures that shape the substitution. You do not have to accept Freudian explanations to find the term useful. Thus people readily talk of a fetish for leather or rubber, implying that these materials have a quality which excites erotic attraction. Freud, as we have seen, saw this as a male phenomenon. Various feminist critics, however, have pointed out the existence of fetishism in female-authored texts, and of female fetishists in the bedroom and on the couches of analysts as well (Schor 1992: 113–16). Some feminists have gone further, and theorized the centrality of fetishism to **Lesbian** sexuality. By disavowing their own castration, women can turn their whole body into the phallus – making the lesbian a successful female fetishist (De Lauretis 1994: chapter 5). It has also been argued that fetishization, by sexualizing the object, is analogous to the common male mode of objectification of women through the 'male gaze'. For this reason, the concept has been widely used in feminist film theory and analysis of **Pornography** (Grosz 1992a: 116–17).

The process of displacing the person, and masking the underlying reality in the object of worship, provides the link with the Marxist use of the concept. Marx argued that fetishism was pervasive in capitalist society. It denoted the process whereby material objects, which had certain characteristics imputed to them by the fact of complex social relations, appeared as products of nature. The elementary form of this was the fetishism of the commodity, as the bearer of value. Under capitalism, although all commodities are products of labour power in a society organized around complex divisions of labour, the value of a commodity appears to be intrinsic to the thing itself. Classically gold, as the measure of exchange in the nineteenth century, seems to have an intrinsic value, and is in effect worshipped, or festishized. But the human labour power that went into it is obscured, so that instead of seeing the object as the product of social labour, the worker seems subordinated to the product itself. The exploitative relationship is hidden (Geras 1983).

By extension, everything can be commodified, including sexuality. Indeed, it is often argued that in the conditions of late capitalism sexuality has been drawn as never before into market relations. The lure of the erotic is deployed to sell everything from motor cars to exotic holidays, while sexuality is locked into fetishized images of what is desirable, especially through a globalized fashion industry and increasingly digitalized representations on the Web. We still want to worship the thing, the object. And as in the original nineteenth-century usage, reason has little to do with it.

FRIENDSHIP

Paeans to friendships echo through philosophy and literature (Vernon 2005), but in the late-modern world they have taken on a new significance. Friendships provide a web of support and security which is particularly important in times of rapid change. They are crucial elements of what Spencer and Pahl (2006) have called the 'hidden solidarities' that underpin social relationships in the contemporary world. Friendships flourish when broad identities are undermined or shattered in periods of rapid social change, or at turning points in people's lives, or when lives are lived at odds with social norms (Weeks 1995: 145–6). Friendships can be sustained over time and place and distance, yet they can allow individuals who live at the margins to feel constantly affirmed and confirmed in who and what they are through evolving life experiences.

Friendships by definition are elective, not given, so they offer the possibility of developing new patterns of **Intimacy** and commitment, based on **Choice** rather than ascription. They also offer the hope, if not always the reality, of relations of equality. Friendships are made between peers; they have tended to be with people from roughly the same class, ethnic and cultural background, and are often also homosocial, that is within rather than across gender. Friendships can also be more readily escaped from than family or sexual/marital relations if differences become divisions. All these features give a special meaning and intensity to friendship in the lives of those who live on the edge. The 'bonding ties' of traditional families can be too restrictive, enclosed, protective and limiting for the post-traditional individual – see **Social capital**. The 'bridging ties' and flexibility provided by friendship or 'personal communities' provide flexible and effective ways of negotiating **Risk** and uncertainty, and of providing care and support (Pahl 2000). Friendships provide the space for the exploration of who or what you are, and what you want to become. This is true at all stages of the life course, from the first tentative stages of exploring sexuality and identity, through the pleasures and crises of relationships, to the problems of ageing and potential loneliness of old age – those **Fateful moments** of a life, which force individuals to reassess who and what they are, and to find ways of adapting to new situations.

Historically friendships have been counterposed to sexuality. Sexual feelings have either been sublimated or sharply denied. W. T. Stead, a contemporary of Oscar Wilde, lamented that his downfall for homosexual offences would threaten friendships amongst men by opening the suspicion of homosexual feelings (Weeks 1977). Homosocial bonding between men, a crucial element of male dominance, has been sustained by an explicit denial of sexuality (Sedgwick 1985). Friendship has also been central to women's experiences, underpinned by an everyday ethic of reciprocity, care and love, but until recently few women would have felt able to express this in a sexual way – see **Lesbian**. Historians have shown the passionate friendships that defined many women's lives in the eighteenth and nineteenth centuries, and underpinned the early rise of **Feminism**, but erotic feelings were ambiguous or denied (Faderman 1981). In the contemporary LGBT world, on the other hand, the relationship between sexuality and friendship has become much more fluid, with lovers, ex-lovers and other friends forming the basis of 'families of choice' (Weston 1991). Lesbians and gay men who may feel excluded from the traditional nuclear family can ground their emotional security and daily needs in strong friendships, where the boundaries between friendships and sexual relationships are often blurred. The non-heterosexual world, it has been argued, is sustained by the intricately woven but durable strands of a 'friendship ethic' (Weeks *et al.* 2001: chapter 3). Peter Nardi (1999), reflecting on the significance of gay male friendships, describes them as the basis of 'invincible communities'. They provide the strength for gays to develop fully creative lives, and the protection against a potentially hostile world. Even more strongly, Michel Foucault saw in gay friendships the really subversive outcome of the gay revolution since the 1970s: 'Society and the institutions which frame it have limited the possibility of relationships [to marriage] because a rich relational world would be very complex to manage' (quoted in Vernon 2005: 134). Gay friendships open up new possibilities of loving, befriending and relating which challenge the narrow solidarities of traditional families, and contribute to the development of a distinctive 'gay ethos' (Blasius 1994). Lovers can become friends, friends lovers, and significant others are not necessarily sexual partners, a 'queering' of conventional boundaries.

The link between friendship, sexuality and changing family forms has been most evident in the developing culture of the LGBT world, but it has had profound implications for wider personal relationships, challenging narrow interpretations of what constitutes family and intimate life. This is increasingly reflected in popular culture. Television series such as *Friends* or *Sex and the City* have focused on young attached (and usually highly attractive people) living or interacting with one another in intense, often family-like, and sexually relaxed contexts. They are popular because they echo new realities about the importance of friendships. Research commissioned by the food manufacturer Dolmio and published in 2006 has found that increasingly the boundaries of friendships and families are dissolving for young people, who often spend more time with friends than family. Apparently 67 per cent of Britons now feel their best friend is part of their family, and whereas 25 years earlier half the population sought to keep friends and family apart, in 2006 only 15 per cent sought to do so. This has given rise to the neologism of 'framilies', which some people apparently feel happy to identify with (Weeks 2007: 178–9).

These trends are likely to accentuate as relations through cyber-space continue to expand exponentially. By 2010 over 500 million people worldwide subscribed to the Facebook social network, some 18 per cent of the global population. The mediation of friendships through cyber-space offers unprecedented opportunities for new links that vastly transcend the limits of friendship ties in the past, making divisions of gender, race, sexuality, class, age and culture if not irrelevant at least attenuated in the virtual world of friendship. It is still too early to predict the full implications of this, but it makes it all the more likely that friendship will have an increasing rather than diminished significance in a globalizing and networked world.

FUNDAMENTALISM

Fundamentalism has been used to describe a disparate range of absolutist religious-political movements that have arisen since the 1970s in a variety of different contexts. The term itself, however, originally had a very specific meaning, deriving from a 12-volume series of pamphlets, *The Fundamentals: A Testimony of Truth*. Published in the USA between 1910 and 1915, it was written by American and British conservative Christians, and gave voice to a growing body of conservative evangelical Protestants (some three million copies of the pamphlets were sold) who specifically rejected the threat to biblical truth represented by Darwinian evolutionism. Against this it affirmed the 'inerrancy' of the Bible, and the centrality of the risen Christ. Its first great moment came – and then went – with the famous 'monkey case', the test case brought against a biology teacher in Dayton, Tennessee, John Scopes, for teaching evolutionism to his classes (though in fact he never reached that part of the curriculum) in breach of the state's prohibition. Though found guilty, he was reprieved on appeal. More significantly the prosecution's case was drowned in worldwide ridicule, and this was soon followed by the debacle of the prohibition of alcohol in the USA, also supported by evangelical Christians, and abandoned with few regrets by the Roosevelt administration in the early 1930s. The movement effectively disappeared from public prominence for another 40 years.

New times saw new dangers, new opportunities and the revival of intellectual currents that many optimists had assumed long dead. From the 1970s we can see the rise of what were broadly described as fundamentalist movements across the globe. And by now the description had a wider meaning, going beyond a resurgent Christian fundamentalism to embrace mass movements of radical Islam, Hinduism and Judaism, as well as more secular absolutisms. Whether in the form of the New Christian Right in the USA, the Islamic revolution in Iran, extreme forms of Hindu nationalism in India, or indeed free-market fundamentalism globally, new challenges developed to established certainties, and newly refurbished verities were loudly proclaimed. The religious movements at least all displayed, despite their profound differences, a number of 'family resemblances' (Ruthven 2004). The core elements were similar to those of the earlier flowering of Christian fundamentalism: textual literalism, a fervent rejection of what it saw as the collapse of morality and a headlong rush towards relativism and secular values, and a passionate belief that the true believers of whatever particular faith they belonged to alone had full access to Truth. There were by now many fundamentalisms, many different claims to truth, but what united them was a passionate absolutism, sharply demarcating right and wrong, striving to banish doubt and uncertainty. And at the heart of this absolutism, in all the religious fundamentalisms, was a passionate preoccupation with gender, sexuality and the body (Bhatt 1997).

In a world of profound, incessant and disruptive change, with the breakdown of traditional patterns of life, and the collapse, especially after 1989, of older grand narratives of change and redemption, especially Marxism, many felt cast adrift. Fundamentalist religious commitment provided an alternative source of meaning and identity for many peoples, a commitment that drew on older beliefs and could plausibly be related to them, but also explicitly challenged Western liberalism, secularism and relativism. The fundamentalisms were, from this perspective, a cry against the radical contingency that has become the hallmark of late-modern societies, and a radical challenge to the diverse ways of life now claiming legitimacy and recognition. In this context it is perhaps not surprising that the gendered and sexed body became the symbolic focus of the deepest anxiety – for it was here that change had been most dramatic and personally experienced. Women who abandoned traditional notions of **Femininity** or women and men who embraced conventionally aberrant sexualities, who blurred the boundaries between men and women, and in doing so undermined the traditional family as the guarantee of social order and reproduction, could be seen to threaten the whole culture, and inherited ways of life. Perhaps even more crucially, they were potent threats to the emotional investment that embattled individuals, especially displaced young men, had in the traditional order. There was a profound sense of anger, embodying, MacCulloch (2009: 990) has suggested, 'the hurt of heterosexual men at cultural shifts which have generally threatened to marginalize them and deprive them of dignity, hegemony or even much usefulness'.

Threats to the integrity of traditional life patterns are very often seen as profound attacks on the integrity of the self (Giddens 1994: 80). This to some extent explains the spectacular emotional fervour of fundamentalist attacks on sexual unorthodoxy: the fierceness of the Culture Wars around abortion and homosexuality in the USA;

the execution of homosexuals and the stoning of adulterous women in Shi'ite Iran; the rise of **Homophobia** in Christian churches in Africa. All such efforts redraw the boundaries and hierarchies, asserting what is good and true, banishing falsity, and affirming a sense of identity and belonging. Sexuality, gender and family become critical boundaries for demarcating community values.

This is generally framed as an attempt to revive ancient verities, a retreat to well-tried values and practices, and it is commonplace for critics of fundamentalist movements to see them as demented attempts to return us all to a past that has thankfully gone. But though they may be in the strict sense reactionary movements, in that they are reacting against the dramatic pace of contemporary change, they are also transparently products of the present. From this perspective, the rise of fundamentalisms from the late 1980s can best be seen as a reaction to the uncertainties generated by **Globalization**, and the profound undermining of traditional patterns of life associated with it. But they have been successful in reaching millions of people across the globe because they use the most modern of means of contemporary communication – from the religious television channels of the Moral Majority in the USA in the 1980s to the highly sophisticated Jihadist use of the Web and other digital technology in the early 2000s – and marry these to a politics of anger and redemption. What the fundamentalist movements have achieved is an effective marriage of political mobilization and religious fervour that utilizes precisely those changes they deplore and which gave them mass energy in the first place: the breakdown of traditional barriers, the global erosion of difference, the creation of multiple identities and the explosion of plural beliefs and truths. The purpose is not a global conversation but a refusal of dialogue, an assertion of truth without regard to consequences.

G

GAY

The widespread use in anglophone countries of gay to refer to same-sex activity dates back to the late 1960s and early 1970s, and is associated with the emergence of the **Gay liberation** movement. Starting in 1969 in the USA, and rapidly spreading to most other Western countries, its defining characteristic was a rejection of the stigma and prejudice associated with **Homosexuality**, and a new willingness on the part of homosexual people to openly affirm their sexual identities. A new term was necessary for new times. The new movement consciously adopted the self-description of gay as a rejection both of the clinical and medicalized category of homosexual, and of the host of pejorative terms, especially the word **Queer**, which had been traditionally used to label and stigmatize homosexuality. The subsequent linkage of 'gay and **Lesbian**' was a powerful signal that the histories of male and female homosexuality were inextricably linked by a common institutionalized hostility, though it soon became obvious that the histories of lesbians and gay men were not the same (Weeks 1977).

This concern with developing a new language can be seen as but a stage of the long effort to put into acceptable words the experience of same-sex eroticism. Just as in the late nineteenth century terms such as homosexual, invert, third-sexers, uranian or the intermediate sex were used to describe a new awareness of same-sex desire, so the adoption of the term gay marks a crucial shift in attitudes, a self-description marking new forms of **Agency**.

Gay in fact has older origins than 'homosexuality', though the meanings have subtly changed. The word gay acquired associations of immorality in the eighteenth century, and prostitutes were commonly described as 'gay women' in the nineteenth century. It is through this link that gay seems originally to have become associated with male homosexuality, largely because the milieu of casual sexual contacts between men and women and men and men overlapped, and certainly in terms of the criminal law, little distinction was made between female prostitution and male homosexuality. Jack Saul, a famous male prostitute of the period, whose ostensible memoirs, *Sins of the Cities of the Plain* (1881) achieved some underground notoriety in late Victorian Britain, gave evidence in the libel trial of Lord

Euston for alleged homosexual offences in 1890. He spoke from the witness stand of his shame, loss of character and inability to get a conventional job. But, he added, 'I occasionally do odd jobs for different gay people' (Weeks 1991: 82). The words are ambivalent but at the very least indicate the close symbiosis of the different underground worlds of prostitution and male homosexuality. From this, gay evolved to become a covert name for homosexual activity. It seems to have acquired a recognizably contemporary meaning in the USA by the late 1920s (Katz 2001: 158). By the 1960s, it was widely used in references, for example, to 'gay bars' in both the USA and Britain, though in the former it was a much more common grassroots term. In Britain it carried an air of what at the time was called 'piss-elegance'.

The evolution of the term reflects the emergence of distinctive sexual identities, and patterns of life. These patterns were constrained and delimited by widespread prejudice, criminalization (of male homosexuality) and institutionalized exclusion, conditions that to a large extent worsened in the 1950s and early 1960s. The emergence of gay liberation can thus be seen as a collective demand for full equality. But the force of that movement was to propel further shifts in meaning. Whilst the terms gay and, to a lesser extent, lesbian, were generally used to refer to homosexuality by the general public, within the lesbian and gay communities themselves, new challenges emerged. The declared aim of gay liberation had been to end the distinction between homosexuality and **Heterosexuality**. The immediate effect, however, of the new movement was to make sharper the distinction between the lesbian and gay world and the institution of heterosexuality. Gay seemed to some to signify an almost ethnic-type identity (Epstein 1992). A further radical challenge to the dominance of gay and lesbian identities as they had developed by the 1980s came from a younger generation of activists who challenged what they saw as the assimilationist tendencies of their predecessors, and resurrected the term queer to signal their transgressive intent (Warner 1993).

Queer activism set itself up against 'heteronormativity', and challenged the rigid categories signalled by the terms lesbian and gay. The queer world embraced bisexuals, ambisexuals, transgendered people, sado-masochists and all who resisted the sexual order. But despite the queer eruption, by the early twenty-first century there were few signs that the word gay was losing its everyday use. On the contrary, it seemed to be on the road to being a global signifier of same-sex activities, appearing in a variety of different languages – though taking on subtly different meanings in different cultural contexts (Altman 2001). It had also, unfortunately, become a generalized term of abuse amongst young people in Anglo-Saxon speaking countries. Despite that, it remains the most widely accepted self-description, either alone, or in the form 'lesbian and gay' or via the more inclusive portmanteau term LGBTQ (Lesbian, Gay, Bisexual, Transgender, Queer, Querying . . .) for non-heterosexual people themselves. Its ultimate significance is that it marked a dramatic transformation in sense of self – from victimhood to full agency – and for this reason the term remains deeply rooted in the consciousness of LGBTQ people themselves.

GAY LIBERATION

The gay liberation movement began, symbolically, with a bang, or at least a riot. The Stonewall riot on New York's Greenwich Village in the early hours of 28 June 1969, the gay novelist Edmund White has written, was like a Bastille day, 'the turning point of our lives' (White 1988: 184). The riot was, in subsequent gay mythology, the day the queers fought back against the police. Over the next few days a riot became, in Edmund White's phrase, an 'uprising'. Gay liberation had founds its moment.

The New York Gay Liberation Front (GLF) was established shortly afterwards, and similar movements soon spread like wildfire across America. Within a year it had crossed the Atlantic and Pacific: the London GLF was founded in October 1970, and similar movements had spread rapidly through North America, Europe and Australasia. There had been a number of homophile reform movements in Western societies from the late nineteenth century (Magnus Hirschfeld's Scientific Humanitarian Committee in Germany from the 1890s to the 1930s, COC in the Netherlands from the 1940s, the Homosexual Law Reform Society in Britain, and the Mattachine Society and the Daughters of Billitis in the USA from the 1950s), but they were not necessarily movements of self-declared homosexuals, and they were certainly not mass movements. Now gay liberationists declared, dramatic, even revolutionary change would be brought about by gays themselves, acting for themselves – the self-emancipation of homosexuals was for the first time, it seemed, a real possibility (Adam 1995).

Gay liberation was first and foremost an assertion of a new **Sexual identity**. The rapid abandonment of the old denigratory self-descriptions of 'queer', 'faggot', 'poufter' in English-speaking countries, and similar terms in other languages, in favour of the new universal signifier of '**Gay**' was an immediate symbol of that. 'Gay is good', 'gay pride', 'gay power' were slogans that marked a new self-confidence in asserting the importance of personal and collective identities, built around newly affirmed sexualities. Gay liberation offered a new form of visibility, with 'coming out' of the **Closet** a central strategy, a mark of pride and self-confidence. By openly declaring their sexualities, gays could begin to show the world they existed, and, as important, show other gays that they were not alone, that through coming out they could come together, and construct new stories about who and what they were.

At the heart of the new politics was a desire for a new sexual freedom. For many gay men especially the revolution was a sexual revolution above all else, the chance to realize desires that had for too long been denied. The 1970s immediately following Stonewall was a period of mass sexual experimentation – exploring pleasure in multiple forms in many different venues, challenging the monogamous norms of the culture, throwing light on what had been a dark secret, confined to shameful silence, in the all too recent past. Sex was pleasure, but it was also political, transgressing against familial and repressive restrictions, and showing different ways of being erotic, and of being human. But as Michel Foucault (1979) pointed out, it is not clear that sex in itself could ever be a founding point of opposition to power. For was not sexuality itself deeply implicated in relations of power? And so-called sexual liberation was a wider phenomenon than simply a gay (especially a gay male) need.

The new gay consciousness partly concealed, partly stimulated an explosive mix of possibilities. It soon became clear that there was no such thing as a single gay identity. Instead there was a dynamic explosion of new identities. **Lesbians** from the start were reluctant to subordinate their own struggles to the sexualized needs and passions of gay men. A whole gamut of other identity positions soon spun off – around **Bisexuality**, **Transgender**, **Sado-masochism**, butch and femme, and, most controversially, **Paedophilia**. Other voices were heard, from minority lesbians and gay men, black, Native American, Chicano, Asian, arguing that the definitions of sexual freedom were too white, male, middle class – see **Inter-sectionality**. Each national experience proved to be subtly different from the dominant American norm (Adam *et al.* 1999). It soon became clear that however powerful the new gay liberation consciousness was it was inevitably refracted through the limits of global circuits of power, the post-colonial experience, and the difficulties of local and regional struggles over sexuality.

Affirmation of identity was the most dramatic aspect of the initial burst of gay liberation, but it was based on a wider notion of **Agency**. The gay liberation movement was a characteristic example of the new social movements that emerged in the 1970s, offering a symbolic challenge to the status quo, erupting from the grass roots, and providing a laboratory for life experiments (Melucci 1989). In the USA from the start the movement saw itself as part of a wider radical, even revolutionary movement. Its immediate inspiration had been in the counterculture, the opposition to American imperialism, the black struggle and second-wave **Feminism**. Much of its initial language came from those movements: 'Gay power' echoed 'Black power', gay liberation echoed women's liberation. The crucial development was the recognition that the experience of insult, injury, prejudice and discrimination was not the result of individual pathology but the effect of systematic processes of oppression and domination. The experience of oppression could now be counterposed to an ideology of 'liberation' (Altman 1993).

Gay liberationists soon began to elaborate their own theoretical categories to explain this dichotomy, from heterosexism and **Homophobia** to the analysis of institutionalized **Heterosexuality**, and contributed significantly to the development of **Social constructionism**. Underlying the personal and political dynamism was a sense of a collective agency. It was through mass solidarity in a movement that individuals felt empowered to come out. It made the construction of powerful individual identities possible. From this developed the strong affirmation of sexual **Community** – a sense of belonging that did not obliterate the individual self but made a positive sense of self achievable. From the early 1970s there was an explo-sion of community expressions in most Western countries, and more widely – neighbourhoods, clubs, bars, self-help groups, campaigning groups, phonelines, newspapers, magazines, political caucuses, faith networks, mobilization around health issues, especially around HIV/AIDS from the early 1980s, sexual subcultures, shops, restaurants, trade union factions, legal campaigns, parenting support groups, campaigns against violence, student groupings, teacher groups, business organizations and so on. The list was potentially enormous, reflecting the dynamism and ever-increasing diversity of the LGBT world. The movement soon morphed into a dense network of sometimes warring, but closely interlinked, loosely organized but emotionally and sexually intertwined social worlds, constituting a form of civil society engaged in a continuous conversation about the meanings and possibilities, hopes and desires, of an ever-growing counter-public. The movement was in many ways about the rights of private life, the freedom to choose how one lived one's sexual life. But the irony was that the best way of protecting private life was to go public on it. Controversies that previously seemed intrinsically about private life became public, a 'public discourse on the personal life', as Plummer (1999) put it.

But the growing presence of such a powerful gay public in most Western countries posed new questions about what direction to go in. On the one hand we can see the consolidation of in effect a gay ethnic identity (Epstein 1992). This was especially true in the USA, where the idea of a gay ethnicity fitted readily into the pre-existing models, and readily gave rise to claims to rights based on claimed minority status. Gay liberation had set out to liberate the gayness of everyone, to make the binary distinction between homosexuality and heterosexuality meaningless. But now gay was in danger of becoming the focus of a narrower identity politics, organized around a very specific type of **Sexual orientation.** For many activists, on the other hand, sexuality was a preference, not a given orientation, a **Choice** rather than a destiny. People could make their own identities and ways of life to fit their different needs. Unity was a matter of political positioning, not of natural affinities. So increasingly there was a weakening of the idea of a single movement. Most GLF groupings had disappeared by the mid-1970s. People could come together in particular crises, like the one developing around HIV/**AIDS** in the 1980s, or against generally repressive backlashes, or for specific rights, as against the sodomy laws in the USA, or for **Same-sex marriage**. But such campaigns had to be shaped and constructed, not assumed to be the inevitable result of a new gay consciousness.

The political and cultural context was also shifting, in large part because of the impact of gay liberation itself. Early gay liberationism had taken for granted that gay freedom was incompatible with the existing sexual order. But since the 1970s there has been a remarkable, if uneven, liberalization of social attitudes, especially in Western Europe, Australasia and North America – even in the USA where LGBT rights continue to be fiercely contested, but the community remains the most vibrant and inventive in the world. In many of these countries formal equality has become the norm, laws have been reformed and same-sex marriage or recognized civil unions have become the strategic goal of gay activists. There has been a major shift in gay politics, from the assertion of identity to the claim of relational rights.

Some critics saw such developments as illusory. For **Queer** activists, the apparent liberalization was a trap, a new form of regulation and control. They could point to the continuation of homophobic attacks, the reality of active discrimination in many areas of life and the continuation of the hegemony of heteronormativity in cultural values and institutions, even in the most liberal jurisdictions. In many other parts of the world, sexual rights are still violently denied, especially under the impact of **Fundamentalism**.

Yet a balanced view would surely suggest that gay liberation had indeed brought about radical change, if not always in the ways anticipated or even desired. There might no longer be a mass movement, or radical mobilization of activists. But beneath the froth of public life something vitally important was happening. Thousands of LGBT people have been quietly building their lives as if they were fully equal citizens, assuming rights and responsibilities often in advance of the law, but creating facts on the ground that the law ultimately has to respond to. It is this sense of people making their own lives, not necessarily in circumstances of their own choosing, and against often formidable odds, but quietly claiming their very ordinariness, that may be the ultimate marker of fundamental change.

GENDER

Gender, in conventional usage, tells whether you are a man or a woman. But this is far more problematic than it seems. Is it possible, the feminist poet and historian Denise Riley (1988) once asked, to inhabit a gender without a feeling of horror? She is clearly distancing herself from the determinism that makes an assigned gender, as male or female, the key determinant of who and what you are, of your identity and subjectivity, and is rejecting the iron laws that trap you within rigid categorizations, and relations of domination or subordination. The common use of the term in this sense is relatively new. The evolution of the term, and of gender theory, reveals the ways in which the question of **Masculinity** and **Femininity** have been opened up to history, and therefore change.

Derived from Old French, the word gender had a long and blameless history in English in two distinct meanings: in referring to differences of 'kind' between words (whether they are 'masculine', 'feminine' or 'neuter') in various languages; and in the sense of engendering, generating, begetting and hence copulating. The modern use of the term, which refers not only to questions of identity but to relations between men and women, and amongst men and women, has echoes of these meanings in that the reproductive sphere is inevitably a key aspect of male/female interactions, and because many users of the term see gender as a concept that is produced within language, that is, it refers to symbolic, social and historical rather than biological or essential differences – and similarities – between men and women. Rather than seeing biological men and women as the fount and origin of gender, gender is now widely seen as a social structure and set of relationships within which masculinities and femininities are produced. As such it has become a key term in feminist analysis, and in wider sexual politics.

The term gender role was first used by the American sexologist John Money in the 1950s, and Robert Stoller (1968) theorized the key distinction between 'sex' and 'gender' in the late 1960s. This was taken up and popularized in the 1970s by feminist anthropologists and sociologists (Oakley 1972). Sex was seen as referring to the basic biological markers of men and women (reproductive capacities, morphological differences) while gender referred to the vast edifice of cultural differences built upon that. This, superficially at least, involved a major break with the theorizations of **Sexology** which had assumed fundamental differences between men and women, and the inevitability of male dominance over women – see **Essentialism**. The genital and reproductive distinctions between biological men and biological women were read not only as a necessary but also as sufficient explanation for different sexual needs and desires. They appear as the most basic distinctions between peoples, deeply rooted in our 'animal natures'.

Theories of gender seek to deconstruct such assumptions. New historical work was effectively demonstrating that within the Western tradition concepts of sexual difference had a traceable history (Scott 1988). The historian Thomas Laqueur (1990) has shown, for example, how in the eighteenth century, in medical discourse, there was a move away from the ancient tradition of seeing women and men as constituting but one sex, with women's bodies an inverted, and inferior, version of men's, towards recognizably modern versions of two polarized, and potentially antagonistic, categories. As this became embodied in social practices so the priority given to gender difference accentuated. Michel Foucault (1980) dramatized this in his famous dossier on a nineteenth-century French hermaphrodite, Herculine Barbin, brought up in the 'happy limbo of a non-identity', who was eventually forced to choose to live as a man. Beset by the increasing need to live a 'true sex', Herculine eventually committed suicide. An obscure French provincial tragedy becomes a metaphor for a culture where affirming your real gender increasingly matters.

Gender theorists have also been able to draw on a growing awareness from social anthropology that gender relations, and masculinities and femininities vary enormously across different cultures. Every society, Gayle Rubin famously argued, 'has a sex/gender system – a set of arrangements by which the biological raw material of human sex and procreation is shaped by human, social intervention and satisfied in a conventional matter, no matter how bizarre some of the conventions may be' (Rubin 1974: 165). Gender, in other words, far from being the stable and eternal basis for the organization of social life was the historically and culturally variable, and potentially unstable means by which different societies organized sexual differences (Moore 2007). The constellation of institutions, beliefs and ideologies and social practices that organize the relations between men and women in any particular society, is not fixed for all time. It constitutes a specific 'gender order' (Connell 2009) that is a product of history, indeed of many histories, and is in constant evolution as new gender projects develop, are consolidated or contested, lived or denied.

From this perspective gender can be seen as a series of social practices which draw on the body and its different capacities – notably reproduction, child care, sexual relations, labour – which appear freely chosen, and do allow **Agency**, but are inextricably bound up with social imperatives. The gender order does not work, as earlier functionalist theorists argued, by imposing inescapable social roles for men and woman. Nor is it monolithic. Anatomy, as Freud recognized, may be a destiny, but the progress to a socially recognized gender position is hazard strewn and constantly disrupted, and resisted – see **Psychoanalysis**. Gender is not a neutral social set-up. It is organized hierarchically, and inscribes difference and division, between women and men, and between hegemonic forms of masculinity and the less unfortunate others. Gender is about power, and historically has been built on the subordination of women and the execration and outlawing of patterns of sexuality which did not readily conform with acceptable forms of masculinity or femininity – especially homosexuality. Of course, the gender order constantly fails – otherwise history would not have witnessed female autonomy or homosexual ways of life. Gender arrangements, Connell (2009: 7) has argued, are at the same time, 'sources of pleasures, recognition and identity, and sources of injustice and harm. This means that gender is inherently political'.

The politics of gender has been at the core of modern **Feminism**, but also of **Gay liberation**, and various forms of men's politics. The meanings of gender, however, have been strongly contested. The social explanation of gender has often been the source of fierce dispute, as many have sought greater security in more essentialist arguments. A strong feminist tradition has sought equality within difference, arguing for the realization of women's distinctive biological needs. From the opposite direction, **Queer** theorists have questioned the sex/gender distinction as covertly reinstating a biological explanation. Judith Butler (1990) has argued that sex is an idea that is produced within relations of gender, rather than the origin or base of them. They are social practices we enact in defined situations, things we do over and over again, often small acts incessantly repeated, cultural productions which 'create the effect of the natural, the original, and the inevitable' (Butler 1990: x). If we accept this radical view, then there is no originary basis for sexual difference. There are only the repetitive acts, imitations of imitations, through which gendered identities are performatively produced in various cultures. Masculinity and femininity, heterosexuality and homosexuality are not emanations of the genes or hormones or anything else: they are regulative fictions and ideals through which conformities are generated, reinforced and 'normalized' by constant reiterations. This points to a politics of subversion and disruption designed to transgress the norms – see **Transgender** – but it is not entirely clear how the social structures of gender can thereby be fundamentally undermined, or whether they can be transcended except by acts of will.

A key element of the gender order is institutionalized **Heterosexuality**, which structures and embodies relations between men and women, and defines culturally distinct masculinities and femininities. This has opened up the question of what the relationship is between gender and sexuality. For an influential radical feminist approach, sexuality is the fulcrum of men's domination over women, and determines gender relations. Catherine MacKinnon (1987: 149), for example, has written that 'feminism is a theory of how the eroticization of dominance and submission creates gender, creates woman and man in the social form in which we know them'. This has led to a particular emphasis on the dangers of **Pornography**, and the centrality of sexual violence to women's subordination. A quite different analysis has come from sex-radicals, who have tended to emphasize the relative autonomy of gender and sexuality (Rubin 1984), and the need to explore the erotic in all its diversity and radical potentiality, for women and men, heterosexuals and homosexuals, and a wide range of sexual dissidents. Clearly, it would be impossible to divorce gender and sexuality, either analytically or politically. The gender order remains resilient, both institutionally and in people's minds. The 'male in the head' (Holland *et al.* 1998) continues to shape female responses, even in the context of rapid social change. But what recent theorizations of both gender and sexuality have demonstrated is that the great edifice of gender can no longer plausibly be seen as an emanation of Nature, but is built on the ever-shifting needs and desires and social practices of millions of people. The gender order may seem immutable, but is subject to constant flux and change.

GLOBALIZATION

The term refers broadly to the process of global integration of economic, social, cultural and communication activities which has gathered pace since the 1980s, and has been seen as the dynamic force that is transforming social relations at all levels on a worldwide scale. Despite its widespread deployment, however, it remains a contested and ambivalent term, whose 'precise meaning remains far from clear' (Plummer 2003: 116). Superficially, it is a neutral term to describe such transformations in global interactions. But since the 1990s it has also been seen as a transnational political and cultural project, closely linked with **Neoliberalism**, which in turn has generated transnational anti-capitalist and anti-globalization movements.

Ideological positioning apart, it is probably most useful as an attempt to describe and account for a series of interlinked processes which together are transforming the context and meanings of human interactions at all levels (Held 2000: 54–5). First it suggests a *stretching* of social, political, cultural and economic relations across frontiers, so that activities in one part of the globe have a potential impact on individuals and communities in every other part of an interconnected world. Second, it implies an *intensification* and growing strength of global interconnect-edness, interactions and flows which go beyond the various societies and state forms that make up the world order. Third, there is a *speeding up* of global interactions, especially through the development of more rapid and accessible transportation, media and information technologies, circulation of goods, capital and peoples.

Sexuality is inevitably subject to these forces of globalization, which are bringing into contestation and confrontation different beliefs, behaviours and assumptions, and in the process is reshaping the context and meanings of intimacy and the erotic. Globalization is not new in the field of sexuality any more than it is in wider economic and cultural relations. The conquests and exploitation by Europeans of the 'new lands' to the west and the east from the sixteenth century in many ways established abiding beliefs and stereotypes about the other which have been constitutive in the shaping of European gendered subjectivities (Connell 2003: 49). The second great wave of globalization from the late nineteenth century to World War I saw intensified colonization, including sexual colonization, international conflict and the dramatic encounter of different erotic cultures, producing in turn international campaigns against sexual exploitation, notably the 'white slave trade', and for sexual reform. These earlier developments are dwarfed, however, by the new waves of global integration since the 1980s, which have produced, in Altman's (2001) graphic phrase, 'global sex'.

While these globalizing processes affect all parts of the world, their impact is uneven on individuals, groups, states and regions because they are enmeshed in huge disparities of power and gross inequalities (Hemmings *et al.* 2006), and this is manifest in persistent inequities between cultures, and in continuing sexual injustices, especially against women, children and lesbian, gay or transgender identified peoples. Globalization in many ways accentuates and dramatizes the inequalities that already existed. Members of new global elites have more in common with each other than with the poor in their own nation states. People with the latest high-tech gadgets rub shoulders with people who have nothing. The new technologies may create new forms of inequality, new desires, wants and needs, while people lose the comforts of their lost worlds, and are forced defenceless or ill-equipped into a global marketplace – including the sexual marketplace. Structural readjustment policies endorsed by the International Monetary Fund (IMF) and the World Bank and Western governments have huge unintended consequences on patterns of everyday life in some of the most disadvantaged countries of the world. Globalization does not abolish difference so much as redistribute it: styles, consumer patterns and identities are internationalized while class divides, often across national boundaries, are strengthened and solidified (Altman 2001:21). At the same time, global perspectives produce new opportunities for transcending the limits and restrictions of tradition, and wide claims for **Human sexual rights** and social justice.

The world of sexuality is being transformed by these new global connections and flows (Weeks 2007). Flows of men and women leaving their traditional homes seeking work and new opportunities, moving from country to towns and cities, from country to country, from the Global South to the affluent West, and even within the West, in pursuit of love, relationships, pleasure. Flows of war, with soldiers crossing countries, causing disruptions, committing sexual abuses and rape, and possibly passing on sexually transmitted infections (STIs), and flows of people fleeing war and extreme violence. Flows of people escaping from persecution for their sexualities or seeking access to reproductive choice. Flows of sexually transmitted infections, including HIV, of community-based organization to combat them and of international mobilization for sexual health. Flows of pornography and sexually explicit materials in a multi-billion dollar global industry. Flows of drugs with erotic connotations, both illicit and licit (**Viagra**, most notably, falls into both categories). Flows of **Sexual tourism**, transforming economies, transporting millions to once exotic and mysterious foreign places, and potentially giving rise to new or intensified forms of exploitation. Flows of communication and media that make sexual information, news, gossip, styles, scandals, personalities, stereotypes, role models, personal dramas, legal changes, reactionary pronouncements, crimes and misdemeanours instantly and simultaneously known everywhere. Flows of popular culture: in films, television, games, music, the Internet (blogs, vlogs, chat rooms, social networks). Flows of consumption, of everything from clothes and gadgets to sex toys. Flows too of financial crises, with incalculable impact on personal and collective life. Flows of **Religion**, and associated moralities, especially of neo-traditionalist or fundamentalist colour. Flows of sexual stories that circulate sexual secrets and confessions, desires, practices, hopes, fears, identities and aspirations, and through their interaction shape new meanings, communities and possibilities. Flows of science that try to interpret and categorize the sexual world, and increasingly to remake it via new technologies, especially reproductive techniques and drug therapies. Flows of social movements, such as global feminist and lesbian, gay and transgender movements. Flows of identities and ways of being, and especially the globalization of lesbian and gay, bisexual and transgendered subjectivities, networks of people living with HIV, sado-masochists, sex workers and the like, but also generating the intermingling of identities, and forms of **Cosmopolitanism** and **Hybridity**. Flows of concern about children – their exploitation, their protection, their rights – and flows of children themselves, through displacement, migration, adoption and sale in human **Trafficking**. Flows of campaigns, from NGOs, international agencies, lobby groups, grassroots organizations, on everything from sexual abuse to sexual infections. Flows of conferences, seminars, academics, activists, experts, medics, psychologists, therapists, all adding to the flow of words, the proliferation of stories, the shaping of discourses and new subjectivities. Flows of sport and leisure, with changing ideals of fitness and health. Flows of literature – ancient, contemporary, mandarin, populist, pornographic, educational, instructional, academic, scientific, religious, moralistic, scandalous, titivating, biographical, historical, political – in millions of books, magazines, journals, pamphlets, in print, online. Flows of **Cybersex**, in ever more extravagant abundance. Flows of reproductive necessities, to prevent and promote births: the Pill, condoms, sperm, donated eggs, adoption, surrogacy. Flows of regulation: on the exploitation of children, marriage rights across boundaries, sex work, crimes, sexual health, medicines, drugs, pornography, Internet posting or downloading. Flows of discourse around rights: human sexual rights, reproductive rights, relational rights, love rights. Flows of transnational friendship, love and relationships. And flows of loss and mourning, dramatized by **AIDS** – a reminder of the costs as well as the gains of global connectedness.

GREAT TRANSITION

Between the 1960s and the 1990s most parts of the Western world experienced a historic transition in sexual beliefs and intimate behaviour, which has had global effects. As the historian Eric Hobsbawm (1994: 320–1) put it, these areas of everyday life had been impressively resistant to sudden change. Yet, 'in the second half of the twentieth century these basic and long lasting arrangements began to change with express speed'. There was no single cause, no regular pattern across regions and countries, no common agenda for its main actors, chiefly members of the baby-boom generation born in the aftermath of World War II. The process was messy, contradictory and haphazard. But in the end it drew in and involved millions of people, re-imagining and remaking their lives in a myriad different ways. Its implications are still working their way through what today is an almost unrecognizable world. This is what has been called the 'great transition' (Weeks 2007: 57).

In little more than thirty years, before the baby boomers had reached middle age, the sexual world had been irretrievably transformed, and attitudes to marriage or non-marriage, to childbearing or non-parenting, to female sexuality, to **Families**, to sexual unorthodoxy, all had changed fundamentally. In most Western countries, marriage rates reached a peak round about 1970, then went into a long decline. Cohabitation, once widely seen as 'living in sin', became normalized. Divorce had become commonplace. Birth control became almost universal. **Abortion** and **Homosexuality** had been at least partially decriminalized in most jurisdictions. New social movements such as **Feminism** and **Gay liberation** paved the way for new claims for rights and **Sexual citizenship**. Censorship of sexually explicit writing and representation was eased, and **Pornography** became a multi-million dollar business.

The period between the 1950s and the 1990s was not a monolithic period: the easy optimism of the early 1960s in America and Western Europe gave way to grimmer times in the late 1960s and 1970s, and moved into new forms of social conservatism in the 1980s. Many of the breakthroughs towards greater liberalism in the 1960s faced reaction in the following decades, especially in response to the **AIDS** epidemic from the early 1980s. There were victims as well as gainers of the changes. But by the turn of the millennium we could see clear shifts in the sexual ecology of late-modern societies. Under the surface of events, at a deep level of popular **Agency**, profound changes had taken place. These can be summed up as follows: a shift of power between the generations, as young people began to redefine the cultural zeitgeist; a shift in power between men and women as women made new claims for rights and equality, and as **Gender** itself began to lose its naturalness and inevitability; the separation of sex and reproduction as more effective birth control made parenting increasingly a choice; the separation of sex and marriage, which was no longer the only acceptable gateway to sexual expression; the separation of marriage and parenting, as couples gave birth outside marriage, and the number of single parents grew hugely; a rebalancing of the relationship between sexual normality and abnormality, as LGBT people claimed

74

recognition; the separation of heterosexuality and parenting, as same-sex parenting, always present, became a key aspect of lesbian and gay domesticity; and the separation of heterosexuality and marriage, as **Same-sex marriage** and civil partnerships were recognized in various parts of the world.

But agreement on what has changed has been accompanied by profound disagreements about the causes of these transformations, and their real meanings and implications (see **Globalization**, **Intimacy** and **Informalization**). Did they represent the widening of the spaces for new personal freedoms and genuine individual choice, freeing people from authoritarian, 'traditional' values; or did they lead to a decisive weakening of the moral conditions for a stable society, imprisoning individuals in an illusory 'liberation'? Both views, and a complexity of shades in between, have been regularly put forward ever since. For the conservative American theorist Francis Fukuyama (1999), the turmoils of the 1960s were at the epicentre of the 'great disruption' which broke the foundations of trust and social capital that sustained Western democracies, and explain the moral confusions and cultural divides that characterize the succeeding decades. Conservative thinkers as a body have generally concentrated on the 'cultural revolution' which fundamentally sapped the traditional values which had underpinned Western civilization, leading, in the words of the conservative American critic Gertrude Himmelfarb (1995), to the 'de-moralization' of society. For the American sociologist Daniel Bell, this was the decade when the Puritan ethic was fatally undermined by an ideological tranformation which put hedonism and ultra individualism and consumerism to the fore (Bell 1996).

From the other side of the political spectrum altogether, other philosophers have been equally pessimistic, and have seen the endless proliferation of speech about sexuality in the 1960s as masking the illusory nature of the freedoms on offer. Herbert Marcuse (1972), who briefly became a radical icon, foresaw the danger of technological rationality working through the erotic to bind the individual to the status quo. Pleasure generated submission. The partial or 'repressive desublimation' offered by advanced consumer societies was a guarantor of the survival of oppression and exploitation. It was now the very form of sexual freedom on offer, not sexual restraint or denial, that binds people to their oppression. We can see similar concerns in contemporary debates about **Commodification**, **Individualization**, **Neoliberalism** and **Sexualization**.

One of the problems with these positions is that despite the ostensible and ostentatious political dichotomies they still tend to rely on a particular model of sexuality, seeing sexuality as like a head of steam that could be either repressed or released. What post-Kinsey sexual theorists like Gagnon and Simon (1974) have called the 'drive reduction' model of sexuality has long coloured both popular and elite writing about the uncontrollable nature of sex – 'if the bridle is removed, sexuality gallops', as a 1933 text put it (quoted in Wouters 2004: 154). But as contemporary sexual theory, itself a product of the upheavals of the 1960s and 1970s, affirms, sexuality should properly be seen as a social production, shaped, organized and regulated in complex social relationships. Rather than attempt to understand what happened in the 1960s to1990s as 'liberation' or 'desublimation' or other variants of metaphors of repression and release, we need to be attentive to the shifts in the social relationships within which sexual activity takes place. Together they led, over this period of the great transition, to the effective demise of the traditional model of sexual restraint and opened the way to a new moral economy – one that was more hedonistic, more individualistic, perhaps more selfish, but also one that was vastly more tolerant, experimental and open to diversity and choice in a way that had been inconceivable just a generation earlier.

H

HABITUS

Habitus is a concept that has been widely deployed in recent years, largely through the influence of the sociology of Norbert Elias and Pierre Bourdieu, though it has also played a part in the radical philosophy of Gilles Deleuze. As an idea it goes back at least to Aristotle, but its modern usage has been heavily influenced by the work of the French social anthropologist, Marcel Mauss. For Mauss, habitus referred to the ways in which cultural attributes such as skills, expertise, styles, tastes, values and habits are deeply internalized, rooted in the lives and bodily practices of individuals and groups, and are lived as innate, the only way to be. The concept has been used as an analytical tool to understand a wide range of embedded and embodied social phenomenon, especially class distinctions and educational attainment, but has also proved significant in theorizing gender and sexual beliefs and behaviour.

Habitus plays a key role in Elias's most influential work, *The Civilizing Process* (2000; first published in German in 1939) to describe those aspects of a personality that are not inherent or innate, but are acquired in the course of development: the thinking, feeling and believing that are learnt from early childhood, so that they become ingrained as a 'second nature' (Mennell 2008: 6), underpinning the process of formalization and **Informalization**. Long-term changes in behaviour become embedded in personality structures and everyday habits so that their social origins are effectively lost. Thus, the development of a new etiquette in Europe from the seventeenth century around defecation and sexual behaviour, so that they became increasingly privatized activities, segregated from daily respectable life, was a process that might have begun in royal courts but became an unconscious rule of ordinary life, policed by feelings of shame that are deeply personal but highly social, marked by power differentials.

Power is central to Bourdieu's use of the concept. For Bourdieu, habitus become 'a way of explaining how power relations are incorporated into the body as physical and psychological dispositions' in the specific locations in which individuals are formed, shaped by class, access to resources and education (McNay 2008: 127). He links the concept more explicitly to a Marxist analysis, to account for the ways in which inequalities are reproduced. The dispositions acquired by a shared habitus become part of the personal and collective unconscious, and are marked by distinctions of culture and taste which have the status of inevitability.

Its value as a concept is that it attempts to escape the twin pitfalls of social theory, an atomistic individualism on the one hand, or a mechanistic social determinism on the other. It seeks to avoid the danger of seeing social phenomena and practical action as the simple effect of freely willed individual decisions. At the same time, the concept allows analysis of the habituation of ways of life and practice that go beyond simplistic ideas of socialization, which have a tendency to see the human subject as the passive recipient of social influences. Its aim is to break down the structure/agency binary by exploring the ways in which the social, with all its class and other divisions, is unconsciously imbibed and lived in **Bodies**. Collective values and norms are not so much consciously learnt as spontaneously absorbed in the form of the physical and emotional dispositions of the habitus, so that it becomes the individual's basic relationship towards the world, even shaping their psycho-sexual disposition in different ways (such as class or racialized differences in sexual beliefs and behaviour). In Bourdieu's use of the concept, through the different relatively autonomous fields that make up the social space – economic, cultural, social and symbolic – individuals are habituated into a hierarchy of practices which bring different forms and weightings of capital and resources, and which make relations of domination and subordination appear natural and eternal, shaping bodily demeanour and appearance (hexis), food likes and dislikes, aesthetic taste, even language use. Language, especially, is a vital medium for the imposition of symbolic violence on people, perpetuating domination by words rather than warfare.

Habitus seeks to explain how societies reproduce themselves in conditions of inequality, division and conflict. It allows connections to be made between ways of living and the experience of class, race, gender and so on. These differences become so ingrained that to challenge them seems to be going against nature, and so embodied that different ways of life seem unthinkable. As with bonding, **Social capital**, of which Bourdieu was an influential theorist, a specific habitus can seem like a castle against the world, a natural order in need of protection against existential threat. Yet Bourdieu was a man of the left, committed to social change and social justice, and alive to the different forms of agency. Defence of existing habits and ways of life opens few doors to transformative change. Whatever the embodied forces of habitus individuals and collectives do resist them and strategize and work to transform them. This is apparent when we turn to gender and sexuality as sites of struggle.

Bourdieu (2001) devotes considerable attention to forms of masculine domination, but has been heavily criticized for suggesting that women are actively complicit in their own subordination (Skeggs 1997). Women have long struggled in a variety of ways against entrenched and naturalized forms of domination, just as lesbians and gays have escaped a habitus which denied or execrated their sexuality. The habitus is not impenetrable, and people can and do break out of habituated behaviour and attitudes.

78

The crucial element of **Agency** is that subjects have a conscious understanding of their conditions of existence, and of the factors that keep them oppressed. This was clear in the emergence of both second-wave **Feminism** and **Gay liberation**, with both movements developing in the gap between lived realities and new aspirations, and in the process casting off many of the embodied practices that had defined their members' lives hitherto. For many influenced by the movements, the habitus became a site of struggle between inherited and entrenched norms and individual hopes and desires, which gave rise to a crisis of legitimacy and to an open rejection of the received order. Here awareness of the contradictions through growing **Reflexivity** is crucial to the possibility of change (Heaphy 2007). At the same time, the alternative communities that develop around sexual identity (see **Community)** develop new forms of habitus, embedding and embodying changing forms of consciousness.

HETEROSEXUALITY

Heterosexuality conventionally refers to sexual behaviour, desires, practices, emotions and identities based on relations between people of 'opposite sexes'. But like all apparently straightforward terms heterosexuality has a complex history and a multiplicity of meanings. The term itself was invented by the same man who invented the word **Homosexuality**, Karoly-Maria Benkert (Karl Marie Kertbenny), in the late 1860s. Originally referring to 'psychical hermaphrodism', what would now be called **Bisexuality**, it only slowly came into general use with its present-day meaning. The historian of the 'invention of heterosexuality', Jonathan Ned Katz (1995) notes its first use in the *New York Times* as late as the early 1920s, and it came into more popular discourse – including in songs and humour – in the 1930s. Only in the late 1940s and 1950s were 'heterosexual relationships' serenaded as the necessary basis for a stable society, though with rare use of the word. Even in the late twentieth century it remained a confusing term. Princess Diana, a famous icon of heterosexual **Femininity**, notoriously confused the words homosexuality and heterosexuality in a recorded phone call with a lover. In popular discourse heterosexuality was a love that did not need to dare to speak its name. It just was.

The absence of a word does not mean the absence of the phenomenon. On the contrary, the very absence is itself prime evidence for the overwhelming, potent unmarked presence of heterosexuality, generally seen as the universal, biologically given basis of reproductive and sexual life. Yet the linkage with homosexuality in the emerging language of **Sexology** and sexual theory at the end of the nineteenth century was no accident and pointed to a persistent problem. Heterosexual behaviour may have been common throughout history. It may have been the necessary means for reproducing the species. But it was less clear what its essence was. Heterosexuality was as much defined by what it was not as by what it was. Anthropologists were already aware from exploring other cultures that many societies were organized around the coexistence of homosexual and heterosexual behaviours. For Freud (1905: 146, n. 1), deeply influenced by sexological theorizing, and by anthropological discoveries, as well as his own clinical experiences, 'the exclusive sexual interest felt by men for women is . . . a problem that needs elucidating'. He noted that the ancient world laid emphasis on the sexual instinct in all its vicissitudes. The modern world emphasizes object choice. In other words, what he called the soldering together of drive and choice of love object was a historical and cultural product rather than an eternal verity. This recognition had profoundly radical implications because it implied that the categories of heterosexuality and homosexuality, and the supposed exclusivity and polarity they suggested, needed interrogation, and could not be taken for granted. This pointed to the later elaboration by Alfred Kinsey and his colleagues (1948) – ironically given Kinsey's general antipathy to Freudian approaches – of a heterosexual–homosexual continuum, with exclusive heterosexuality a minority experience at one extreme, and a similar small percentage of exclusive homosexual behaviour at the other, with most people scattered along the scale in between. What the work of Freud, Kinsey and others underlined was that homosexuality and heterosexuality were relational terms: each existed because of the other. They had little meaning on their own. For a long time, however, this remained a minority opinion. In biology, psychology and the social sciences heterosexuality and its other, homosexuality, were defined increasingly as distinct sexual categories. From the 1970s, as with homosexuality, efforts were made to define a heterosexual **Sexual orientation**. The paradox of the efforts in the late nineteenth and early twentieth centuries to give heterosexuality and homosexuality names was that it suggested an essence rather than variety, polarity rather than a continuum, and the effect of writing about sexual 'abnormalities' and **Perversion** was to bolster and confirm the norm, heterosexuality.

Feminist theory from the 1970s began to change the terms of the debate – see **Feminism** and **Gender**. Gayle Rubin's (1974) theorization of a sex/gender system pointed to the fact that heterosexuality was much more than a sexual practice; it was a social institution based on a binary division of sexuality and a hierarchical ordering: of men over women, and of heterosexuality over homosexuality. Heterosexuality was a key element in constituting and maintaining both the gender order and ideas of sexual normality (Rubin 1984). Adrienne Rich's (1980) discussion of 'compulsory heterosexuality' as a systematic denial of female emotional and sexual existence, underlined that here was an expression of social imperatives rather than natural evolution. Other writers tested out a range of metaphors and neologisms to make the same point: from Christopher Isherwood's 'heterosexual dictatorship', through heterosexism, hetero-patriarchy, the heterosexual panorama, heterosexual hegemony, heterosexual privilege, the heterosexual imaginary, the heterosexual assumption, to the heterosexual matrix and heteronormativity. The theoretical underpinnings of these accounts varied considerably but all sought to go beyond the traditional **Essentialism** of discussions of heterosexuality, and to elaborate the ways in which it was invented and institutionalized in specific social and historical circumstances, reproducing sexed and gendered hierarchies.

Queer critics have put these arguments at the centre of their theory. For Judith Butler (1990) the heterosexual matrix of discourses, institutional forms and practices positions heterosexuality as the normal, natural, inevitable and legitimate sexual expression. It is maintained by the promotion, assertion and performative re-inscription of discursive tropes, by the erasure of alternative lives through their unacknowledgement, and the forceful policing and regulation of alternative sexualities. Warner (1993, 1999) elaborated the concept of heteronormativity to account for the ways in which such efforts become embedded in everyday norms, taming radical challenges by accommodating them in acceptable ways. So, it has been argued, lesbians and gays who embrace **Same-sex marriage** are in danger of assimilation into heterosexual norms and values – what has been called 'homo-normativity'.

Feminist critics of heterosexuality have taken a variety of positions. For some it is not only represented in, but reproduced through, such phenomena as **Pornography**, **Trafficking** and **Violence** against women. Some radical feminists have seen genital intercourse between men and women as itself equivalent to an act of violence (Dworkin 1989). Other researchers have demonstrated how hetero-sexuality is embedded in the heads of women as well as the hearts (Holland *et al.* 1998). Women may seek to break away from traditional notions of how they should behave with men, but are constantly dragged back into emotionally and sexually subordinate relationships. This process goes beyond sexual relationships. Heterosexual hegemony is not only about ordering sexual lives but structures the domestic and extra-domestic division of labour and resources between men and women (Jackson 2000). But it can also be argued that many of these arguments go too far, obscuring diverse forms of resistance and as well as the possibilities of sexual exploration for women. As well as being an institution that locks men and women into relations of power and subordination, and creates and excludes the other, heterosexuality is also a series of sexual practices (Segal 1999). It embraces loving relationships as well as rape, **Choice** as well as coercion. It covers a multitude of sexual activities, that give pleasure as well as pose dangers.

Heterosexuality brings together sexual activity, gender, masculinity and femi-ninity into a complex set of relationships. Some have argued that heterosexuality as a social institution shapes gender. Others have suggested that gender is the logical prior category, which produces hierarchical relations that shape hetero-sexuality. Yet others have given priority to sexuality in shaping both gender and heterosexuality. The argument is surely rather metaphysical. The historical reality is that heterosexuality is inextricably bound up with and shaped by evolving discourses and practices of gender and sexuality, reinforced and ritualized by multiple practices of everyday life. Heterosexuality is not a unitary or monolithic structure. It is a site of struggle and contested meanings. It has changed throughout history, and continues to change today. One example of this is the way hetero-sexuality has become the basis for distinctive **Sexual identities** (Seidman 2002). There may seem a paradox here: surely heterosexuality has shaped and defined identity through history. That may be the case, but it has tended to be dissident identities that have expressed themselves forcefully. The emergence of people explicitly declaring their heterosexuality, or straightness, may be a testimony to continuing fear of the other. But it also indicates a growing pluralization of sexual subject positions and identities that requires the articulation of what was hitherto unspoken.

HOMOPHOBIA

Homophobia has become the most commonly used term to describe anti-homosexual prejudice and discrimination, a conceptual tool and theoretical resource for individuals and collectivities to name and respond to homosexual oppression (Bryant and Vidal-Ortiz 2008: 387). The popularization of the concept is generally attributed to George Weinberg (1972), writing in the early stages of the **Gay liberation** movement, and was elaborated as a reaction to the view that **Homosexuality** was a problem of individual pathology. Traditionally, same-sex desire was seen as the problem to which society had to react. The idea of homophobia neatly reverses the discourse. Now the problem was attributed to anti-homosexual prejudice and societal hostility. As a tactic in the campaign for homosexual rights the concept of homophobia had many 'splendid ironies', as Plummer (1981: 62) pointed out early in the concept's history. Whereas in the past the homosexual was regarded as sick, now it was those hostile to homosexuality who were thus labelled. Whereas homosexuals were often seen as having an irrational fear of the opposite sex, now heterosexuals could be portrayed as having their own irrational fear, 'homosexual panic'.

Homophobia, Weinberg argued, describes a phobia prevalent among most non-homosexuals, taking the form of a 'dread of being in close quarters with homosexuals' (Weinberg 1972: 23). It was inculcated in early life, producing a revulsion against homosexuals and frequently a desire to inflict punishment or retribution on them. Amongst homosexuals themselves this led to a chronic self-denial, guilt and what gay liberation described as self-oppression.

It was thus initially a psychological concept, developed via a dialogue with **Psychoanalysis**. Weinberg argued that the institution of psychoanalysis was itself a major agent for the reproduction of homophobia. At the same time, roots of the idea can be found in psychoanalysis itself. As one analyst put it, 'irrational, anxious, hostile responses may be activated not only amongst people who are threatened by their own homosexual impulses, but also in any one whose aggressive and sexual feelings are barely repressed' (Friedman 1988: 187).

The principal problem with the concept is that it too often stays within the problematic of mental illness, simply reversing the terms. It individualizes the issue of anti-homosexual feelings, making it a problem of personality rather than societies. Weinberg partially recognized that by listing a number of motives for homophobia, including **Religion** and the threat to dominant cultural values, particularly those relating to family life. Such explanations are clearly historical and social in focus rather than psychological, and pointed to fuller analyses that attempted to theorize the structural and cultural factors that shaped hostility towards homosexuality. Theories of heterosexism, compulsory heterosexuality and hetero-normativity were obvious moves in that direction (Adam 1998), and with homophobia were the key concepts that shaped gay theorizing. All of them suggest that the royal road to understanding hostility towards homosexuality is through understanding the structures and institutionalization of **Heterosexuality** and the ways in which it inscribes **Gender**.

From this perspective, homophobia could be theorized as deriving from personal insecurities amongst heterosexually-defined men about their ability to meet conventional gender expectations – giving rise to a gender panic (Herek 1986). Anti-gay activities, ranging from school playground taunts, jokes and threats through to physical violence, police the gender boundaries and strengthen male heterosexual bonding. For **Queer** theorists homophobia is intrinsic to contemporary heterosexual masculinity. Disavowed male homosexual desire contributes to a heightened sense of masculinity, and male homosexual panic becomes a normal condition of male heterosexual privilege (Butler 1990) – though it is not clear how this explains hostility towards lesbianism. The emphasis on heterosexuality has, however, allowed a broadening of the idea of homophobia, to describe hostility towards other sexual and gender unorthodoxies, such as **Bisexuality** and **Transgender**, giving rise to concepts of bi-phobia and trans-phobia.

The concept of homophobia has proved a popular and easily graspable way of accounting for continuing hostility towards homosexuality. It has been deployed in relation to the playground and streets, schools, universities, the law, prisons, families, employment, politics, religion as well as everyday life. It has become a catch-all idea, though perhaps better as a *descriptive* term than as a coherent theoretical and analytical concept. The major problem is that as a generalizing term, still vestigially rooted in a psychological disposition, homophobia also assumes a common experience of homosexuality, assuming a universal structure for both. All the evidence, however, is that structures of homosexuality vary enormously across the globe; so, it follows, do attitudes towards homosexuality, and therefore the meanings and salience of a concept like homophobia. The accounts of homophobia as they have been theorized since the early 1970s have overwhelmingly been based on the dominant structuring of same-sex desire in Western industrial societies since the nineteenth century. Even so, they do not readily explain significant variations of attitudes across such societies (Robinson 2008), nor variations within each society, particularly those based on differences of race and ethnicity – see **Intersectionality**.

The real value of the concept lies in the way it directs attention to a continuing feature of societies across the globe, despite widespread liberalization in many parts of the world: deep-seated and irrational hostility towards homosexuality involving both symbolic and physical violence. The concept of homophobia can be seen as a key borderline idea, bridging the psychological and social. It poses urgent questions for both.

HOMOSEXUALITY

The term homosexuality, an uneasy blend of Greek and Latin parts, was invented in the 1860s by the Hungarian writer Karoly Maria Benkert, to describe sexual attraction to, and physical and emotional involvement with, someone of the same gender. It represented a conscious attempt to break with the traditional language which had execrated and condemned (usually male) same-sex experiences, especially sodomy, the crime too awful to be named among Christians, and subject to often drastic legal constraints, including the death penalty. The invention of the word, alongside others with similar implications, such as invert, urning or third-sexer, during the late nineteenth century, can be seen as a public sign of the articulation of distinctive identities and subjectivities organized around same-sex desires. As Foucault (1979) famously put it, the sodomite was a temporary aberration, expressing a potentiality in all sinful creatures. The homosexual belonged to a species, with a singular set of personal characteristics and sexual desires.

The term was intended to be a more neutral, less pejorative, alternative to the traditional language of sin, degeneracy and perversion which had dominated thinking about same-sex activities in the Christian West, and which had their roots in biblical prohibitions. But the word soon became part of the new, would-be scientific language of **Sexology**: homosexuality moved from being originally a sin, then a heinous crime to being a scientific problem, and a medicalized condition. There has been a long controversy about the role of sexology in achieving this, and particularly over whether it helped constitute homosexuality as a distinctive category. Certainly there is plentiful evidence of a rich and complex history of same-sex activity that was not simply invented by sexologists. Many of the pioneering theorists of homosexuality were themselves homosexual, like Karl Heinrich Ulrichs, Edward Carpenter and Magnus Hirschfeld, all anxious to give meaning and humanity to the new descriptions. Moreover, the pioneering writers on homosexuality were often in dialogue with, and learnt from, people who were gradually defining themselves as inverts or homosexuals (Oosterhuis 2000). But sexology helped provide a language which was crucially important in a significant new development: the hardening of the binary divide between homosexuality and **Heterosexuality** that is characteristic of the late nineteenth and early twentieth centuries, with the latter the dominant term and homosexuality the deviant other (Sedgwick 1990). This binarism has dominated the sexual imaginary ever since, and taken as rooted in nature. A full historical understanding has shown that, on the contrary, it was the result of a complex process of definition and self-definition, a process that has been explored particularly by scholars influenced by **Social constructionism** and **Queer** theory. The invention of the term did not create homosexual life histories or subjectivities. But it contributed to the shaping of a discourse in which homosexuality appeared as a wholly distinct experience, a category apart. In so doing it helped construct 'the homosexual' as a distinct being.

The definition of homosexuality as a specific medical or psychological condition led to a preoccupation with the 'causes' of homosexuality which has tended to dominate thinking about it. The fact that few people have bothered to enquire into the causes of heterosexuality indicates the dominance of the view that homosexuality was an abnormality that needed to be explained. However, after a century of debate and scientific enquiry the question of causation remains as inconclusive as ever. The biological explanation argues that homosexuality is an inbuilt and probably hereditary condition that affects some people and not others. Negatively, it can be seen as a pathological distortion of the natural sexual drive, caused perhaps by hormonal imbalances or chromosomal accidents, or more recently, in a surprising rebirth of biological explanations, the result of a 'gay gene' or a 'gay brain', as suggested by the American scientists Dean Hamer and Simon LeVay and others (Wilson and Rahman 2005). Such explanations have led in turn in some quarters to more positive views of homosexuality. If homosexuality has a biological explanation, and is a specific **Sexual orientation**, might it not be as 'natural' as heterosexuality? Many homosexual activists have in fact argued this since the nineteenth century. However attractive such explanations are to homosexual activists, they, like the negative views, have the misfortune of being completely unproven, and one suspects un-provable.

A second approach has concentrated on understanding the psychological reasons for homosexuality. The most famous name associated with such explanations is Sigmund Freud, the founder of **Psychoanalysis**. Building on earlier sexological explanations, Freud attempted to understand what he called sexual inversion in terms of the universal bisexuality of human beings rather than in the biological make-up of a distinct group of people. It resulted from the specific patterns of interaction with parents and the complex and universal processes through which the bisexual infant became an adult. So homosexuality, like heterosexuality, resulted from an inhibition of the sexual drive. As a working hypothesis this has been enormously influential, though in subsequent debates it has also led to enormous confusions. Does a child become homosexual because of a weak father and strong mother, or because of an over dominant father and a weak mother? Both explanations have been frequently offered, and equally often fail to match the biographical facts of individual homosexuals. As a result, psychoanalysis has often been seen as hostile to homosexuality as other theories of the mind, a picture unfortunately confirmed by the practices of many individual psychoanalysts.

One further problem is what is claimed as a universal process can be refuted by the sheer variety of patterns of sexuality on a world scale. Recent approaches, under the rubric of social constructionism, have tended to try to understand homosexuality in social and historical terms, concentrating less on what causes homosexuality and more on what shapes attitudes towards it. Different cultures respond to same-sex practices in different ways, and this in turn helps to determine whether it is possible to live a homosexual life or develop a distinctive homosexual identity. On a world scale there seems to have been two social patterns which allowed a certain acceptance of some aspects of (usually male) homosexuality. The first, which can be seen historically in cultures as far apart as east Asia, Melanesia, the Islamic world and the ancient Mediterranean, more or less tolerated homosexual behaviour as long as it was between an adult male and a youth, usually as part of the processes by which the young male was accepted as a full man. It did not normally affect traditional family life. The second great pattern, embracing cultures from the Philippines to Madagascar, and some tribal societies in Africa and North America, accepted some forms of same-sex behaviour as long as the homosexually inclined man 'became' a woman, or the woman a man. The Native American berdache is the classic example.

Neither of these patterns allowed the emergence of what has become the dominant Western pattern in the twentieth and twenty-first centuries: the idea that homosexuality forms the basis for a separate sexual and social identity and way of life, based on resistance to the dominant heterosexual norms. This idea probably first emerged in the new urban cultures that developed from the early modern period. Cities allowed groups of people who felt different to come together in relative anonymity, and develop alternative lifestyles. At first these subcultures, usually of what were seen as effeminate men, and to a smaller extent masculine women, were secretive and subject to strong persecution. But during the twentieth century, they gave rise to ever more complex social networks, and to a strong sense of **Community** amongst self-identified homosexuals, who were beginning to resist the hostile labelling of them as sick or inadequate. This was the basis for the **Gay liberation** movement which powerfully emerged in the United States in 1969, and asserted the validity of positive **Lesbian** and **Gay** identities, in the process developing a strong critique of 'compulsory heterosexuality'.

The strength of these new identities, and the communities that were built around them, was demonstrated in the early 1980s with the sudden emergence of the HIV/**AIDS** epidemic. In combating a frightening epidemic, the lesbian and gay community came of age. But the experience had also demonstrated the vulnerability of the non-heterosexual world to strong backlashes against liberalizing tendencies. This was especially the case among conservatives in some Western countries (notably the USA) and in large parts of the former USSR's sphere of influence in Eastern and Central Europe, and in the Global South, where same-sex activity became a focus of opposition to Westernizing tendencies. **Fundamentalism**, especially, demonstrated fierce and frequently violent hostility towards same-sex activity.

There have been various attempts to assess the percentage of the population that is predominantly or exclusively homosexual. Alfred Kinsey's work in the late 1940s has been used to suggest that as many as 10 per cent might be, though more recent research has tended to suggest a much lower figure, perhaps 1 to 2 per cent in Britain, France and the United States. The worldwide evidence suggests that this is quite the wrong way of posing the issue. Though Western-style identities have begun to spread throughout the world, they are by no means the dominant or only ways of living homosexuality. In many parts of the world, ranging from Turkey to large parts of East Asia, Africa and South America, homosexuality remains tabooed. Even in Western countries, prejudice remains, and the legal systems are often discriminatory. In all these parts of the world there is no necessary link between homosexual practices and homosexual identities. The idea that lesbians and gays are a distinct group of people has been challenged radically by social constructionist and queer theorists who argue that sexual identity, if not sexual desire, is a matter of **Choice**, and that the divide between homosexuality and heterosexuality is a social and historical one, not one based in any fundamental or essential reality. This returns us to the question of causation. It is possible that some people develop predominantly homosexual desires as a result of a variety of factors: possibly genetic, possibly psychological, possibly social opportunity; we still do not know. But in the end that is not the important question. What ultimately matters is whether homosexuality offers the possibility for viable life choices, and a fulfilling way of living. The evidence of recent years is clearly that it does, though resistance to this evidence is still very strong on a world scale.

HUMAN SEXUAL RIGHTS

The idea of 'human rights' had its origin in the American and French revolutions of the late eighteenth century, and has had a complex and tortured history ever since. To be *human* rights as opposed to natural or particularist rights, all humans across the world must possess them equally, and only because of their status as human beings (Hunt 2007: 20). But the construction of the idea of a common humanity, and what a full humanity might embrace, has had to be struggled for in the past two tumultuous centuries. It certainly had an ambiguous relation to the sexual. Prior to the early 1990s, sexuality was strikingly absent from international human rights discourse. The Universal Declaration of Human Rights, adopted by the United Nations General Assembly in 1948, had famously declared the 'inherent dignity' and 'equal and inalienable rights' of all members of human society, but its protection of family life and privacy proved limited in practice in supporting any claim to sexual rights. Over time the universal subject of human rights has been seen as having different racial or ethnic origins, different faiths or none, varying health needs, and as being gendered in complex ways, but for long the UN (or rather its diverse members) proved reluctant to acknowledge issues of **Sexual diversity** or **Transgender**. The international argument for a wider agenda embracing sexuality in its broadest sense only began to emerge fully into international debate with the Vienna conference on Human Rights in 1993, the UN declaration on the Elimination of Violence against Women later that year, the world population conference in Cairo in 1994 and the women's conference on Beijing in 1995 (Petchesky 2000).

International movements on sexual issues date back to the late nineteenth century, focusing particularly at first on prostitution and the white slave trade (that is, **Trafficking** of children and women). The Hague Convention of 1907 had outlawed rape as an act of war (though tragically with limited effect). The World League for Sexual Reform, led by Magnus Hirschfeld developed in the 1920s an agenda, on homosexuality and reproductive rights especially, which foreshadowed later campaigns, but the League perished with the Nazi rise to power and the descent into war. Issues of sexuality were only explicitly revived from the 1970s, under the impact of second-wave feminism, the internationalizing of the LGBT movement and the global HIV/**AIDS** epidemic. Sexuality came onto the international human rights agenda, at first, mainly through debates over privacy and reproduction (Waites 2005: 55). There are obviously strong links between reproductive rights and wider questions of sexuality, especially in relation to core themes like bodily integrity, personhood, equality and diversity, and to the social and cultural contexts which encourage injustice and violence. While a strong international discourse on reproductive rights has emerged powerfully, its history underlines the difficulties in negotiating common meanings across different societies, dependent on different traditions, circumstances and relations of power between men and women, and women and women (Petchesky and Judd 1998).

Reproductive rights and sexual rights are not, however, necessarily the same, and conflating them can lead to the disenfranchisement of non-reproductive sex in general, and non-heterosexual sex and questions of transgender in particular (Miller 2000). Two influential reports by Amnesty International (2001b, 2004), building on the work of grassroots women's organizations across the globe, documented a painful stream of stories of violence and abuse of women, ranging from harassment, enforced female circumcision and forced marriages to rape and murder. One legal expert (Bamforth 2005: 3–10) has observed five commonalities across such experience. First, the acts of violence they highlight are intimately related to social conceptions of gender and appropriate gender roles. This involves the denial of basic human rights to women, and often extreme violence to LGBT people and women when they are seen to infringe locally enforced norms. Second, the violence inflicted on minorities and women itself has strongly sexual dimensions – notably in the high incidence of rape. Third, these actions are often justified by reference to local religious or cultural factors, and interventions are often rejected as neo-colonial. Fourth, many of the laws in countries where violence and abuse of human rights are rife often play a role in justifying abuse, and state agents, especially the police, often play a part in inflicting violence. Finally, although the role of the state is critical in permitting violence, much of the violence against women and sexual minorities is conducted by private actors, in the home or the locality. Denial of basic rights is deeply embedded in many cultures.

As this suggests, denial of rights to women are inextricably linked with denial of rights to LGBT people. The UN Commission on Human Rights' call in 2003 upon all states to promote and protect the human rights of all persons regardless of their **Sexual orientation** was a major breakthrough, long fought for, though its main effect was declaratory rather than substantive. The intervention of other NGOs alongside LGBT organizations has also been very important. Two reports at the turn of the millennium made a major impact. Amnesty International's *Breaking the Silence* (1997) examined the various ways in which individuals can be targeted for their sexual orientation – real or alleged – and how a rights framework can be developed. A second report, *Crimes of Hate, Conspiracy of Silence:*

Torture and Ill-treatment Based on Sexual Identity (2001a) provided further detail. The main push, however, has come from within the international LGBT movement itself, which gave rise to organizations such as ILGA (International Lesbian and Gay Association, founded 1978), the International Gay and Lesbian Human Rights Commission, and various transgender organizations such as the UK's Press for Change (Kollman and Waites 2009). Two documents have particularly focused debate and campaigning in the early twenty-first century. The Yogyakarta Principles, published in 2007, in effect argued that LGBT rights were already inherent in existing international human rights law, and assumed the fixedness of **Sexual identity** categories. The **Essentialism** of many arguments about gay and lesbian politics poses the danger of limiting their international impact. The Declaration of Montreal, presented at the International Conference on LGBT Human Rights in 2006, went further, calling for the creation of a UN convention on elimination of all forms of discrimination on grounds of sexual orientation and gender identity, and attempted to go beyond Western definitions of sexuality (Swiebel 2009).

It is clear from these examples that struggles over human rights are themselves not unproblematic. As Petchesky (2000) notes, while the claim to rights can be enabling, it can as easily lead to an intensification of conflict over which rights and whose rights have priority. If sexual cultures vary enormously and have specific historical formations, how do we distinguish those claims to right that have a universal resonance, and those which are highly culturally specific – and possibly distasteful to large numbers of citizens around the globe? A recognition of the human rights of women, for example, does not mean that as yet it is possible to develop a common assumption about what those rights mean in practice, as controversies over the legitimacy of women wearing the veil, enforced or arranged marriages, access to birth control and the like underline. Okin (2005: 84) warns of the dangers in a **Multiculturalism** or cultural relativism that protects different cultures that discriminate against women. Others, however, see dangers in imposing 'Enlightenment values' on the Global South (Rajan 2005). Similarly, **Cosmopolitanism** as the ideal of establishing dialogue across chasms of difference depends on breaking down the structures that separate people off from one another, and often seem utopian in a divided world.

Such debates within the discourse of human rights illustrate the core problem: human rights do not exist in nature. They are not there to be discovered, already written on tablets of stone. They have to be invented, in complex historical conjunctures and contestations, as part of the making of minimal common values. They are the result of sustained dialogue. And in a divided, often violently polarized world, that is not an easy task (Corrêa *et al.* 2008; Plummer 2010).

Yet, as Butler (2005) argues, specifically in the context of LGBT issues, claims of human sexual rights are not just particularist aspirations: they pose profound questions about what it means to be human in a globalized world which in many parts still seeks to deny the humanity of non-heterosexual or gender challenging people. To assert sexual rights means that 'when we struggle for rights we are not simply struggling for rights that attach to my person, but we are struggling *to be conceived as persons*' (Butler 2005: 69). Sexuality is more than simply an attribute of an individual. It has come to define a relationship with the self and with others, one's very humanity. LGBT people *have* to raise questions about the injustices they face because if they did not do so their very humanness would continue to be questioned. Thus the central challenge of international gay and lesbian rights is to assert the reality of homosexuality, not as inner truth, not as sexual practice, 'but as one of the defining features of the social world in its very intelligibility' (Butler 2005: 64–5). To assert the value of LGBT subjectivities and ways of life is to challenge existing realities, and to show that there are many different ways of being sexual – and of being human. More generally, we can equally argue that the struggle over human sexual rights is in the end a struggle about what it is to be human. Just as discrimination, prejudice, oppression and exploitation are denials of full humanity, so a positive claim for sexual rights is an assertion of the rich diversity of human possibilities.

HYBRIDITY

The term hybridity, like so much in the conceptualization of sexuality, has its roots in nineteenth-century botanical and biological language. It suggests a cross-fertilization of natural elements to create a new entity (as with plants and animal breeds). Applied to historical and social scientific analysis, as it has been increasingly, it offers a powerful metaphor for the personal and cultural inter-mingling that is characteristic of the late-modern world, especially under the impact of **Globalization**. Closely related terms can carry both heavy overtones of disapproval or prejudice (as with mongrelization, miscegenation, bastardard-ization), and more neutral or positive meanings (for example, fusion, translation, blending, creolization or **Mixedness**). In these forms it has been widely applied, *inter alia*, to food, music, architecture, fashion, art, languages, writing and religious forms. Since the 1930s, however, it has been most powerfully deployed in explorations of ethnic and racialized identities, and most recently in post-colonial studies by writers such as Homi Bhaba, Stuart Hall, Edward Said and Paul Gilroy (Burke 2009).

They all argue that cultural identity is neither fixed nor inevitable, but fluid and negotiable, a process rather than a final achievement. All identities in this sense are hybrid, always combinations of disparate elements. Historical examples of cultural hybridization abound. Amongst many possible examples, historians have noted, for instance, the Hellenization of the Roman Empire, the (historically obliterated) construction of early modern Spain as an encounter between Islamic, Jewish and Christian cultures, the various intellectual encounters, Islamic, Jewish, Byzantine as well as Western European that contributed to the European Renaissance, or the making of Latin American and Caribbean cultures from an extensive and conflict-ridden exchange between African, European and indigenous peoples and cultures. Such encounters are often marked by confrontation, exploitation, discrimination and inequity as well as reciprocity, exchange and dialogue, but the point is that new cultural formations can and do emerge from these intense interminglings, to create new, hybridized social – including sexualized and gendered – actors in an increasingly complex world. Hybridity is a key idea in the development of contemporary ideas of **Cosmopolitanism**.

The concept of hybridity has been used for analysing specific sexual and gender configurations. Contemporary **Bisexuality**, for example, has been presented as a hybridization of patterns of modern gay, lesbian and heterosexual culture, while hybridization has been deployed to theorize **Transgender**, and especially intersex identities (Hird 2004: 97). But it also offers an understanding of the ways in which sexuality is shaped by and drawn into wider social conflicts. As pejorative words like miscegenation suggest close encounters of ostensibly different cultures can arouse strong fears about the sexual mingling and the transformation of the gender and family/kin order that hybridity may produce. Fear of mixing can produce fierce boundary drawing and the defence of the pure breed. A related, though contradictory, fear is of cultural – and sexual – homogenization as global flows allegedly lead to the McDonaldization or Coca-Colonization of the world, and local differences and cultures disappear. Defence of traditional ways of life, especially concerning issues around the body, gender and sexuality, and the fear of indeterminacy or uncertainty that arise in moments of profound change, has been a strong feature of contemporary **Fundamentalism**. And yet the evidence suggests that dialogue and adaptation as much as contestation is a characteristic feature of cultural encounters. Altman (2001) has spoken of the 'global gay' as a major element in the contemporary sexual world, referring to the emergence on a global scale of similar same-sex identities and ways of life based on Western models. But the evidence is less of a takeover by such models as of creative borrowing – see for example the ways in which in the Philippines the term gay 'signals a range of semantic possibilities, including that of transvestism and transgendering' which are shaped by a very specific history of sexuality and gender (Johnson 1997: 89). We can see a similar process of cross-fertilization in the global dialogue over reproductive rights where, as Petchesky (2003) has shown, the different historical experiences of women across the globe, and conflicting views of the meanings of bodily integrity, have nevertheless fed into an emerging international discourse of **Human sexual rights**.

Peter Burke (2009: 54), who has offered an incisive history of the concept, admits hybridity is 'a slippery, ambiguous term, at once literal and metaphorical, descriptive and explanatory', and yet it clearly has been useful as a way of trying to understand the complex formations that constitute the sexual. As sensitivity to the ways in which sexuality is shaped on the fluid boundaries of the biological, the psychological and socio-historical grows, it is likely that the concept of hybridity will continue to be valuable in theorizing such rich and varied patterns.

I

INDIVIDUALIZATION

Individualization has become a key term in accounting for social and cultural transformations in the contemporary world. It is clearly closely related to terms such as individualism (the belief in the central importance of the individual in political, economic, social and moral life), and individuation (the process of becoming a fully fledged individual in society), but has different connotations. It is, according to two of its main theorists (Beck and Beck-Gernsheim 2002), a *social* and *historical* process, leading to *institutionalized individualism*. Individualization means 'First, the disembedding and, second, the re-embedding of industrial society ways of life by new ones, in which the individual must produce, stage and cobble together their biographies themselves' (Beck 1994: 13). It is a concept that is closely linked with detraditionalization, **Globalization** and **Neoliberalism**.

Disembedding implies that in late-modern societies individuals are being increasingly freed from the weight of traditional structures and authorities under the impact of juggernaut-like change. Ties that link people, such as work, community and especially the family, become ever more tenuous. In such a world people have no choice but to choose their own ways of life, and in that process sexuality and love assume ever-increasing importance. Individuals are forced reflexively to organize and calculate the pros and cons of their future action, and that can bring a sense of isolation, the loneliness of moral choice. In that context sex and love can become a source of meaning, an anchor against drift. But such bonds are inherently more fragile than the 'ties that bind' of old, so that a sense of contingency and heightened risk increasingly surrounds interpersonal relationships. Theorists disagree on the implications of this. The mild pessimism that surrounds Beck and Beck-Gernsheim's (2002) analysis, reaches the verge of despair in the writings of Bauman, who forecast a new 'dark age' characterized by rampant individualism and consumerism (2005). Such views are balanced by the more optimistic analysis in the work of Giddens (1992) who sees in this process the potentiality for new forms of **Intimacy**.

The thesis of individualization has been widely challenged on a number of grounds. Have most people, even in the late-modern West, genuinely broken free of traditional structures and life patterns? Do they really have the freedom to choose their own ways of life? Are contemporary relationships as friable as they are presented? The obvious defence is that what individualization theorists are describing are ideal types rather than everyday reality, historical tendencies rather than final achievement. But the main value of the concept is that it sees contemporary individualism not as constitutive of the social order but as a product of it. In many ways the theory is an attempt to address older concerns of social critics, especially in relation to the intricate connections between the social, the individual and the intimate in the culture of capitalism.

Critics of the 'new individualism' (Elliott and Lemert 2006) tend to emphasize its emotional costs The belief that capitalism distorts and damages individual potential, creating a manipulated self, has had a long history, culminating in the critiques of the Frankfurt School, Marcuse and others of **Commodification**. The trends of contemporary culture dissolve the human bond, replacing authentic reflective subjectivities with narcissistic, hedonistic values. Psychology sustains the fiction of the autonomous subject in such a culture. But this is at best a regulatory fiction itself, and is no more liberating than the traditional ties and relationships it is replacing, leaving individuals 'stranded'. We live in a 'therapy culture', 'distracting people from engaging with the wider social issues in favour of an inward turn to the self' (Furedi 2004: 203). But this is a confessing self, part of a therapeutic culture in which everyone confesses to every other self, manifested in 12-step therapy programmes, personal counselling, memory recovery work, phone and cyber therapy, peer counselling, not to mention the confessional extravaganzas of television programmes and the like (Elliott and Lemert 2006: 130).

All this is pretty despairing, and does not bode well for solid relationships. Against this, feminist and other critics have made a number of powerful points. First of all, it is not at all clear that the bonds of family life have dissolved in the ways portrayed. **Families** may have changed, but there is plentiful evidence that shifting patterns of **Relationality** continue to offer care and commitment, especially to children (Smart 2007). It is also clear that for many people the new individualism is about more than doing your own thing. It is about developing forms of autonomy that are also profoundly social. As Heller and Feher (1988: 36) argued, 'If the end of the individual is self-determination, then the higher purpose to which the individual is committed is likely to be the self-determination of others'. If individualization is a profound social process that is reshaping the world, and individualism is an ambiguous philosophy that embraces everything from the pursuit of civil rights to neoliberal economics, then what David Held (1987: 290) has called 'democratic autonomy' is perhaps more about the pursuit of individuality, the expansion of individual freedoms and the broadening of life chances in full awareness of the opportunities that promote and the limits that restrict. This is a relative form of autonomy in the sense that it is individuality in and through our relations with others (Weeks 1995: 66). But that is perhaps the most important truth about contemporary individuality, that it is a profoundly social phenomenon.

INFORMALIZATION

Some theorists have sought to explain the changes in Western sexual mores since the 1960s in terms of a process of 'informalization'. The leading proponent is the Dutch sociologist Cas Wouters, who has produced a series of articles and books on the theme (2004, 2007). Informalization is the twentieth and twenty-first century manifestation of the long-term process of social and psychological change theorized by the influential sociologist Norbert Elias (2000) in his masterwork, *The Civilizing Process* (first published in German in 1939), which he described as 'formalization'. Wouters is a close disciple of Elias.

Formalization is a tendency in Western societies, since the sixteenth century at least, towards a more orderly and rule-driven way of life, based on increasing control over impulses and the development of a culture of self-control and restraint and an internalized authoritarian conscience and values. These new instinctual controls become so habituated that they create new personality types, a 'second nature', whose origins are social not biological (see **Habitus**). The notion of a second nature is not dissimilar to Freud's concept of the super-ego. It basically plays a key role in a disciplinary phase of social development, traceable in Western Europe especially, which projects wildness on to the other, characteristically on strangers, the lower classes, or racial and sexual others. Once widely accepted behaviours, such as farting, burping, spitting, urinating or defecating in public, or semi-public, eating with your hands or sharing utensils, sharing beds, having sex in semi-public, were increasingly seen as transgressive or unacceptable. There was increased discretion around sexual activity, growing taboos against people of the same sex sharing beds, growing segregation of the genders, and the separation of or sequestering of areas of life regarded as disagreeable or threatening. The increasing privatization of death from the nineteenth century provides a classic example. Similarly the sequestration, categorization and hierarchical classification of sexual behaviour in the nineteenth century had lasting results in shaping contemporary mores, with sexuality becoming the dark secret of individual lives.

Elias recognized that this culture was punctuated by periods of relaxation, or informalization, as in the scandals of the *fin de siècle* at the end of the nineteenth century, the alleged excesses of the Jazz Age and the 'flappers' of the 1920s, to some extent in the personal disruptions of World War II, and above all in the permissiveness of the 1960s. He saw these, however, as temporary loosenings of the long-term process. Wouters goes further. He sees informalization as a decisive shift in both 'sociogenesis' (the relations between individuals and groups) and 'psychogenesis' (the ways in which individuals manage their emotions and relate to themselves).

Wouters has argued that gradually from the 1940s, but with a strong spurt forward in the 1960s, a 'controlled decontrolling' (2004: 9) of emotion management and personal morals became dominant in Western societies. Social conduct became increasingly less authoritarian, more differentiated and varied for a wider public, with an increasing variety of emotional and sexual patterns of behaviour becoming socially acceptable. There is, for example, an increased informality in the use of first names and of familiar pronouns, a break from rigidities in clothes, hair styles, dancing and popular music, a growing toleration of the use of what used to be regarded as 'bad' or vulgar language, and a general relaxation of personal behaviour. Above all, there is a growing acceptance of what were traditionally seen as sinful, perverted or unacceptable sexual behaviours, such as homosexuality, pre-marital and extra-marital sex, informal unions, as well as less authoritarian relations between adults and children (see **Great transition**).

At the heart of this is a tendency to greater self-control over behaviour, a process of responsibilization and self-regulation, a move from conscience to consciousness, leading to the emergence of a 'third nature'. Self-regulation, it is argued, can only become dominant in societies with a high degree of interdependency and social integration, and a broadening democratization of interpersonal relations. Only in such a culture can there be sufficient trust to allow a relaxation of well-established constraints on behaviour.

In some ways Wouters' argument appears close to Herbert Marcuse's theory of a 'repressive desublimination' in consumer society, but whereas for Marcuse this represents a manipulation of erotic possibilities, for Wouters what is hap-pening is more a mutual acceptance on the part of growing numbers of people of the necessity of self-restraint. This is his counter to those social conservatives who would castigate the permissive revolution precisely for the weakening of external and internal controls. It is a little ironic that Wouters in part bases his argument on an increase in trust when the period from the 1960s on has been generally seen by conservative critics like Fukuyama (1995, 1999) as one of declining trust precisely because of the breakdown of traditional values and restraints. But though certainly not a social pessimist, Wouters is reluctant to fall into the trap of over-optimism or inevitability. The twin processes he sees at work in contemporary society, of social differentiation (for example, the appearance of new social and sexual identities) and integration of social functions and groups as a result of growing interdependency, can produce social conflicts. Moreover, informalization is in a spiral relationship to processes of reformalization, where attempts are made to re-establish social contraints – the 1980s offers a prime example, with socially conservative movements and governments dominant in many countries, especially the USA and the UK. Yet, there is a sense of the long-term durability of the process Wouters describes, and his position can be linked to a number of related theories.

Giddens (1991, 1992), for example, is clearly in many ways influenced by the Elias approach (and is indeed a former student and colleague of his), and is certainly interested in psychological shifts, and emphasizes other elements of the 'trans-formation of intimacy', particularly 'detraditionalization' under the impact of profound economic and social change and globalization. Similarly the theorization of **Individualization** as a process makes many of the same assumptions. Whatever the qualifications one might make, the thesis of informalization provides an impor-tant insight into a process of unprecedented sexual change, linking it to long-term changes in the relationship between biology, psychology and society, as well as the growth of responsibilization.

INTERSECTIONALITY

Intersectionality is concerned with the overlapping, interlocking, interweaving, multidimensional forms of power that inscribe individual and collective lives and experience of domination and resistance. Individual identities and social positions are shaped by and at the intersection of a host of often conflicting forces, typically for theorists of intersectionality, dynamics of class, gender, race and ethnicity, but also embracing a host of other determining influences including nationality, faith, geography, age and generation, ability and disability, and sexuality (Taylor *et al.* 2010).

The roots of intersectional analyses are firmly in the social movements of the 1970s and 1980s, especially at the point where **Feminism** and anti-racism met. The interlocking, mutually reinforcing impact of various forms of power and domination around race, gender and sexuality was first articulated by black feminists as it became clear that the universalizing tendencies of white feminist analyses, especially around issues like the family, did not speak to the experience of all women. The black lesbian Combahee River Collective (1982: 14) wrote of the difficulty of separating race from class from sex oppression, because in their lives they were experienced 'simultaneously'. The term intersectionality itself seems to have been first used by Crenshaw (1989) in a discussion of the discrimination facing black women workers. The concept proved enormously influential amongst black feminist writers, especially as it foregrounded racism and anti-racist struggle, but it had a significant impact also on wider feminist thinking, especially as questions of difference came to the fore, bringing a recognition of the complexities of social positioning and of forms of political struggle. It had been apparent since the early days of second-wave feminism that women experienced oppression as women differently depending on their social location, and that there were multiple forms of domination. This had given rise to an additive notion of oppression: a woman was oppressed as a woman, as an African-American (or Chicana or Latina), as a lesbian, as a disabled person, and so on. The danger of such an approach was that it reinforced a tendency towards developing hierarchies of oppression, and victimhood and lack of agency. What intersectionalist analyses sought to do was to show how such experiences worked together to reinforce one another in the uniqueness of subject position: they were lived not as separate forms of oppression but as inextricably interlocking and densely lived experiences, producing their own forms of resistance. As Nash (2008: 13–14) notes, the force of these analyses was to highlight the reality that 'identity is complex, that subjectivity is messy, and that personhood is inextricably bound up with vectors of power'.

One obvious response to this messiness was to affirm ever more precise hyphenated identities as the focus of personal realization and collective struggle,

96

which had the effect of fragmenting the hitherto unified categories of 'woman' or 'lesbian' or 'gay' that had emerged from feminism and **Gay liberation**. But there was another inherent push in intersectional analyses, towards the querying of fixed identities: a recognition that identity categories were socially and historically constructed, were always provisional, and were themselves potential vectors of power as well as the basis for resistance to oppression. From this perspective what mattered was not so much the articulation of precisely defined identities as the performance or doing of forms of resistance to the experience of mutually reinforcing forms of power. There was an overlap here with **Queer** critiques of identitarian politics, though in practice for queer theorists the challenge to identity categories took precedence over the lived experience of multiple oppressions.

Early intersectional analyses were above all preoccupied with the interplay of race, gender and class. These were seen as the key mutually constitutive social divisions. Critics of the concept have, however, suggested that sexuality has often been under-emphasized in intersectional writings, not least because many theorists were reluctant to see it as itself a major social division (Erel *et al.* 2010). Against this relative neglect, it can be strongly argued that it is impossible to understand contemporary sexuality without grasping the ways in which it is shaped by intersecting forces; nor is it possible to understand gender, class or race without a recognition of the ways in which they have been heavily sexualized. Historical work has increasingly shown the ways in which sexualities are constructed at the juncture of diverse relations of power.

Foucault (1979) suggested that the very idea of 'sexuality' is an essentially bourgeois one, which developed as an aspect of the self-definition of a class, both against the decadent aristocracy and the rampant 'immorality' of the lower orders in the course of the eighteenth and nineteenth centuries. It was a colonizing system of beliefs which sought to remould the polity in its own image. The respectable standards of family and domestic life, with the increased demarcations between male and female roles, a growing ideological distinction between private and public life, and a marked concern with moral and hygienic policing of non-marital, non-heterosexual sexuality, and non-white was increasingly the norm by which all behaviour was judged. 'Respectability', argues Skeggs (1997: 3), 'has always been a marker and burden of class.' Despite the gradual erosion of class boundaries, the work of Skeggs and others shows the continuing salience of class assumptions about female sexuality, especially the sexuality of working-class women. The literature abounds with images of relations between men and women (and indeed between men and men, and women and women) where class, power and sexual fantasy and desire are intricately interwoven.

Sexuality is similarly constituted in a highly gendered world. This is structured by and through shifting patterns of **Masculinity**, in its hegemonic and subordinate forms, and **Femininity**, also in complexly varying patterns. Masculinity and femininity are relational terms, given meaning only through the existence of the other. But this means that inevitably normative definitions of sexuality are struc-tured by this relationship, and by the privileging in particular of heterosexuality.

Categorizations by class or gender intersect with those of ethnicity and race. Behind this is a long history of the encounters between the imperial heartlands and the colonized peoples in which the latter's erotic patterns were constituted as 'other', and inferior. The process has been encoded in a series of practices, from immigration laws to birth control propaganda, from medical attitudes to the pathologizing in psychology and sociology of different patterns of family life. As Stoler argues, via the colonial encounters, an 'implicit racial grammar underwrote the sexual regimes of bourgeois culture' (Stoler 1995: 9). Western notions of racial purity and sexual virtue – that is, norms of white sexuality – were in large part constituted by rejection of the colonized 'other'. This sexualized racism has been crucial in shaping local sexual cultures.

Intersectionality offers a space for analysis of such linkages rather than a theory that explains them. It has been an umbrella concept for different theoretical and political emphases. In particular, it leaves open the question of what differences matter. The originating concern with racialized experience has been vital in broadening feminist analyses, and in demonstrating the absences in lesbian and gay politics. More broadly, it has encouraged the recognition of other dimensions of inequality, and the ways they interact with each other. At the same time it is important to recognize that the fact that different identities are intertwined and bound inextricably together does not mean they come into play together. Some identities and experience of oppression are more important at one particular time rather than another, giving rise to different forms of political struggle. The simultaneity of forms of oppression that the Combahee River Collective identified in the late 1970s points not so much to the equal weight of different forms of domination but to the ways in which they are lived together in different specific locations in specific historical situations. This points above all to the importance of respecting the lived realities of oppression in all their complexity, and of listening to the diverse stories of intersecting experiences of power and resistance that people tell one another.

INTIMACY

Intimacy is a term that has long been associated with **Sexuality**, a polite euphemism for (often illicit) sexual intercourse. The *Oxford English Dictionary* dates this usage back to 1676, though more generally the word implies warm and close relationships, emotional, intellectual as well as physical, ranging from **Love** and **Friendship** to relations between parents and children. Historians of lesbianism have described non-sexual intimate friendships as a characteristic form of female relationships in the eighteenth and nineteenth centuries which bonded women in a world of love and ritual, 'surpassing the love of men' (Faderman 1981) – see **Lesbian**. Not all intimate relations are sexual, and not all sexual interactions are intimate.

Some theorists have suggested there has been a 'transformation of intimacy' (Giddens 1992) in recent years, as part of a major restructuring of interpersonal relationships in the late-modern world. The model contemporary relationship, it has been argued, is increasingly based on choice and equality. Freed of traditional constraints that locked marriage, family, sex and reproduction together, individuals can freely choose their partners, decide whether to get married, cohabit, or love together, separately or apart. They do so in the context of greater egalitarianism between the genders, and greater informality between adults and children (Weeks 2007). Giddens has talked of the development of the 'pure relationship', or what Jamieson (1998, 1999) calls 'disclosing intimacy', based on an openness to the other, and on 'confluent love', an active, contingent **Love** which takes for granted a high degree of equality in emotional give and take. Pure or disclosing relationships, the argument goes, are sought and entered into for what the relationship can bring to the individuals concerned. They are mediated through a host of socio-economic and gender factors. They survive often through inertia, habit and dependency. But ultimately the relationship is based on mutual trust between partners, which is in turn related to the achievement of the desired degree of intimacy, and the forms of love which develop. If trust breaks down, so in the end does the relationship. As the divorce figures and the rates of breakdown of cohabiting relationships suggest, this can lead to a high degree of instability in personal relationships. But at the same time, the emphasis on personal commitment and trust as the key to emotional satisfaction has radical implications.

Chosen commitment, freely entered into, implies the involvement of consenting individuals, with equal rights and responsibilities. It assumes open communication and dialogue and a willingness to negotiate. Trust has to be worked at and not taken for granted. The relationship must be free of arbitrary imbalances of power, and of coercion and violence. Because it is freely chosen it has the possibility of enduring, and of being stronger because of the personal investment in it. This egalitarian relationship underlines the democratizing impulse in intimate relationships: the stress on individual autonomy and freedom of choice provides a radicalizing dynamic that is transforming personal life (Weeks 1995: 37). In particular, it has been argued, women are leading the way, both in seeking more equal relations and in ending old ones. For the first time, Beck and Beck-Gernsheim (1995: 62) suggest, 'two people falling in love find themselves both subject to the opportunities and hindrances of a biography designed by themselves'.

This has been an influential argument, but has provoked a major debate. Giddens (1992) has optimistically seen in these changes evidence of growing agency amongst women, perhaps the greatest social change of the twentieth century. From a different, more cautious perspective, Beck and Beck-Gernsheim (1995) have detected in the new forms of intimacy a response to the emptiness opened up by the breakdown of traditional familial patterns, a functional response to the decline of old meanings and religion. Individuals, in this vision, are less like newly empowered agents than forced to be free (Smart 2007). Where some theorists see radical opportunities for better relationships, others paint darker prospects. Bauman (2003) detects in the contingency and 'frailty' of contemporary relationships a terrible indictment of the disposable culture.

But more fundamental than such theoretical debates is the more empirical question of whether there has indeed been as profound a transformation of intimacy, one way or another, as theorists would suggest. Feminist critics have pointed to the absence of strong evidence for the development of fully disclosing relations between men and women (Jamieson 1999), and while agreeing that there is a greater degree of egalitarianism in heterosexual relationships than in the past, argue that there are persistent asymmetries between men and women (Jackson and Scott 2004). The 'male in the head' still shapes female psychic subordination to men in sexual behaviour (Holland *et al.* 1998). Even lesbian and gay relationships, which it has been suggested are more likely to approximate to the pure relationship because of the absence of structural inequalities between couples made up of individuals of the same gender, have been criticized for the persistence of power imbalances (Weeks *et al.* 2001: 114–18). And whatever the changes in relationships between adults, relationships between adults and children remain clearly differentiated. There is a great deal of evidence that though parents and their offspring have much more informal and easy relations than in the past, adults continue to feel a strong sense of duty towards their children, with little sign of the pure relationship based on mutual consent.

The main burden of the criticisms is that the thesis of a transformation towards more egalitarian and open intimate relations is over-reliant on evidence drawn from Western, affluent middle-class individuals, downplaying the strong persistence of traditional gendered inequalities between men and women, and ignoring the considerably different patterns of relationships across class and minority ethnic populations. On the other hand there is plentiful evidence of major shifts in adult relationships, leading to new forms of **Relationality**. One sign of this is a broadening definition of intimacy itself. The main focus of the debate has been on couple relationships, but many people now choose to explore intimacy in multiple relationships – see **Polyamory**. More broadly, it can be argued that the very idea of intimacy is shifting in a networked world. Forms of 'public intimacy' (McNair 2002) bring into open discourse what used to be fiercely guarded as highly personal. The Internet opens huge possibilities of virtual intimacy, including through vast possibilities of social networking. A confessional culture encourages people to disclose individual secrets to mass audiences. An 'intimate public sphere' (Berlant 1997) now exists on the borders between public and private realms constructed by a multiplicity of human relationships – criss-crossed by many potential conflicts as well as opportunities for new types of relationships. All this suggests that there has been a transformation of intimacy, but in radically more varied ways than suggested by earlier theorists. The concept of intimacy has a long history but has become a crucial site for talking about changing human relationships and life experiments in the contemporary world.

L

LESBIAN

The word lesbian can be traced back in English usage to the early seventeenth century, referring to inhabitants of the Greek island of Lesbos, home of the poet Sappho, whose verses celebrated love between women. Sapphism by the late nineteenth century was used to describe 'unnatural' sexual relations between women, and lesbianism was becoming a commonly accepted descriptor in literary and sexological discourse for same-sex relations between women. Radclyffe Hall's famous novel *The Well of Loneliness* (1928; initially banned in England) provided an abiding image of the male-attired self-identified woman-loving woman, 'from birth set apart in accordance with some hidden scheme of Nature' (quoted in Weeks 1977: 107). By the 1930s lesbian had become commonly used as a noun, for example the 'mannish women' could now be described readily as 'a lesbian'. Definitions of lesbianism were inevitably inextricably linked with wider definitions of (mainly male) **Homosexuality**, and understood within its terms, though it was striking that early **Sexology** was able to offer few examples of lesbian lives. Richard von Krafft-Ebing provided but a handful of case studies in his encyclo-pedic *Psychopathia Sexualis* at the end of the nineteenth century, while Freud confined himself to a few references and one major case study in the 1920s, which suggested the masculinity of lesbians. While pioneering sexologists sought to dispel the automatic association of male homosexuality with effeminacy, les-bianism was generally seen as an assertion of masculinity in women. This in part reflected the emerging lesbian subcultures of cities such as New York or Paris where sharp distinctions were drawn between butch and femme roles well into the 1950s (Nestle 1987; Kennedy and Davis 1993). As in Hall's novel, the butch partner was regularly seen as the true lesbian; at the end of *The Well of Loneliness*, as the title suggests, the femme partner departs for a male lover, leaving the heroine struggling on alone. The reality was more complex, with abundant evidence, as Nestle suggests, of creative and fulfilling relationships, and pleasures. But it remains the case that lesbianism was defined, and to a large extent lived, within the rigid and polarized gendered divides of the time, and the specifics of lesbian history were often obscured by wider discourses on homosexuality. This was in part because of the lesser social salience of lesbianism compared to male homo-sexuality. Notably few jurisdictions historically, for example, had penalized lesbian sexuality as such, and attempts to do so in inter-war England were only partially successful (Waites 2005).

The situation changed dramatically with the rise of second-wave **Feminism** and **Gay liberation** from the late 1960s. Although many in the women's liberation movement sharply distinguished themselves from lesbianism, others saw lesbian-ism and feminism as decisively linked: 'Lesbianism is the practice and feminism is the theory' was a rallying cry for many self-identified lesbians, large numbers of whom had come out within the context of the women's movement, often making a conscious political **Choice**. This was in tune with early gay liberationist ambitions to realize the homosexuality in everyone, and with trends, especially in French feminist thinking, associated with writers such as Luce Irigaray, Hélèn Cixous and Monique Wittig, to delineate specific female, and in the latter case lesbian, forms of pleasure (see **Femininity**). But for many lesbian feminists lesbianism was much more than a sexual category. Lillian Faderman (1981: 142) suggested that most lesbians did not see lesbianism as a sexual phenomenon first and foremost; it was a relationship in which two women's strongest emotions are directed towards one another. Her book, *Surpassing the Love of Men* traces the intense relationships between women in the eighteenth and nineteenth centuries that only the inter-vention of male sexual science in the twentieth century insisted in defining as sexual. Adrienne Rich (1980) in a similar vein made an influential distinction between the 'lesbian continuum' and a 'lesbian existence'. The lesbian existence is equivalent to a lesbian identity, but it is not defined by sexual practice but rather is the sense of self of women bonded to other women who are sexually and emotionally independent of men. This in turn is an expression of the lesbian continuum, which bonds all women together in sharing an inner life, resisting male power, providing practical and political support and resistance to marriage, and in building female support networks and communities. Lesbianism, in this defini-tion, is the essential point of resistance to 'compulsory **Heterosexuality**', which underpins male dominance. It is fundamentally different from male homosexuality, which Rich regularly identifies with male privilege and male lust. Political lesbians influenced by such arguments emphasized the dangers of male sexuality, and the complicity of heterosexual feminists, and of other lesbians, with patriarchal domination.

For many other self-identified lesbians all this was a denial of their sexuality, and of a sexualized history. They argued that it romanticized and naturalized the bonds between women, presented male power as monolithic, and above all de-eroticized lesbianism. For a well-established lesbian like Joan Nestle, political lesbianism, 'cheated our history'. For such lesbians it was crucial to recover the notion of lesbianism as an erotic category and **Sexual identity** and way of life. In the debates that followed, butch–femme relationships were re-evaluated as offering the potentiality of female pleasure and choice, and lesbian **Sado-masochism** was defended as offering challenging and creative ways of exploring the play of power and eroticism (Samois 1982). The pleasures as well as the dangers of sexuality were stressed (Vance 1984). For these sex-radicals lesbian sexuality was much more than a political stance. It offered possibilities for exploring erotic choice and increasingly varied forms of identity.

While these arguments of the 'sex wars' sharply divided feminist sexual politics into the 1980s, important shifts at the grass roots of lesbian life were taking place in late-modern societies. In inner cities and suburbs, in small towns and in the countryside lesbian networks and communities were developing affirming strong lesbian identities (Ponse 1978). 'Lesbian' had begun its twentieth-century history as a deviant label. The sexual politics of the 1970s had politicized the term, either as the definition of anti-patriarchal politics or as sexually transgressive. But for thousands of women it simply described their personal and social identity and culture. Lesbianism might, as theorists suggested, be socially and historically constructed, like other sexual categories – see **Social constructionism** – but it was increasingly lived as the core of complex ways of life, a 'necessary fiction' (Weeks 1995).

The new **Sexual stories** that emerged from these lesbian worlds told of many different ways of being, of diversity rather than singularity (Stein 1997). The new positive lesbian cultures might provide a common space, but it was the play of differences that was shaping lives – differences of class, race and ethnicity, of geography, age and generation, of taste, consumption and erotic preference. The 'lipstick lesbian' who appeared in the 1990s apparently lived in a different world from the earnest political lesbian of the 1970s. New concerns, or new formulations of older preoccupations, such as parenting came to the fore (Lewin 1993). The lesbian feminist movement of the 1970s had fervently critiqued marriage; now recognition of **Same-sex marriage** was a passionate demand (Lewin 1998). Lesbianism was acquiring different meanings in different contexts. By the end of the first decade of the new millennium some lesbian theorists were wondering whether the very idea of a lesbian identity and community had had its day. At one end of the scale, some political lesbians of the 1970s had drifted back to hetero- sexual ways of life. At the other, some butch lesbians were choosing to transition towards **Transgender** identities. More generally, a growing liberalization in most late-modern societies saw a growing overlap between heterosexual and non- heterosexual life concerns, with sexuality only one aspect of an over-determined social identity (Stein 2010). Increasingly what mattered were the specificities of lesbian lives rather than generalities.

An inherent tension was built into lesbian politics from the early 1970s. On the one hand was a universalizing tendency which saw a lesbian potential in all women, and sought to realize this potential, either in a directly political sense or in the more challenging form of transgressing traditional female sexual norms. On the other hand, there was a strong tendency towards particularist demands arising from the consolidation of a strong lesbian identity. A third alternative was never fully envisaged by early activists and theorists: that lesbianism would become an ordinary part of the texture of late-modern societies. This need not imply that an emphasis on specific lesbian needs are redundant. The growing hostility towards homosexual people in parts of the Global South, as well as continuing **Homophobia** in the late-modern societies of the North, is a testimony for the continuing relevance of a global politics of lesbian and gay rights. But such politics will necessarily be based on the complexities of sexual identifications, and their intersections with other vectors of power.

LOVE

Love may make the world go round but it seems to do so in a variety of different ways. Native Americans reputedly have some six hundred categories of love experience (Douglas and Atwell 1988: 35). The Western tradition as a whole has confined itself largely to four major types: *filial* (the love of parents for children); *philia* (the love embodied in friendship); *agape* (the love of God); and the *erotic* (the urge for union with another, which embraces passionate sexual love). It is the last of these that has come to symbolize the full power of love, becoming 'the primary vehicle for self-realization, transformation, and transcendence' in contemporary society (Person 1989: 354).

Romantic love, based on sexual passion, with **Desire** often in stark conflict with social norms and conventional commitments, has been a key motif of Western ideology for centuries, and the supreme ideal since the Romantic movement of the early nineteenth century. In the twentieth century the ideal was harnessed to the ideology of heterosexual marital happiness, providing the erotic charge which (it was hoped) kept couples together. The reality was usually more mundane, most couples muddling through with little concern for the more abstract glories of passion, but the romance of love has continued to shape personal hopes and aspirations even as the social basis for traditional **Marriage** and **Intimacy** has eroded. In the post-traditional world, love has become more, not less, important, the essential integrating glue, according to Beck and Beck-Gernsheim (1995: 170), of an era of **Choice** and **Individualization**: 'For individuals who have to invent or find their own social settings, love becomes the central pivot giving meaning to their lives.' But these bonds, disenchanted social critics have argued, are inherently fragile, insecurity incarnate, in a culture of 'liquid love' where relationships are dispensable, readily begun, easily ended, underlying the frailty of human bonds (Bauman 2003). Feminist writers have detected a continuing incitement of love, but a cultural thinning out of its meaning. Love, Mary Evans (2003: 55) argues, 'is now more clearly encouraged and endorsed than at any time in its history by a social culture of entitlement and personal fulfilment', but the power of love to enrich has been diminished because it has become an inflated currency, no longer bounded by inhibitions, constraints and necessary obligations (such as to children).

The meanings of love have ever been multiple, and the priority given to its varied forms have shifted through time and in different cultures. The possibility of love may be a constant of human psychological make-up, but the forms in which it is expressed are necessarily social and historical. Love – even romantic love – is not a fixed thing but is heavily culturally coded. In the late-modern world, love has become more fluid, less a prescription for eternal devotion, more a matter of personal choice and self-making, a mode of communication rather than an eternal truth. Heterosexual romantic passion is no longer seen as the acme of erotic love, nor is marriage seen as its ultimate home. Love between men, and between women, in their complexities and often strong resistance to monogamous norms, have been newly celebrated (Weeks *et al.* 2001: 119–31). 'Confluent love', Giddens (1992) has argued, based on the freely chosen 'pure relationship' between autonomous individuals, whether heterosexual or homosexual (with homosexual lovers indeed seen as pioneers), is both the basis and result of more democratic relationships, and is generating new forms of intimacy. The emphasis now is less on an ideal of eternal love, but on contingent love, on the pleasures and satisfactions that can be found in a particular relationship – so long as it lasts. When passion fades, so a relationship may end – only for the individuals to start all over again. Love no longer just happens; it has to be worked at, negotiated and renegotiated, as individuals construct meaning, and seek the pleasures of sexuality and intimacy, however ephemeral.

Confluent love is a cool notion of love. It does not deny passion and commitment, but is reluctant to give a transcendent meaning to love. Critics have readily seen in such analyses an acceptance of contemporary hyper-individualism, and a failure to acknowledge the continuing asymmetry of relations between men and women, and the wider forms of inequality which keep people in the economy of needs rather than the consumer world of choice (Evans 2003). But it is important not to exaggerate different positions. Most sociological writers on love recognize the shifting ideologies of love in the late-modern world, though they might differ on how generalized the practice of confluent love might be. Nor is it a quality that is exclusively the product of conventional individualism. Advocates of **Polyamory**, for example, make similar arguments about autonomy and choice in defence of multiple, committed relationships. On the other hand, more traditional notions of love as growing after (often arranged) marriages remain strong amongst minority ethnic communities from East Asia and elsewhere. Giddens's analysis is not prescriptive, and can be seen as an observation of current trends, an ideal type, rather than a new model. More crucially, a recognition of the contingency of love need not lead to an abandonment of wider social relations, but in fact may be a spur to work harder at them.

Love may seem pre-eminently an individualizing emotion, but there are approaches that highlight its wider social and bonding significance. The psychologist Erich Fromm (1971) critiqued the self-sufficient individualism that leads to 'an egoism *a deux*', love as a haven from aloneness, the couple contra the world, which he sees as much of a pathology as the individual who refuses any love at all. Against this he advanced a notion of love which reaches out to others. He saw four qualities which are common to all forms of love: care, responsibility, respect and knowledge (Weeks 1995: 177–85). Love as care involves an active concern for the life, hopes, needs and potentialities of the person, or people, we love. 'Caring' has been an intensely gendered activity, with women traditionally identified with the caring role. But there are plentiful examples where care reaches out beyond such stereotypes – one thinks, for example, of the loving care by gay men for the sick and vulnerable that was characteristic of the response to the **AIDS** crisis. A truly loving care can be built on the recognition of the autonomy of the other, and an ability to enter sympathetically into the life of others. That in turn requires that we love responsibly. A responsible love is based on mutual commitments, and on the recognition that what each does has consequences for others. Carol Gilligan, in her influential book, *In a Different Voice* (1982) sees an ethics of responsibility as characteristic of female psychological and moral development, but there is no reason to believe that this is an exclusively feminine quality. AIDS again provides an example. The discourse of **Safer sex** was a way of recovering the erotic based on the minimization of risky behaviour in relations of mutual responsibility. Love as responsibility implies accepting that we are not isolated individuals, sufficient unto ourselves, but part of a web of reciprocity which brings mutual responsibilities and respect for the other.

Respect involves taking seriously the dignity of others. Respect is impossible when people are locked into forced relations of domination and submission, when men and women, or indeed men and men, and women and women, attempt to impose their sexual and emotional needs on their partners, and engage in violence, whether symbolic or real. Respect involves accepting the full humanity of the other as a condition of one's own humanity. That requires openness to others, mutual disclosure and mutual knowledge, a sensitivity to the needs of our significant others.

Love based on care, responsibility, respect and knowledge is a recognition that we make our individual lives meaningful through our involvements with, and love of, others. The language of self-fulfilment, self-determination, autonomy and authenticity, so prevalent in the contemporary discourse of love, contains within it some notion of our being-with-others. The ability to love others, Fromm (1971) argued, depends on one's ability to love oneself; but one's ability to love oneself in turn depends on one's recognition by others. Love may still be the highest ideal of individuals, but its fulfilment requires a continuing commitment to others.

M

MARRIAGE

The historian John Boswell has compared marriage in pre-modern Europe with marriage in the modern West. In the earlier period, he argues, marriage conventionally began as a property arrangement, in its middle was chiefly about raising children, and ended about love. Western marriage, on the other hand, begins about love, in its middle is still largely about raising children, and often ends about property – 'by which point love is absent or a distant memory' (Boswell 1994: xxii).

Despite (or perhaps because of) the rather disenchanted tone, Boswell is suggesting several highly significant points. First, marriage, generally seen as a universal of human history, and widely touted as the cornerstone of Western societies – the seventeenth-century philosopher John Locke called marriage humankind's 'first society' – has changed its meanings and implications dramatically over time. Marriage is not a fixed, stable institution. There are diverse marriage practices across cultures, formalized in a host of different ways. In our contemporary plural, multicultural societies different patterns of marriage coexist more or less happily, whether based on sexual attraction, marriages arranged by families, or currently same-sex marriages. Marriage links people on the basis of custom, law and frequently religion, but its forms are in constant development, even flux.

Second, marriage has been as much about people's relations with the wider society as it has been about the wishes and desires of autonomous individuals. There are always more than two people in any marriage. It carries status, rights and responsibilities, and obligations, above all for children, and links you to other families in ties of blood and affinity. Yet marriage was often also a privilege, not a right. Many countries have had taboos, rules and laws against inter-marriage, whether between people of different faiths or ethnic and racial groupings. Most states of the USA passed laws against miscegenation, at the same time as traditional marriage was imposed upon freed slaves as a condition of citizenship: 'white heteropatriarchal middle class families became the standard against which other families were judged' (Ferguson 2004: 86).

Third, marriage's link to property is inescapable, even for the propertyless. One of the functions of marriage in many cultures is precisely to ensure legitimate heirs to property and titles. But it is likely that this has always been a minority concern. For the disadvantaged, marriage was too important to depend on mutual affection alone. It was needed for rather more mundane reasons, to consolidate a multitude of other relationships without which the survival of the couple and their family was threatened (Gillis 1985). This was particularly true for women who at various times have themselves been seen as property, and yet for whom marriage provided a degree of economic protection and social position. Historically, women have always been subordinated in marriage, but marriage was nevertheless an inescapable destiny for most.

Fourth, marriage has been concerned with legitimate access to sex, to reproduction and parenting. In many traditional societies, amongst the masses who were not rich or privileged, marriage often only took place after the woman became pregnant. Community pressures usually worked to ensure that marriage did happen, though as varying illegitimacy rates demonstrated at crucial moments of transition, these pressures often did not work. Taboos against unmarried mothers and bastardy ensured that the victims were women and children, which in turn worked to generate a cautious moral climate around sexual behaviour. Women's sexual conservatism had a rational basis prior to effective birth control and greater economic and social autonomy.

Marriage is widely touted as both fundamental to human existence, and essential to well-being. Yet at the same time this apparently natural institution is regularly seen as fragile, and an endangered species. Since the 1970s moral conservatives in the West have inveighed against the decline of marriage, which they see as a potent explanation for societal ills: family breakdown, high divorce rates, an exponential increase in lone-parenthood, teenage pregnancy and feral youth. Marriage, they argue, is rooted in our genetic make-up; is sustained across cultures by religion, rites and sacraments; has vital economic foundations for consumption, exchange and production; and plays a central social role in regulating relations between men and women, bridling male lust, and sustaining children. Couples who do not get married are less likely to stay together, and their offspring are more likely to have poor educational attainments, economic prospects and relationship prospects. For cultural conservatives, marriage, as the cornerstone of a stable and moral society, is in possibly terminal crisis (Morgan 1995). Yet at the same time as politicians, religious leaders, moralists and journalists lament the collapse of this key social institution, the very same people are often in the vanguard of the opposition to **Same-sex marriage**, which in the early twenty-first century has become the single most important issue for LGBT activists, amongst whom clearly the demand for marriage is not in decline but very much on the rise. This underscores that ultimately what moral conservatives fear above all is less the decline of marriage as such as the threat to marriage as the cornerstone of heterosexual normality. This was made clear in the USA in 1996 by the passing of the Defense of Marriage Act (DOMA) which explicitly defined marriage in federal law as between a man and a woman, and allows states not to recognize same-sex marriages effected in other states. This has been subsequently followed up by vigorous attempts to outlaw same-sex marriage in federal law, and most of the states currently outlaw same-sex marriages. Marriage matters because it promotes and naturalizes heterosexuality as the norm, and thus by definition excludes non-heterosexual people.

To put this another way, jeremiads about the decline of marriage are not so much about the eclipse of an age-old institution, as about the nature of interpersonal relations and **Intimacy** today. The pinnacle of marriage's popularity and social significance was not in the dim and distant past, but coincided with that very 'sexual revolution' that conservative critics have thought was destroying it in the 1960s. In 1990, 95 per cent of women and 94 per cent of men in the USA aged between 45 and 54 either were or had been married. It was practically universal marriage in the three decades after World War II that fostered growing opposition to compulsory marriage, especially for baby boomers (Weeks 2007).

In most Western countries the past forty years have seen a dramatic shift in patterns of relationships. Already by the early 1970s most couples in Sweden cohabited rather than getting married, and this trend has become general, with high rates of cohabitation, increasing numbers of births outside marriage, delayed marriage and high rates of divorce. In the USA between 1970 and 1990 the percentage of married adults decreased from 72 per cent to 62 per cent. The percentage of non-marital births increased from 5.3 per cent in 1960 to 39 per cent in 2009. The general pattern was of what Cherlin (2009) called a 'marriage-go-round', with rather than lifetime monogamy a pattern of serial monogamy. Marriage was still taken seriously, but no longer as a mark of status, or the only legitimate access to sex. Rather, it was increasingly a marker of commitment. Since the 1970s marriage and divorce have increasingly come to be seen as issues of a couples' own making and unmaking rather than subject to higher moral codes (Williams 2004: 30). In Britain as elsewhere, what has increasingly come under scrutiny by governments of various political colours is less the relationship of husband and wife and more their roles as fathers and mothers, and hence the welfare of their children. While marriage has become less an issue of public regulation, and cohabitation both before and instead of marriage has become commonplace, parenting, previously largely a private matter, has become increasingly a matter of public concern.

Alongside the reworking of old norms and values, we can also see the emergence of new norms, involving a refashioning of the meanings of commitment, to partners, significant others and dependents. And a broad conclusion is incontestable. Across the board, far from exhibiting signs of amorality or irresponsibility, most people are living lives of extraordinary ethical intensity, creating a relational ethics in which individual needs and desires are balanced by commitment to the other.

These commitments are not so much obligatory as negotiated, driven by concern about 'the right thing to do' rather than a sense of duty – except in the case of dependents, where a sense of duty remains absolute. Yet the sense of mutual responsibility provides a steady guide to action, precisely because responsibilities seem freely chosen, and are neither predetermined nor contractual (Finch 1989; Finch and Mason 1993). Beck and Beck-Gernsheim (1995: 98) argued that freed of all outer constraints about whom you can like, and can marry, it paradoxically turns out that you may need new kinds of mutual control, for example though pre-nuptial contracts that may regulate everything from property rights to who does the washing up, or through the vogue for self-help books. But Lewis (2001: 182) in her study of marriage in Britain found little support amongst her interviewees for purely contractual views of marriage. Even those in the minority who were in favour of a more contractual model were not clear what it would be about. Instead, people increasingly have to make it up as they go along, adapting traditional patterns or shaping new ones. At stake are decreasingly the binary cultures of heterosexuality and homosexuality, which traditional marriage set in stone, but rather the forms of mutuality appropriate to the conditions we find ourselves in. Various forms of cohabitation, or non-cohabitation as in the case of living apart together (LAT) couples, commitment to **Friendships** and personal communities, as well as the possibilities and challenges of **Polyamory**, have increasingly become choices open to people. These choices are not always absolutely free choices precisely because of the web of relationships within which they must be exercised, but they signal the different ways of committing yourself in relationships of reciprocity and care. Marriage is no longer a social or moral imperative. It has become one way amongst others of signifying commitment.

MASCULINITY

What we take for granted as natural and inevitable is more likely than not to be historically specific, and therefore contingent, and changeable. So it is with masculinity. After an extensive survey of men's history across cultures and time, the sociologist R. W. Connell concludes: 'I am forced to wonder whether "masculinity" is in itself a culture bound concept that makes little sense outside Euro/American culture' (Connell 1993: 605). The argument she is making is that there is no essence of masculinity which transcends time and space, no single quality which is a biological or psychological constant in men, which dictates their behaviour. Ideas of Iron John, the proto-masculine man of the woods, or the fairy tale that women are from Venus and men from Mars, that is incommensurably different, say more about our contemporary insecurities and fantasies than about any fundamental truth.

Masculinity and **Femininity**, like the organization of sexualities into heterosexual or homosexual categories, are historically specific, and are socially constructed. Because of the impact of **Social constructionism**, it is difficult today for a social scientist to argue seriously that the apparent differences between men and women mechanically dictate social difference, or that personal and cultural identities are automatic products of inner propulsions (though many sociobiologists or evolu-tionary psychologists, drunk on the excesses of the genetic revolution, still try to do so). We are aware of the complexities of historical processes, the power of discourse and the intricacies of power. But that broad brush hides a complex debate.

110

Some constructionist accounts have tended to give the impression that society mechanically imprints its necessities on the blank page of nature, and some theorists may have overemphasized the entrapping effects of discourse rather than the energizing impact of agency. Others offer more complex analyses, stressing the importance of **Bodies**, but not as a biological imperative, nor as a barren landscape on which the social imposes its demands. Masculinities, like femininities, are social practices, not eternal truths. They are shaped in the interaction between the biological, the social and the psychological. So 'masculinity', to the extent it can be clearly defined at all, is at the same time a place in gender relations (that is defined by its placing in relation to the parallel shaping of femininity), the practices through which men and women place themselves in relation to **Gender**, and the effects of these practices in bodily experiences, personality and culture. Gender relations are organized in the intersection of power, production, and emotion, resulting in a host of masculinities coexisting and interacting at the same time: hegemonic, subordinate, marginalized and oppositional, all of which are shaped in specific historical circumstances (Connell 2005).

The particular dominant patterns of masculinity that have underpinned Western thought for the past five centuries had their origins in two world historical changes. The first is the breakdown of the medieval order, in which the position of men and women was dictated by hierarchy and status, and the consequent long, painful and still unfinished rise of individualism. Masculinity gradually came to be seen as less a quality of social position and increasingly something that was possessed by an individual, in terms of strength, ability, sexual prowess, power over women, and other men. Of course, one of the consequences of seeing this as a historical process is that we can now see that the creation of the modern individual is itself a social production, shaped by very complex processes: changes in the economy, in the distribution of class power, in the new role of Europe in the global system, and later by the revolutionary changes that transformed the world from the eighteenth century. The industrial and urban revolutions reshaped the patterns of gender, and of masculinity, as they did everything else, reordering the dominant forms (for example, the shift from aristocratic to industrial and technological hegemony), and producing new, subordinate forms of masculinity (for example, in the complex images of the male industrial worker from the nineteenth century) (Mosse 1996).

The second world historical shift helped shape these massive changes. This was the encounter with the non-European world, through the imperial and colonial expansions from the sixteenth century. European masculinity, it can be argued, has been defined against the other, provided by the subordinated peoples of the colonized world. Connell (1993) has suggested that the first masculine cultural type in modern European history was provided by the conquistadors. Throughout the history of European empires, normal masculinity was defined against the subordination and inferiority of native peoples. Black men, both in Africa and through their diaspora in the Americas as a result of slavery, have historically been stereotyped as both closer to nature, and hypersexual, with little control over their passions. Oriental men, by contrast, have been stereotyped as sensual, effeminate, androgynous,

111

devious, perverted in their sexual tastes. Mixtures of these images have been used to describe other colonized peoples. All such images have served to confirm the sanctity of Western imagery of masculinity, which has therefore been built around whiteness, force, power, and exclusion of the feminine and the perverse.

Masculinity and femininity only exist in relation to each other. One cannot exist without the other. As Western ideologies of masculinity emerged, therefore, we see a redefining of femininity. Thomas Laqueur (1990) has traced one crucial element in this process during the eighteenth century: the emergence of the notion that men and women were two distinct types, complementary but fundamentally different. For the past two hundred years the dominant discourses have constructed a binary notion of gender, in which men and women are radically separate. This has been central to the emergence of the dominant myth of our culture: that the institution of **Heterosexuality** is the only natural form of human life. Masculinity has in large part since the eighteenth century been defined through the exclusion of homo-sexuality. Since the nineteenth century, a new binary divide came to dominate our thinking about sexuality: a radical opposition between heterosexuality and **Homosexuality**, which defied all historical evidence by suggesting their funda-mental opposition.

We are talking here of images, stereotypes, beliefs. They attempted not simply to describe the world, but also to construct it in a particular way. Of course, their relationship to the real world of living, breathing, feeling men and women was very complicated. There have always been a variety of ways of living gender relations, and these in turn have changed in an ever more complex history. Representations do not necessarily tell us how people lived. But they did set the boundaries within which normality was defined. To live outside the boundaries inevitably produced acute tensions, in social relations (such as the marginalizaition and oppression of effeminate, cross-dressing or homosexual men), in personal lifestyles and in psychic conflict.

The social practices of masculinity are lived through the body. But embodiment is not only about the physical, it is also about the psychic, the often missing link between the natural and the socio-cultural. Sociological theories too often assume that socialization works. **Psychoanalysis** assumes that it cannot fully work. The work of Freud at the end of the nineteenth and in the early twentieth centuries is so important precisely because it documents the acute conflicts around gender and sexuality of a society which seemed to treat masculinity and femininity as unproblematic. Psychoanalytical theory, on the contrary, tells us that masculinity and femininity are both precarious achievements, constantly struggled for, continuously undermined. In Western culture, the discourses of gender and of sexuality are so locked together (to be a real man is to be definitively heterosexual) as to be virtually indistinguishable. But we also know that this apparently perfect marriage of gender and sexual identities is a constant source of tension, fear and threat, providing a potent brew of psychic energy.

Both masculinity and femininity are 'gender projects' (Connell 2009), through which social practices over time construct and transform the relations between men and women. The projects are now being disrupted as never before by dramatic social change. Many men still have a strong emotional and material investment in the current order (the 'patriarchal dividend'), even as it shows strains; others are complicit with it; while some are in one way or another striking oppositional notes. The meaning of what it is to be a man is problematic as never before.

Which is why new narratives of masculinity are now emerging. They speak of vulnerabilities as much as of power. They speak of fear and anxiety as much as of strength. They speak of reconciliation with women as much as conflict. They speak of the pluralism of men, and their different needs and desires, as much as true manhood. It is no longer appropriate, if it ever really was, to think of a monolithic entity called masculinity in a world of 'new men', reinvented 'straight men', many types of gay men, bisexual men, transgendered and inter-sex peoples – the list is potentially endless. Segal has argued that 'it is an understanding of the *differences* between men which is central to the struggle for change' (Segal 1990: x). At the same time, men are more like women than anything else, and the binary division within masculinity between heterosexuality and homosexuality can now be seen as an historical fiction which conceals a much more confused mixture of fears, anxieties and desires about what being a man means. All of this has been historically confused by the hierarchical ordering of gender and sexual relations which has done violence to men's as well as women's life experiences.

Even in Western cultures, with already several decades of the feminist challenge behind us, the myth of masculinity continues to constrain men. The continuation of male violence against women is one index of this. Just as the myths of masculinity had a long and complex historical development, and have been embodied physically and lived psychically, so the deconstruction of the myths will require long and complex change. The dramatic social and cultural changes of recent years provide conditions for reinventing masculinities. They will only produce the necessary changes if they are seen as part of a wider political project in which concepts of human rights and social justice take on board the reordering of gender and sexual relations.

MASTURBATION

The distinguished Swiss doctor Samuel Tissot believed it to be more dangerous than smallpox. The philosopher Immanuel Kant thought it was worse than suicide. Other distinguished luminaries of the Enlightenment saw it as the cause of general debility, moral corruption and premature death. Masturbation, the solitary, secret vice, had a dramatic career, from round about 1712 to roughly World War II, as the gateway to numberless, often nameless horrors, particularly for boys and young men. High amongst these was **Homosexuality**, which generations of moralists and school masters feared was the inevitable result of self-abuse. 'Manliness and self-reliance', the sexologist Richard Krafft-Ebing wrote, 'are not the qualities which adorn the impotent onanist' (Weeks 1977: 25). Quacks and pornographers made fortunes from the new taboo. Philosophers constructed moral systems around the obloquy that sex with oneself produced. Meanwhile, generations of young people, male and female, had their sexual lives blighted by the fear inculcated in vulnerable minds by the torrents of medical expertise, moral instruction and popular mocking targeted at the most common, probably least harmful and certainly most privatized erotic activity in the world.

Historians have long been puzzled by what might be called the moment of masturbatory madness. Beginning with the publication sometime between 1708 and 1716 of *Onania*, a sensationalist tract probably written by John Marten, an English surgeon and quack, a new sexual pathology with an awesome ability to generate guilt, shame and anxiety emerged (Laqueur 2003). After a murky but rapidly growing adolescence, the new disease reached maturity and respectability in 1760 with the publication of the French edition of Tissot's *Onanism*, which became a literary sensation across Europe. Thereafter, there was no holding back. Masturbation was launched into the mainstream as a serious malady, and the solitary sex became the target both of passionate polemic and of medico-moral intervention. Only in the twentieth century, and then unevenly, were the doubts aroused by the anxiety makers listened to. As late as the 1990s President Clinton in the USA was forced to lose a Cabinet member who had apparently endorsed masturbation. More broadly today, in a culture of omnipresent pornography and the Internet which consecrates practically universal incitements to solitary sex, the idea of masturbation as an appalling disease seems an insanity, a testimony to a more oppressive and repressive age.

What emerged in the early eighteenth century, Thomas Laqueur (2003) argues, was a whole new way of conceptualizing masturbation, fundamentally different from the ways in which solitary sex was seen in either Classical, Jewish or Christian traditions – and different again from the contemporary view. Ironically, the new preoccupation coincided with the dawn of the age of Enlightenment. Far from being the product of irrational repression, the best minds of the age, and the most fervent advocates of unshackling the chains of unreason, were enthusiastic supporters of the new understanding of masturbation. The fear of masturbation was more than a temporary aberration of a dark past. Rather it can only really be understood as integral to the Enlightenment project itself, to the birth pangs of modernity.

Masturbation is the sexuality of the modern self. It is protean, unbounded, limited only by imagination. It is the sexuality of secrecy, of privacy, of excess. It is self-governed, autonomous, autarchic. It is the sexuality of fantasy. It is a denial of, or at least outside, the social. All this is what made sex with the self seem such a threat to the doctors, theorists, moralists, ethicists of the eighteenth century. It represented the pursuit of pleasure without social ties or mutual obligation. It threatened the delicate ties of civil society that the Enlightenment worthies sought to strengthen to moderate the stark opposition of state and society. It represented the genie of selfishness unleashed by the new world of commerce and individualism. The onanist, in this interpretation, was the alter ego, the nasty brother and sister, of the modern self struggling to be born. Masturbation was the vice of individuation in a society where the old ramparts against uncontrolled desire had crumbled. It pointed to a world of solipsism and anomie which denied moderation, real autonomy and reason.

Yet the effect of this often well-intentioned tirade against meaningless freedom was to blight countless lives, inhibit sexual happiness, impose a medico-moral hegemony over the erotic as a replacement for clerical interference, and delay rather than speed up the working through of an individual, secular, sexual ethics to replace the vacuum left by the decay of religion and of a hierarchical social order. So powerful was the legacy of Marten, Tissot, the Encyclopaedists who enthusiastically embraced their ideas, of Rousseau, Kant and countless doctors, schoolmasters, scoutmasters and other zealots, that it became virtually impossible to escape their embrace. Even Freud, who rewrote the story of autoeroticism to make it the root of all sexuality, could not escape the feeling that masturbation *must* have some harmful effects. Not until the 1960s did the taboos melt away in a new sexual world, and masturbation began to find its new destiny, especially for women whose clitoral sexuality and multiple orgasms were freshly rediscovered.

Solitary sex was consistently seen as a problem in the context of the cultural flux produced by rapid social and economic change. Today we are in the midst of ever more massive cultural transformations, but it is a world where sex with the self has found its role: not as the gateway to vice, but as the royal (super) highway to private pleasures and infinite fantasy. The joy of masturbation, as the wit Quentin Crisp once quipped, is that you don't have to dress up for it. That was what Enlightenment polemicists feared. In the world of global sex that has become its justification.

MELANCHOLIA

The term, which first appeared in English in 1607, has an ancient lineage. It is rooted in the classical idea that bodily health and illness is shaped by the balance between bodily fluids – the four humours. Melancholia was produced by an excess of black bile. This has become a nice image for the spectrum of depressive ills associated with the term – apprehension, despondency, gloom, low self-esteem, a feeling of impending doom, lack of enthusiasm, sadness, a sense of anomie or meaninglessness, and deep pessimism about the future. Such terms readily lend themselves both to individual crises and to social conditions. Cultural historians have noted various periods in Western history when a generalized melancholia can be detected – for example, the early seventeenth century in the midst of agonizing religious strife and acute social disruption, and the early nineteenth century with the revolutionary upheavals and romantic awakening: John Keats wrote an 'Ode on Melancholy' which evoked the 'wakeful anguish of the soul'. More prosaically, contemporary commentators have also deployed the term to describe aspects of the present, both in relation to sexuality (especially in the wake of **AIDS**) and more generally to account for a cultural climate marked by a sense of loss, detachment and thwarted grieving. For this they have relied heavily on readings, and creative adaptations, of Freud and **Psychoanalysis**.

Freud's classic text 'Mourning and Melancholia' was published in 1917 in the midst of the first, devastating world war. In the midst of so much death and grieving, Freud attempted to understand the process of mourning, and put it onto a clearer psychoanalytic basis, going beyond the traditional attitude that grief at the loss of a loved one normally fades with time, and that time heals everything. On the contrary loss is not a more or less prolonged phase of suffering, but a profound psychic crisis. Grief can only fade through a psychical working out of the pain caused by the loss of a loved one. Melancholia is on a spectrum of possible responses, where time cannot easily heal. In both mourning and melancholia the subject characteristically at first loses interest in the external world, is unable to choose a new love object and loses all appetite for living. Eventually most mourners are able to work through the pain by detaching, decathecting, element by element, from the love object and eventually achieving a new relationship with reality. But in melancholia the ego identifies so completely with the love object that it is unable to detach itself, and continues to live the pain, because the love object continues to live with the self, albeit unconsciously and unacknowledged. What is particularly interesting about this psychoanalytic narrative is that Freud explicitly includes within the idea of the lost love object not only the individual mourner, but also social and intellectual phenomena, such as one's country or beliefs and ideals. One could mourn to the point of melancholia national defeats or radical transformations, or the collapse of ideologies. The way was open for psycho-social explanations for cultural moods as well as personal grief.

Melancholia has particularly been deployed in **Queer** theory, notably in Judith Butler's (1990) engagement with psychoanalysis. The inability of the child to mourn the loss of the love of a parent in the Oedipal drama, leads to the internalization of the lost love object. Heterosexual melancholia, she argues, is the price of stable gender identities, because it involves the repression of homosexual feelings in the Oedipal process. The enforced rejection of homosexuality in a regime of compulsory heterosexuality inevitably colours heterosexual relations with a sense of loss of the potentiality of same-sex love. By extension, it can be argued that homosexuality is similarly haunted by a sense of the loss of a heterosexual component, and is shaded by melancholia (Derbyshire 2008). Both are compromise formations, rendered necessary by the historical structures of heterosexual hegemony, but which are nevertheless limitations on the flux of desire. The loss of wider potential lingers in the contemporary organization of sexuality, which is inevitably caught up with melancholic strains.

A less abstract use of melancholia can be found in response to the AIDS crisis. The overwhelming nature of the impact of AIDS especially amongst the gay male community in the USA, has produced, it has been argued, an identification with the dead that readily lends itself to a complex web of feelings of fear, anger, and loss. The community grieves not only at the death of friends and loved ones, but also at the demise of the sexual freedoms and experimentations that characterized the earlier history of the gay community (Crimp 2002). For many this mourning is the spur to militancy. For others within the gay community it leads to a state of melancholia, and an assertion of conservative values, disavowing the sexual creativity which had defined the gay world.

Social critics have also found the concept of melancholia useful in attempting to diagnose the state of the nation. Gilroy (2004) evokes a post-colonial melancholia marking and marring British life. Hoggett (2008), pursuing the same theme, sees a country haunted by loss and decline. The end of empire, loss of great power status, the collapse of community, the decline of civility, respect and decency, a 'broken society': these are losses that cannot be fully thought about, fuelling an inchoate sense of grievance, self-reproach, irritability and despair. 'Like a melancholic, Britain is stuck in a process of arrested development' (Hoggett 2008: 116). Whether this is an accurate portrayal is at least debatable. The irony of such a diagnosis is that it partakes of the disease it is attempting to describe. One has to ask whether this ultimately reveals better the state of Britain, or the state of mind of Britain's public intellectuals. It demonstrates the hazards of applying the concept of melancholia to whole cultures or countries.

MIXEDNESS

Racialized minority ethnic and faith communities are the sites where the tensions and ambiguities of different regimes of sexuality are most fiercely contested. Sexuality, gender and family are critical boundaries for demarcating community values, and women's bodies are often the crucial battleground for the assertion of belonging and difference (Weeks 2007: 113). Mixed relationships, or mixedness, a term increasingly used to describe sexual and intimate bonding, and parenting, between people drawn from different racial, ethnic and religious backgrounds, is therefore an important area for contestation and the development of new values and attitudes.

Most cultures have developed customs, taboos, regulations or laws to control, limit or absolutely prevent sexual relationships across racial, ethnic or religious boundaries. Sometimes the prevention of miscegenation becomes more or less part of the constitutional make-up of a society, as in the USA through slavery and into the 1960s, or in Apartheid South Africa until the 1990s. Marrying 'out' – of your caste, or class, or faith, or even local community – has been fraught with difficulties and danger in countries and regions as wide apart as India, Northern Ireland and Israel. Even radical opponents of racism and discrimination have, in their assertion of the importance of identity politics, challenged people who seek to inter-marry, fearing identity confusion or even identity loss. In the 1980s in Britain, social workers sought to limit inter-racial adoption on the grounds that it would undermine cultural belonging. In turn critics of **Multiculturalism** across Europe especially have lamented the exclusivity and inward nature of minority communities who hold to their own traditions and never mix.

The paradox in all this, is that different groups have always mixed to create the jumble of DNA that makes up the current world population. Purity in an essentialist sense has never been possible, but as the mixed populations in every society indicate, love and passion, as well as rape and forced sex, have often been stronger than tall fences and popular prejudice. The mixing of populations is a reality, but it has been occluded by local norms, fear or prejudice and various forms of occupational, housing and cultural segregation. This makes all the more important evidence that the boundaries are not only being reinforced as people affirm their cultural difference, as in many Western cities, but people are reaching across the divide to establish mixed relationships.

In 2010 the Pew Research Center in the USA reported that one in seven new marriages were inter-racial or inter-ethnic, a record high. These figures were six times the rate in 1960, and double what it was as recently as 1980. In the 1960s fewer than one in a 1,000 American marriages were between a black and a white person. In 2010 the figure was one in 60 (McGurn 2010: A17). The figures are even more striking in the UK. Connolly and White (2006: 5) have noted the emergence of a new British-born ethnic group, comprising some 700,000 people in 2001, those born of mixed parentage. This is scarcely one ethnic group because as the authors themselves point out there were distinct groups in England and Wales: those born of mixed white and African Caribbean parents, the largest group; those of mixed white and Asian origins; and a smaller group of mixed white and African. African Caribbean people were most likely to be involved in mixed relations, South Asians least. But of all the minority groups they list, the highest proportion of under 16s are from the mixed population, suggesting an increasing rate of inter-group relationships (Caballero *et al.* 2008). The rates of inter-ethnic relations were higher in Britain than in any comparable country in Europe, as well as than in the USA. This need not imply a breakdown of old barriers. A 1997 survey showed that 32 per cent of Asians and 29 per cent of Jews claimed they would have a problem if a relative married an Afro-Caribbean compared to 13 per cent of white Britons (Collins 2005: 224). Yet whatever the hardening lines of division in many urban centres, and whatever the continuing evidence of racism, white on black but also across other ethnic divisions, some sociologists have seen in growing mixing evidence of new forms of 'conviviality' that look to a different future.

Both the absolutist affirmations of separate identities that underline the attitudes of socially conservative ethnic leaders and official policy, and their liberal critics who advocate a new push for integration and new cohesive definitions of national identity are challenged in favour of a new project which is open to 'the chaotic pleasures of the convivial postcolonial urban world' (Gilroy 2004: 167). The 'radical openness' that conviviality points to does not abrogate the reality of racism (or of other forms of domination and subordination, especially around gender and sexuality). On the contrary it points to the importance of identifying the forces which inhibit and deny the possibilities of more egalitarian and just lives. But it also suggests the importance of valuing the everyday life experiments that very many are already engaged in, and our ability to live with difference, and the mixing of differences, without becoming anxious, fearful or violent.

MORAL PANIC

Moral panics are flurries of cultural anxiety and social fear, which usually focus on a condition or person, or group of persons, who become defined as a threat to accepted social values and assumptions. They arise generally in situations of uncertainty, confusion and ambiguity, in periods when the boundaries between legitimate and illegitimate behaviour seem to need redefining or classification. Characteristically, the mechanisms of such a panic follow a broadly similar path. A threat is defined in a particular event (a youthful riot, a sexual scandal, a new disease); 'folk devils' are stereotyped as main culprits for the problem (feral young people, the fallen woman, the single mother, the homosexual, the paedophile, the carrier of disease); public fear is whipped up and channelled by moral entre-preneurs, religious leaders, politicians, media columnists; a spiralling escalation of fear leads to the manning of the moral barricades, sides are taken and absolutist positions are adopted; symbolic resolutions emerge (a dramatic court case, tougher laws, moral isolation, increased social surveillance); followed usually by a subsidence of the panic, if not of the underlying source of tension and anxiety, with its victims left to survive the carnage (prison, physical assault, exile, moral obloquy, increased regulation) as best they can.

The term was popularized in the early 1970s by the British sociologist Stan Cohen in his book *Folk Devils and Moral Panics* (1972), and was used specifically to analyse the reaction to youth revolts of the period. But with the development of a new politics of sexuality from the 1970s, it soon became apparent that this concept could be used fruitfully to explore a recurrent phenomenon of panic responses in the history of sexuality (Weeks 1981). For the erotic sphere is a fertile source of cultural anxiety, touching as it does on sensitive and highly personal intimate issues about the body and its pleasures, but also on critical issues of culture, social well-being and public policy.

Moral panics around sexuality abound in the history of sexual modernity since the eighteenth century. Typical sexualized panics over the past couple of centuries include obsessions with the dire effects of **Masturbation** on children and adolescents from the eighteenth century to the early twentieth centuries, the fears that young European girls were being trapped into the 'white slave trade' in the late nineteenth century, and recurrent scandals around homosexuality, most famously the Oscar Wilde trial and its aftermath in 1895, but there were many others, in Germany, France, the USA. Since World War II there has been an apparently endless series of moral panics focusing on moral and sexual issues: venereal disease, over-population and population decline, **Prostitution**, human **Trafficking**, homosexuality, single mothers, sex education, child sex abuse and **Paedophilia**, teenage sex, **Pornography**, and so on. They become more acute when there are fundamental divisions in society over moral direction, as in the so-called 'culture wars' in the USA from the 1970s. There have been suggestions that such 'sexual panics' (Herdt 2009) have become more frequent as a general social uncertainty and cultural anxiety become entangled with wider social divides. They have certainly been more prominent, suggesting that sexual issues have become more and more central to cultural preoccupations and social regulation.

A significant feature in many of them has been the connection that has been made between sex and disease, disease becoming a metaphor for dirt, disorder and decay. Not surprisingly, panics have emerged over the social and moral connotations of genital herpes, cervical cancer and, most dramatically of all, HIV/**AIDS**. The early response to AIDS in the USA and to a lesser extent elsewhere in the early 1980s had many of the characteristics of a generalized moral panic. There was the identifying of a new, devastating and mysterious set of illnesses, obviously linked to sexual behaviour; there was a ready-made scapegoat in the newly liberated gay man, already the subject of a backlash for the alleged excesses of the 1970s; there was a newly organized moral majority ready to blame rapid social and cultural change on the sexual revolution; there was a generalized fear manifest in media hysteria and political position taking; and there was the emergence of various symbolic solutions – border controls, isolation, rituals of decontamination, compulsory blood tests and the like. The immediate panic did of course dissipate, and new treatment therapies began to emerge, though in this case the syndrome itself did not disappear, soon achieving pandemic status, with the focus moving away from the rich countries of the West to the Global South. Amidst such a global crisis, for many the concept of moral panic seemed too feeble a tool to explain what was going on (Watney 1987). It has been widely critiqued for its lack of explanatory power. Moral panic theory has offered a useful focus for exploring the sexual and moral economy of different periods and cultures, but it does not tell us why certain issues come to the fore at particular times and touch a cultural nerve.

This suggests that moral or sexual panics need to be seen in a dual context: of long-term shifts and modalities in the culture and regulation of sexuality, and in specific conjunctural events. It is, for example, difficult to understand the increased surveillance of homosexuality in the USA and Britain in the early 1950s outside the context of the Cold War and its drawing of new boundaries around acceptable behaviour. But specific panics arose from events – the McCarthyite witchhunts in the USA, or spy scandals in the UK. Anxieties about young people's sexualities in the 1960s can be seen as one result of the tsunami of baby boomers hitting the crisis of moral order shaped by a messy collision of consumerism, new social movements and identities and a crisis of the state as a result of a failing and unpopular war. The AIDS crisis of the early 1980s erupted as a new political hegemony of the New Right confronted an unpopular minority in the midst of fervent culture wars.

Such examples suggest two thoughts about sexual/moral panics. First, their impact can only be fully measured if we grasp that they are local manifestations of wider social shifts, most notably the rapid rise of sexuality as a focus of social, political and cultural divisions since the 1960s. Sexuality has become a terrain of acute uncertainty, and moral panics are spaces where certainty is fought for.

But the second thought is that the resolution of moral panics is never unambiguous. The agents of surveillance, regulation and social order might win local battles and symbolic victories. But the unanticipated consequences of the course of events are often as significant as the intended. In the examples above, it is impossible not to observe that the anti-homosexual mood of the early 1950s fed directly into a new spirit of resistance and agency in the 1960s and 1970s. The baby boomers of the 1960s became the social, cultural and moral leaders of the 1990s and 2000s, with often radically different attitudes from those of their parents. And people living with HIV/AIDS refused the label of victim and survived. Sexual/moral panics are a significant feature of late-modern societies, but their outcomes are usually ambivalent and contradictory.

MULTICULTURALISM

In 1966 the British Home Secretary, Roy Jenkins, confronted by the increasing racial and ethnic diversification of British society, defined integration not as a 'melting point' or assimilation but as equal opportunity coupled with cultural diversity, in an atmosphere of mutual toleration (Jenkins 1970: 267). This he saw as the definition of a 'civilized society'. It was also for a long time as good a general definition of multiculturalism as emerged. Through the 1970s and 1980s a wide range of Western countries, from Canada to Sweden, Australia to the Netherlands, as well as the UK and USA, developed a range of policies at national and local level that broadly followed the multiculturalist rubric. Many were responding to the dawning awareness of cultural diversity in their societies, often as a result of post-imperial migration to the former metropolitan homelands, and each society developed approaches in accord with their own social and political traditions. In the Netherlands and Belgium policies were based on the long tradition of recognizing distinctive group identities, religious or linguistic. In the UK there was a cautious pragmatic adjustment to shifting demographics within a policy framework that had traditionally assumed homogeneity and common citizenship. In the USA affirmative action policies targeted at African-Americans attempted to respond to the historic legacy of racism by developing policies based on the recognition of different needs in an unequal society. Multiculturalism to a large extent became a polite way of referencing racial and ethnic differences in all these countries. But whatever the variations of form, what multiculturalist policies had in common was a recognition of unequal power relations between minority and majority groups, and of the unfair disadvantages citizens from minority communities experienced in unitary frameworks (Phillips 2007).

States can harm individuals, the philosopher Charles Taylor argued, having in mind the examples of the Québécois and First Nations in Canada, if there is a 'failure of **Recognition**' (Taylor 1992a). The core of multiculturalism was a recognition of the distinctiveness of cultural identities, with policies directed at finding ways of acknowledging and respecting different ways of life within a common national framework. The difficulty for multiculturalist advocates was agreeing on what was implied by different ways of life and a common framework. Gender and sexuality were central to the definition of difference, and amongst the most contested aspects of it. Critics of multiculturalism, including feminists, had quickly noted that respect for difference might involve tolerating practices that they had long challenged, especially entrenched patterns of gender inequality, female subordination in marriage, forced marriages, sex with minors, genital mutilation of women and deep hostility towards sexual unorthodoxy, especially homosexuality. Multiculturalism rapidly became a scapegoat for the continuation of such practices. On the other hand, developing a common framework could readily be seen as imposing Western norms on different cultures, claiming universal validity for what was very historically specific. The tensions inherent in multi-culturalism became more acute as national debates became inextricably entangled with international tensions, especially around a resurgent Islam with strong elements of **Fundamentalism** (Modood 2007). Many states that had pioneered multiculturalism, such as the Netherlands and the UK, began to retreat in the 1990s and 2000s, often under intense political pressure, as they perceived threats to their long-standing commitment to gender and sexual equality, and a threat to national identity (McGhee 2008). In France, the use of the veil by some Muslim women was seen as a threat to Republican values, and banned in schools, a move echoed in other European countries (Scott 2007). Opponents of multi-culturalism worried about the loss of national cohesion as members of minority cultural communities seemed entrenched in their own traditions, failing to learn the majority language and accentuating their isolation and sense of bitter embattlement as they affirmed their allegiances elsewhere, to Islam. Even the more sympathetic supporters of multiculturalism wondered whether government support for minority cultures had in fact contributed to entrenching both difference and impermeability, especially by assuming the holistic nature of the cultures and relying on often self-appointed leaders to articulate the traditional needs and values of their communities – usually at the expense of the different needs of women and young people.

But even as the policies and values of multiculturalism faced mounting criticisms, the underlying issues that it had attempted to respond to became if anything more rather than less acute in the early 2000s, especially after the 9/11 calamity in 2001. For some the correct response was the elaboration of forms of **Cosmopolitanism** that broke away from the inhibitions of national traditions and local cultural ties. Others argued that multiculturalism need not assume the equal worth of all cultures, regardless of the way they treated women and their own minorities. It was possible to reconcile respect for difference with adherence to agreed minimum human standards, the rights of exit and voice, and to develop a multiculturalism that was more sensitive to the complexity of different cultures. Minority cultures were not radically other.

Just as theorists question the **Essentialism** that underpins concepts of 'race' and 'ethnicity', so the notion of culture needs to be radically queried. Cultures are always multifaceted and complex, and shaped in specific historic circumstances. Even as the (usually) male leaders of some minority communities might assert the eternal verities of traditional gendered and sexual values and structures, dissident women and homosexually-inclined people find forms of resistance and self-expression. Members of diverse cultures are not enslaved to their determining traditions, but exercise **Agency** – which is why, from this perspective, multi-culturalism is best seen as referring to individual claims to full citizenship against cultural barriers rather than a claim for the group rights of specific cultures (Phillips 2007).

The reality of cultural diversity is of ambivalence, ambiguity, tensions and contradictions rather than fixed or determining boundaries. Cultures, minority and majority, change under the impact of shifting social realities and human practice. They are not fixed for all time. Complex processes of racialization of new minority populations continue to work around ideas of otherness. But minority communities also intermingle, and are a locus of cultural **Hybridity**, in which new identities and ways of life are being forged. Gilroy (2004) questions whether the emergence of essentialized racial and ethnic identities has contributed anything worthwhile to the struggle against racism, and sees the hope for genuine change more in the development of 'multiculturality', rather than the forms of multiculturalism – based on the reification of group identities – that have characterized official attitudes. The multiculturality that Gilroy defends is based on the idea of conviviality, arising in the multiplicity, diversity, interminglings and pleasures of everyday life. It is the very ordinariness, banality even, of vibrant coexistence in family life, popular cultures and sexual interactions that is the real answer to the impasse reached by contemporary multiculturalism.

N

NEOLIBERALISM

Neoliberalism has been widely seen as the intellectual precursor and ideological buttress of the restructuring of global capitalist markets and values since the 1970s. It refers specifically to refurbished free-market economics, but has developed a wider set of meanings. As a concept it is closely associated with others such as **Globalization** and **Individualization**, and has been attributed with a dramatic impact on the ways in which public and private life are perceived and organized. But it has a high degree of elasticity, a term that is at once 'intriguing and infuriating' (Davies 2009: 88).

Originating in the 1920s to refer to free-market economics, from the 1930s the term was increasingly used to describe the work of economists who were developing a large-scale critique of Keynesian and welfare and collectivist policies in the name of individual and market freedoms. Such critiques came into their own with the economic and social crises of the 1970s and the rise of New Right politics, especially in the USA and the UK, which led to large-scale economic and social restructuring. Both 'Thatcherism' in the UK and 'Reaganism' in the USA have been seen as neoliberal regimes, though uneasily combining economic liberalism with social and moral conservatism. From this perspective, neoliberalism is the ideological face of globalizing forces, which critics argue undermine welfare policies that protect the individual against the depradations of international capital. The impact of the 1980s structural adjustment programmes enforced on debtor countries, usually in the Global South, by the International Monetary Fund and the World Bank provide a classic example of this. These cuts inevitably had a massive impact on the poorest, with women and children particularly affected, and having often devastating effects on personal life. The cutting back on educational opportunities for women, for example, had a major impact on population policies, inhibiting women's opportunities to control their own fertility. Similarly, cutbacks in health spending inhibited efforts to curb the spread of HIV/**AIDS** in sub-Saharan Africa (Okin 2005).

Not surprisingly, neoliberalism has become a generalized term of abuse amongst many in the anti-capitalist and anti-globalization movements, and a handy catch-all explanation for radical opponents of the status quo. More specifically, it has been deployed by a number of sexual theorists to link changes in the economy, society and culture to the transformations of sexual and intimate life since the 1970s. This amounts to arguing that the considerable liberalization of sexual codes evidenced in most Western and other societies from the 1970s is either a direct effect of neoliberal strategies or can be readily articulated with them.

The late-modern individual, the argument goes, is forced to live the illusion of individual freedom and personal choice whilst actually being wrapped in the gilded cords of late capitalism, seduced by the wiles of a globalizing consumer capitalism, exploiting and commercializing the most precious human bonds, including the sexual and intimate (Hennessy 2000; Binnie 2004). Ideas of individual autonomy and self-responsibilization so central to contemporary secular liberalism are not so much illusory or deceptive as the very forms of regulation which can most effectively fit with the current form of capitalist organization. Critics often deploy a particular reading of the work of Michel Foucault to explain this: neoliberalism is a new form of governance through which the individual is 'forced to be free', to manage his or her self. Under neoliberal imperatives, individuals become 'entrepreneurs of themselves, shaping their own lives through the choices they make among the forms of life available to them' (Rose 1999: 230). This elaborate and sophisticated form of subjectivity/subjectification does not lead to the abandonment of governance; rather it substitutes self-governance as the principle form of social regulation.

Recent liberalizing sex reforms have been read in this light. Critics of **Same-sex marriage** have seen it as a move toward creating the respectable gay as opposed to the transgressive, disruptive and challenging **Queer**. Respectability involves a voluntary regulation of the sexual self in the interests of full acceptance and citizenship (Richardson 2004: 393). Some have seen this process working its way through the management of HIV in the 'post-crisis' world (in the West at least). People with HIV learn to calculate and manage **Risk**, using their know-ledge of their HIV status, their T cell count and blood viral load count, and the likelihood of infection to negotiate sexual partnerships (Adkins 2002:108ff.; Davis 2005: 251).

From this position the self-reflexive person is the ideal subject of neoliberal discourse. An emphasis on individual freedom and rights, and the importance of self-surveillance and regulation for the individual who has internalized the norms and goals of liberal forms of governance, is central to the new society. In the contemporary world such forms are all the more potent for seeming to be so dispersed, underplayed and voluntarily chosen.

Powerful as such arguments appear there is a slipperiness about them which raises strong doubts. For example there is a lack of clarity about the exact relationship of neoliberal tendencies and wider social changes. Is neoliberalism the cause of the liberal changes? Are they a necessity of the globalized free-market economy? Or is there merely a contingent relationship between neoliberal economic and social restructuring? There is also a real problem about the implicit determinism of many critical accounts of neoliberalism, the assumed cause and effect between the needs of international capitalism and developments in personal life. Marxist theorists in the 1960s and 1970s expended huge energy in deconstructing the causal links between economic base and social and cultural superstructures. Now many seem willing to reaffirm them with a vengeance. But there are obvious contradictions in such analyses, particularly with regard to sexuality. The most highly developed neoliberal society, the USA, is also one of the most conservative in reshaping public policy in relation to sexuality and morality, while at the peak of Thatcherism and Reaganism it was moral conservatism not social liberalism that was allied to economic liberalism, suggesting at the very least the complexities of such linkages. Above all, many of the arguments advanced by critics of neoliberalism tend to obscure one of the most crucial reasons for the shift in sexual values: the power of grassroots **Agency**. Collective struggles – of **Feminism** and **Gay liberation** especially – have contributed to, complemented but also often obscured the reality of myriads of individual struggles by women and men over many years to gain control over the conditions of their lives – in controlling fertility, entering into freely chosen or escaping oppressive relations, challenging sexual ignorance, battling against sexual violence, affirming sexual identities, having sexual pleasure, avoiding sexual pain (see **Great transition**). Such changes are not the simple results of neoliberalism, however important the tendencies it embodies, the forces it represents and its ideological successes have been in shaping the modern world. Sexuality has a tendency to elude simple forms of determination, and conscious and deliberate efforts at reshaping and regulating.

P

PAEDOPHILIA

Few issues arouse as much fear, anxiety and loathing in late-modern societies as paedophilia, the sexual attraction of adults for children. The 'paedophile' has become a potent embodiment of evil, a synonym not only for the child sex abuser but also in many cases for child abductor and even murderer, and a powerful generator of **Moral panic**. The especial horror invoked by the abuse of innocence, by the imposition of adult desires on the vulnerable, powerless child, suggests a culture that is profoundly anxious about the boundaries and differences between adults and children, and has become increasingly concerned with protecting the young as long as possible. Yet this has not always been the case.

The term was first defined as a sexual disorder by Richard von Krafft-Ebing in his *Psychopathia Sexualis* (1886), and by the early twentieth century had become widely used within sexology and medicine. There was an older tradition, however (especially amongst men grounded educationally in the Classics), that lauded intergenerational friendship and love, especially for its pedagogic possibilities – the so-called Greek love justification: in the passage from childhood dependence to adult responsibility, it was suggested, sexual and moral guidance by a caring man for an adolescent boy could be invaluable. Subsequently, apologists used the evidence of social anthropology, that a number of tribal societies had complex rites of passage for adolescent boys which involved sexual relations with older men, to attempt to justify paedophile relationships. **Sexology** itself, especially the work of Freud, had offered evidence for the existence of **Childhood sexuality**. For some advocates of paedophile love there was but a short step from this to the attempted legitimation of intergenerational relationships. In the wake of the sexual liberation movements of the 1970s a number of groups emerged in Europe and North America to argue this case – for example, NAMBLA (North American Man-Boy Love Association) in the USA, PAL (Paedophile Action for Liberation) and PIE (Paedophile Information Exchange) in the UK (Weeks 1977). They soon attracted hostile responses in the media and from the law (a number of paedophile activists ended up in prison), but also produced strong opposition from feminist and lesbian and gay activists.

The alleged link with paedophilia has been one of the most difficult areas in the progress of lesbian and gay acceptance. The largely unfounded association of gay men with sex with minors has long shadowed discussion of lesbian and gay rights, and represents perhaps the last great taboo in the full integration of LGBT people. It has been noticeable that as European countries moved towards recognition of **Same-sex marriage**, rights to adoption were at first excluded. The fear of sexual abuse by the 'predatory homosexual' lingered long after traditional prejudices had ostensibly eroded. In fact, contemporary cultures, from Australia to Europe to the USA, have preferred to focus on the figure and otherness of the anonymous paedophile rather than on the hard reality that most abuse of children is carried out by a close relative or family friend, or perhaps by a priest, as a wave of scandals involving the Roman Catholic Church, from the UK and Ireland to Australia, various parts of continental Europe and the USA, has dramatically revealed. Child sex abuse is usually heterosexual in nature, and a surprising number of abusers are women (some estimates suggest between 5 and 20 per cent).

The growing sensitivity to abuse of children is the result of long campaigns, often led in Western countries by feminists, or by survivors of abuse themselves. This has become a global phenomenon, with international campaigns to end **Trafficking** in children and the worst excesses of **Sex tourism**. In the process, the distinction between paedophilia and sexual abuse has tended to become eroded. What the debate on paedophilia in the 1970s began to discuss were the meanings and implications of sexual and intimate relations across the generations. Were they invariably exploitative? Given the variety of different minimum ages for sexual activities across the world, is there an ideal age at which consent becomes free and possible, rather than abusive, and a relationship becomes consensual, rather than coercive? Did intergenerational sex have different implications for male and female young people? The developing sociological literature pointed to the existence of paedophilias, not a single paedophilia, and the need to be sensitive to distinctions in the context of protecting the young and vulnerable (Taylor 1981). These important issues became increasingly difficult to explore and debate as the discourse shifted to sexual abuse. The **Sexual stories** of self-declared paedophiles are no longer heard as tales are told of abusers, and the voices of survivors have become more prominent (Plummer 1995).

The focus on child abuse has thrown light on a historically grossly neglected subject, but is important also for what it reveals about current attitudes to childhood. Children have become increasingly a focus of meaning in family life. Children, O'Connell Davidson (2005: 18) suggests, 'are the "gift" that couples can give to each other in order to secure their own relationship as well as to establish social links with each other's kin'. To achieve this, children need to be different from adults, to be in a morally bounded and protected realm, where they are absolutely dependent on older people. Yet the boundaries between adults and children have never been so contested. The dialectic of agency and dependency on the part of young people, and duty and anxiety on the part of adults, makes for a potent brew of tensions and anxieties about the sexual activities and vulnerabilities of young people. But public anxiety is not simply about the sexual behaviour of young people. It is also about adults' own behaviour: 'Today's fears emanate from the sexual desire of the parents, not of the children' (Bauman 1998: 29).

It is precisely the implications of adult desire for young children that has been at the heart of controversies over paedophilia since the nineteenth century. The focusing on sexual abuse in more recent years has pinpointed the entanglement of power and desire that inevitably structure intergenerational relations. In the process paedophilia has become the distorted mirror in which our culture sees reflected back the difficulties and dangers of growing up in a highly sexualized world.

PERVERSION

The term perversion, suggesting a turning away from what is right and proper, has always had a strongly moral implication. It was seen as an upsetting of the natural order of the world, converting men to vice and corruption (Roudinesco 2009). Its incorporation into the language of the nascent **Sexology** of the late nineteenth century, therefore, represented a significant moment in the classification and categorizing of sexual behaviours. Prohibitions and taboos that were rooted in ancient Christian codes were transferred to the ostensibly, and ostentatiously, scientific language of the sexological textbooks, providing definitions, Kinsey sharply commented, nearly identical with 'theologic classifications and with moral pronouncements of the English common law of the fifteenth century' (Kinsey *et al.* 1948: 202). **Homosexuality**, transvestism, fetishism, voyeurism, kleptomania, sadism and masochism, coprophilia, undinism, frottage, chronic satyriasis and nymphomania, necrophilia, pederasty: the list was potentially endless, and destined to grow in the twentieth century. Each perversion was investigated with zealous care and its causes were endlessly speculated upon. Was it a degeneration or a harmless anomaly, congenital or acquired, the result of tainted heredity or the effects of moral corruption, a product of psychic trauma or free and wilful choice?

The pioneering Austrian sexologist Krafft-Ebing suggested a distinction between a *perversion* and a *perversity,* the latter a product of vice, the former a psycho-pathological condition. Havelock Ellis distinguishes between *inversion,* a turning inwards and a more or less random biological 'sport', and *perversion*, which sprang from moral indulgence. Magnus Hirschfeld and his followers distinguished *perversions* from *anomalies*, the latter suggesting almost benign variations. But at the same time as case studies were tidily labelled, and forensic experts offered neat explanations to display before the courts, the perverts themselves began to walk out of the pages of the sexological writings, speaking in authentic tones of self-confession (though often rendered in Latin for the sake of decency), marked by their badges of sexual unorthodoxy. Those excluded by the sexual order began to assert their own normality, engaging in dialogue with sexology (Oosterhuis 2000), and beginning to write their own **Sexual stories**.

This was what Foucault (1979) has described as the 'perverse implantation'. On the positive side, the description of these exotic types of sexual being considerably expanded the definition of what could be considered as 'sexual'. Freud, the founding father of **Psychoanalysis**, opened his *Three Essays* in 1905 with a discussion of homosexuality and other 'sexual aberrations' precisely because he believed that their existence transformed conventional views as to what constituted sex. He used them 'as a weapon with which to throw the traditional definitions of sexuality into question' (Laplanche and Pontalis 1980: 307). The new sexological definitions extended backwards to include the most modest whispers of infantile sexuality and outwards to the farthest reaches of human behaviour, to embrace not only common or garden variations but also esoteric manifestations that had little obvious connection with orgasm or even pleasure at all.

The negative side of this classificatory enthusiasm was a sharp reinforcement of 'the normal'. The categorization of the perversions, debates over their causes and the detailed categorization of their most exotic manifestations worked to emphasize their pathology, their relationship to degeneracy, madness and sickness, and helped to reinforce the normality of heterosexual genital relations. This was the case even with Freud and psychoanalysis. It was the tragic destiny of humankind necessarily to forgo the infinite range of **Desire** in order to ensure survival in a world of scarcity. For Freud, the term 'perversion' had a precise technical meaning, as an aspect of all our lives we could not escape. All of us were heirs to the polymorphous perversity of infancy. It was a problem only when it became an end in itself and blocked the road to 'mature sexuality'. But it was very difficult to separate that meaning from the wider moral and political meanings attached to it. Freud believed that the germ of perversion is present in us all, yet the notion of a 'mature' sexuality clearly implies a normal developmental route, necessitating leaving behind those infantile urges. The language of perversion cannot avoid dividing the sexual world into the normal and the abnormal, the elect and the damned.

As was clear from the ambiguities of the pioneering sexologists themselves, implicit in the definitions of perversion were other potential meanings. Homosexuality, 'scarcely a perversion' in Freud's terms, led the way as those radically excluded by medical and psychological discourses fought back, culminating in its removal from the American Psychiatric Association's *Diagnostic and Statistical Manual* (DSM) of mental illnesses in 1974 – after sustained campaigning from the gay community (Bayer 1981). As this suggests, pure science had very little to do with the de-classification: it was highly political. Which is why, under pressure and in a liberalizing climate, the language has gradually changed, except in the more rabidly religious parts of the world. Few mainstream sexologists would now feel easy using the language of perversion to describe the variety of sexual behaviours. For one leading sexologist in the late twentieth century, Robert Stoller (1977), perversion is best described as, and limited to, the 'erotic form of hatred', defined not so much by the acts themselves as by the content, hostility to others. A new term, the paraphilias has come into general use to describe the sexual spectrum, which fits more readily into a discourse of **Sexual diversity**. The zeal to categorize, however, has not ceased. As this was being written the American Medical Assocation issued a draft of its revised DSM. The paraphilias listed, from exhibitionism to voyeurism via frotteurism, paedophilia, sexual masochism, sexual sadism and transvestic fetishism, are remarkably similar (minus homosexuality) to those in Krafft-Ebing's *Psychopathia Sexualis* in the 1880s. What is different is that the voices of the science now have to compete with the loudly speaking perverts themselves.

A 'perverse dynamic', Dollimore (1991) has argued, lies at the heart of Western constructions of sexuality. The striving to produce and regulate the norm inevitably produces the other, the feared and execrated or merely despised, which simultaneously denies and confirms the norm. The political and sexual ordering is always internally disordered by the very perversities it produces and sets up against itself. That disorder provides the elements of resistance, subversion and transgression. The perversions assume a hierarchical ordering of sexuality. Contemporary perverts have a radically different vision of the erotic, marked by sexual diversity, pluralism and **Choice** rather than prohibition and condemnation.

PLEASURE

The intense, exquisite, addictive and escapist delights of the erotic have always lain uneasily alongside the challenge of mundane reality. Sexual mores have been built precariously across the chasm between unbounded expectation and the harsh realization of limits, and at the ultimate between Eros (the drive towards life) and Thanatos (the drive towards death). In the world of sexuality, there is an eternal tension between attraction and repulsion, hope and threat, fascination and fear, pleasure and danger. Societies have in various, intricate ways attempted to find the right balance. The ancient Greeks sought an art of life (at least for male citizens, excluding women, the young and slaves) in which temperance balanced excess, and self-discipline kept pleasures in order. The aim was to define the uses of pleasure in a way which neither ignored it, nor surrendered to its intoxicating force. The Christian tradition was shaped, in contrast, by a sense of the dangers of sexuality, focusing on the sins of the flesh rather than the pleasures of the body, with the marriage bed offering an uneasy place of armistice, and this continues to shape the Catholic tradition of morality to the present (Hawkes 2004).

Today, many argue, hedonism, the pursuit of individual pleasure unbounded by moral restrictions, has triumphed in late-modern societies. But even as **Secularization** has eroded the certainties of religious traditions, sexual pleasures continue to be shrouded by a sense of encroaching threat. Sexuality may have been separated from its reproductive justification, and a new world of 'plastic sexuality', or 'polymorphous non-perversities' (that is sexualities whose only purpose is pleasure) may have opened up (Giddens 1992) but contemporary cultures worry about the **Commodification** of the erotic, the **Sexualization** of the young, the threats posed by **Pornography**, **Prostitution**, human **Trafficking** and **Sex**

tourism, and the spectre of love without commitment, pleasure without responsibility. While popular culture in the West offers a positive incitement to the pursuit of sexual pleasure, commentators, from traditional moralists to radical critics of the status quo, continue to evoke the dangers. Sex may be pleasurable, but pleasure remains problematic, especially in demarcating limits and boundaries.

A powerful justification for this can be found in the Freudian tradition. For Freud, the pursuit of pleasure, or at least the avoidance of unpleasure, was a, if not the, driving force of civilization and of individual life. The libido, the sexual drive, provided the energy of human development. But it could never be unbounded, because it came up against the restraints necessary for the building of civilization. The tragedy of human existence was that pleasure had to be constrained by necessity (see **Psychoanalysis**). Freudo-Marxism, via the work of Wilhelm Reich and the Frankfurt School, especially Herbert Marcuse, looked to a future society that went beyond the necessity of repression, and where the extraordinary energy of the libido could liberate individuals, and fuel a healthy, pleasurable eros. But in the very moment of seeing the potentialities and necessity of pleasure, Marcuse and his colleagues identified the subtle, corrosive effects of capitalist consumerism in distorting and perverting those possibilities, and in effect locking them up again. Although these thinkers soon became deeply unfashionable, we can still trace their moral emphasis on the wiles and cruelties of capitalism in the contemporary critiques of **Neoliberalism**. But if pleasure can so readily be colonized, where is the focus of resistance? For a thinker who is sceptical of the idea of the liberation of sexuality, Michel Foucault, and who sees the apparatus of sexuality as a locus of power, governance and surveillance, the site of resistance lies in new forms of relationships, and in the body and its multiple possibilities for pleasure (Foucault 1979). Pleasure it seems is both corruptible and beyond corruption. Pleasure continues to have protean potential in the contemporary imagination.

The transformations unlocked in the **Great transition** provided new permissions to seek pleasure, and **Feminism** and **Gay liberation** promoted new attitudes towards bodies – seeking autonomy, health and well-being as well as enjoyment of sexual possibility. The feminist trajectory, however, oscillated perilously between foregrounding danger and pursuing pleasure from the 1970s to the 2000s, and the resulting tensions ultimately fractured the movement's unity. Pleasure, it was obvious, was highly gendered, but the meanings of that proved both contested and divisive (Vance 1984). For gay men, on the other hand, apparently endless possibilities for pleasure opened up in erotic spaces from New York to old Amsterdam, from San Francisco to London, from Toronto to Sydney, from Bangkok to Berlin, with many hot spots in between.

Unfortunately, Thanatos continued to chase Eros as the HIV/**AIDS** epidemic made its deadly way across the globe from the gay communities of America. As the balance of pleasure and danger tipped again in the 1980s, some gay men bravely sought ways of finding sexual enjoyment in an epidemic, and elaborated a new etiquette of **Safer sex**. Sexual desire could put many at risk of death, but careful pleasure could enhance life. But as the phenomenon of **Barebacking** reveals, some gay men found their pleasures by dicing with death. For the American gay writer, Leo Bersani, barebacking was both a terrible danger and a site of intense, overwhelming pleasure – of jouissance, in which subjectivity and subjection could be obliterated (Bersani and Phillips 2008).

Jouissance is a term that has played a significant part in the psychoanalysis of Jacques Lacan, and has had an impact in the **Queer** theory of Bersani and Judith Butler, as well as the philosophy of Slavoj Žižek. It signifies the bliss of sexual orgasm, but also a pleasure that is in excess of what can be endured. It is too much, taking the subject beyond pleasure to the point of intense suffering. Jouissance is what has to be sacrificed by the human animal in the entry into the Symbolic Order, the order of language and culture. It is, for Lacan, the opposite of pleasure. It is where normative subjectivity fails. This is precisely the attraction of the notion of jouissance for a queer theorist like Bersani. Jouissance as a transcendent bliss, attained through taking the erotic to the ultimate, is where conventional ideas of the self, identity, subjectivity dissolve. It is the great refusal of straight definitions of the normal.

But what can sexual pleasure mean to the impoverished woman struggling to escape domestic sexual violence; or to female or transgender sex workers in the most excluded settings in the Global South; or to marginal youths getting by on the peripheries of world cities (Corrêa *et al.* 2008: 146)? The rise of **Human sexual rights** embraces a complex of hopes and ideals: negatively, of escape from oppression, violence, injustice; positively, of new forms of freedom, from condom use to the ability to explore different sexualities. Pleasure is not easily susceptible to right claims. It carries its own ambiguities. But for those cruelly denied them the possibilities of pleasure point to the affirmation of our common humanity rather than the pursuit of its dissolution.

POLYAMORY

Polyamory, as a term, has been widely used since the 1990s to describe *consensual* non-monogamous sexual, intimate and emotional relationships with a range of partners – though all these descriptions are ambivalent and challenged. Polyamorists consciously reject the hegemony of traditional monogamy, that is, normatively heterosexual, male-dominated couple relationships based on exclusive love and sexuality, with strict regulation of extra-couple or non-couple relations and of unorthodox sexualities. What has been called 'mono-normativity' is deeply embedded in Western cultural beliefs and structures, encoded in institutions such as **Marriage** and the orthodox family, policed by the green-eyed goddess of jealousy, and ideologically justified as natural, deeply rooted in our biological heritage.

Against this polyamorists argue for open, egalitarian (especially gender equality), democratic, mutual and freely chosen relationships based on the potentiality of multi-partnerships where rules and boundaries are negotiated rather than given or assumed. At its most radical, polyamory poses a fundamental critique of existing relationships in the name of non-exploitative, non-dyadic forms of living and loving. Such hopes and dreams are reflected in a flowering of self-help groups, networks and communities, a vocabulary of neologisms, websites and advisory, counselling and support services, as well as a considerable media hype, especially in the USA and to a lesser extent Britain (Barker and Langdridge 2010).

There is nothing new in critiques of compulsory or compulsive monogamy, or in the experimentation with various forms of non-monogamy. It can be traced in Western fiction since at least the seventeenth century, and from the nineteenth century a number of pioneering radicals and socialists and middle-class Bohemians self-consciously experimented with new forms of relationships, often under the guise of 'free love'. Building on these earlier efforts, the counterculture of the 1960s and second-wave **Feminism** and the **Gay liberation** movement of the 1970s offered sustained critiques of 'straight', capitalist, sexist, patriarchal or heterosexist relations (the enemy varied) and explored alternatives to normative couple relationships and the traditional family, with varying degrees of ingenuity and success. Supporters of the commune movement that was contemporary with these other movements often attempted to live the dream of alternatives to coupledom, but the dreams were usually deferred under the cold winds of property disputes, questions of who did the cooking, conflicts over child care and the resilience of pair-bonding. But the dream of less exploitative relationships than those offered by the monogamous norm never quite died in the feminist and gay movements. 'For some, like ourselves', write the feminist sociologists Jackson and Scott (2004: 151), 'the critique of monogamy remains central to living as heterosexual feminists while challenging the institutionalization of heterosexuality.' From this historical perspective polyamory can be seen as an attempt to pick up the pieces of a well-established critique, though in changed historical circumstances.

What is new is the transformation of patterns of intimate life in the **Great transition** since the 1960s in most Western countries (Weeks 2007). The gender revolution, the shifting patterns of **Family** life, the decline of marriage, the frequency of divorce, the widespread acceptance of cohabitation, the bending of the heterosexual/homosexual binary divide, the emergence of new sexual subjectivities and identities – all these have had uneven effects but have contributed to the undermining of the traditional organization of relationships, and opened spaces for new lifestyle choices and life experiments, some fully in line and complicit with societal trends, others claiming radically to subvert or transgress them.

Polyamory has to be distinguished from traditional forms of non-consensual non-monogamy – such as infidelity, adultery, casual promiscuity, swinging and dogging – and from polygamy in various forms (though interestingly customary forms of polygamy have been legitimized by the model South African constitution, alongside **Same-sex marriage**). They may easily be condemned for embodying deceit, abandonment of commitment, male exploitation and the dominance of heteronormative values. But radical polyamory can also be differentiated from contemporary 'open' relationships, heterosexual or non-heterosexual, which are usually bounded by tacit or explicit rules to safeguard the core couple. One husband cited in a study of heterosexual couples observes that 'If my wife had a quick screw it wouldn't upset me, but an affair would'. A wife made a similar comment: 'I don't mind if he *fucks* them, as long as he doesn't *talk* to them' (Duncombe and Marsden 2004: 143). These offer carefully calibrated distinctions to safeguard the core relationship. Similarly, a common feature of gay male couple relationships is the downplaying of *sexual* fidelity as the marker of commitment and fidelity. Emotional faithfulness tends to be valued much more highly than sexual (Heaphy *et al.* 2004), but is usually policed by agreed or understood rules about casual affairs: 'don't ask, don't tell', 'never on your own, always the two of us' or 'always catch the last bus home'.

The problem with such relationships is that they also assume the primacy of the pair-bonding couple, with other relationships placed as secondary or peripheral. So same-sex-marriage has been critiqued by advocates of radical polyamory for reaffirming coupledom and sexual exclusivity. For many polyamorists, their relationships are a matter of principle not pragmatism or opportunism, representing a refusal to be trapped within traditional concepts of monogamy, or coupledom. For **Queer** activists, polyamory may be seen as a way of escaping heteronormativity, though Adam (2006: 24) suggests that this may be more of a lesbian than male gay preoccupation. The editors of a volume on lesbian polyamory suggest that it 'compels us to question traditional definitions of fidelity, family and intimacy', and includes many different forms of multiple intimate relationships (Munson and Stelboum 1999: 2). This is an arena of complex distinctions. For some polyamory is a lifestyle choice opening new possibilities for more exciting sexual explorations. For others, the unifying ideal is that 'polyamory frees up each partnership from having to meet all the needs of the other' (Bettinger 2005: 104). For yet others it opens up more utopian avenues for transforming human relationships whilst recognizing the diversity of intersecting needs and possibilities (Finn 2010). On the other hand some radical critics have seen in the emphasis on love and intimacy in polyamorous relationships a danger of appropriation into normative and assimilationist discourses (Klesse 2007: 114). Polyamory remains a highly contested concept.

There are no reliable figures for those engaged in polyamorous or more broadly non-monogamous relations. A British report in 2001 estimated that 14.6 per cent of men and 9 per cent of women had concurrent relationships, though these tended to decline with age, and they by no means signify any principled commitment to non-monogamy (Johnson *et al.* 2001: 4). A 2009 estimate for the USA suggested that some 500,000 people were involved in polyamorous relationships. For most people, however, it is the couple that remains the norm, perhaps indicating not so much the naturalness of pair-bonding as its convenience. Couple relationships remain difficult enough to maintain in a world of transformed intimacy. Polyamorous involvements are infinitely more complex, and are especially difficult when children are involved. Yet it can be argued that something fundamental has changed in the late-modern world. What has become the norm is the practice of serial rather than lifelong monogamy. People go on trying to make relationships work, and when necessary try again and again, but usually with one rather than multiple partners. Monogamy may not be enough, or sustainable for a lifetime, but for most people polyamory remains a step too far.

PORNOGRAPHY

Etymologically, pornography refers to the description of the life and manners of prostitutes and their patrons, and thus by a simple extension the suggestion of 'impure', 'unchaste' and explicit erotic expression in writing or pictorial form. Hence one possible definition of pornography is illicit activities designed to stimulate sexual desire (with the implicit suggestion of masturbatory activity). It links the term to another word, obscene, which has an older history, and a more general application, suggesting lewdness, indecency, disgust and, in varying degrees, illegality. Most attempts at controlling pornography are done under anti-obscenity legislation, which in the English jurisdiction at least has been concerned with controlling representations which have a tendency to 'deprave and corrupt' – a notoriously subjective and culturally shifting rubric.

Explicit erotic representations are as old as human civilization, as sexual imagery scraped on the walls of Stone Age caves vividly suggests. The invention of the term pornography in the mid-nineteenth century (its first recorded use is in the early 1860s) can be seen as part of the zealous Victorian urge to label and categorize sexual behaviour which went beyond the norm. But there was more to it than that. The appearance of the word at this time reflects the technological revolution that was making possible the rapid dissemination of photographic images; and a cultural and political climate where the issue of how to regulate illicit sexual behaviour, especially female prostitution, was coming to the fore. We can also postulate the creation of a new market (amongst men) for the explicit circulation of sexual fantasy (usually, though not exclusively, about women) – this is also the period when private collectors took pride in collecting the choicer examples of erotic material, creating a mystique around the erotic, and stimulating a demand for a new industry to supply their fantasies.

But the difficulty of distinguishing the pornographic and the obscene from the merely erotic or explicit has bedevilled attempts either to control or tolerate it. The appearance from the 1950s of mass circulation, sexually titillating magazines, such as *Playboy*, *Penthouse*, and *Mayfair*, and the creation by the 1970s of a multibillion dollar international industry in print, film and video suggested both a high demand and a high degree of social acceptance for at least what became known as 'soft porn'. Reactions varied. For the moral traditionalist pornography represented a defilement of sexuality. For the social liberal, pornography might be something to be disliked, even disapproved of, but was generally seen as a matter of personal **Choice**, as long as its manifestations did not unduly sully the public sphere. For some feminists, on the other hand, pornography represented something far more dangerous. In Robin Morgan's famous phrase: 'porn is the theory; rape is the practice' (Morgan 1980: 139).

During the 1970s and 1980s, pornography became redefined by many radical feminists as essentially about male violence against women. For some, pornography, by its explicit degrading of women in representations, caused violence towards women. For Andrea Dworkin (1981), however, pornography *was* violence against women: male power over women was exercised through heterosexual penetrative sex, which was violence, and pornography was the main vehicle for male colonization of women. Thus in their attempt to introduce an ordinance outlawing pornography in Minneapolis in the 1980s, Dworkin and her co-campaigner, Catherine MacKinnon, proposed that it be defined as 'the graphic, sexually explicit subordination of women whether in picture or in words' (Dworkin and MacKinnon 1988) – a not so subtle shift from the original dictionary definition.

A fierce debate subsequently erupted over the meanings and implications of pornography. All feminists could probably agree that pornography tended to objectify the female body, the main focus of pornographic representations. They could also agree that the distinction between private and public spheres, which was central to liberal attempts to draw a line between toleration and banning, was inadequate. Many crimes against women were committed in the home, and the power relations of men and women were complex, so there was no answer by saying pornography was a matter of personal choice. But as Dworkin's feminist opponents pointed out, not all pornography was violent, or led to violence. A great deal of pornography did not even relate to heterosexuality: gay porn grew exponentially during this period, and that could hardly be described as being about the violent subordination of women. The scapegoating of porn, moreover, obscured the distinction between representation, which potentially demeaned the subject, and erotica, designed simply to arouse emotions and bring pleasure. There was a domain of fantasy which needed to be recognized, and which could not be simply identified as 'reality'. Above all, the anti-porn campaigners, in wanting to ban pornography, risked allying themselves with right-wing moral conservatives in narrowing the boundaries of acceptable sexual behaviour. Many feminists, in turn, whatever their personal feelings about porn, allied themselves with anti-censorship campaigners (Segal and McIntosh 1992). Behind this was a strong belief that pornographic representations were a complex product of male-dominated societies, and targeting pornography alone would not touch the roots of continuing inequalities of power between men and women.

Definitions which play on the illicit nature of pornography, or on its harmful effects, inevitably construct pornography as in itself harmful. This could be said to be both the radical feminist position and that explicitly underlined in the 1986 (conservative) Meese Commission in the USA. The Williams Report (1979) in the UK, on the other hand, explicitly attempted a definition which stressed the function of pornography (sexual arousal) and content (sexually explicit representations). It then set aside questions of morality and of legal restriction to be addressed separately. This was in tune with a liberal strategy of **Regulation** which held that it was not the function of law to lay down what was moral or immoral in relation to sexuality. All society could legitimately do was preserve public decency and prevent harm. This in turn simply reopens the debate in another way. What constitutes harm? What are the limits that could or should be set on public representations of explicit sex?

Such questions have become more rather than less pointed as pornography has exploded on the Internet and become a major element of **Cybersex**. Child porn, and the ways in which it underpins **Paedophilia**, has become a huge focus of moral anxiety and attempts at regulation, with recurrent sweeps on alleged perpetrators who are often caught by their credit card numbers. More broadly, the cyber revolution has promoted what has been called Porn2.0, a new economy of explicit erotica, with new types of sexual labour and professionalism, extreme imagery, a multiplication of specialist sites, online fan communities and the rise and rise of the amateurs, not least the sex bloggers and video posters (Attwood 2009a). As throughout its history, pornography continues to exploit the many fissures and opportunities in contemporary regimes of sexuality. Regulation and control, moreover, however keenly pursued, get more and more complex in the digital world, and little seems to limit pornography's ineluctable growth.

PROSTITUTION

The conventional definition of prostitution is as the exchange of sexual services for cash, and/or other material benefits. Prostitution has, however, always involved more than this because the cash nexus and exchange are rarely simply arrangements between equals. The market is never a level playing field. Prostitution is also about power differences embedded in complex social relations. Feminist theorists have therefore argued that prostitution is best conceptualized as a social relationship which allows the power of command over one person's body to be exercised by another (O'Connell Davidson 1998). This is usually male power over women, even in many cases when the worker is male, as in 'gigolo' arrangements. Male–male prostitution is common, female–female rather less so, but both raise slightly different questions, not least because both client and prostitute belong to the same sexual caste. But in all cases power differentials are at stake.

Traditionally, prostitution has been seen as a response to male sexual needs, a biological necessity which shapes the inevitability of selling sex and makes it a universal institution (McIntosh 1978). This has tended to let men off the hook, and penal codes and social obloquy have generally focused on the female prostitute rather than the male client. She has been the target of endless prosecutions, exploitation and violence, seen as the vector of disease, up to and including HIV, and has been the subject of hostile labelling, recurrent stereotyping and high-minded pathologization. The organization of prostitution has varied enormously across historical periods and cultures, from independent workers to highly organized brothels and international flows. Different jurisdictions have equally varied in their forms of surveillance and control, from state regulation to turning a blind eye. In England prostitution as such has not been illegal over the past two hundred years as local bye-laws, common law and national statutes have punished the 'common prostitute', closed brothels, limited street walking, but tacitly accepted a large-scale selling of sex. It has been seen as the necessary other of respectable, familial, heterosexual norms.

Since the nineteenth century feminists have campaigned vigorously against the double standard of morality inherent in social attitudes towards prostitution, giving rise to several different responses and strategies (see **Feminism**). For some early, first-wave feminists, often in alliance with social purity campaigners, the target was male sexuality, linked to campaigns against the state regulation of vice (Walkowitz 1980). For others, the main concern was the 'rescue' of 'fallen women', often overlapping with the protection of women's rights. These shades of emphases have been replicated in the attitudes of second-wave feminists. It is fair to say that feminist interventions have radically transformed thinking about prostitution since the 1960s, but the debates have frequently been most heated amongst feminists, and with prostitutes or sex workers themselves. For radical feminists there is a continuity between socially respectable institutions and prostitution: marriage has often been seen as a licensed prostitution. For polemicists like Kathleen Barry (1979, 1995) prostitution is a product of male sexual violence and an inherent assault on the dignity of women, and has taken a particularly vicious form through the international sex trade, or human **Trafficking**. The main targets of this sort of critique are male power structures and the ready acceptance of male violence, but there is also a strong message for women involved in the sex trade. Women, Barry argues, have no inherent right to prostitute themselves nor can they give meaningful consent to the violation of their own rights. For this reason radical feminists are usually vehemently opposed to self-organized groups of sex workers and their supporters campaigning for their sexual rights.

The widespread adoption of the term sex worker by those involved in the sex industry implies a rejection of the traditional shame associated with selling sex, and of the sense of 'victimhood' sustained by radical feminist discourses. Prostitute rights groups, such as the English Collective of Prostitutes in the UK and COYOTE (Call Off Your Old Tired Ethics) in the USA emerged in the 1970s, and have inspired international networks defending women's rights, calling for changes in penal laws and for the decriminalization of sex work. The core message is that involvement in the sex industry is a form of labour like any other, and requires the same rights and protection as any other form of work. On this principle, many sex workers have joined trade unions, or become involved in campaigning groups. Internationally, activists have defended the right of sex migrants to cross borders in pursuit of work (Agustin 2007).

While the defence of sex workers' rights and the rejection of victimhood have been vital gains against the prejudice and discriminations of the past, there is a danger that they obscure the potential discrimination and exploitation of any worker in a highly competitive market economy. It is at least debatable how free any **Choice** to enter the sex industry can be in a world of advanced capitalism, embracing dramatic economic and social inequalities, extremes of poverty and wealth, and the continuing subordination of women and children, both within rich countries and between the West and the Global South. These are conditions in which choices are confined to a set of alternatives which are not of the sex worker's choosing. Sex work is not separate from but an integral part of wider social relations.

Contemporary prostitution is a global phenomenon, and illustrates the uneasy coexistence of many different forms, from the individualized casual selling of sexual favours, through more collective forms akin to small businesses, to large-scale brothels and vast international criminalized networks. Like the social relations of production generally, as well as the rapidly changing world of sexuality, sex work is rapidly changing in the conditions of **Neoliberalism** and **Globalization**. Sex work itself is rapidly diversifying, no longer necessarily hidden in the violent shadows of cities and towns, but glossily advertised online, no longer just confined to specific sexual acts, however versatile, but offering diverse forms of entertainment and even the promise of new forms of intimacy authenticity (Bernstein 2007). Sex work offers services to match the changing needs of mobile populations, whether migrating vast distances for work, in escape from war or poverty, travelling in pursuit of business opportunities globally, or searching for diverse pleasures, fantasies and utopian dreams as in **Sex tourism**. These changes affect male prostitution as much as female as old taboos against homosexuality decline in the West, and male sex work become routinized and barely stigmatized.

As sex work changes, so the search continues for more effective forms of regulation, local, national and international. Experiments in decriminalization of prostitution are tried, and then retreated from under pressure from local inhabitants, moral campaigners or radical feminist enthusiasm. Abolitionism, originally concerned with abolishing the international white slave trade, has increasingly become concerned with eliminating prostitution, overlapping with new forms of prohibitionism that seek to cut off the supply and the demand. More humane attitudes towards the sex worker are increasingly accompanied by more draconian attitudes towards the (male) clients (Sanders 2008). The 'Swedish model' developed in the early 2000s in social democratic Sweden under feminist pressure, deliberately focuses on the male punter, leading, as Kulick (2005) has vividly put it, to the creation of a new type of deviant, the ordinary user: 'Four hundred thousand Swedish perverts'. This has proved an influential new approach, followed in a diluted form in Britain and elsewhere in Europe, if with mixed results. The problem is that these various attempts to grapple with the protean forms of prostitution might seek to end gender injustice but tend to end up reinforcing spaces of exclusion and increasing the vulnerability for many of the sex workers involved (Hubbard *et al.* 2008). It is difficult to believe that societies have yet found the best means of balancing opposition to exploitation with recognizing the sexual rights of sex workers. The ultimate reason for that, perhaps, lies in the continuing ambivalence of attitudes towards prostitution across countries and cultures.

PSYCHOANALYSIS

Psychoanalysis has made a major contribution to the theorization of sexuality since the early twentieth century, though its impact has often been ambiguous and contradictory. Sigmund Freud's own writings themselves provide a treasure house of possible interpretations, while the work of his successors has pointed in a variety of destinations that the founding father might have had difficulty in recognizing. As a result the meanings of psychoanalysis remain fiercely controversial. It has been seen both as the essential theory of **Desire** and as its prison guard, opening new ways of interpreting the erotic, and foreclosing sexual and gender possibilities.

The importance of psychoanalysis, at least in the work of Freud himself, lies in the fact that it simultaneously proclaimed the significance of sexuality to psychic and social life, and challenged the received definitions and meanings of the erotic. The core of psychoanalysis is the theory of the unconscious, a psychic realm, with its own dynamic, rules and history, where the biological possibilities of the body acquire meaning. The unconscious is a sphere of conflict: between ideas, wishes, and desires – above all sexual desires – denied access to conscious life by the force of mental repression, yet 'returning' all the time to disrupt consciousness in the form of dreams, slips of the tongue, jokes, neurotic symptoms or perverse behaviour. What fundamentally constitutes the unconscious are those wishes or desires which are repressed in the face of the demands of reality, and in particular the repressed, incestuous desires of infancy: 'What is unconscious in mental life is also what is infantile' (Freud 1916–17: 210).

This suggested that sexuality extended back into earliest childhood – in the form of 'polymorphous perversity' and an original common **Bisexuality** – and could not be readily straitjacketed by either genital or reproductive aims. In the *Three Essays* (originally 1905 but frequently and successively added to thereafter) Freud simultaneously acknowledged his debt to contemporary **Sexology** and problematized its rigid categorizations and the assumption that they resulted from straight-forward biological instincts. He went further than anyone else in incorporating **Perversion** within the acceptable range of sexuality. The effect of the *Three Essays* was to suggest that the perversions were part of everyone's sexual make-up. Their negative was revealed in neurotic symptoms, which were displaced representations of repressed sexual wishes. Their positive presence was demonstrated in fore-pleasures, and by the social existence of perverts themselves. These perversions represented the re-emergence in adulthood of component instincts to which we are all heirs.

Alongside the broadening definition of sexuality, Freud also questioned the automatic nature of object choice. He argues that the reduction in the choice of partner to one of the same sex in **Homosexuality** parallels a similar reduction in **Heterosexuality**. As a result, he suggests, 'from the point of view of psycho-analysis the exclusive sexual interest felt by men for women is also a problem that needs elucidating' (Freud 1905: 146, note 1, added 1915). Homosexuality could not be regarded as a thing apart. Its roots were to be found in the universal bisexuality to which we human animals are born, and in the mental processes by which each individual negotiated the hazards of castration anxiety and the Oedipus crisis to obtain a precarious, conflicted subjectivity. For Freud, there is no inevitable, biologically determined progress to the altar of accepted adult gender or sexual identities. Attaining subjectivity and final object choice is the result of a struggle that we all have to enter and that by no means ends in a victorious capture of the position allotted to us by reason of our anatomy, or the demands of culture.

On the other hand, as Freud notoriously wrote, 'Anatomy is destiny' (Freud 1916–17: 178), and this is at the core of the radical objections to Freud's theories from the first and ever since. The phrase appears to underpin the intractability of our social arrangements, to justify sexual division, to impose a tyranny of the body over the mind. 'Anatomy', as Denise Riley has argued, *given everything as it is, points us irresistibly along certain paths, to certain choices.*' (Riley 1983: 4), but this has not been how Freud was read, nor is it clearly what he finally meant. For Freud, the relationship between the dynamic unconscious and the drives and the demands of civilization was always complex, unfinished, never fully resolved, and yet structured by necessity. This is encapsulated in his famous letter to the American mother of a young homosexual. Homosexuality, he wrote, is assuredly no advantage. It is nothing to be ashamed of. It is a variation of the sexual function, produced by an arrest of sexual development (Jones 1961: 308). Here we have the tensions in his work clearly articulated. On the one hand, we have the demythologizing effects of Freud's theory of psycho-sexual mechanisms. On the other we can see a clear and irreducible normative stance in that little word 'arrest'. Freud in the end does believe that civilization requires a normal progression to a heterosexual object choice, and any failure to achieve that is a problem – for the individual and the culture. Once a goal-directed version of sexuality is introduced, however surreptitiously, then the whole laboriously constructed edifice of sexual variety begins to totter.

These ambiguities shaped Freud's legacy. The theory of bisexuality, for example, was rejected by later psychoanalysts who sought to pathologize homosexuality. For a later generation of ego psychologists, psychoanalysis provided a basis for a normative (heterosexual and genital) vision of a healthy sexuality. Even those theorists, like Wilhelm Reich and Herbert Marcuse, who from the 1930s and 1940s attempted, in different ways, an uneasy marriage of Freud with Marx, abandoned key elements of Freud's radicalness. Reich assumed that the character-structure demanded by capitalism repressed an essentially healthy natural heterosexuality that would surely flourish in a socialist society. Marcuse went further than Freud in seeing the perversions as the great refusal of repression, and the germs of a desublimated sexuality. But both relied on biologically essentialist views of the sexual instinct or drive. Reich and Marcuse had different views of what the sexual drive is, but they agreed on the existence of a common instinctual structure across all cultures. Sexuality is not shaped within history, but outside and beyond it, whatever its contingent forms. The release of sexual energy is seen as beneficent and liberating in a way which is strongly reminiscent of pre-Freudian romantics.

It was the perceived inadequacy of this approach that directed many sexual radicals in the 1970s and beyond in new directions. The rise of second-wave **Feminism** and **Gay liberation** from the late 1960s offered a whole set of new political subjects, with different preoccupations from earlier radicals – and they were often strikingly hostile to psychoanalysis, especially its uneven history around female sexuality and homosexuality, and what was seen to be its latent biological **Essentialism**. The anti-essentialism and the critique of psychoanalysis have been seen most clearly in the work of Michel Foucault (1979).

When, against this trend, some feminists moved towards a re-engagement with Freud it was in two different directions. The influence of Melanie Klein proved especially influential in theorizing parenting and the gendered characteristics associated with that (Chodorow 1978). The school of the French analyst Jacques Lacan, on the other hand, offered a 'recovery' of Freud from the biological encrustation of both immediate post-Freudians and the Freudo-Marxists; and a critique of the dominance of the psychoanalytic institution. The most telling aspects of Lacan's work related to his account of the complexity of subjectivity, the fragility of sexed identities and a theory of desire based on lack. Juliet Mitchell's *Psychoanalysis and Feminism* (1974) became the main conduit for this approach in the anglo world, and was especially important in offering an account of the patriarchal construction of femininity under the 'law of the Father'. Mitchell added to the power structures of capitalism, as explained in fairly orthodox terms, another set of relationships, those of patriarchy. This proved enormously influential, and has offered a productive, if frustrating, space for subsequent feminist theorizing, especially under the impact of French theorists such as Irigaray and Kristeva (Evans 2005: 47–9) – see **Femininity**. There has also been a revival of interest in Freud in **Queer** theory, especially the work of Judith Butler, though this remains highly contested (see entries on **Abjection** and **Melancholia**).

Psychoanalysis is now so encrusted in the barnacles of conflicting interpetations that it is difficult to see an original Freud. But he remains a powerful presence precisely because of the tensions, ambiguities and contradictions in his writings. They point to the difficulties and complexities of theorizing the relationship between the biological, the psychic and the social, especially in understanding sexuality. The challenge his work posed a century ago remains a live one.

Q

QUEER

Queer is a word that has had a spectacular journey, from a signifier of the peculiar, odd, twisted, bent to a descriptor of the highest of high abstract theory, by way of militant sexual activism. Queer as a concept about sexuality is as fluid and full of multiple meanings as the world it has referred to.

Queer 1 was the word commonly used in Britain, and to a lesser extent in other English-speaking countries, until the almost universal adoption of **Gay**, after 1969, to describe both **Homosexuality** as a condition and homosexual people themselves. Significantly, it was also the most common self-description amongst people who identified as homosexual. To say 'I am queer' in the London of the 1950s or 1960s was to tell of who and what you were, and how you positioned yourself in relation to the dominant, 'normal' society. It signalled the internalization of a particular set of meanings about homosexuality (Houlbrook 2005). Like common alternative words such as 'bent' it signalled the general perception of same-sex desire as something eccentric, strange, abnormal, perverse and (from thieves' cant) bad and worthless. It also carried the perhaps more subtle meaning of to puzzle, query or ridicule, hinting at the play many queer people had with dominant meanings, especially through camp and demonstrations of effeminacy (in men) or butchness (in women).

Queer 2, referring to the rise of new forms of lesbian, gay, bisexual and transgender militancy in the late 1980s, especially in the USA but also elsewhere, marks the spectacular return of the repressed in new forms of militancy. The immediate stimulus was anger amongst young activists at the ways in which the **AIDS** crisis had been neglected by conservative administrations in the USA and elsewhere, but beyond this was a yet more radical challenge, to what was seen as the assimilationist and ethnicizing politics of the gay movement as it had consolidated in the 1980s. As Warner (1993: xxii) put it, queer activists 'reject a minoritizing logic of toleration or simple political-interest representation in favour of a more thorough resistance to regimes of the normal'. A deep sense of political and cultural alienation at the direction of gay politics led to a reappropriation of the stigmatizing term 'queer' as a confrontational gesture in a militancy that sought inspiration in the radicalism of early **Gay liberation**. What was strikingly different from earlier uses of queer, however, was the reversal of the meanings of the term. It had shifted from being a negative, individualizing description to a signifier of collective agency and militancy, such as Queer Nation and Act Up! in the USA and Outrage! in Britain, both countries which had seen sharp moves towards conservative moral politics in the 1980s; a new militancy was less obvious in countries which were moving rapidly in the direction of more liberal attitudes towards same-sex activities, such as Denmark and the Netherlands. The emergence of a new queer politics provided new opportunities for dialogue between those who had found the direction of gay life generally problematic: between men and women, gays and straights, black and white, bisexual and transgendered, able-bodied and disabled people, people living with HIV/AIDS and community activists. It was consciously a politics of the streets, but it also fed into a wider cultural politics, notably in a new queer cinema.

There is an obvious link between this new (if relatively short-lived activism) and the new theoretical directions indicated by Queer 3. Both radically questioned the fixity of lesbian and gay (or indeed other) **Sexual identities**, and embraced a politics of subversion, dissidence and transgression. But in fact they pointed in quite different directions. Queer theory became a new, and often esoteric, language in the academy rather than on the streets, despite its radically transgressive commitments. The lesbian and feminist theorist Teresa de Lauretis is generally credited with first using the term in 1990, but renounced it three years later, largely because it had been taken up by those it was designed to challenge. The lineage of queer theory lies in early gay liberationist and feminist theory and in the radical implications of **Social constructionism**, in post-structuralist theory, in the deconstructionist writings of Jacques Derrida, and in the analyses of discourse and power of Michel Foucault (Seidman 1996). But whereas the earlier works had been largely historical and sociological in focus, queer theory was originally much more closely aligned to literary theory and philosophy, though its influence has spread rapidly back into sociology, as well as into critical theory, cultural studies, post-colonial and critical race studies, human geography, even psychology and biology.

Queer theory acquires its meaning from its oppositional stance to the norm. 'Queer is by definition whatever is at odds with the normal, the legitimate, the dominant' (Halperin 1995: 62). This gives the concept a certain elusiveness, and an ability to encompass a variety of positions. Its most characteristic concerns in the early days, in the writings of Eve Kosofsky Sedgwick (1985, 1990), Jonathan Dollimore (1991), Judith Butler (1990, 1993), and others, were with the dynamics of the emergence and inscription of the homosexual/heterosexual binarism as evidenced in works of literature or theory. Whereas early constructionist theory had focused, for example, on the evolution of the category of the homosexual, queer theory was concerned to explore the power of the binary divide that gave rise to the category in the first place, and with the embeddedness of heteronormative values and structures (Warner 1993, 1999) This was a productive emphasis, but had the odd effect of reasserting rather than deconstructing the binary divide, now seen as a, if not the, principle dynamic of social organization (Weeks 1995: 115). Queer theory worked to stress the arbitrary, fictional nature of identities and subject positions, but also had to tackle the apparent intractability of the sexual and gender categories and subjectivities as performatively ritualized and lived. Building on the British philosopher J. L. Austin's speech act theory, Butler sought to show how gender is produced as an effect of regulatory regimes: 'instituted in an exterior space through a stylized repetition of acts', which create the idea of the natural, the original and the inevitable (1990: 141).

If the binary is so fundamental to Western culture, if it works by constantly reaffirming its naturalness and inevitability and is experienced not only in representations but by being embodied in individual subjects and in the values and structures of heteronormative culture, can it be challenged and changed? The early work of Butler and other queer theorists pointed to a politics of subversion and transgression – through carnivalesque challenges to the existing order, through radically transgessive sexualities, through the subversive undermining of gender fixity as in **Transgender** – which dramatized the fluidity and changeability of sexual meanings. Critics rapidly pointed out that carnival is licensed freedom, that there is no necessary link between sexual radicalism and social progressiveness, and that transgender does not necessarily undermine gender but in some circumstances might require its institutional confirmation (as in 'sex-change' operations).

The ambiguities of queer theory are most evident in its response to recent liberalization of attitudes towards homosexuality in most Western countries, especially the legalization of **Same-sex marriage**. Queer analysis, Brandzel (2005: 195) argues, suggests that 'marriage is a mechanism by which the state ensures and reproduces heteronormativity, and absorbing certain types of gay and lesbian relationships will only further this process'. The logic of such apparently widely approved reforms, therefore, is to move towards assimilation into the sexual status quo, and to undermine the radical challenge offered by queer politics. To install same-sex marriage or domestic partnerships as the model for sexual legitimacy is, Butler (2005: 59) argues, to 'constrain the sociality of the body' in ways which are acceptable to the dominant order. But surely there is something a little odd in queer radicals finding themselves on the same side as deeply conservative opponents of LGBT rights in opposing same-sex marriage? It suggests that queer theory has become so wrapped up with academic subversion that it is in danger of forgetting the sexual worlds it grew out of and originally sought to address.

R

RECOGNITION

The political theory of recognition has come to prominence because of the major reconfiguration of the social, cultural and political landscape since the 1970s. The rise of various forms of identity politics, associated especially with questions of race and ethnicity, gender, lesbian and gay politics, and various other forms of difference and **Diversity**, has at the very least challenged, and in some places displaced, more traditional forms of political mobilization, especially a politics of class and economic divisions.

The politics of recognition is above all concerned with developing appropriate forms of acknowledgement of the disparate claims of the identity groups that have proliferated and flourished since the emergence of anti-racist politics, second-wave **Feminism** and **Gay liberation**. The main theorists argue that recognition both holds the key to contemporary politics, and is central to the meanings of justice today (Thompson 2006: 3). It is a politics for a pluralistic world, and is closely linked to, but not coterminus with, ideas of **Multiculturalism**. The central focus is to defend and promote the idea of a society where individuals and social identities enjoy appropriate recognition, which in turn implies a politics of equality, difference and mutual acceptance.

The roots of the idea of recognition lie in Hegelian philosophy – though not all theorists of recognition accept a Hegelian position – and the notion that the identity of the self is always dependent on its recognition by others. It has also been strongly influenced by the emphasis of the Frankfurt School of critical theory on a dialectic of *immanence* and *transcendence,* which assumes that a critical stance on the existing order must be rooted in that order, so that the seeds of an alternative can be detected and promoted. What has given a particular energy to the perspective are a series of crucial events, from the civil rights movements in the USA to the claims of Quebec for linguistic and cultural autonomy, through to key moments in sexual politics, such as the politics of the veil and **Same-sex marriage**. Each of these has given rise to new claims to rights and acknow-ledgement deeply rooted in the culture but within an established order that was (initially or continuously) resistant or hostile to such claims. This in turn gives rise to struggles for recognition – a key concept – through which identities are developed and affirmed.

As such a list of crucial mobilizing events suggests, the politics of recognition has diverse roots, and varying implications in complex, polyvocal, globalizing societies. There are, however, key preoccupations of recognition theory, which have defined the debates. A central concern is with the link between identity and recognition, particularly through a dialogical concept of the self. For Charles Taylor, whose writings from the early 1990s helped shape the political theory, human identity is formed through dialogue with others, especially 'significant others' in the case of intimate life – what Benjamin (1990: 16) called 'mutual recognition'. Through interaction with, and recognition by others, people can make sense of their lives, achieve a sense of self-realization and self-fulfilment, and of authenticity (Taylor 1992a and b). For Axel Honneth (1995), the desire for recognition is so central to individual self-realization that it becomes the motivating force behind social development. Affective recognition, love, traditionally through the heterosexual family, but increasingly through other foci of care and affec-tion, such as lesbian and gay relationships and 'families of choice', is the bedrock from which autonomous participation in public life becomes possible (McNay 2008: 128–9).

Though there have been strong critics of such dialogical theories of the self (Fraser 1995) they have provided the basis of a wider social and political engage-ment. If we assume that failures of recognition, or 'misrecognition', cause harm, damage and oppression, then a politics of recognition requires respect for the rational autonomy of human beings, and esteem for the diversity of possible forms of action. That is, recognition requires both universalistic values and a recognition of difference, potentially contradictory ambitions, but both central to a politics of recognition.

The difficulty with the identity focus of the theory is that it obscures questions of resources, and hence of material inequalities. Nancy Fraser (1995; Fraser and Honneth 2003) has attempted to address this by balancing a 'politics of difference', concerned with questions of identity, with a 'politics of equality', concerned with issues of redistribution and class. Cultural struggles are inevitably linked to economic struggles. Both, she suggests, are necessary to achieve the full and equal participation of all individuals in society. The danger of such a position is that it leads to a dualistic politics, a politics of identity in uneasy tandem with a politics of class, and in the process reproducing the old Marxist base–superstructure dichotomy. This, it has been argued, distorts the complex relationships involved. Lesbian and gay struggles for legitimacy may be primarily cultural but they inevitably become bound up with questions of material inequality. The forms of power that they confront are not separate but inextricably linked (Butler 2004: 30).

There is an inherent problem with any form of identity politics. The processual, contingent, hybrid and fluid nature of contemporary **Sexual identities**, and the potentialities thus opened up for different forms of politics, are obscured by a politics based on the assumed truth of identities. There is a constant danger of fixing in stone what is potentially more open and creative. One of the merits of the dialogical emphasis which lies at the heart of the political theory of recognition is that it leads to an acknowledgement that contemporary identity politics are not simply about the viability or legitimacy of particularist identity claims. They are part of an endless process of struggle against injustices of various forms, and a key aspect of practices of freedom and of human **Agency** (Tully 2001: 22). As long as people are vulnerable to the cruelty of others, and experience shame, humiliation, violence and the various forms of 'disrespect' (Honneth 2007) then struggles for recognition will necessarily continue.

REFLEXIVITY

Sociologists have defined reflexivity as a key feature of the late-modern world, closely linked to **Risk**. 'Risk society' and 'reflexive modernization' (Beck 1992) are often used interchangeably, and refer to a society where 'self-identity becomes a reflexively organized endeavour' (Giddens 1991: 5). For Beck, reflexivity is more like a reflex action as social actors respond in a host of ways to the disruptive sweep of social change in late-modernity. Reflexivity involves self-confrontation and potential confrontation with social institutions and systems which seem impermeable but have their own degree of institutionalized reflexivity themselves (Beck 1994: 5). Giddens, more concerned with the shaping of the self in conditions of late-modernity, stresses the ability of individuals facing the juggernaut of change to reflect on their situation, to weigh up risks to them and the wider society, deploying their own particular knowledges, and the expert knowledges they can draw on, and acting in the light of all this (Heaphy 2007: 89). Action in the world is a crucial element of the theory. Individuals are not passive observers of a rapidly changing world, but act in and are transformed by it.

Reflexivity is crucially related to the process of **Individualization**, a social process that imposes its imperatives on individuals, but which also provides the context by which individuals can fashion their lives. What Giddens (1991) calls 'the reflexive project of the self' requires the individual to sustain a coherent, but continuously revised narrative of the self in the context of multiple choices. Self-identity is the self as reflexively understood by the person in terms of his or her life story (see **Sexual stories**). The more traditional values and structures weaken, and the more life is reshaped by the interplay of the local and the global, the more individuals are also forced to negotiate their ways of life, in the process creating new patterns of **Intimacy**. Even **Bodies** are not immune from the dialogue with the self as what Connell (2009) calls body-reflexive practices shape and reshape the gendered body. Late-modern individuals have no choice but to choose – their lifestyles, relationships, their sexualities and embodied identities. Individuals are forced reflexively to organize and calculate the pros and cons of their future action, and that can bring huge new opportunities for developing a strong sense of self, but may also generate a sense of insecurity and isolation and the loneliness of moral choice. The choice biography is essentially a risk biography.

Sexuality is a critical domain of reflexivity because it has a central symbolic role in late-modern cultures. The erotic can be the basis of pleasure, self-fulfilment and intimacy, but it is also a source of meaning: as other traditional bulwarks of the self seem to crumble, sexuality often becomes the glue that holds relationships together and offers an anchor against drift. Sexuality is also a key to modern identity formation – see **Sexual identities** – and a domain of **Choice**. Most people, of course, do not feel they can choose their sexual desires, which seem to be theirs by instinct or wired into the genes. More crucially, this freedom to choose is always constrained, and limited. Is it a genuine freedom when you are forced to be a free agent? The reality is that choice is always limited by the same social forces that have made it available. Nor is choice without its dangers – of violence, disease, anxiety, uncertainty.

Some critics have seen in this theory of a reflexive, choosing, self-making self an ideal subject of **Neoliberalism** (Adkins 2002), able to fit nicely into a free-market world of autonomous individuals governing themselves believing themselves to be free, making their own choices, whilst actually conforming to wider cultural imperatives. Perhaps a more fundamental problem is whether the reflexive project of the self accurately describes the ways in which most people live in the contemporary world. The theory tends to play down the ways in which individuality is lived in specific social worlds, which generate their own loyalties and commitments. From this perspective moral choices may not be lonely: they have their own social context and significance – see **Relationality**. This points to a major criticism of theories of reflexive modernity. There is an acute danger that the reflexive self in this sociological approach is akin to a universal subject of late-modernity, and in the process the class, gender and racial differences that shape everyday life are largely ignored. To put it bluntly, the reflexive self has been seen as an ideal type of the Western, white, middle-class male.

This goes too far. At the heart of the idea of reflexivity is an important emphasis on the active **Agency** of contemporary individuals in shaping both their sense of self and practice in the world. It is right to stress that agency is never totally free, and that there are limits to the free play of self-making and social experimentation. On the other hand, against the settled pessimism of so much contemporary theory it is important to recognize that individuals are not passive in the face of social change. Reflexive self-awareness is a critical aspect of everyday practice. The stories we tell each other about who we are, and how we want to live, become active agents in remaking the self and reshaping the world.

REGULATION

All societies regulate sexuality. It is the very process of regulation that produces what is culturally defined as sexual – norms, values, institutions, laws, domestic arrangements, and the demarcation of what is acceptable or unacceptable, moral or immoral, healthy or diseased. Each culture makes 'who restrictions', concerned with the gender of the partners, the species, age, kin, race, caste or class which limit whom we may take as partners; and 'how restrictions', which are concerned with the organs that we use, the orifices we may enter, the manner of sexual involvement and sexual intercourse: what we may touch, when we may touch, with what frequency, and so on (Plummer 1984). These regulations take many forms: formal and informal, legal and extra-legal. They derive from family and kinship patterns, economic and social organization, **Religion**, the role of the state and sub-state organs, the political balance of power at particular moments, the impact of ideologies and belief systems, social movements and cultures of resistance (Weeks 2009a: 23–31). Many of these in the past have been shaped at national level, but increasingly international or transnational structures are shaping a global discourse with incalculable effects. International organizations such as the IMF and World Bank impose polices that may have dramatic effects on intimate life. Global religious organizations like the Roman Catholic Church shape policies towards abortion and birth control. Transnational bodies like the European Union and other European institutions such as the Court of Human Rights are increasingly involved in shaping sexuality. The United Nations has intervened in relation to the role of women and children, and less successfully on homosexuality.

These forces of regulation tend to apply in highly differentiated ways to different elements of society. Historically, different patterns of regulation have applied to men and women, shaped in ways which subordinate women's sexuality to men's. There are different rules for adults and children. Unorthodox sexualities elicit a range of different (and often highly discriminatory and violent) responses. There may be forms of regulation (for example, over **Marriage**) that affect the majority more favourably than racial, ethnic or sexual minorities, or, as was the case in Apartheid South Africa, favour the minority over the majority populations. Even within one national space there may be a variety of differentiated **Sexual cultures**. Contrariwise, many sexual cultures cut across national, political and geographical boundaries. The rules are often more acceptable as abstract norms than as practical guides. But they provide the permissions, prohibitions, limits and possibilities through which erotic life is **Socially constructed**.

Societies, in their urge to regulate, organize and control sexuality, have adopted various strategies, which may in fact uneasily coexist within one society, remnants of battles long fought, or re-kindled, about how people should live their sexual lives. Historically, we are heirs of the absolutist tradition. This has been based on a fundamental belief that the disruptive powers of sex can only be controlled by a clear-cut morality, derived from religious injunctions and codes, and intricately embedded in key social institutions: marriage, **Heterosexuality**, family life and (at least in the Judaeo-Christian traditions) monogamy. This absolutist morality is deeply rooted in the Christian West and in the Islamic East, and has shaped the general culture, and forms of legal regulation. The major set of legal changes in countries like Britain and the USA in the last decades of the nineteenth century and the early part of the twentieth century (on obscenity, prostitution, age of consent, homosexuality, incest) were pushed for by absolutist social morality movements, propelled in many cases by a religious fervour, and frequently in alliance with moral feminism. Countries like France and other countries under the aegis of the Napoleonic Code may have tempered moral authoritarianism in legal codes (such as by decriminalizing homosexuality) but remained strongly wedded to absolutist patriarchal values in relation to family and inheritance. Since the 1970s there has been a significant revival of absolutist positions allied both to the political rise of a religious conservatism in the USA and to the wave of **Fundamentalism** across the globe.

Like the absolutist approach, the libertarian tradition embraces various strands of belief. It can be found as much on the political right as on the political left. One important element has a surprising affinity, in its fundamental assumptions about what sex is, to moral absolutism. A major literary tradition, from the Marquis de Sade through the 'decadents' of the late nineteenth century to twentieth-century writers such as Georges Bataille and Jean Genet, celebrate sex as danger and transgression. Like the Christian absolutists they appear to see sexuality as threatening the self, society and even the universe. Unlike the absolutists they believe it should.

Another libertarian strand holds that sexual liberation is a (perhaps *the*) key to social freedom, a disruptive energy that can help break the existing order. The difference is that these libertarians believe that sex is fundamentally good and healthy, a force blocked only by the power of 'civilization' or capitalism. Wilhelm Reich and Herbert Marcuse are the classic theorists, and they had an enormous influence in the developing sexual politics of the late 1960s. It is on the opposite side of the political spectrum from a third strand of libertarianism, which has grown in significance since the 1970s, a right-wing libertarianism linked to an absolutist individualism. If, as many right-wing theorists argue, the state and its colonizing agenda is the real enemy of individual freedom, then the less the weight of prohibitions and restrictions on individual action the better. Hence an agenda which is willing to deregulate hitherto tabooed sexual behaviour, as well as other forms of tabooed behaviour, such as illicit drug use.

The problem with the absolutist and libertarian traditions is that they lean towards **Essentialism**. Sexuality is seen not only as a powerful energy which is outside and opposed to society, but also, because of this, a natural force which appears to embody its own morality. Values and theoretical assumptions about the nature of sex are closely related. In this sense, libertarianism and absolutism are mirror-images of one another: both are committed to a view of sexuality which transcends the bounds of history.

In practice, the regulation of sexuality in most late-modern societies has increasingly shifted away from legal moralism, whilst avoiding the dangers of an anything-goes libertarianism, and has been increasingly shaped by varying forms of the liberal tradition in which the role of the state and law is to hold the ring for private decisions. In the United States the central organizing idea has been that of 'rights', including the right to privacy. In the debates over **Abortion** each side uses the language of fundamental rights, the rights of the unborn child versus the rights of the mother to exercise control over her body. As this illustrates, to speak of rights does not end the discussion. We are still left with the problem of which person's rights are paramount in what specific situation, and whose rights are taken up can often be a clearly political rather than an a priori moral issue. In the case of abortion there are conflicting values at play, and the state and law finds itself battered by conflicting forces. In Britain, where the idea of rights is less institutionalized, the liberal tradition has developed more pragmatically. It was most famously articulated in the Wolfenden Committee report on prostitution and male homosexuality, published in 1957 (Wolfenden 1957). It was, it argued, the duty of the law to regulate the public sphere, and in particular to maintain public decency. There were limits, however, in its obligation to control the private sphere, the traditional arena of personal morality. Churches might strive to tell people what to do in their private lives. It was not the task of the state to attempt to do the same. The state, therefore, had no place in the enforcement of private standards. In such an approach there was a tacit acceptance that society was no longer – if it ever had been – governed by a moral consensus, and that there was in practice a plurality of alternative moral views abroad. The law should therefore limit its role to the maintenance of common standards of public decency, and only intervene in private life to prevent harm.

This leaves open the questions of what the contents of those 'common standards' are at any particular time, and what is meant by 'harm'. Implicit was a recognition that attitudes change over time in relation to both public and private life, and that the law would necessarily need to evolve too. Within liberal societies we can in fact see two characteristic developments. The first is towards forms of **Neoliberalism**, through which, it has been argued, ideas of individual autonomy and responsibilization, at the heart of liberal discourse, become the very means by which forms of regulation can most readily fit with the requirements of advanced capitalism. The second development is towards a welfarist/protectionist regulatory form in which the state intervenes ever more actively to promote rights and prevent harm. The difficulty here is in defining whose rights and what harm. Protecting children may be universally accepted (but what is a child? At what age should they be able to consent to sexual activity?) but how do we balance the rights of sex workers against those who wish to prohibit **Prostitution**? There are no obvious solutions to such dilemmas in liberal discourse itself.

The limitations of the liberal position have led to the theorization of a radical pluralist approach (Weeks 1995). Radical pluralism begins with an assumption that sexuality in itself is neither good nor bad, but is rather a field of possibilities and potentialities, all of which must be judged by the context in which they occur. It opens the way then, to acceptance of diversity as the *norm* of contemporary cultures and the appropriate means of thinking about sexuality. At the same time it recognizes the multiple ways in which sexuality is entangled in and defined by various forms of power. This does not, of course, still all difficulties: in many ways, in fact, it compounds them. It is far easier to confront each difficult area of choice with a moral code which tells us exactly, and invariably, how we should live. In a social climate of rapid social – and moral – change, and of the emergence of new social possibilities, identities and lifestyles, it is a temptation to seek once again the security of absolute moral standards, which fixes us in a world of certainty where personal and social identities are given. The radical pluralist approach, in sharp distinction to the absolutist tradition, is tentative, provisional, open-ended and alive to contingency. It can be seen as partaking of some of the elements of the libertarian tradition – especially what may be called its 'sex-positive' attitudes – while at the same time it shares with the liberal tradition a recognition of the need for careful distinctions, for a grasp of meaning and context, and of the importance of the discourse of rights and choice. Where it differs from both these traditions is in its decisive recognition of the social production of sexualities, and their complex embeddedness in diverse power relations. Its aim, consequently, is to provide guidelines for decision making rather than new absolute values. It rejects the temptation of a 'radical morality'. Instead it places its emphasis on the merits of dialogue and **Choice**, and the conditions which limit choice.

RELATIONALITY

The concept of relationality, together with closely linked terms such as related-ness and relationism, is an attempt by social scientists to grasp the density and intricacy of contemporary relationships, particularly in Western, late-modern societies. It seeks to go beyond the limitations of traditional ideas of kinship, usually rooted in universalistic assumptions about the significance of blood relatedness, and at the same time to demonstrate the inadequacies of current theories of **Individualization**, which tend to exaggerate the erosion of significant bonds (Smart 2007: 46–9). The essential insight is that subjectivity, individuality and identity are not the products of bounded individuals, acting in isolation, nor are they dictated by rigid rules of kinship rooted in the natural: they are constituted within, through and by complex, culturally variable social relationships, in changing historical circumstances. The reality of everyday lives is not atomized individuality but connectedness.

Anthropologists have long been concerned with the significance of kinship in shaping family systems, individual and social identities, and gendered and sexual meanings. The incest taboo at the heart of kinship, prohibiting sexual activity within certain degrees of blood relationships, especially between parents and children and siblings, has been seen as a universal law, marking the passage from a state of nature to human society. For Freud the myth of Oedipus – who unknowingly killed his father, then married his mother, and had to pay the dire consequences of breaking the law – expressed a fundamental truth both about the painful necessities of human society and of individual subjectivity. Yet there is plentiful evidence that forms of this ostensibly universal taboo have varied enormously. The incest taboo might indicate the needs of all cultures to regulate sexuality, but not how it is done. Even blood relationships, it is now generally agreed, have to be interpreted through the grid of culture (Weeks 2009a: 23–4). Anthropologists have increasingly recognized that kin ties are not natural links based in biology, but are social relations between groups, often based on residential links and hostile to genetic affinities (Sahlins 1976: 75). They have increasingly stressed that it is less the formal structures of kinship that are crucial than the shifting patterns of relatedness (Carsten 2004). Close on-going relationships are indeed fundamental to the constitution of a sense of personhood, but the forms of those relationships need not be biological or genetic. Anthropological and sociological studies, for example, have recently shown the significance of elective kin in shaping non-heterosexual relationships, and these are today part of a wider phenomenon of 'families of choice' that go beyond lesbian and gay lives (Weston 1991; Weeks *et al.* 2001) – see **Families**. Relationality also directs us to other forms of relationship besides those of the dyadic couple or children – towards relations between siblings for example (Mauthner 2005), or the significance of **Friendship**. As intensely social creatures rather than isolated monads we both make and are made by the bonds of relationships, often the result of active **Agency**, and many of which we choose.

The concept of relationality, therefore, 'takes as its starting point what matters to people and how their lives unfold in specific contexts and places' (Smart 2007: 47). Such a position is a valuable antidote to those cultural conservatives of both right and left who lament the decline of the family and the breakdown of **Community**, with individuals apparently thrown back on their individual resources. Against this, theorists of relationality stress the incessant sociality of human beings, constantly inventing and reinventing forms of relating that work for them. Family is what we do rather than a fixed institution we either belong to or feel excluded from, and we live and do family-type things – loving, caring, living together or apart – in various ways. From this perspective there is no reason to exclude non-heterosexual or any other conventionally unorthodox form of relationship from legitimacy and **Recognition**, and whether such relationships are called family, kin or friendship networks is neither here nor there. What matters are the realities of mutual support.

The standard criticism of such arguments is that these fluid and pluralist everyday relationships lack the sense of commitment and obligation that were at the core of traditional kin and family patterns. Two major studies of the meanings of kin and family responsibilities in Britain (Finch 1989; Finch and Mason 1993) have demonstrated both the continuing strength of genealogical links, and the constantly negotiated nature of day-to-day relationships. The blood kin does indeed have a reality in most people's lives, providing a minimum safety net, especially in crises. On the other hand while people have a strong sense of obligation and duty towards dependent children, and have a sense of the 'right thing to do' in relations with adults, they generally operate pragmatically in day-to-day interactions. Commitments have to be worked out through negotiations between consenting adults not assumed or simply based on lineage. Responsibilities are created rather than flowing automatically from specific ties of blood. The resulting commitments are not, however, any less strong than more traditional obligations and duties. On the contrary, because they are freely negotiated they have the potential to be more resilient and adaptable in shaping the reciprocal responsibilities of everyday life.

The reality is less of an atomized and anomic population than of strong and evolving patterns of reciprocity, care and cultures of intimacy in everyday life. These vary across class and are shaped by differences of ethnicity and race. They are affected by economic advantage and disadvantage, and are bisected by continuing and divisive inequalities. The values remain highly gendered, with women still taking on the majority of caring responsibilities, especially with regard to children. We are not talking about pastoral or utopian relationships, but about constant, often conflict-ridden, negotiation about the needs of everyday life. Yet across the diversities of late-modern societies, people continue to strive to make relations work. Far from seeing the erosion of **Social capital**, as cultural pessimists argue, contemporary forms of relating give rise to new social and cultural resources.

All this suggests that while individualizing trends are strong, people are still firmly committed to relational values. They remain energetic moral actors, embedded in webs of personal relationships, working to sustain the commitments that matter to them (Weeks 2007: 171–8). People may not express grand ethical schemes but live by highly contextualized, practical values, concerned with the appropriate thing to do. It is an ethic based on interdependence, in which mutual care is a key, defining element. Individual autonomy, the capacity for self-determination, appears to be a vital strand of everyday common-sense values, but it is exercised in and through our involvement with and commitment to others. This appears to be the key feature of contemporary relationality.

RELIGION

Since the European Enlightenment in the eighteenth century many have dreamt that religion would decline under the impact of reason, science and the progress of humanity. None of the giants of social science of the late nineteenth century – Marx, Durkheim and Weber – were believers, and they believed the power of religion would wane. Marx famously proclaimed that religion was the opium of the masses, and while Weber and Durkheim believed religion had key social and historical functions, neither expected it could survive modernity and the 'disenchantment of the world'. Nietzsche believed God was dead, and every value was up for grabs, while Freud saw religion as a response to infantile needs, and would disappear as the fruits of knowledge were more widely dispersed. The challenge to religious dominance reached a disastrous failure in attempts by *soi-disant* Communist regimes to abolish religion as best they could, and create new forms of humanity. More realistically, scepticism about religious claims, allied with rapid social and economic development, led to the widespread **Secularization** of modernizing societies in the West. If God was not quite dead, He seemed to be increasingly confined to special niches.

156

But the surprising feature of the late twentieth and early twenty-first centuries is that faith has made a comeback in a big way. Religion is at the heart of cultural clashes and political divides from the USA to India, taking in large parts of Latin America, Africa, the Middle East and large chunks of Asia. The old monotheistic faiths of Christianity and Islam are in fierce competition in Africa; are vigorously, if separately, growing in different parts of China; while Islam has become a major and sometimes contentious presence in European urban centres. Religion also fuels the rise of various forms of **Fundamentalism** across the globe. Secularization is not dead – it has a vigorous and expanding life in many parts of the world – but its triumph is no longer assured, for 'God is back', as recently affirmed by two prominent journalists (Micklethwait and Wooldridge 2009). And sexuality is at the heart of this apparent religious revival on a worldwide scale.

All religious systems have in one way or another always been preoccupied with bodies and their unpredictable desires. Religions take various forms, ranging from polytheisms to monotheisms and many that have no concept of gods though a key sense of the divine or transcendence. There is no consistency in dogma, ethics or attitudes towards sexuality. But what all religions tend to have is an array of beliefs, rituals and celebrations that affirm the community of the faithful and firmly differentiate the group from others. Religion thus generally asserts a group identity and various rites of passage confirm membership and belonging, often marking key sexual moments: births, puberty and transitions to adulthood and weddings especially.

Some religions, like Judaism are highly prescriptive and proscriptive about family, gender and sexual ethics. Others rely on self-discipline and meditation: the pursuit of Nirvana in the Buddhist tradition is based on the renunciation of desire. Other faiths are more lyrical, if only in a very specific fashion: one expert has written of the 'radical legitimacy of the practice of sexuality in the Islamic world', as long as it was not homosexual – 'violently condemned' by Islam – or involved extra-marital sex by a woman, who even in the twenty-first century may be stoned to death in certain militantly Muslim countries (Bouhdiba 1985: 159, 200). In the mainstream Christian traditions there has been a deep suspicion of the body, and until comparatively recently a legitimization of sexuality only when linked to reproduction. Canon law in the Middle Ages developed a list of sexual sins which put masturbation, sodomy – anal intercourse between men or sex between humans and beasts – below rape, because at least rape could lead to conception. Only from the sixteenth century do we see a new eroticism entering the conjugal relationship, largely at first within Protestant groups, but this often led to an intensification of taboos against non-marital, and non-heterosexual sex (MacCulloch 2009).

Even as laws against sexual misbehaviour began to move out of the hands of the Church into that of the state from the early modern period they continued to carry the connotation of sin as well as crime. Sodomy, too awful to be named amongst Christians, according to an English jurist in the seventeenth century, remained both into the nineteenth century, and only in the twentieth century did religion and the law gradually separate. It was the early twentieth century before incest became a

157

statutory crime in English law, while birth control and divorce, like abortion, remained entangled in religious beliefs until the late twentieth century across Europe, the most secularized part of the world.

Faith systems work to confirm orthodoxy and guard against transgression. This has generally involved the subordination of women within the faith and the punishment of homosexuality. Religions like Islam, Judaism and Christianity tend to proclaim the radical equality of women within their faiths, and there have indeed been highly respected female figures in their traditions and iconography. But practices are more complex and contradictory. Muslim men in the twenty-first century are allowed four wives under sharia law, a wife one husband. Men are allowed to marry outside the faith, women can only marry into the faith. In Islam and Orthodox Judaism, segregation of worship is still normal. Women are respected, but overwhelmingly in their domestic roles as mother and wife. In the Christian churches women's admission to the priesthood has been a hazardous journey. The Roman Catholic Church formally declared women ineligible for the priesthood as late as 1977, but it has become an article of faith rather than simply a matter of discipline and tradition. In the Church of England the issues of the ordination of women and then of women bishops have proved deeply divisive.

But it is not just women's formal role within faiths that evoke a sense of crisis. The ultimate issue is that of women's sexual autonomy. The re-imposition of the veil on women in orthodox or radical Islamic countries such as Saudi Arabia, Iran or Taleban-controlled Afghanistan marks an often violent rejection of the contemporary world, and the effect it has had on women (ironically, the adoption of the veil by Muslim women in West European countries is often justified as a mark of their autonomy, a breakaway from the sexualizing influences of Western culture).

If women's sexuality is a continuing problem for many faiths, the emergence of new sexual subjectivities, especially affirmative lesbian and gay identities, has proved virtually impossible to cope with. Homosexuality has always coexisted, albeit uneasily, with various religious systems. The existence of taboos and often draconian penalties against it is a testimony to its continuing vigour. Islamic countries in North Africa famously combined religious traditions and forms of homosexual activity amongst men that were tacitly tolerated as long as they did not impinge on a man's gender identity. In England, the Anglican priesthood in the late nineteenth and twentieth centuries were well known to be full of gay men. Yet the question of homosexuality and religion has proved to be especially fraught. Both the Episcopalian Church in the USA and the Church of England have reached the verge of schism over gay priests and bishops (Bates 2004). This is in large part because LGBT members of those churches are no longer prepared to accept discretion as the price of acceptance in the Church. Since the 1970s various movements have arisen in and outside the Christian churches of North America, Western Europe and elsewhere to affirm the faith of LGBT Christians. Similar groupings have emerged amongst gay Muslims and Jews. At the same time, the great expansion of more evangelical or militant forms of religion across all the major faiths has regularly focused on anti-homosexual themes to mobilize the faithful, and redraw the boundaries around the true faith, whatever it may be. In the West this has produced appalling problems for the Catholic Church as it has proclaimed its hatred of the (homosexual) sin, if love for the sinner, at the same time as it has had to cope with its own manifest sins in the explosion of accusations of child sex abuse by priests across the various continents. For many this smacks of a hypocrisy at the heart of a universalistic ambition. In parts of the Islamic world hostility to sexual aberrations has taken a more violent turn as men have been murdered for homosexual activities.

Post-Enlightenment thinkers looked forward to modernity eliminating the need for religion. Micklethwait and Wooldridge (2009) have seen the return of God as the Americanization of religion (paradoxically, given the anti American fervour of much religious militancy in the Middle East and elsewhere). America in its history has demonstrated that religion and modernity can march together. By the late twentieth and early twenty-first centuries modernity and religion had become allies across the globe as many religious groupings, whether the born-again Christians of the USA or the Shi'ite radicals of Iran, or the Hindu militants of India, or the house Christians of China, deployed the most modern technologies to mobilize the masses (Bhatt 1997). Millions of people were drawn to the faiths, in part as a haven from the insecurities and ambiguities of a rapidly transforming world. Affirmation of traditional values, and the certainties of family, gender difference and sexual conformity, offered a badge of belonging. It has proved a potent force, largely for conservative moral and political ends.

Does it suggest the end of the hopes of a secular world? Many of the new religious certainly hope so as they fervently proclaim their truths. But the nature of the late-modern return of religion points to a different conclusion: it may be turbo-charged by anxiety and fear of change, it may proclaim to know the secrets of the good or moral life, it may believe in its own ultimate truth, but it has not led to a universalizing system of beliefs but rather a proliferation of faiths, a free market in religion. Many religious groups may seek moral hegemony, but regularly proclaim their vulnerability, and embattlement, minorities alongside other religious and non-religious minorities. The paradox of the return of God is that it is occurring in an irredeemably plural world, whose very diversity both feeds and ultimately limits the power of religion.

REPRODUCTIVE TECHNOLOGIES

Reproductive technologies refer to the growing array of scientific and medical interventions to control fertility, to combat infertility and to generate new life. The technologies include a range of birth control devices, including the familiar condom, the contraceptive pill, patches, injections, implants, intrauterine devices (IUDs) and sterilization (including female tubal ligations and male vasectomies). Fertility treatments for men and women attempt to make up for where nature may have failed, or when ill-health or accidents prevent successful pregnancy, and include various treatments against male impotency (see **Viagra**). Various techniques to create new life includes donor and self-insemination, *in vitro* fertilization (IVF), producing so-called 'test-tube babies', and surrogacy, where a woman agrees to deliver a baby for someone else, sometimes altruistically, often for payment; she may be the genetic mother or a carrier following the implantation of an embryo. Much of this was made possible by growing knowledge of the body, its physiology, hormonal and above all genetic make-up. The genetic revolution has opened up the possibility of genetic screening, embryological manipulation and of human cloning. In doing so it has created vast new opportunities for human control of the body and life processes. It also opens up challenging questions about who regulates and controls the new technologies.

For millennia the central issue, especially for women, was how to control births. A host of traditional methods, including prolonged lactation of children, which it was widely accepted would delay further pregnancies, were supplemented by **Abortion**, and early barrier methods. The campaigns for birth control (a term invented by the American feminist Margaret Sanger before World War I) were long and hard in most Western countries, and often unresolved in other parts of the world. The Roman Catholic Church continues to oppose artificial birth control globally (and refuses to support the use of condoms even as protection against sexually transmitted infections on the grounds that their secondary effect is to prevent births). But since the 1950s technological breakthroughs and their mass marketing globally have transformed the ways in which conception has been controlled, especially with the widespread use of the Pill and related hormonal controls, and more effective IUDS. The use of the Pill has been widely seen as a major factor in the sexual liberation of women. The history is rather more complicated than that (Weeks 2007). Women in many Western countries were already dramatically limiting family sizes before the new technologies. The new birth control technologies were, however, more effective and largely safer (though the Pill generated a number of health scares, and various other chemical treatments had to be withdrawn from the market because of dangerous side-effects). They also put greater control of their reproductive capacities into the hands of women, and have provided a vital symbol as well as practical support of female autonomy.

If birth control techniques are historically deeply rooted, efforts to create new life were until recently the subject of utopian dreams or dystopian fears rather than scientific possibility. When the early second-wave feminist Shulamith Firestone (1971) looked forward to conception without heterosexual copulation few thought this was little more than a radical feminist fantasy. Barely a generation later its reality is deeply reshaping reproductive possibilities. There is a deep paradox here, because at the same time as Western women, the main beneficiaries of the technological breakthroughs, are delaying and concentrating child birth, or avoiding it altogether, the new reproductive technologies to create life are in high demand. Whether through infertility, the hopes of lesbians and gay men to parent, or the choice of older women, even into their sixties, to conceive, new possibilities have produced a vast new medical industry, and in the case of grassroots self-insemination, especially by lesbians, a sort of flourishing cottage industry (Saffron 1994). What started through IVF as a medical aid to help the infertile has become a multibillion dollar industry chasing a huge demand for different ways of making a baby. It was estimated in early 2006 that there were one million customers and $36 billion revenue in the United States alone, with the costs of top quality eggs, from highly educated women, reaching around $50,000, and surrogate mothers charging up to $59,000. It is hardly surprising this quickly became a global market. Guatemala generated around $50 million per annum by exporting babies at around $25,000 a time. Denmark became the world's largest exporter of sperm. And if this should ever run out, now artificial sperm has been produced to fertilize mouse eggs, and promises eventually to end male infertility.

The United States has become the global centre for fertility treatment because there the industry remains largely unregulated. Other jurisdictions have a variety of differing regulations. Britain anguished over the implications of this revolution probably longer than any other society, and established ethical standards and acceptable practices through the Human Fertilization and Embryology Authority. But the explosion of technological possibilities is in danger of outstripping the cautious utilitarianism of the approach (Weeks 2007: 156–7). What rights does a woman have to use the frozen sperm of a long-dead husband? How can you regulate gay men fathering children with a surrogate mother outside the UK? How do you control women over 60 using fertility treatment to conceive? What priority should health providers give to satisfying an exponentially growing demand for fertility treatment when there are abandoned babies in their millions across the globe? How, on the other hand, do you control the traffic in eggs and sperm as well as babies? Is there not a new spermatic economy developing where women are reduced to little more than wombs? Could the new technologies lead to a new violence against women and even gynocide? (Plummer 2003: 41–2). Above all there is the spectre of human cloning, and the possibility of breeding out not only harmful genes but also 'unwanted' types in a new form of eugenics (the baby with inherited genetic disabilities, the offspring of the 'underclass' or ethnic minorities, those feared to have the 'gay gene'). New dilemmas arise all the time, some of them all too painfully real, but all creating new potentialities of regulation and difficult decisions, by the state, by courts and by individuals. The Pill helped separate sex and reproduction. The new technologies go further, splitting repro-duction from blood kinship, with incalculable effects.

RISK

Sexuality has long been associated with risk: risks associated with conception and birth; with growing up, first sexual awakenings and finding an erotic identity; risks of pregnancy, of sexually transmitted diseases, of HIV and AIDS; risks of violence and abuse, and of discrimination and persecution for your sexual nature and choices; risks of love, relationships and loss. If sexuality in the contemporary world is in large part about living with uncertainty (Weeks 1995) – uncertainties of identity, beliefs, behaviours, values, health and well-being – then how to achieve a sense of security, and balance dangers and pleasures, desires and duty, opportunity and risk become paramount issues for individuals and societies.

We live today, the German sociologist Ulrich Beck has argued (1992, 1999), in a risk society, which is substantially different from earlier forms of society, and is becoming increasingly globalized. In the pre-modern world threats to individual and collective life were seen as beyond human control, the result of natural disasters, fate or the hand of God. Things happened to people, and they rode the waves as best they could. Modern societies have been concerned with exerting control over natural forces, imposing a rational ordering over the whims of nature. The result has been huge human advance. But contrary to the hopes of Enlightenment philosophers progress has not destroyed the irrational or eliminated threats of many kinds. On the contrary modernity has produced risks that no other type of society has had to face, including the possibility of the ending of life on Earth through nuclear or ecological disaster by manmade actions, or inactions. As society moves towards attempting to eliminate risk – and regularly failing to do so – risk becomes a key element in defining an era of 'reflexive modernization', a form of society where individuals are actively involved in interrogating themselves and others. Weighing risk becomes highly political. Societies strive to minimize risk, through public order, health provision, welfare systems, expert advice, but such forms of collective insurance are themselves often at risk (of ideological shifts, of changes in regulation, of financial cutbacks and simply of failure to manage risk), and do not remove the fears and anxiety generated in a risk society (Edwards and Glover 2001).

A heightened sense of insecurity and risk is associated with two interrelated transformations: the undermining of traditional ways of life, especially family forms and sexual mores, and the growth of **Individualization**. These changes have increased opportunities for new ways of life and greater personal freedom, but also bring new anxieties as people are disembedded from old securities and have to negotiate the hazards of everyday life without fixed guarantees. This can increase risk-taking, as in the pursuit of aimless sexual encounters, the weakening of a sense of responsibility to others, or the pursuit of extreme sexual pleasures. It can also make everyday decision-making more difficult, as social issues are individualized, seen as problems that need personal decisions and actions, and ethical guidelines are few and far between We can now control births, eliminate birth defects, manipulate the embryo, engineer life, artificially stimulate or dampen the libido; we have drugs to control, if not prevent, STIs, and prolong the life of people with HIV; we can transform gender, we can engage with each other globally, in the media and online. But we also have to calculate the hazards and contingencies, balance the pronouncements of doctors, sex experts, therapists, traditional moralists, parents, peers, in cyber-space and in embodied life, and make fundamental decisions about how we should live in a world of growing but fraught **Choice** and **Reflexivity**.

Taking charge of your life, making life-changing or life-confirming decisions, involves risk, because it means facing a host of open possibilities (Giddens 1991: 73). For this reason the reflexive biography is a risk biography. Risk is built into the very texture of the modern self. This position has been widely criticized as overtly individualistic, ignoring both the uneven impact of individualizing processes, and the complexity of power relationships on different social worlds (Elliott 2002). Whatever the merits of grand, generalizing theories about the nature of modernity or post- or late-modernity, in the multiple experiments in everyday living that most people engage in decisions about how to confront risk are not made in splendid isolation. They are shaped by local commitments, cultural norms and the sheer contingencies of everyday life in many different social worlds.

True as this may be, it does not in the end in any way weaken the perception that facing risk is an inescapable necessity in the contemporary world. As one interviewee on a research project on perceptions of risk put it, 'Risk is part of your life, that's part of the definition. It's always there – you can't walk anywhere without taking a risk' (Lupton and Tulloch 2002: 324). Nowhere are risks more acutely perceived today than in relation to sexuality. One reason why **AIDS** had such a cultural significance is that it dramatized the new risks emerging in a transformed sexual world. Here was an epidemic where the people most affected in the early stages of the crisis became heavily involved in organizing a response to it, in campaigning, care and support, promoting the adoption of **Safer sex**, challenging expert opinion, treatment activism and embracing new therapies. The epidemic epitomized the risk environment, and the reflexive response to it. It crystallized the uncertainties inherent in contemporary sexualities.

S

SADO-MASOCHISM

Sado-masochism emerged as a sexual category in the late nineteenth century and was a key concept in the new **Sexology** of the period. Richard von Krafft-Ebing first defined it in the 1886 edition of his *Psychopathia Sexualis*, and the term itself was based on the names of two infamous literary figures, the Marquis de Sade and Leopold von Sacher-Masoch, the one representing a desire to inflict pain and humiliation in the interests of sexual pleasure, and the other to experience it. From the start, however, there was an ambivalence about how pathological these sexual practices were. For the sexological tradition sado-masochism was clearly a **Perversion**, but its roots lay in an exaggeration of the normal relations intrinsic between men and women. Krafft-Ebing saw sadism as 'nothing else than excessive and monstrous pathological intensification of phenomena – possible too in normal conditions, in rudimental forms – which accompany the psychical sexual life, particularly in males' (Weinberg and Levi Kamel 1983: 27). Freud, paying due homage to Krafft-Ebing's coinage, saw it in his *Three Essays* as a 'sexual aberration', but believed it occupied a special position amongst the perversions because the contrast between activity and passivity that underlay it was amongst the universal characteristics of sexual life. Krafft-Ebing himself had recognized that a pathologized description of this sexual practice was insufficient. One of his early case studies, from whom he apparently learnt a great deal in an ongoing dialogue, was an articulate advocate of sado-masochism (Oosterhuis 2000). The clinical definition, which remained influential for a long time in psychology and psychiatry, was from the start, ironically, shaped by sado-masochists themselves.

Since these pioneers, there have been various attempts to articulate sado-masochism as a benign sexual variation and **Choice**. Increasingly since the 1970s, consensual sado-masochism has become the basis of a viable personal and collective **Sexual identity**, with associated networks, communities and subcultures, especially though not exclusively associated with the lesbian and gay world, focused on the eroticization of power relations. As an early lesbian advocate put it: 'we select the most frightening, disgusting or unacceptable activities and transmute them into pleasure' (Califia 1979: 19). Alongside this the pathologizing echoes of the term 'sado-masochism' have been increasingly rejected. Preferred descriptions have included SM, s/m or s&m. More recently some practitioners have adopted the hybrid BDSM as a self-description, made up of B&D (bondage and discipline), D/s (dominance and submission) and S&M (sadism and masochism), embracing the key aspects of the practice. It is a catch-all label for a range of activities, including 'all sexual identities and practices involving pain play, bondage, dominance and submission and erotic power exchange' (Langridge and Barker 2007: 6).

Not all practitioners would wish to see these activities as the basis for identity, nor would even those who go public on their activities and identities see them as necessarily radical or transgressive. It is simply an aspect of their sexual life. Yet for many advocates of BDSM from within the sexual cultures of the West, there is a larger agenda. Consensual BDSM, it is argued, provides unique insights into the nature of sexual power, therapeutic and cathartic sex, revealing the nature of sexuality as ritual and play. This has proved highly controversial. A lively controversy erupted in the 1980s between lesbian advocates of SM and their opponents in the USA that dramatized conflicts over the politics of female sexual pleasure (Samois 1981; Linden 1982), and the relationship between BDSM and wider sexual politics and culture has remained complex.

A wide range of sexual stories around SM have proliferated in recent years, and these stories are clearly expressing new needs and a wider sense of identification around once outlawed and execrated sexual activities. On one level there is no necessary link between the various possible practices, iconographies, uniforms, fetishisms (leather, rubber, etc.) and sexual pleasures that huddle under the general label. Sado-masochism is as arbitrary a sexual category as any other. But its growing public profile may also be seen as indicative of a wider shift: as a logical extension of severing the link between reproduction and sexuality, and the recognition, even celebration, of **Sexual diversity** which is a characteristic feature of the contemporary world. A study of the gay male BDSM world (Chaline 2010) has described an evolution over the past half-century from a secretive subculture, to the growth of open SM institutions, through a commercialization of the scene to a pluralistic world where the label covers a host of different erotic activities and identity practices. But this trajectory has a wider resonance for all SM practitioners. What was once seen as transgressive has become mainstreamed, opened up like all other aspects of the erotic to commercial exploitation and **Commodification**, and to the opportunities and challenges offered by the **Globalization** of sex and the ever-growing availability of **Cybersex**.

At the same time, SM in all its diversity remains a 'laboratory' where critical issues about the erotic can be explored (Beckmann 2009). What the radical advocates of consensual SM can do is pose very dramatically the question of where the limits of sexual experimentation and pleasure can be drawn. If pain, domination and submission, ritual and power play are not in themselves intrinsically wrong, and are all enacted in the context of informed choice, then we need to think again about the relationship between context and choice, subjectivity and consent in talking about sexuality. To what extent should people be able to consent to activities that are conventionally regarded as painful and potentially harmful? What are the conditions that make such choices valid? Such questions challenge us to reflect on limits of normality, the boundaries of valid sexual activity, and what are the extremes to which we can go in the pursuit of pleasure.

SAFER SEX

Safe or safer sex refers to the range of sexual practices adopted initially by gay men to avoid transmission of disease in the early days of the **AIDS** crisis, including avoiding exchange of bodily fluids, condom use and the exploration of various forms of non-penetrative eroticism. Beginning in the increasingly embattled gay communities in American cities, it rapidly spread to other gay communities across the world. In a period where governments turned their backs on the burgeoning epidemic, epidemiology of the epidemic was in its infancy, medical authorities had a range of speculative theories about causation (ranging from amyl nitrate to sexual overload and a blood-borne agent), and there was acute danger of **Moral panic** in society at large, the adoption of safe-sex techniques was a practical response from communities now at risk.

The notion of safe sex is not itself new. Sex workers had long been aware of the risks of unprotected sex, and sought various means to minimize risk. Men throughout the centuries have adopted a variety of primitive protectives, from rags to sheep bladders, until the invention of vulcanized rubber and hence the modern condom (regularly used more for the prevention of disease than against conception). What was distinctive about the new messages of safer sex in the gay communities of the USA in the 1980s was that it was a public and collective discourse that emerged directly from the people most at risk. It was pioneered by gay men to protect themselves and their loved ones, and to learn 'how to have sex in an epidemic' (Callen and Berkowitz 1983). As national agencies belatedly began to respond to the crisis, and in the absence of drug preventatives, effective treatment or a magic bullet cure, safe sex took on a different tone, basically about how the wider (that is, heterosexual) population could be protected from risk groups. But in the gay communities, still most at risk, the term retained its earlier sense. Safer sex was a means of negotiating sex and love, of building a respect for self and others, in a climate of ignorance and fear. It offered a way of recovering the erotic, based on the minimization, if not complete elimination, of risk, in relationships of mutual trust and responsibility (Weeks 1995: 181).

By the end of the 1980s it was estimated that the majority of gay men in leading urban centres in North America, Australasia and Western Europe were regularly using safe-sex techniques, resulting, according to leading epidemiologists, in 'the most profound modification of personal health-related behaviors ever recorded' (quoted in Halperin 2007: 18). Despite the duration of the crisis, and the advent of effective combination therapies, there is evidence that safer sex continues to be the norm in urban gay communities, even as many gay men revolt against what they see as its restrictions – see **Barebacking**. Ideas about what constitutes safe sex have, however, evolved considerably over thirty years as gay men continue to define and redefine the meanings of risk and the limits of safety in a process of continuing experimentation and mutual debate. In the richer countries gay men regulate their sexual practices pragmatically depending on context – whether with regular partners, or casual pickups, whether they are HIV-positive or negative – and in relation to prevailing community norms, and evolving medical knowledge (Kippax 2010: 188). Safer sex is reflexively negotiated by a community that has to an extraordinary degree been in the vanguard of debates about HIV and responses to it. In the process a subtle etiquette has evolved to ensure negotiated safety. A couple might, for instance, abandon protected sex between themselves, if both are HIV negative, but ensure protected sex if either had casual sex. There is still risk (condoms are only estimated to be at best 95 per cent safe) but it is minimized, assuming trust and honesty. Disclosure of status, once sharply tabooed even within the gay community, has become an important part of managing risk. Sero-concordance (that is, people of the same HIV status) has become a critical determining factor for many gay men in deciding whether or not to use safe-sex techniques. Other approaches to minimize risk include dispensing with condoms when a positive partner has an undetectable viral load, or ensuring that the positive partner always takes the receptor position in anal intercourse. None of these practices are 'safe' in the sense that risk has been eliminated. But they represent practical ways of reducing risk in a continuing epidemic.

None of these safe-sex techniques can succeed in isolation. They are predicated on wider community ties, complex webs of relationships, through which know-ledge is transmitted and personal and collective safer-sex strategies can evolve. Effective prevention strategies throughout the AIDS crisis have relied on com-munity mobilization, through which safer sex becomes part of community norms. What is striking about safer-sex practices is that they began as an emergency grassroots response to an overwhelming crisis, and have become rooted in gay community values, a testimony to the ways in which sexuality can be re-imagined through practical **Agency**.

SAME-SEX MARRIAGE

Historians and anthropologists have traced culturally approved and ritualistically embedded same-sex unions in a variety of historical settings, ranging from ancient China and Rome to various African cultures. Blessed by the Church, they existed both in Catholic Western Europe and in Orthodox Eastern Europe in early modern Europe, and even later, though their meanings remain obscured by the mists of history (Boswell 1994). They have, however, only become a central focus of lesbian and gay politics, and of public controversy, since the 1980s. This reflects major shifts in the discourses of sexuality and intimacy, not only in the West, where debates began, but much more broadly in a globalizing world. The idea of same-sex marriage has stimulated sharp and often divisive debates, not least amongst lesbians and gays themselves. Is same-sex marriage necessary because it will mark the full integration of lesbians and gays into society, as some gay conservatives argue? Or desirable because it mimics, undermines and transgresses the heterosexual institution, as some activists propose? Is it, as many **Queer** theorists polemicize, an accommodation to the existing order, an assimilation strategy which drains any challenge to the existing sexual order? Or is it simply the next logical step in the recognition of LGBT rights, a crucial move towards full **Sexual citizenship**, as many ordinary lesbians and gay couples might feel.

Whatever the controversies, recognition of same-sex marriage or civil partnerships has rapidly spread (Descoutures *et al.* 2008; Sexualities 2008). Since Denmark pioneered the legal recognition of same-sex unions in 1989, most West European countries have followed suit in one way or another, the majority since the millennium. By 2010 the countries that fully recognized same-sex marriage included Belgium, Canada, the Netherlands, Norway, Portugal, Spain, Sweden, South Africa and Argentina. The only major Western democracies without some legal recognition of same-sex unions, though falling short of marriage, were Italy, Greece and Australia and the United States as federal wholes, though five US states had legalized marriage, and others had enacted some form of recognition of domestic partnerships. In the United States, especially, same-sex marriage had become a major symbolic issue, and the target of fierce debate and divisions.

This has been a major and largely unexpected transformation. In the 1970s, with the rise of **Gay liberation** ideas across most Western countries, but particularly in the United States, no one, whether inside or outside the movement, raised the possibility of same-sex marriage. It seemed beyond the horizon of possibility, desirability and intelligibly in the context of fierce lesbian and gay critiques of the family and heterosexual marriage. But by the turn of the millennium it had become the key issue in the LGBT world, and a hot political issue more widely throughout Western democracies. The rise of same-sex marriage as an issue signals two important, intertwined changes: shifting priorities within the LGBT world itself, and changes within national cultures that were clearly liberalizing their attitudes and laws.

The change amongst lesbians and gays marks a significant move beyond the original 1970s preoccupation with issues of **Sexual identity** towards a concern with the nature and ethics of relationships. This can be seen, for example, in the rise of debates about 'families of choice' (Weston 1991), and in widespread discussion of lesbian and gay parenting. The concern with caring relationships was stimulated above all by the **AIDS** crisis amongst gay men, which had dramatized the absence of relationship rights, and a growing concern over parental rights, especially amongst lesbians, in a culture where gay parents were often denied parental rights on the break-up of previous heterosexual relationships. The felt need for same-sex relationship rights grew from the ground upwards, a genuine grassroots response to changing realities. This fed into an emerging discourse of

Human sexual rights, through which networks of LGBT activists committed to the recognition of 'love rights', and cross-national political elites, educated in new rights discourses, seized the initiative, even in the absence of high-profile campaigns (Kollman 2007).

Whatever the common patterns and underlying trends, however, each country has taken its own path, reflecting its own cultural bias and political balance. The same-sex unions legislation in France, commonly known as PACS, for instance, followed classic republican traditions by refusing to recognize the separate cultural identities of lesbians and gays (Johnston 2008). It allowed civil partnership arrangements for heterosexuals and homosexuals alike, and was clearly distinguished from marriage, whose legal status was not affected: no new legal entity was created, and no challenge was offered to the permanence of sexual difference (the 'symbolic order') or the legitimacy of kin relations ('filiation'). It was opposed by conservatives of left and right, but has bedded down as a normalized and widely accepted reform, favoured in fact more by heterosexuals than by LGBT people. In the Netherlands radical changes came about through an incrementalism which fitted in easily with the tradition of 'pillarization' that assumed the coexistence of different rights claims, and was committed to recognizing them. The legalization of same-sex civil partnerships and then of marriage in the early 2000s therefore seemed a logical next step in the Netherland's institutionalized liberalism (Waaldijk 2001).

The experience of the United Kingdom shows another variant. For a long time, it was classically hesitant in pursuing the legalization of same-sex partnerships – or indeed any liberalization of attitudes towards homosexuality. Yet within a very short period at the beginning of the new millennium a bundle of legal reforms belatedly modernized British sexual law, culminating in the Civil Partnership Act in 2004. The approach adopted bypassed many of the controversies which arose elsewhere. Instead of a principled debate about the merits of same-sex marriage, the UK simply reproduced civil marriage law wholesale but called it something else, thus avoiding much religious opposition. It was a classic case of 'liberalization by stealth', and a very British compromise (Weeks 2007).

It is the United States which has become the epicentre of controversy about the politics of same-sex marriage. As the most neoliberal of cultures, it has also produced the most fervent and fundamentalist opposition amongst Western democracies. As the society with the most affirmative LGBT identities and communities, it has produced both the most energetic campaigns for same-sex marriage and the most sustained critiques from the heart of those communities. Same-sex marriage, critics have argued, makes claims to racially constructed ideas of sexual respectability and the naturalization of a racially stratified welfare state (Brandzel 2005; Kandaswamy 2008). Given the heat of the debate it is surely relevant that the United States is also the most religious of Western societies. That largely explains the degree of opposition to same-sex marriage from conservative Christians. It might also help explain the fervour with which LGBT activists in the United States stand out for full recognition of same-sex marriage, compared to the more secular British or Scandinavians. Where religion is in decline, the LGBT population seems more likely to be satisfied with less than marriage, because marriage itself is less sanctified; where religious traditions remain strong, as in Spain and the USA, so it is likely to go for full marriage rights when same-sex unions are recognized.

Same-sex unions touch powerful chords in their national cultures which is why the strands of the current major preoccupation of the LGBT world have to be knitted into local languages. But at a deeper level what we see in the new stories about same-sex relationships is a common desire across cultures for equal relationship rights, and for a full **Recognition** of same-sex relationships. This is a vote for validation, not absorption, and for the ordinary virtues of care, love and mutual responsibility for which same-sex marriage has become a symbol.

SECULARIZATION

Secularization as a general process involves three interrelated processes. First, there is an emptying of God from the spaces of everyday life, so that the idea of the divine or transcendent no longer suffuses and gives meaning to all aspects of life. Second, it is associated with the decline of formal worship, so that fewer and fewer people formally acknowledge a superior being even if they hold to a vague religiosity. And third, it leads to the growth in what can be called a 'public secularity', a situation where 'Belief in God is no longer axiomatic. There are alternatives' (Taylor 2007: 3). The process of secularization has gone further in some countries (for example, Britain and Scandinavian countries, despite having national churches, and most other parts of Western Europe) than in others (especially the USA, despite a formal separation of church and state, and in vast tracks of the world where religion seems to be on the rise). But in those parts of the world where secularization has gone furthest religion has become privatized, the focus of personal belief rather than public policy, and, for the non-religious especially, attitudes and behaviour, apart from a vague sense of good and evil, have largely floated free of direct religious influence altogether.

Given the centrality of **Religion** to the definition of morality and the organization of sexual behaviour, its relative decline has had profound effects on the way sexuality is lived. There has been a progressive detachment of sexual values from religious values – even for many religious people. This has a long history, since at least the rise of humanism in the Renaissance, but a key moment in its development was the process, gathering strength from the mid-nineteenth century, whereby the initiative for judging sexuality passed from the churches to the agents of social and mental health, especially in the medical profession. Feminists in both Britain and the USA bitterly complained that doctors were becoming a new priesthood, especially in the ways they dealt with female sexuality, and this was accentuated by the growing prestige of expertise and science. The new **Sexology**, in the wake of post-Darwinian biological breakthroughs, and a new more rigorous psychology, especially after Freud, attempted to provide a new scientific patina to the under-standing of human sexuality. This has been an unfinished revolution in the sense that moral, medical and scientific matters remain inextricably linked. It is still easy to be simultaneously denounced as evil, immoral and sick if you offend against local norms. Nor, of course, have the religious given up their attempts to regulate sexual behaviour. The power, of, say, the Roman Catholic Church, to set the sexual agenda on birth control, **Abortion** and **Homosexuality**, remains immense across Western and non-Western countries. In the USA religious conservatives have achieved significant political power, and have shaped public responses to a wide range of sex-related activities, from abortion to sex education and **Same-sex marriage**. More widely, fundamentalist movements across the globe have put issues around sexuality, gender and the body at the heart of their agenda – see **Fundamentalism**.

Yet the fact that so many of these challenges focus on the secular nature of sexual change – 'secular liberalism' and 'secular humanism' have become potent terms of abuse – is a backhanded tribute to how far secularization has gone. Humanists might gripe at the continuing force of religious moralism, but churches in many European countries tend to complain that no one listens to them anymore, and they are in danger of becoming an embattled minority. And to a large extent the churches are right, in the sense that liberal democracies increasingly wish to ensure that church and state, faith and public morality, remain separate, whatever the role of religion in forming individual morality. Formal demarcations of what is right and proper, appropriate or inappropriate, have become increasingly the province of non-religious experts – in sexology, psychology, medicine, welfare services and social policy. Even in the most traditional of churches, such as the Roman Catholic, many of the faithful routinely ignore their leaders' teaching on birth control, homosexuality or celibacy. From America to Australia, Austria to Ireland, the Church hierarchy itself, under the most fiercely traditionalist of popes, has been devastated by accusations of paedophilia in the priesthood. Similarly, the puri-tanical moral codes of the Islamic kingdom of Saudi Arabia have not stopped its princes haunting the pleasure pots of Western Europe, while the young people of the Islamic Republic of Iran have begun their own sexual revolution within the absolutist codes propounded by their religious leaders (see Mahdavi 2009). It is also worth remembering that the new theocracies of the Islamic world may be resisting the whole thrust of modernity, but are doing so with the full panoply of late-modern technology which itself is contributing to the decline of the sacred.

Strong social and economic forces in the contemporary world are simultaneously propelling the dissolution of ancient religious verities, and also paradoxically generating militant religious movements in reaction. The new surge of expansive energy of world capitalism from the 1980s, linked to the wider process of **Globalization**, served to accelerate the dissolution of traditional structures, and to encourage the process of secularization. There is a great historical irony in this. Some of the most prominent proponents of 'setting the individual free' to exploit the new market forces (Margaret Thatcher in Britain, Ronald Reagan in the USA) were moral conservatives and social authoritarians with regard to personal life, even if they were not profoundly religious themselves. For such radical conservatives religion was a crucial support of social order. However, the very success of their economic ideologies served to fundamentally undermine their moral traditionalism. If you extol individual choice in economic matters, how can you resist the tide towards individual choice in matters concerning personal life? Ironically, some of the most prominent religious Right leaders in the USA, like Catholic priests, have been beset by sexual scandals, demonstrating at the every least that secular sexual values may have penetrated deeply into the heart of conservative religiosity.

A secular age does not proclaim an alternative moral framework to the ones that have dissolved. Secular humanism has a historical association with the wider process of secularization, but not all supporters of secularization are humanists. Some may indeed be personally religious. The main thrust of secularization has been to challenge the primacy of a single authority in saying how we should live, and to separate private action from social moralism. Its logic is to point to pluralism and to institutionalized **Toleration**. But, paradoxically, in the absence of any alternative world outlook to that of religion, sexuality itself has become an arena for thinking about personal destiny and belonging, and for personal transcendence. The effect has been to place on sexual relations themselves a greater burden of expectation than ever before. Whether they can or should carry such a weight of expectations is, at the every least, dubious.

SEX ADDICTION

Sex addiction is a characteristic product of late-twentieth-century blues that by the new century had become a major therapeutic industry, especially in the USA. Given publicity by the rush of celebrities faced by sexual scandals to specialized clinics for 'treatment', it became a handy alternative description for what in a less frenetic therapeutic culture used to be covered by such ill-defined but resonant terms as promiscuity, 'Don Juanism', priapism or nymphomania. These were moralistic or medico-moral words which carried heavy cultural condemnation. Sex addiction, contrariwise, suggests a personal problem that can be addressed by clinical treatment or finely tuned 12-step self-help programmes. It speaks of a post-traditional culture which is saturated by sexuality, but in which it is difficult to find widely acceptable norms of behaviour. Compulsive, apparently out-of-control sexual activity, whether with partners, casual pickups or prostitutes, with oneself through **Masturbation**, and/or by overindulgence in **Pornography** or obsession with **Cybersex**, is now seen not as a problem of morals or lack of self-discipline, but as an addiction (Carnes 2001).

Addiction itself is an ambivalent term. It has been widely used since the late nineteenth century to describe compulsive, patterned, repetitive indulgence in what John Stuart Mill described as 'bad habits', usually alcohol or drugs. Debate has raged at various times over whether it marks a physical pathology, a chemical imbalance or a psychological state, but the common assumption is that it is beyond an act of individual will to control. The individual is trapped in a state of utter enslavement to whatever the object of the addiction is. The search for the high, the escape from the self or everyday reality is followed by satiation, release, shame or remorse, and the relentless repetitive pursuit of a new fix. He or she has lost control of the present, and has surrendered options for the future. The invention of the concept has been seen as a form of social regulation in a culture which could no longer rely on traditional forms of control to shape individual behaviour (Giddens 1992). It displaces concerns about the morality of certain types of extreme behaviour, traditionally condemned as breaches of communal norms, and replaces them with a medicalized and individualized condition, with all the varied and attendant possibilities of intervention that that might apply.

One of the interesting features of the category of sex addiction is that it arose just as older medicalized categories of sexual behaviour – **Homosexuality** most notably – began to disappear from the diagnostic registers. As societies apparently became more tolerant of certain sexual practices and ways of life, and stressed the importance of autonomy and choice, they became more concerned with patterns of behaviour that seemed beyond choice, that undermined genuine autonomy. Sex addiction was a label readily thrown at gay men with multiple partners in the wake of the **AIDS** crisis, though the majority of people seeking professional help appear to be heterosexual men. Undoubtedly, there have been many casualties of greater sexual freedom, the transformation of gender relations and of personal life, and many who feel they need help to regain control of their sexual lives – the thousands who attend clinics or are members of groups such as Sexaholics Anonymous, Sex Addicts Anonymous and Sex and Love Addicts Anonymous (the echo with Alcoholics Anonymous is self-conscious and deliberate) or access the Sex-Help website and the like attest to this. Some estimates suggest that as many as 6 per cent of the population of the USA might be sex addicts, though the evidence base for this is weak. But there is clearly a felt perception amongst many people that they lack the social or psychological resources to deal with sexual difficulties and obsessions without external support. Whether subsuming all such issues under a label such as sex addiction helps or hinders is more debatable.

SEX TOURISM

Sexual adventure and experimentation has long been an enticing partner of tourism. The Grand Tours of aristocratic British young men from the eighteenth century onwards involved not only immersion in the archaeological and artistic wonders of great European cities but also pleasurable exploration of the various sins of the flesh – though frequently with rapid punishment from endemic venereal disease. Foreign travel meant an escape from narrowness and hypocrisy at home. In the 1920s, for British homosexual writers such as Christopher Isherwood, Berlin meant boys. By the later twentieth century a quick trip to Amsterdam or Copenhagen represented for many European men an escape from the continuing puritanism and legal restrictions of their homelands, especially if you were gay or had a passion for pornography (or both). With the explosion of rapid, and relatively cheap, air travel since the development of the jumbo jet the possibilities of the few became the opportunity for the masses, women as well as men, old as well as young, seeking time out from the routines of everyday life, seeking the exotic other, or just exotic sex, or sex without commitment, or possible new partners, or the pursuit of the illegal or what was tabooed back home. But the other side of the pursuit of pleasures far from home is darker. For many critics of this new sexual world, sex tourism has come to be seen as coterminus with sexual exploitation, especially of women and young children, which requires new forms of regulation across national boundaries (O'Connell Davidson 2005).

Many of the countries at the forefront of sex tourism in the Global South have themselves been fully complicit in these developments, adopting active policies to encourage not only conventional Western tourism but a consciously sexual tourism, often with dramatic effects (Weeks 2007: 209–10). The early stages of Thailand's economic miracle was fuelled by the country's role as a 'rest and recuperation' centre for US troops in the Vietnam war, and easy sex become a major element in the Thai repertoire of pleasure. Even when sexual servicing is less explicit, the end result may be the same. Alexander (1997: 63–100) has analysed the way in which the Bahamas restructured its own economy as a service economy, with a large part of its capital invested in the tourist industry (hotels, airlines, services and tour operators, international finance capital, real estate). But it remains a service economy predicated on huge disparities of power and opportunity, and the formal tourist economy slips easily into a more informal, sexualized economy. Sex tourism can potentially unbalance fragile economies, with complex impacts on local populations.

That is not normally the major preoccupation of the tourists themselves. In the new sexual playgrounds of Asia or the Caribbean, Western (usually, but not invariably, male) punters can explore their fantasies to the limits of their imaginations and pockets, and distance themselves from both local conditions and their discontents with contemporary civilization (Seabrook 2001). In a study of the male heterosexual tourist in the Dominican Republic, O'Connell Davidson (2001) found that their desire for the other is less a wish to love them for themselves but rather to proclaim what many feel they have lost: a certain form of male privilege. In the third world, even the third-rate American or European tourist is king or queen (O'Connell Davidson and Sanchez Taylor 2005: 87). But it is not just so-called developing countries that welcome the sex tourist. American cities such as San Francisco, Los Angeles and New York have famously become a magnet for sex tourism, and especially the gay tourist. The local governments of Manchester and London in the UK have actively promoted the gay-positive attractions of their cities. While European cities such as Amsterdam have long been a haunt of sex tourists, others such as Rome, Barcelona and Madrid (and other attractions such as Lesbos) have rapidly followed suit.

Lesbian and gay tourism has often been seen as more progressive than hetero-sexual tourism, challenging colonial patterns and striving for new forms of identi-fication across distance. Yet there has been an insistent note of sexual colonialism throughout modern gay history (see Weeks 1977) and queer critics have seen a continuing trend in which the entitlement to travel, and to resist homophobic pressures, has to be balanced by an ethical concern for the local cultures which have become desirable destinations (Binnie 2004: 86–104). Some indigenous pro-gay organizations, as in Hawaii, have questioned 'the "hidden" or "unnoticed" violence of tourism', which depends on low-waged labour that exploits many workers, especially women and young people, and which in the long run displaces poor peoples from their own lands and neighbourhoods (AFSC 2002: 211). Even the internationally famous Sydney Mardi Gras has been challenged for its mar-ginalization of working-class gays and lesbians, people of colour, and of bisexuals, transgender people and queers (Markwell 2002: 81–100).

So sex tourism is not an innocent phenomenon. It has offered glimpses of different ways of life to millions of travellers, at best challenging their culture-bound assumptions. It has provided great potentialities for play and enjoyment. At the same time, it is inevitably deeply implicated in continuing patterns of exploitation, and the economic, social and cultural restructuring associated with **Commodification, Globalization** and **Neoliberalism**. As ever pleasure has to be measured against pain and exploitation, the potentiality for agency against the intricate patterns of domination and subordination.

SEXOLOGY

Sexology, the scientific study of **Sexuality**, was born in the last decades of the nineteenth century with striking ambitions. The key pioneer, the Austrian foren-sic psychiatrist Richard von Krafft-Ebing, wrote in a preface to his landmark *Psychopathia Sexualis,* which went though 12 editions between 1886 and 1903, that his task was no less than to reduce the manifestations of erotic life to their 'lawful condition'. Just as contemporary sociology in the hands of Marx, Durkheim and Weber was seeking to lay bare the laws of society, so sexology set itself the task of uncovering, describing and analysing the 'laws of nature'. In carrying out their ambitions, the Founding Fathers of sexology – there were few women involved – also helped to shape the categories and meanings of the sexual in ways which continue to be influential into the twenty-first century (Weeks 1985: 64–72).

We can trace the earliest manifestations of a new would-be scientific zeal in relation to sexuality to the theorists of **Masturbation** in the eighteenth century. Tissot's fulminations against onanism marked a crucial transition: what you did was now something more than an infringement of divine law; it told the world what sort of person you were. By the 1840s Henricus Kaan was writing about the modifications of the *nisus sexualis* (the sexual instinct) in individuals. Other formative works followed: on prostitution, childhood sexuality, hysteria and the sexual aberrations. Karl Heinrich Ulrichs published 12 volumes on **Homosexuality** between 1864 and 1879, which influenced Carl Westphal's 'discovery' of the 'contrary sexual impulse' in 1870, and Krafft-Ebing's work on the sexual **Perversions**. It was the latter who pulled together the scattered trails into a new approach (Oosterhuis 2000). A host of investigators of the highways and byways of the erotic soon followed, aided by the new prestige of the biological sciences following the publication of Charles Darwin's work on the origins of species and sexual selection. In his *Three Essays* (1905), which was itself a major influence on the course of sexology, Freud acknowledged the particular influence of nine writers, including Krafft-Ebing, Havelock Ellis and Magnus Hirschfeld. There were many others, drawn from penology, law, psychiatry, psychology, anthropology and medicine.

At the heart of the new approach was a conviction that underlying the diversity of individual experience was a complex natural process – the 'sexual instinct' – which needed to be understood in all its forms. This led in the first place to a major effort of classifying and defining sexual pathologies, which gave rise to a dazzling array of neologisms and sexual taxonomies, from the antipathic sexual instinct and **Bisexuality** to zoophilia, taking in coprolagnia and urolagnia, festishism and kleptomania, exhibitionism and **Sado-masochism**, frottage and chronic satyriasis, inversion and transvestism, and many, many more. Second, this concentration on the perverse threw new light on the 'normal'. Havelock Ellis began his life's work on the psychology of sex with a detailed study of the secondary, tertiary and other characteristics of men and women. Sexology came to describe the study both of the sexual instinct in all its variations and of relations between men and women, for ultimately they were seen as necessarily linked: **Gender** and sexuality were locked together as a biological imperative.

Kinsey later compared these pioneers to Galileo and Copernicus in making it possible to see the world in new ways: 'they broke new ground'. This certainly fitted with the early sexologists' own self-evaluation. They saw themselves as in the vanguard of modernity, marrying science and sexual enlightenment. In his Presidential address to the 1929 Congress of the World League for Sexual Reform, Magnus Hirschfeld declared that: 'A sexual ethics based on science is the only sound system of ethics' (quoted in Weeks 2009a: 140). Hirschfeld, like other luminaries of this first phase of the sexological revolution, looked forward to a new enlightenment in which prejudice, religious moralism and authoritarian sexual codes would dissolve before the light of reason as provided by the new science of sex. Sexual knowledge and sexual reform marched hand in hand. 'Through science to Justice', Hirschfeld famously proclaimed as the watchword of his Scientific-Humanitarian Committee. Many subsequent sex researchers, from Alfred Kinsey and his colleagues, via the sex therapists William Masters and Virginia Johnson to contemporary investigators of penile response, other things being equal, might have proudly echoed this.

But there is another way of seeing the role of sexology: not as a neutral investigation of the dark continent of sexuality, but as constitutive of it (Foucault

1979). Modern sexuality, it can be argued, is in large part at least a product of sexological writing not so much discovering sexual types but helping to invent them. As is clear from the work of Krafft-Ebing, Havelock Ellis and Magnus Hirschfeld, much of their taxonomic efforts and attempts to understand particular sexual types developed in dialogue with their patients and clients (Oosterhuis 2000). Concepts of the invert, the masochist, sadist or the transvestite did not simply emerge ready-formed from the heads of sexologists. But they provided much of the language and helped shape the discursive forms through which meanings and emergent **Sexual identities** were articulated (Bland and Doan 1998). It is also indisputable that they also lent their weight to normalizing institutions, to attempts at 'cures', and to eugenic solutions to the 'problems' of overpopulation and the proliferation of the 'feeble-minded'. Havelock Ellis was not alone in being a sexual reformer, and also a supporter of the eugenic breeding of 'the best' (inevitably defined by class and racial criteria). The proliferating literature on married love might encourage the belief that women, too, were sexual beings deserving of satisfaction and pleasure. But these marriage experts also managed to pathologize the single woman and to sustain a burgeoning literature on the inadequacies of 'frigid' women. By the 1920s social purity organizations were looking to the writings of Ellis, Freud and others to underpin their fundamentally normalizing positions.

Over the decades since, the science of desire has been drawn upon to justify a huge variety of moral positions, from passionate advocacy of sexual revolution to fervent endorsement of sexual orthodoxy. Today, we can call on an encyclopedia of would-be scientific arguments to sustain our reasoning, from hormonal theories, evolutionary psychology and the 'silent whisperings' of sociobiology for explaining sexual difference and perversity and to justify the inevitability of inequality – or indeed of equality. Sexual knowledge has expanded exponentially, and has become a cornucopia of potential meanings.

But sexology's pretensions to being the royal road to truth have long been dispelled; like every other would-be science, it is enmeshed in the web of social relations, and has specific conditions of possibility and impact. We need to treat its more imperialistic claims with caution and a sensitivity to their origins (Lancaster 2003). As Steven Epstein (1996) has demonstrated in relation to the science of HIV/**AIDS**, the subjects of scientific investigation have their own voices, and are not prepared to simply accept what they are told. This has always been the case. A history of the science of sex shows that human sexual nature is more recalcitrant and resistant than the taxonomists and labellers and the sexual experts generally would often have us believe.

SEXUAL CITIZENSHIP

The language of sexual citizenship has come to the fore since the 1980s as a way of focusing claims to sexual rights within a viable and widely recognizable moral and political framework. It has been especially linked to LGBT rights, but as a concept it is open to a wide range of claims to recognition and entitlement around the erotic. A rights discourse has a long history in Western traditions, and the feminist and lesbian and gay movements from the 1970s identified clear lacunae in current practice – especially with regard to gender and sexual equality and relationship choices. Claims to full citizenship provide a way of articulating claims to sexual equality, rights and **Recognition** within the context of national politics, and through the related idea of **Human sexual rights** to wider transnational and international recognition.

The concept of citizenship speaks of involvement and belonging in a political society, and consequential rights and attendant responsibilities. Its roots lie in ancient Greek city states, where citizenship meant to be a full member of the polis (and was universally the prerogative of adult men, excluding women, children and slaves). By the time of the European and American revolutions of the late eighteenth century citizenship had come to encompass basic civil rights, certainly for white men, and in the course of the nineteenth and twentieth centuries, in a series of stops and starts, brought full political rights as well, though only belatedly to women. Women's right to vote was only achieved well into the twentieth century in the liberal democracies, after prolonged struggles – after World War II in France, and approaching the millennium in Switzerland. The welfare state settlement after 1945 in most Western countries brought a broadening of the concept to incorporate new social rights, around full employment, access to education and health and welfare entitlements but these remained predicated on a gendered division of labour and the pre-eminence of the heterosexual family (Marshall 1950). Both major strands of citizenship theory – the republican which stressed individual involvement in the polis as the key to realizing a full humanity, and the liberal, which emphasized entitlements and social protection – ignored the issues around gender and sexuality which came to the fore from the 1970s in response to the new social movements of **Feminism** and **Gay liberation**. Since then there has been a major theoretical effort to broaden the scope of citizenship theory, to include the class and racialized assumptions which have all too often been ignored, as well as the dimensions of culture, gender and sexuality which have remained implicit in citizenship discourse.

It is in this context that theories of sexual citizenship have developed, with a wide range of claims for ending discrimination against LGBT people: for equality under the law, employment rights, full access to social entitlements, the right to serve in the armed forces, spousal and parenting rights and the like. The would-be sexual citizen has come into being because of the new primacy given to sexual subjectivity since the 1970s, and has been seen as a harbinger of a new politics of intimacy and everyday life (Weeks 1998: 35). Sexual citizenship is a sensitizing concept which alerts the world to new concerns, largely ignored in traditional political debates, around the body, its possibilities, needs and pleasures; with new sexual identities; and with the forces that inhibit their free, consensual development in a democratic polity. It offers the opportunity to incorporate new realities in intimate relationships into political discourse and puts on the agenda issues that have traditionally been seen as highly personal. The sexual citizen is therefore a hybrid being, bridging the private/public divide. Her/his emergence signals the partial removal of sexuality from the private sphere, where it had historically been sequestered, into the public domain where it can become fully political.

There is certainly no general agreement on the meanings or implications of the idea of sexual citizenship. Evans (1993), a pioneering user of the concept, has deployed a broadly materialist framework to emphasize the processes of **Commodification** which both structure and delimit new sexual categorizations and subjectivities, not only of gays and lesbians but also of paedophile and trans-gendered people. Richardson (2000) has emphasized the limitations of citizenship claims when confronted by the dominance of heteronormative structures and values. Others have questioned whether it is ever possible for LGBT people, always ambiguously placed as sexual strangers and outsiders, to be full citizens (Phelan 2001). 'Queer citizenship' might be a radical ideal, but could it be a contradiction in terms (Bell and Binnie 2000)?

Plummer has developed his analysis of **Sexual stories** to deploy the concept of intimate citizenship, which 'flags a proliferation of debates about how to live a personal life in a late-modern world' (2003: 68). A cacophony of sexual narratives, old and new, compete to be heard – about families, partnerships, sexual pleasures and pains, identities and differences, faith and unbelief, freedom and imprisonment, adults and children, parenting and childlessness, health and illness, living together and living apart, living and dying well, individuality and collective belongings. In the process people in diverse communities are producing new stories about the types of relationships they want, and narrative frameworks which articulate and configure emerging values.

As might be expected in the diverse, pluralistic world that Plummer vividly describes there is no necessary agreement about which way citizenship should go. Whilst many see citizenship discourses as one necessary focus for thinking about what it means to bear rights and to belong, for others it carries the danger of accommodation to the traditional order (Brandzel 2005). **Same-sex marriage** and the wish for gays to serve in the military have been interpreted as little more than an abject surrender to heteronormativity. Such policies, it is argued, are in danger of creating new divides, between 'good' citizens and 'bad' citizens, between respectable gays and transgressors. This is accentuated by a tendency in sexual citizenship theory to emphasize lesbian and gay claims to full citizenship, and ignore the claims of other 'sexual minorities'. This poses the danger of reifying gay identities, ignoring the fluidity and changeability of **Sexual identities**; and it plays down dissident sexual and gender practices, such as **Sado-masochism** and **Transgender**. Concepts of citizenship, it is suggested, are indelibly heteronormative, and are criss-crossed by assumptions about gender, race and nationality, limiting what belonging ultimately means (Yuval-Davis 2005).

Whilst acknowledging these dangers, defenders of sexual/intimate citizenship theories would argue that their ultimate function is not to sustain the status quo but to offer a critical stance on it, by emphasizing the realties of social exclusion in even the most liberal of polities, and by delineating the policies and politics that would lead to full social inclusion. If citizenship is about full belonging, then advocates of sexual and intimate citizenship are voicing basic claims to recognition and inclusion that have too long been ignored.

SEXUAL CULTURES

The concept of sexual cultures has come into use to describe the multiplicity of contexts and social worlds in which the sexual is lived, practised, enjoyed and feared in an erotic economy which is marked by diversity and ever-growing complexity. It has long been recognized by writers on sexuality that each continent, nation, region, geographical area, local culture and city, as well as different nationalities, ethnicities, religious groups and even classes, status groups and political movements have different moralities, ethics, rituals, norms and values, and even diverse forms of behaviour. These have traditionally been conceptualized in terms of overarching ideas of what is right or wrong, moral and immoral, normal and abnormal. For most early theorists of sexuality in the Western tradition the dominant assumption was that the prime purpose of sex was reproduction, its natural location was between men and women, and its legitimacy was guaranteed by church and state through marriage and the family. Other forms – whether extra-marital love, prostitution, homosexuality, non-genital and non-reproductive sex, some of them individualized practices, others increasingly organized in local subcultures – could scarcely be ignored but were overwhelmingly seen as aberrations, immoralities or perversions of the sexual instinct. These were the dubious others of true sexuality.

Since the nineteenth century such a belief system has become increasingly untenable. Anthropological findings of non-Western cultures demonstrated conclusively that there were many different ways of being sexual, and of being men and women, though reception of these insights were generally obscured by ethnocentricity and racism. The new science of desire, **Sexology**, sought to show how varied the patterns of sexual behaviour were, while social studies from the Chicago School in the USA in the early decades of the twentieth century through to the work of Alfred Kinsey and his colleagues in the 1940s and 1950s give abundant evidence of the existence of diverse sexual subcultures beneath the patina of conventionality and orthodoxy.

What is new is not so much the fact of sexual variety, as the way it is conceptualized. **Social constructionism** has sought above all to show that sexuality is shaped at the level of both individual practices and cultural values and norms by historical and social processes. Sexualities (and the plural is crucial, denoting the range of different forms of sexual life) are culturally specific, and are constructed in a host of different ways. There are commonalities across cultures, and constant flows and interactions between cultures, and these need to be

180

understood. But the erotic is practised and lived within distinctive sexual cultures, and these have increasingly become the focus of serious investigation (Eder *et al.* 1999a and b).

An emphasis on the social shaping of sexual cultures does not mean they are ephemeral, or easily changed. A striking feature about sexual cultures is how deeply embedded they are, taking on the air of naturalness and inevitability, even when they are near neighbours or coexist with one another. An example of this is provided by the religious divides within Europe, which persist even as the continent has become increasingly secular, and which continue to shape different sexual cultures. Four distinct religious-moral patterns have been detected (Eder *et al.* 1999a: 6–10). North-western Europe, largely Protestant since the sixteenth century, with strong individualism, has tended to emphasize the nuclear family, taboo extra-marital sex, execrate homosexuality, while condemning but tacitly accepting **Prostitution** as an inevitable accompaniment of male lust. The Catholic countries of southern Europe tended to have strict moral codes but relatively lenient attitudes, condemning sins, but condoning the sinner. The extended family has been a continuing feature of these cultures, as was a covert acceptance of homosexuality, as long as it did not breach gender norms. For English travellers of the eighteenth and nineteenth centuries, Italy was both the site of the Papacy and a wonderland of sexual possibilities. The Orthodox Christian countries of Eastern Europe were at earlier times famed for sexual licentiousness, but since early modern times the Church has been morally very conservative, and the value system has been very familial, with strong divisions between men and women; this conservatism also became part of the Communist regimes that ruled in these countries until 1989. The fourth religious system, Islam, was dominant in south-western Europe, and now through extensive migration is influential in north European cities, though in Britain the influence comes from South Asia rather than from within Europe. The countries under its sway had strict moral codes, but with a marked gap between theory and practice amongst men, as long as behaviour remained private and gender norms were not publically violated.

This schematic description has broad truth, but obscures great complexity. Even within the confines of Great Britain, Wales has historically had a distinctive sexual culture, closer to France than to northern European patterns (Weeks 2007). France, Spain and Italy, three Catholic countries, have diverged significantly. Each national culture in Europe has developed its own distinctive ethos within overarching structures. All have changed under the impact of the **Great transition** since the 1950s, though at uneven paces. Spain's sexual codes froze under General Franco's regime, and burst into exotic life from the late 1970s. Britain had one of the most conservative sexual cultures in Europe in the 1950s, and one of the most liberal by the 2000s. Time is a critical variable. Another vital factor is the interaction between different cultures. The European Union has been a major influence in liberalizing attitudes towards homosexuality across its members and beyond. If continuity is a marked feature of many sexual cultures, it is important to remember that they can and do change. And new sexual cultures continue to emerge.

Most major urban centres across the globe, even some of the most conservative and repressive, now have a multitude of distinctive sexual worlds growing out of and reinforcing diverse sexual practices and tastes. The World Wide Web has countless sites catering for every conceivable desire. Altman (2001) has well described the interlocking nature of global sex in the contemporary world. It is now best understood as a network of an ever-increasing variety of distinctive sexual cultures.

SEXUAL DIVERSITY

The concept of diversity, the condition of being 'diverse', concerning 'difference' or 'unlikeness', resonates in the late-modern world. Diversity – in terms of race, ethnicity and nationality, faith, politics, culture, taste, consumption, economic and social opportunity, reproduction patterns, health opportunities, education, family life, ability and disability, sexual identity – has a high profile, and is the potential site of conflict and division. *Sexual* diversity is perhaps the most controversial and contested area, not least because of the origins of the concept. It is closely related to **Perversion**, each term suggesting a move away from a strict 'normality'. The *Shorter Oxford English Dictionary* acknowledges the link by recording as one meaning of 'diversity' the word 'perversity', a usage it dates back to the sixteenth century. There is a common history. Yet a huge divide has opened between them, signifying a major shift in the language of sexuality and the way we think about our needs and desires. Diversity suggests a continuum of behaviours in which one element has no more fundamental a value than any other. Such an idea is threatening and deeply challenging to many traditional notions of what sexuality is, or should be.

Sexology played its part in the emergence of a discourse of diversity. As early as the 1930s Havelock Ellis suggested that the term perversion 'is completely antiquated and mischievous and should be avoided' (Ellis 1946: 127). He offered instead the less opprobrious phrase 'sexual deviation', and whatever its own limitations this became a commonplace description in psychological and sociological discussions in the half-century or so afterwards. Latent in such shifts of terminology was a recognition of sexual pluralism and the emergence of what Gayle Rubin has described as the concept of a 'benign sexual variation' (Rubin 1984). Aspects of this were already there in the work of the early sexologists and in **Psychoanalysis**, but Kinsey was perhaps the key figure in the transition, arguing that biologically there was no right or wrong (Pomeroy 1972). The biologism was probably less important in the long run than the weight of evidence he offered. The two vast volumes he largely wrote, *Sexual Behavior in the Human Male* (1948) and *Sexual Behavior in the Human Female* (1953), provided an unparalleled insight into the variety of sexual behaviours under the carapace of sexual respectability in American society. When it became possible to say, on the basis of what was then the most thorough investigation ever done, that 37 per cent of the male sample had

had sexual contact to orgasm with another male, then homosexual activity could no longer be seen as a morbid symptom of a tiny sick minority. And if this was true of homosexuality, then it was potentially true also for a wide range of other sexualities, from bestiality to **Paedophilia**, from **Sado-masochism** to a passion for **Pornography**. From this flowed a profoundly important and influential sociological – and political – point. If people had such a wide range of sexual needs, desires and experiences, then a yawning gap existed between moral codes and sexual behaviour.

If transformations within mainstream sexology provided a theoretical framework for a recognition of diversity, the political energy came from a different source: the 'sexual minorities' themselves. There has been an explosion of public expressions of sexual diversity in recent years. New categories and erotic minorities have emerged. Older ones have experienced a process of subdivision as specialized tastes, specific aptitudes and needs become the basis for proliferating sexual identities. The list is potentially endless as each specific desire becomes a locus of political statement and possible social identity. The example of **Homosexuality**, as Gayle Rubin has argued, has provided a repertoire of political strategies and organizational forms for the mobilization of other erotic populations (Rubin 1984). Transgender people, bisexuals, sado-masochists, fetishists, man–boy lovers, sex workers and others have vocally emerged, clamouring for their right of self-expression and legitimacy, with varying degrees of successful recognition. And it is not just social movements that claim a progressive lineage and agenda that make their claim to recognition. Powerful fundamentalist or conservative movements, like anti-abortionists or fathers' rights organizations, claim their place in the pluralistic universe, regularly presenting themselves as vulnerable victims of liberal intolerance and 'political correctness'.

This 'pluralization of the public spheres' (Plummer 2003: 73) has generated proliferating voices and **Sexual stories** of feminists, gays, traditionalists, fundamentalists, faith groups, environmentalists, sexual dissidents and subversives, moral conservatives, health professionals and patients – debating, shouting, reasoning, experimenting, preaching in multiple social worlds, in social movements, on the streets, in newspapers and journals, via the Web and the blogosphere, on television and radio – all making different and often conflicting claims. Diversity causes trouble.

This is largely because recognizing the fact of diversity is not the same as valuing diversity as a good in itself. Even many who wish to affirm their own distinctive identity are reluctant to hear the voices of others. And even the most ardent defenders of diversity have to accept that not all forms of diversity are equally valid. A recognition of sexual variation cannot preclude debate about how to evaluate the many forms of diversity, demarcating the acceptable from the unacceptable, the harmful from the harmless. There are two particularly troublesome forms of diversity: those involving differences of power, especially when organized around gender, race and sexuality, or involving intergenerational relations; and social and cultural practices perceived as harmful or undesirable

(Cooper 2004: 190–1). The first are often underplayed, but frequently represent the critical intersection of forces and inequalities that reinforce each other. The second have been the source of some of the most intractable battles in the 'sex wars', for example around sado-masochism and pornography, and the concept of harm is fiercely contested.

The problem here is that sexuality in itself no longer embodies any obvious rights or wrongs. The days when it was possible to argue that a particular act was 'unnatural' have long gone. We can no longer understand the sexual, despite the best efforts of some contemporary theorists influenced by the new genetics, in the biological terms adopted by Kinsey. So inevitably, we need to draw on ethical standards that are largely external to our perception of the erotic. Awareness of sexuality does not in and of itself tell us how we can or should intervene – even if we wanted to – to promote the benign and prevent the perverse (both of which are themselves ambivalent terms). Which is why the question of sexual diversity is at the heart of contemporary sexual debates – and is likely to remain there.

SEXUAL ETHICS

Ethics are concerned with how we should live. Sexual activity has throughout cultures and histories raised profound questions about how to live the life of desire. Some societies have seen the erotic as secondary, subordinate to other issues. Others – as in the Christian tradition – have attributed sexuality with prime moral significance, carrying with it a weight of prescription about how people should act, and think, in order to achieve the good or moral life. Sexuality continues to raise questions about duty and desire, morality and immorality, goodness and evil, truth and falsity. Perhaps sex acts, as Gayle Rubin (1984: 285) has suggested, 'are burdened with an excess of significance'.

The revolution in thinking about the sexual since the 1970s (see **Sexuality**) has put such questions into a wider perspective (Weeks 2009a: 139–40). If we reject the hierarchy of sexual values laid down by the science of sex (see **Sexology**), how can we distinguish between the normal and the abnormal? If, as Foucault said with reference to Sade, 'sex is without any norm or intrinsic rule that might be formulated from its own nature' (Foucault 1979: 149), how do we determine appropriate and inappropriate behaviour? If we can no longer regard sexuality as either intrinsically threatening and evil, or liberating and good, on what basis can we judge the value of sexual restraint or sexual liberation? Recent liberation movements, Foucault observed in a late interview, 'suffer from the fact that they cannot find any principle on which to base the elaboration of the new ethics . . . [other than] an ethics founded on so-called scientific knowledge of what the self is, what desire is, what the unconscious is, and so on' (Foucault 1984: 343). He is here referring to a reliance on psychoanalytical theory but it could equally apply to an ethical system based on sociobiology or evolutionary psychology. The problem is that this 'scientific knowledge' is full of divisions and contradictions about what the self is, what desire may be, and even whether there is such a thing as 'the unconscious'.

Foucault's own late attempt to grapple with this dilemma, in the two volumes of his *History of Sexuality* published at the very end of his life, is characteristically indirect. The two volumes are superficially at least simple exegeses of ancient Greek and Latin texts on how people should live (Foucault 1985, 1986). But their very lack of obvious contact with today's problems serves to clarify what is at stake. He likens the world of the Greeks and Romans to our own in one key respect. Like us late-moderns, they were faced with the task of elaborating an ethics that was not founded in religion or any other a priori justification, least of all science. Like people today they were troubled with moral questions around what we term sexuality (the nearest equivalent for them was called *aphrodisia*). Many of the concerns have in fact been continuous for over 2,000 years: with the body, the relations of men and women, of men and men. Unlike people today, however, they did not attempt a codification of acts which made sex itself the bearer of negative values and moral anxieties, nor attempt a subordination of individuals to external rules of conduct based on such values and anxieties. They sought instead an 'aesthetics of existence', an art of life in which temperance balanced excess, self-discipline kept pleasures in order.

The ancients were preoccupied with methods of self-knowledge, with techniques of the self, rules of conduct organized around dietary matters (the individual's relation with his body), economics (the conduct of the head of the household) and the erotic (the relations of men and boys). They were seeking modes of life which derived not from a central truth about sex, but from the set of relations in which the individual was embedded. The aim was to define the uses of pleasure in a way which neither ignored it, nor surrendered to its intoxicating force. This was an ethics for 'free men', from which women, children and slaves were excluded, and is hardly directly applicable to today. What Foucault is doing in examining a time so different from our own is to throw our own needs and aspirations into relief. What we lack, he is suggesting, is not a transcendent truth, but ways of coping with a multiplicity of truths. We need not so much a morality based on absolute values, but an ethics and politics which will enable us to cope with a variety of choices.

This is an issue that is very much in tune with the preoccupations of the late-modern world, with its diversity, flux, **Individualization** and increasing emphasis on the loneliness of moral choice. The weakening or absence of a widely accepted foundational ethic, whether based on received religion or science (which should not be taken to mean that there are no true believers in these systems) does not lead straightforwardly into a moral swamp. Instead we can see development of a late-modern ethics based on a recognition of ambivalence, conflict and constraints, which is particularist and contextual, but which strives for a minimum or thin universalism (Weeks 1995). This is evidenced in a range of theoretical and political debates around 'life politics' (Giddens 1992), a politics of 'living well' (Rutherford 2005), a political ethic of care (Williams 2004: 28), 'dialogic citizenship' (Plummer 2003) or a 'love ethic' (Weeks 1995). These come from different starting points, but cohere around a series of concerns, with intimate relationships, care, how to relate to others, how to honour the body, how to be erotic, how to respect the natural world.

Living grounded moralities, in the solidarities of everyday life, Plummer (2003: 108) argues, provides shared stories through which we can learn of moral and ethical dilemmas that people experience, and begin the necessary dialogue. People work through their problems in their own ways, following their own values and guidelines, telling their own moral tales. But it is through sharing these stories that people can begin to reflect upon their lives in reflexive ways. What makes people moral agents, Smart and Neale suggest (1999: 114), 'is not whether they always make the right decision, but whether they reflect upon the decisions they take and weigh up the consequences of their actions'. **Reflexivity** becomes the hallmark of ethical action as, in Foucault's terms, 'practices of the self' begin to shape ethical lives as practices of freedom (Foucault 1988). But these practices are not isolated actions, but always situated, ultimately based on norms and values of reciprocity and solidarity.

This is the context for what has been described as radical or critical humanism (Weeks 1995). As one of its leading theorists in relation to sexuality, Ken Plummer (2003: 162) has put it, 'The humanism I would like to see developed would encourage a view of human beings as an "embedded", dialogic, contingent, embodied, universal self with a moral (and political) character'. This is humanism as a 'regulative ideal' rather than a metaphysical concept, with 'humanity' as a project of political construction not something that has always been there (Weeks 2007: 223). One of the most vital features of globalization, and of the discourse of human sexual rights, is a growing sense of what Butler (2005: 54) calls vulnerability to others, in both their pain and their pleasures. Critical humanism involves a recognition of the frailty of humanity in the vast cosmos, and the ease with which we can suffer pain, insult and rejection. But that offers a challenge to hope rather than a counsel of despair. 'The grand abstraction and the search for universals is bound to falter and we are usually better working with a theory of the human being that is grounded, practical and charged with doing things, usually together with others' (Plummer 2010: 46). This pragmatic stance has profound implications. It involves making the 'human gesture', affirming the human bond which links us beyond the chasms of difference.

SEXUAL IDENTITY

Although the ideas behind it are not new, the idea of a sexual identity only emerged fully in the 1970s, notably from second-wave **Feminism** and **Gay liberation**, as a way of affirming a positive sense of self by those whose sexualities had been rejected by an oppressive culture. It now has a more general application, but sexual identities still matter above all to the sexually marginalized. They refer to our sense of self and subjectivity, who we believe we really are, but also to our relationship with others.

The concept of identity came into general use in the 1950s, usually in relation to the 'identity crises' faced by young people in the transition through adolescence to young adulthood. But it has become a central idea in the contemporary world. Identity tells us about what we have in common with some people, and what differentiates us from others. Identities provide individuals with a sense of who and what they are, where they belong, and where they want to go. They tell us a story about ourselves, and provide a sense of security. They can also divide people, sometimes murderously, as with some forms of ethnic or nationalist identities. Identities create boundaries. They provide comfort and support; but they can also cause trouble (Butler 1990).

Few identities cause as much trouble as sexual identities. In Western societies since at least the nineteenth century, as Michel Foucault (1979) famously put it, sex has become the 'truth of our being'. We frequently as a matter of course define people by their sexuality – he is homosexual, she is bisexual, he is 'normal' (that is, heterosexual). Similarly people define themselves as sexualized beings. **Gay** has become a self-description with a powerful public resonance. Sexuality has become something that matters in telling the stories of who we are, and has mattered to societies who want to impose disciplinary meanings on its subjects. There is a long history to this, inextricably linking sexual to other social identities. Concepts of national identity have long been inextricably bound up with notions of proper gendered or sexual behaviour. The forging of new class identities from the industrial revolution onwards was linked with battles over the meanings of 'respectability', and what it was to be a real man and a feminine women in the shifting division of labour. The refinement of a racialized Western identity in an age of imperialism was closely bound up with distinct sexual classifications and typologies, and the identification of the colonized of the world as distinctly 'other', more primitive, less sexually controlled, which in turn served to confirm the West's supposedly superior sexual patterns. Now in a post-colonial world we see a return of the repressed as many formerly colonized societies, and fundamentalist movements, react against Western liberal ideas. We also see from the late nineteenth century the marching on to the battleground of history of alternative or oppositional sexual identities, the so-called 'perverts', each claiming their place in the sun, and from the 1960s onwards making their vocal claim for justice.

Sexual identities matter above all to the sexually marginalized. Take the example of homosexuality. In a world where same-sex love and marriage divides churches and societies, where new forms of toleration of sexual difference in most Western societies have to be set against fierce intolerance, persecution and even murder of homosexuals in large parts of the world, clearly sexual identity has become more than an individual quirk, variation or taste. It provides the basis for resistance, subversion and social action. Sexual identity is a concept that bridges the divide between public and private. It refers to our sense of self and subjectivity, who we believe we really are, but also to our relationship with others, and our membership of sexual communities and social worlds. It is a term that speaks of our individual being, of our collective involvements with others, and about the way societies regulate sexuality, and allow (or try to forbid) sexual differences to flourish. Sexual identities tell us about power and resistance, control and agency.

For second-wave feminists and lesbian, gay, bisexual and transgender people and other self-defined sexual minorities who were finding a public voice in the 1970s, it became important to affirm a new sense of self and collective involvement. Identities built around one's sexuality became a central focus both of a personal sense of agency and of a new politics around gender, sexuality and the body. To come out as lesbian or gay was to do more than state a sexual preference; it was to position yourself in a new way in relationship to a hostile society. And the key point is that you were not doing this on your own: the sense of a movement and developing sense of **Community** provided a context in which you could affirm your sexual being and involvement with others like yourself. It allowed new stories to emerge about sexual oppression, personal struggle and finding yourself in a new world of personal and collective agency.

Sexual identities are paradoxical. They assume fixity and permanence – 'I am what I am' – yet all the evidence suggests that they can and do change. Theoreticians debate whether **Sexual orientation** or preference is inborn or socially shaped and organized. But the reality is that there is no necessary relationship between what your desires or sexual practices or behaviour are, and how you identify yourself. Many self-defined heterosexuals have gay sex, without it changing their sense of identity, as the HIV/AIDS crisis revealed. Similarly many self-defined gay people have heterosexual sex without necessarily shifting their sense of who they are. On a global scale sexualities are organized in a huge variety of different ways, and the Western categories of **Heterosexuality** and **Homosexuality**, gay and straight, have no historic meaning. Even in Western societies they have a specific, time-defined history.

Identities are basically social and historical phenomena which have only a contingent rather than necessary relationship with how people actually behave. Theorists have therefore argued that they are best seen as stories we tell about each other, or are told about us, narrative structures, invented realities, in effect 'fictions' (Weeks 1995). Post-structuralist and **Queer** theorists have taken this to its ultimate conclusion by arguing that sexual identities are arbitrary impositions on the flux of sexual possibilities, and constrain rather than enable sexual possibilities. Subjectivities may be produced within discourses, but the ways individuals recognize themselves within these are not determined. Sexual identities are always ultimately expressions of **Hybridity** rather than uniformity, and are built at the intersection of many possible meanings, structures and ways of being. A variety of critics have argued that rather than explore the genesis and effect of sexual identities in all their complexity, it would be more useful to understand the psychic and social structuring of individual subjectivities or the social interactions that produce a sense of self. What can surely be agreed is that there is no essential identity that expresses the ultimate truth about an individual. Sexual identities are inevitably and always relational: they exist because of the existence of an often feared or threatening other; masculinity and femininity only have social meaning because of the existence of the other term. Similarly homosexuality and hetero-sexuality are concepts that define the other. Such terms are historical inventions which gain meanings in specific historical contexts. These meanings are always the subject of struggle, negotiation and change.

And yet people hold to their sexual identities with passion and intensity. Like other identities, sexual identities offer what the sociologist Anthony Giddens (1991) has called a sense of 'ontological security' which places the individual in a narrative structure that is both individual and social. They give meaning to individual lives, and they locate the individual in a wider history. They have provided the basis of complex cultures, spatial organization (as in gay areas of major cities), distinctive sexual and relational patterns, and political mobilization. Sexual identities may be fictions, but they seem to be necessary fictions.

Sexual identities have become key actors in a globalized society. Progressive governments especially increasingly listen to political movements organized around sexual identities. Conservative movements and states frequently scapegoat the sexually unorthodox. Concepts such as **Human sexual rights** as a matter of course refer to the legitimate claims of sexual minorities. Yet at the same time it is important to remember that in complex societies a sexual identity does not exhaustively define a citizen. People have multiple social belongings, defined by gender, race, ethnicity, nationality, geography, language, age, ability/disability, and so on. Sexual identities lie at the intersection of many potential social posi-tionings. Which is prioritized at any particular moment depends on a range of social, cultural and political factors. What we can say with some certainty, however, is that the rise and rise of sexual identities since the 1970s, starting in Western countries and now global in scale, testifies both to an increasing recognition and acceptance of **Sexual diversity**, and to a world where sexual justice still has to be struggled for.

SEXUAL ORIENTATION

Sexual orientation is a much used but fundamentally ambiguous concept. It came into use in discussions of sexuality in the 1970s largely as a synonym for **Homosexuality** and object choice, less frequently if at all for heterosexual patterns, though logic would suggest that if it is true for one form of sexuality it must be true for the other. But logic has little to do with the popularity of concepts. 'Sexual orientation' suggests an essential sexual nature which shapes human subjectivity. As such it has been extremely valuable in arguments for homosexual equality and justice: if something was fixed and given by Nature, then surely it should not be the subject of hostile legislation, discrimination and **Homophobia**. This type of argument has a long history.

The definition of homosexuality by **Sexology** as a specific medical or psychological condition at the end of the nineteenth century led to a preoccupation with the 'causes' of homosexuality which has tended to dominate thinking about it ever since. The fact that few people bothered to enquire into the causes of **Heterosexuality** indicates the dominance of the view that homosexuality was an abnormality that needed to be explained. Heterosexuality, on the other hand, was the taken-for-granted, natural state, from which other forms of sexual expression were a **Perversion**, deviation or at best variation. However, after a century of debate and scientific enquiry the question of causation remains as inconclusive as ever. The biological explanation argues that homosexuality is an inbuilt and probably hereditary condition that affects some people and not others. Negatively, it can be seen as a pathological distortion of the natural sexual drive, caused perhaps by hormonal imbalances or chromosomal accidents. More recently, evolutionary theory – via sociobiology and evolutionary psychology – has led to a rebirth of biological explanations. Studies of DNA have led some to see evidence of a 'gay gene' or a 'gay brain', as suggested by the American scientists Dean Hamer and Simon LeVay and others (Wilson and Rahman 2005).

If homosexuality has a biological explanation, and is a specific sexual orientation, then it can easily be argued that same-sex desire is as natural as heterosexuality. Homosexual activists have in fact argued this for over a hundred years. Many of the late nineteenth-century pioneers of sexology, amongst whom were many early advocates of homosexual rights – Karl Heinrich Ulrichs, Magnus Hirschfeld, Edward Carpenter – deployed ideas of a third or intermediate sex precisely on these grounds, and were extremely influential. Unfortunately, when the Nazis sought to wipe out sex reform movements in Germany after 1933 they used exactly the same arguments of a biological variation to justify attacks on homosexuality. Science has had little to do with it.

A second approach has concentrated on understanding the psychological reasons for homosexuality. The most famous name associated with such explanations is Sigmund Freud, the founder of **Psychoanalysis**. Building on earlier sexological explanations Freud attempted to understand what he called sexual inversion in terms of the universal bisexuality of human beings rather than in the biological make-up of a distinct group of people. It resulted from the specific patterns of interaction with parents and the complex and universal processes through which the bisexual infant became an adult. So homosexuality, like heterosexuality, resulted from an inhibition of the sexual drive. As a working hypothesis this has been enormously influential, though in subsequent debates it has also led to enormous confusions. Does a child become homosexual because of a weak father and strong mother, or because of an over-dominant father and a weak mother? Such explanations have been frequently offered, and equally often fail to match the biographical facts of individual homosexuals. Subsequent psychological theories have failed to clarify the mechanism at work.

Against this **Social constructionism** has argued that it is this preoccupation with etiology or causation that needs investigation. Few people ask what causes heterosexuality; why are we so concerned with the causes of homosexuality (McIntosh 1968)? Instead, it was suggested that homosexuals should be seen as a social category, rather than a medical or psychiatric condition. Kinsey *et al.* (1948) had shown that there was no necessary connection at all between what people did sexually and how they identified themselves. If, in a much disputed figure, 37 per cent of the male population sample had had some sort of sexual contact with other men to the point of orgasm, yet a much smaller percentage claimed to be exclusively homosexual, identity had to be explained by something other than sexual proclivity or practice. Following such insights, sociologists began to make a critical distinction between homosexual behaviour, desires and identities. Homosexual behaviour is widespread; but distinctive roles, categories and ways of life have developed only in some cultures, and do not necessarily encompass all forms of homosexual activity. From this perspective, the creation of the homosexual category was a form of social control designed to minoritize the experience, and protect and sustain social order and traditional sexual patterns. Plummer (1975), for example, explored the impact of hostile labelling in creating sexual stigma, which in turn supported the construction of sexual identities. Sexual activities of all kinds, Gagnon and Simon (1974) argued, were not the results of an inherent drive but of complex psychosocial processes of development, and it is only because they are embedded in **Sexual scripts** that the physical acts themselves become important. The new sexual history added an extra dimension by exploring the evolution of ideas of a distinct homosexual condition. The process of medicalization, in particular, was seen as a vital explanatory factor shaping the new social category (Foucault 1979).

Many of these ideas inspired or were stimulated by **Gay liberation**. However, despite its initial enthusiasm for ending the distinction between homosexuality and heterosexuality, the most immediate impact of the new movement was to consolidate a sense of **Sexual identity** built around a fixed orientation. Many believed clearly that homosexuality was intrinsic to their sense of self and social identity, essential to their nature. In this climate a critique of **Essentialism** could readily be conceived of as an attack on the very idea of a homosexual identity, a fundamental challenge to the hard-won gains of the lesbian and gay movement, and the claim to recognition of homosexuals as a legitimate minority group (Stein 1992). This was the source of the appeal of subsequent theories of a 'gay gene' or 'gay brain', which suggested that sexual orientation was wired into the human individual.

But such anxieties seem misplaced. The distinction between behaviour, categories and identities need not necessarily require the ignoring of questions of causation; it merely suspends them as irrelevant to the question of the social organization of sexuality. Foucault himself stated that: 'On this question I have absolutely nothing to say' (cited in Halperin 1995: 4).The really important issue is not whether there is a biological or psychological propensity that distinguishes those who are sexually attracted to people of the same gender from those who are not. More fundamental are the meanings these propensities acquire, however or why ever they occur, the social categorizations that attempt to demarcate the boundaries of meanings, and their effect on collective attitudes and individual sense of self. Social categorizations have effects in the real world, whether or not they are direct reflections of inherent qualities and drives.

Queer critics have gone further, in challenging and deconstructing the social categorizations, emphasizing the ways in which they distort the fluidity and complexity of sexual subjectivities. Arguments for rights and justice based on the idea of a fixed sexual orientation ignore the underlying structures of heteronormativity, and trap people into rigid identities and categories. From this perspective, theories of sexual orientation, however pragmatically useful in particular controversies, limit radical thinking about sexuality (Waites 2005).

SEXUAL SCRIPTS

Sexual scripts are key elements in social theories of **Sexuality**. Sexual **Essentialism** assumes the fixity of our sexualities, on their resilience in the face of all efforts at modification. Social and historical explanations, contrariwise, assume a high degree of fluidity and flexibility in 'human nature', in its potentiality for change – not overnight, not by individual acts of will, but in the long haul of history and through the complexities and agencies of social interaction – see **Social constructionism**. The evidence of other cultures, and of different periods and social worlds within our own, demonstrates that there are many different ways of being 'men' and 'women', many alternative ways of living social and sexual life. These variations are not, however, random, they are highly patterned arrangements of language and symbols, expectations and practices that arise in social interactions. It is here that the idea of the 'script', used by interactionist sociologists to account for the way we take our sexual meanings, provides a powerful, if inevitably ambiguous, metaphor: 'Scripts specify, like blueprints', John Gagnon has suggested, 'the whos, whats, whens, wheres and whys for given types of activity. . . . It is like a blueprint or roadmap or recipe, giving directions' (Gagnon 1977: 6).

Scripts work in some ways like the earlier sociological concepts of roles in delineating possible ways of acting and being, but fundamentally break with the deterministic assumptions and functionalism of most role theory. Scripts are not the slaves of social needs but emerge in the incessant process of human meaning-making. We do not, of course, follow absolutely these guidelines, or we would all be the same, and 'immorality', deviance or transgression would scarcely exist. There are oppositional as well as regulatory scripts, multiple forms of agency as well as blind obedience. But the 'scripts' laid down in social practices set the parameters within which individual choices are available. In society generally there is little that is spontaneous – and this is especially the case with the erotic. Scripts offer signposts for sexual activity.

Sexual scripts are central to the theory of 'sexual conduct' developed by John Gagnon and William Simon (1974). They argue that far from being the fundamental 'natural' activity that early **Sexology** theorized and popular opinion takes for granted, sexual activities are the outcome of a complex psychosocial process of development, and it is only because they are embedded in scripts that the physical acts become possible.

The theatrical metaphor of scripts suggests an acting out or performance of erotic life rather than an expression of a deeper, essential urge, which relates the approach to the dramaturgical sociology of Erving Goffman, as well as the later work on sexual and gender performativity as theorized by Judith Butler (1990 – see **Queer**). Where it differs from the latter is the absence of any assumed structuring impulse. There is no fully written play which individuals are expected to act out word for word, only a variety of possible forms of expression through which social meanings are mediated.

Sexual scripts work on three possible levels: the interpersonal, the intra-psychic and the cultural. The interpersonal refers to the everyday interactions through which sexual meanings and practices are negotiated and acted out by individuals in society. The intra-psychic is the space where a sense of self is shaped, routinized and stabilized (or destabilized and reshaped). The cultural provides the wider permissions and prohibitions, about whom you may have sex with, what sort of sex you can have, for what purposes, under what conditions and in what circumstances, that Gagnon spoke about.

Unlike a post-structuralist approach, in which subjectivity is produced within and through discourse, sexual scripting strives for a reflexive and flexible understanding which stresses both contingency and agency in shaping sexual practice, identities and meanings (Brickell 2006: 95). The weakness of the approach lies in the absence of a wider historical sense of how and why sexual regimes change over time, which is why for a time the approach tended to be eclipsed by the more overarching theories of Foucault (1979). Its continuing strength lies in its ability to help us understand the complexities of the social creation of sexualities, and of **Sexual stories**, from the ground up.

SEXUAL STORIES

Stories are basic to human culture. Human beings are above all narrators and story tellers, Plummer (1995: 5) argues, and society can be interpreted as a seamless web of stories emerging everywhere through social interactions, helping to make society work. *Sexual* stories, narratives of intimate life, focused on the erotic, gender and relationships, play a crucial role in shaping cultural meanings, and have always done so. They are as old as human society, embodied originally in folk memories and oral tales, and then in epic and lyric poetry, fictional romances, religious tracts, diaries, confessional autobiographies, pornography and, from the nineteenth century, quoted in scientific compendia, though often encoded from full public view by discreet Latinate or heavily abstract prose. In the famous case studies presented by the pioneers of **Sexology**, from Krafft-Ebing to Freud and beyond, we can hear the voices of the apparently normal sexual person, with all their peculiarities, and of the sexually unconventional – homosexuals, sado-masochists, fetishists, transvestites – in all their ordinariness struggling to be heard. In the twentieth-century texts on 'married love', we hear stories of the struggle to have pleasure, to protect oneself from unwanted pregnancies, tales of anxiety, fear and the hope for fulfilment. And in the closing decades of the twentieth century and as a new millennium opened we heard new sexual stories: coming out stories from a multiplicity of sexual beings, stories of women affirming their sexual autonomy, and of men asserting their privileges or lamenting their inadequacies, harrowing accounts of abuse, of violence and rape, narratives of survival, of well-being and illness, of living and dying with **AIDS**, of love and mourning, of relationships and the pursuit of virtual ecstasy. Once hesitant and nervous, today these voices and their diverse stories are everywhere.

Though sexual stories may have a long history, their volume and significance have dramatically changed. We can now tell our sexual stories in a huge variety of different ways. Michel Foucault (1979) has famously written of the discursive explosion since the eighteenth century which produced sexual modernity. It generated new forms of knowledge deeply implicated in the coils of power, producing new subjectivities, social positionings and disciplinary patterns. But it also produced counter-knowledges, resistances and new voices. Far from censoring sexual discussion, as historic myth once suggested, the nineteenth and twentieth centuries have seen a positive incitement to talking about the erotic. But this proliferation of sexual narratives, the urge to talk about sex, was for long constrained by rules on who could speak, in what circumstances and on whose authority. The private sphere was jealously guarded, shrouded in discretion, while the public sphere was regulated and controlled by prohibitive laws or religious sanctions, shrouded by media silences, popular prejudice and organized hypocrisies everywhere. From the 1960s the impermeable divides between personal and public life in most Western countries began to dissolve and the democratization and **Informalization** of sexual life opened up new possibilities for speaking about the body and its desires. Now we can hear everyone who wants and is able to speak – on reality or confessional talk shows, in parliaments and in the multiplying media, on the streets and in chat rooms, via personal blogs or vlogs, and through social networks – and there is a mass audience for this babel of voices, ready and willing to talk back. Today in the late-modern world there is no privileged elite of authorities effectively telling us who or what we are as sexed or gendered beings. There are many would-be authorities competing cacophonously, especially in the anarchic democracy of cyber-space, telling their own stories.

It has been famously said that homosexuality, the love that once dare not speak its name, now can't shut up. But that is true of all forms of the erotic. Through stories – of lust and love, of hope and mundane reality, of excitement and disappointment – told to willing listeners in communities of meaning, people imagine and re-imagine who and what they are, what they want to become. Through personal narratives we give meaning, stability and ontological security to the flux of our individual lives (Giddens 1991). In stories we tell each other in the various social worlds we inhabit (and are shaping by this endless story telling) we can make and remake the realities of **Desire**, **Intimacy**, **Sexual Identity** and **Sexual citizenship**. Sexual stories are deeply implicated in moral and political change,

and shifting stories of self and relationships carry the potential for radical transformations of the social order (Plummer 1995, 2003). They are circulated in and
through social movements, communities and networks, and become the focus for
thinking through and reorienting the needs and aspirations of everyday life. Late-
modern stories particularly reveal and create a multiplicity of new projects, new
constituencies, new forms of agency and new possibilities for the future. These are
stories of human life chances, of emotional and sexual democracy, of **Sexual
diversity**. There are also many other stories, equally late-modern but achingly
searching for a world that has gone, warning of the dangers of pluralism and fearing
the anarchy of change – there are evangelical Christian, or radical Islamicist, or
many other morally conservative stories proclaimed as loudly as any progressive
accounts, telling of fear and threat and of cultural decline.

Many stories want to offer the security of final Truth: this is how it was, this is
how it is, this is how it must be. But the never-ending explosive expansion of story-
making tells us something else. There are many truths, none of which can legitimately claim final authority. Stories are by definition fictions, attempts to make
sense of and bring order to the constant flux of reality. But that does not make them
any less significant. Contemporary sexual stories contain their own narrative truths,
offering meanings and understandings that enable us to navigate the rapids of
everyday life.

SEXUAL VIOLENCE

Sexual violence involves forceful physical or mental violation of a person's space,
body or being by another or others. It is most commonly inflicted by a man or men
on a woman. The United Nations Declaration on the Elimination of Violence
Against Women in 1993 defined it as 'any act of gender-based violence that results
in, or is likely to result in, physical, sexual or psychological harm or suffering to
women, including threats of such acts, coercion, or arbitrary deprivation of liberty,
whether occurring in public or in private life'. Such a definition covers a whole
gamut of activities from beating to sexual harassment to genital mutilation.
Violence in this definition is a core element in women's subordination by men,
though it is important to remember that violence against sexual minorities is also
common, and is a key element of **Homophobia**. Men on men, women on men,
women on women, and adult on children sexual violence is also well documented
– see **Paedophilia**. Sexual violence is an act of power which deploys sexuality to
ensure the perpetuation of relations of dominance and subordination.

For many feminists rape is the quintessential manifestation of sexual violence,
embodying the essence of male violence against women. Rape, Susan Brownmiller
(1974: 15) influentially argued, expresses the deep-rooted, transhistorical and
transcultural will on the part of men to dominate women. It 'is nothing more or
less than a conscious process of intimidation by which all men keep all women in
a state of fear'. Many men of course do not rape, but they do not need to. Their

supremacy is assured by the rapists, who are the 'shock troops' of patriarchal domination. This polemic had a powerful impact because it brought to light the reality of endemic violence, the continued silence of men in discussing it, and the failure of the authorities in many jurisdictions to take rape seriously. In the ostensibly liberal countries of Western Europe and North America police and prosecutors characteristically minimized rape accusations, women were regularly seen as having brought attack upon themselves by provocative behaviour, and the victims of rape often felt that after being hauled through courts, facing hostile questioning, they had undergone a second horrendous assault. Rape in marriage was rarely a crime. It was not until 1984 that marital rape was recognized in Britain; and the number of successful rape prosecutions remains notoriously low. Sexual violence against women has been constantly underplayed, so it is not surprising that the Brownmiller message about male violence has continued to influence much feminist thinking about the inherently violent nature of male sexuality. Its influence can be seen in radical feminist critiques of **Pornography** (Mackinnon 1987 and Dworkin 1981), **Trafficking** and child abuse, which focus on the centrality of violence in defining the oppression of women.

The difficulty lies not so much in the call to action and recognition of such critiques as in the basic **Essentialism** of the underlying analysis. One of the difficulties in the central argument on rape, for example, is that it assumes that the incidence of rape is common and consistent across all cultures, ignoring the evidence that its extent varies enormously, particularly at different historical periods. That is to say, rape can be best seen as a heavily historicized experience, depending on the specific balance of power between men and women. That is not to minimize the significance of rape as an act of domination, nor to ignore its impact on women's life, but rather is an attempt to understand it as a social rather than biological phenomenon that can be explained, and is susceptible to transformation. The alternative is to see it as an eternal, essential aspect of all male relationships with women, which by definition is beyond the possibility of change, and puts women in the position of permanent victims of men's violence.

Rather than seeing sexual violence as the inevitable by-product of an inherently aggressive masculinity, many feminists have found it more useful to see it as the ritualistic enactment of power relationships that play on cultural meanings about sexuality. If this is so, then we must find the explanation of violence in the social and psychic conditions in which **Masculinity**, **Femininity** and **Heterosexuality** are acquired. As Segal (1990: 252) put it, 'The wider causes of men's violence must be located in societies which construct "masculinity" in terms of the assertion of heterosexual power . . . locating the object of sexuality in women, and the subject of sexual desire in men'. It is not that men's sexuality is by its nature violent. Rather, male sexuality becomes a focus for the expression of male power, especially when that power seems vulnerable and threatened. A blend of factors lies at the heart of male aggressiveness, ranging from psychic repression and the conditions of family life to social expectations concerning male behaviour. But if this is agreed, and male sexual violence is not at all a product of an unproblematic

196

biology but of complex social practices and psychological structuring, the changes needed to transform the relations between men and women can only be brought about by equally complex processes, ranging from new methods of child-rearing to radically different economic, legal and social conditions for women.

The fact that sexual violence can also be frequently observed in other relationships underlines that we need to find its source in the complex power dynamics at play in particular situations. There has, for example been a growing recognition in recent years of the prevalence of male rape, which probably has its source in homophobia and fear of repressed homosexuality amongst men. Dominating other men sexually is a way of affirming your own real masculinity and confirming the victim as other. Violence in lesbian and gay relationships has also been more widely acknowledged (Renzetti and Miley 1996), with suggestions that it is at least as common as in heterosexual relationships. The roots of such violence must be found in frustrations, suppressed anger, repressions, and disparate resources and power. Despite radical changes in patterns of **Intimacy**, inequalities persist not only between men and women, but also between men and men and women and women, and the normal and the transgressor. The question of male sexual violence against women can from this perspective be seen as an extension of a pervasive culture. Such violence is endemic, enacted in a series of sexualized situations from adult rape to child abuse, from sexual harassment at work to domestic violence.

Sexual violence has become a key element in global debates on **Human sexual rights**. Reports and experiential accounts document an endless stream of stories of violence and abuse, ranging from harassment, enforced female circumcision, forced marriages to rape and murder (Amnesty International 2001b, 2004). Bamforth (2005: 3–10) has observed five commonalities. First, the acts of violence they highlight are intimately related to social conceptions of gender and appropriate gender roles. This involves the denial of basic human rights to individuals simply because they are women, and often extreme violence to LGBT people and women when they are seen to infringe locally enforced norms. Second, the violence inflicted on minorities and women is refracted through strongly sexual dimensions – notably in the high incidence of rape. Third, these actions are often justified by reference to local religious or cultural factors, which claim communal approval for acts of violence. Fourth, many of the laws in countries where violence and abuse of human rights are rife often play a role in justifying abuse, and state agents, especially the police, often play a part in inflicting violence. Finally, although the role of the state is critical in permitting violence, much of the violence against women and sexual minorities is conducted by private actors, in the home or the locality. These, rather than an assumed inherently male violent sexuality, are the commonalities that define sexual violence on a global scale.

SEXUALITY

The word sexuality conveys a host of meanings. On the one hand it appears to refer to one of the most basic features of human life, 'our sexuality', the most natural thing about us, the 'truth of our being', in Foucault's (1979) phrase. On the other, it is so heavily encrusted by historical myths and entrenched taboos, by culturally specific meanings, that sexuality appears more a product of history and the mind than the body. Perhaps, as Vance (1984) once suggested, the most important human sexual organ is located between the ears. Sexuality as a concept is uneasily poised between the biological, the social and the psychic. Even Freud confessed to the difficulty of agreeing 'any generally recognized criterion of the sexual nature of a process' (1916–17: 323).

The earliest usage of the term sex in the sixteenth century referred to the division of humanity into the male section and the female section; and the quality of being male or female. The subsequent meaning, however, and one current since the nineteenth century, refers to physical relations between the sexes, 'to have sex'. What we know as **Masculinity** and **Femininity**, and what came to be labelled from the nineteenth century as **Heterosexuality**, with **Homosexuality** as its aberrant other, are thus inscribed into the meanings of sex from the start. Sexual, a word that can be traced back to the mid-seventeenth century, carries similar connotations – pertaining to sex, or the attributes of being male or female, is one given meaning. The word sexuality itself emerged in the early nineteenth century, meaning the quality of being sexual, and it is this meaning that is carried forward and developed by the sexual theorists of the late nineteenth century.

Sexologists sought to discover the 'laws of nature', the true meaning of sexuality, by exploring its various guises and manifestations. They often disagreed with one another; they frequently contradicted themselves. But all concurred that sexuality was in some ways a quality or essence underlying a range of activities and psychic dispensations (Weeks 1985). Thus the Austrian psychiatrist Richard Krafft- Ebing became a pioneer in seeing sexuality as something that differentiated different categories of beings – so opening the way to theorizing **Sexual identities**. Freud went further. His *Three Essays* (1905) began with a discussion of homosexuality, thus severing the expected connections between sexuality and heterosexual object choice; and continues with a discussion of the perversions, so breaking the link between pleasure and genital activity. In the early development of **Psychoanalysis**, sexuality was seen as central to the workings of the unconscious. More broadly, sexuality was becoming a distinct continent of knowledge, with its own specialist explorers. When people spoke of 'my sexuality', they meant those desires and behaviours which shaped their sexual (and social) identities, as male or female, heterosexual or homosexual, or whatever.

Against the certainties of this tradition the late twentieth century saw the emergence of an alternative way of understanding sexuality. 'Sexuality' was a social construction, a 'fictional unity', that once did not exist, and at some time in the future may not exist again. The sexual theorists John Gagnon and William

Simon (1974) have talked of the need that once may have existed to *invent* an importance for sexuality. Michel Foucault (1979: 105) queried the very category of 'sexuality' itself: 'It is the name that can be given to a historical construct.' Sexuality was a discursive unity that emerged in the transition to modernity from the eighteenth century, and was a critical locus of power-knowledge over individuals and populations.

Following on from these conceptual shifts, contemporary theorists question the naturalness and inevitability of the sexual categories and assumptions we have inherited. They suggest, following Foucault, that the concept of sexuality unifies a host of activities that have no necessary or intrinsic connection: discourses, institutions, laws, regulations, administrative arrangements, scientific theories, medical practices, household organization, subcultural patterns, ethical and moral practices, the arrangements of everyday life. The idea of sex, that seems so foundational to the very notion of sexuality, is itself a product of the discourses. For the interactionist sociological tradition, nothing is sexual, as Plummer (1975) suggests, but naming makes it so. So sexuality can be seen as a narrative, a complexity of the different **Sexual stories** we tell each other about **Bodies** (Plummer 1995); a series of **Sexual scripts** through which we enact erotic life (Gagnon and Simon, 1974); or an intricate set of performances through which the sexual is invented and embodied (Butler 1990).

These radical redefinitions of sexuality have, inevitably, aroused intense controversy. Historical construction seems to deny the whispers and desires of the body itself, as sociobiologists and evolutionary psychologists argue. It appears to question the validity of the sexual identities (homosexual/heterosexual/bisexual, etc.) by which many people have set so much store. This however is precisely the point. A historicized approach to sexuality opens the whole field to critical analysis and assessment. It becomes possible to relate sexuality to other social phenomena. New questions then become critically important. How is sexuality shaped, how is it articulated with economic, social and political structures? Why do we think sexuality is so important, and to what extent does it now have a global meaning (Altman 2001)? What is the relationship between sexuality and power? If sexuality is constructed by human **Agency**, to what extent can it be changed?

These theoretical issues have been played out in a historical situation where sexuality as never before has become the focus of cultural and political struggle. The rise of radical sexual social movements such as **Feminism** and **Gay liberation** since the 1960s has been paralleled by the rise of conservative fundamentalist movements equally concerned with the body, gender and sexuality. Issues such as **Abortion**, homosexuality and sex education have become bitterly contested political issues on a global scale. At the same time, the HIV/**AIDS** epidemic has dramatized the significance of sexual health and its inextricable linkage with issues of identity, diversity, social division and opposing values. There is a new uncertainty about the meanings of sexuality. In such a situation, we can no longer seek a solution in the definitions of sexual scientists or self-styled experts, however well meaning. Only by problematizing the very idea of sexuality as a given of nature does it become possible to rethink the meanings of the erotic.

SEXUALIZATION

The concept of 'sexualization' has come into wide use in recent years to describe the situation, starting in Western societies but increasingly manifested on a global scale, where the erotic in its various forms has become both more accessible than ever before to ever-greater numbers of people, young and old, and has permeated a vast range of personal and cultural activities hitherto discreetly protected from explicit **Sexuality**. Critics have spoken of the pornification of the culture, and have been concerned with its impact on children, and particularly girls and young women (Paul 2005). Social theorists such as Bauman (2005) have described a condition where intimacy and love have been corrupted by a disposable culture: an easy come, easy go sexuality can be readily enjoyed and immediately forgotten. Other commentators have spoken of the mainstreaming of sexual imagery, where the traditional confinement of sex to the private sphere has melted under the impact of massive cultural change, and new opportunities, threats and challenges have opened up (Attwood 2009b). As with all aspects of sexual life, the meanings and significance of sexualization have been fiercely contested, and new battle lines have emerged.

The historical context is the explosion of sexual meanings and possibilities in the late-modern world. The neat sequestration away of sexuality into the secrecies (and lies) of private life that, superficially at least, characterized the nineteenth century, and defined sexual norms for much of the twentieth century, has collapsed in the contemporary world. The boundaries between private life and public life have become more permeable and new forms of 'public intimacy' have developed in what has been called a 'striptease culture' (McNair 2002). Some of this is long established. Film has circulated highly sexualized imagery since its inception. Critics have complained since at least the 1950s about the sexualization of women in advertising. Cultural conservatives have long inveighed against the trivialization of the erotic, the undermining of the 'specialness' of sex, and the sleaziness of public spaces. But the pace has accelerated dramatically in recent years, heightened by the communications revolution. The media generally has become much more sexually explicit, in imagery and content. It has become easier for many people to discuss the convolutions and disasters of their most intimate lives in front of millions of watchers of television confessional programmes or reality shows than with their ostensible loved ones in the confines of the bedroom. There has been a burgeoning of **Sexual stories** about sexual needs, desires, hopes, fears, identities, intimacies. The Internet has provided protean opportunities for **Cybersex**, democratizing sexual expertise, inflating fantasy and opening vast new possibilities for sexual networking and action. **Pornography** and sub-pornographic imagery have become pervasive and routinized. Sexual life generally has been drawn into the marketplace in the process of **Commodification**. Underlying all this are the ways in which sexuality has become the defining feature of identity and **Intimacy**, in a world where sex has become the truth of our being. All these have been seen as clear enough markers of a process of sexualization coursing through myriad aspects of the late-modern world.

It is perhaps not surprising, as Paul (2005: 11) comments, that many 'have no idea what this means for ourselves, our relationships, or our society'. Nor is it surprising that, increasingly, professional and government bodies have felt it necessary to explore the likely effects of this process. An American Psychological Association (2007) task force worried about the ways in which people are sexually objectified, valued only for their sexual attractiveness, with children especially developing inappropriate sexual knowledge and behaviour, with indeterminate but negative consequences for their self-image, self-esteem and future development. In a report produced for the British Home Office, Linda Papadopoulos (2010) expanded on these themes. She defines sexualization specifically as the imposition of adult sexuality on children and young people before they are capable of dealing with it, putting pressure on them that children have never experienced before. While children are 'adultified', women are 'infantilized', and men are 'hyper-masculinized'. Experts agree, she argues, that all this puts young people in danger of particular risk and harm, potentially leading to depression, eating disorders, bullying and violence.

That there are dangers in an incessant process of sexualization few would want to deny. Where critics of these alarming warnings would disagree is on the scale and nature of the problem. If, as Papadopoulos and others would argue, the situation is so potentially perilous, it is not at all clear that the recommendations for action – new advertising guidelines, more controls of imagery on television and video games, better sex and health education, further research and a new specialist journal – quite measure up to the problem. The danger of focusing on sexualization as the major issue is that it avoids the wider social context – of inequalities of power, including gendered inequalities, economic disadvantage, lack of opportunities for many young people – in which sexuality is deeply enmeshed. It potentially displaces deep-seated social problems which seem insoluble, onto an area which is a fruitful focus for moral anxiety. This is one of the traditional ways in which a **Moral panic** emerges, giving rise to magical solutions but leaving the underlying problem unresolved. The reality is that sexuality has become a central space where debates about the nature and future of late-modern culture is played out. Sexualization offers an umbrella concept through which many of the issues can be argued over – but not resolved.

SOCIAL CAPITAL

The concept of social capital refers to the values, norms, degree of trust, social networks, collective ties and relationships, and resources that groups of people have in common in specific historical, cultural and economic circumstances, and that give them a social advantage – or disadvantage (Edwards 2004). Though most theorists of social capital have paid little direct attention to sexual life, it is an important and relevant concept because of the emphasis on family and intimate relations, and the strong interest in the significance of moral issues. As an idea it is an obvious extension of the idea of economic capital, which has been such a dominant idea in twentieth-century (especially Marxist) thought, to other social attributes, notably physical, cultural, symbolic, human and even emotional and erotic capital. A recent theory of erotic capital (Hakim 2010) focuses on specifically sexual allure and attractiveness, which it is suggested women have more of than men, but have been prevented from realizing fully by patriarchal moral restraints. More generally erotic capital normally refers to the sexual attributes and confidence that can be deployed in sexual situations.

Each of these forms of capital suggest specific capacities and resources that people derive from their personal and social lives, and which position them favourably in relation to others in their social worlds. The utility of *social* capital as a working concept is that it directs attention to the significance of a range of social involvements, including family, gender and intimate relationships, to the well-being of a given society. During the 1990s and early 2000s the concept had a major impact on social thought and political practice in a number of Western countries, largely because of the impact of Robert Putnam's best-selling book, *Bowling Alone* (2001), although the literature and debate were much wider. Putnam's work resonated with a general social mood, especially in the USA and Britain, that was concerned with the breakdown of family ties and communal values – interpreted as evidence of the decline of social capital The evidence he put forward – symbolized by the apparent collapse of membership of local bowling clubs – argued for a weakening of participation in the local community, which in turn could be blamed on the corroding impact of excessive individualism (see **Individualization**), leading to an enfeeblement of principles of responsibility, obligation, reciprocity and trust. The attraction of this thesis is that while it shared a sense of decline with many social and cultural conservatives, it opened up the possibility of a mildly progressive and communitarian politics focused on strengthening social capital – examples of which were tentatively manifest, for example, in the Clinton Presidency in the USA in the 1990s and during New Labour supremacy in the UK between 1997 and 2010. The major difficulty lay with how exactly one measured social capital – what was it exactly that was being measured, and what tools could do it? – and assessing its impact.

Two aspects of the theory have proved especially influential in analysing the experience of social change: the idea of 'bonding' and 'bridging' social capital. Bonding social capital, deriving from intense family and community loyalties and solidarities, provides a strong sense of belonging and identity, and has provided the basis of strong sexual and intimate cultures, for example in working-class and minority communities (Weeks 2007: 32–3). The obverse is that it also potentially generates a deep cultural conservatism, promoting intense internal trust, but an equally fervent distrust of the outside world. This can lead at worst to an embedded commitment to highly gendered and traditional relational values, a fear of moral pollution from the outside world, and a punitive view of more diverse patterns of life – aspects of which are witnessed in the rise of **Fundamentalism**. Bridging social capital, by contrast, offers weaker but broadening ties, which go beyond the local solidarities and build links with a wider range of people. Characteristically men are better able to use bridging social capital, through greater social mobility and closer involvement in work and other social involvements, than women historically have been able to do. Though they may open up communities to new ideas, the downside of such bridging links is that they can undermine communal values, heighten individual rather than collective achievements, and do little to change gender relations for the better.

Followers of the French sociologist Pierre Bourdieu, including feminist theorists, have emphasized the absence of class analysis from the mainstream exponents of social capital theory, and the lack of attention to gender, sexuality and race (Edwards *et al.* 2006). Laments that social change since the 1950s have undermined social unity and cohesion ignore, such critics suggest, the profound reorganization of social life during the past generations, and the unfinished revolution which has produced a complex, multicultural and sexually diverse late-modern culture in Western societies. Despite these changes, a critical analysis would stress the limits to the achievement of social justice because of continuing class and racial inequalities. Others have stressed the emergence of new forms of social capital that more than balance the alleged decline of more traditional forms, and that enhance the possibility of more democratic and open relationships (Holland *et al.* 2003). A good example of this is provided by the impact of **Gay liberation**, which has strengthened the social networks and sense of **Community**, and hence social capital, amongst LGBT people. Some evidence of this was provided by the **AIDS** crisis, which generated an unprecedented grassroots response, including community-based support mechanisms and a culture of **Safer sex**, in the communities most affected. There is also strong evidence of the strength of social capital ties amongst diasporic minority ethnic communities, such as for example between people of Caribbean descent in Britain and extended families in the various islands of the Caribbean (Goulbourne *et al.* 2010). African-Caribbean communities, with a tradition of female-headed families, have often been stigmatized as having weak social capital. But concentrating on family structures obscures the richness of family meanings and bonds, the importance of personal values of care, affection and mutual support, the strength of family-type rituals and customs, and the strength of neighbourhood and community that transcend physical distance.

Theorists of social capital have not produced a consensus. Their various analyses have suggested at least three key positions: a decline in social support networks, especially the family; the intractability of power relations, where despite massive social change class and racial divides remain strong; and the potentiality for new forms of **Relationality** in the conditions of late-modernity. The value of the concept has been in the focus it forces on the factors that make for strong social relations. What it has not been able to do is suggest any consistent measure of success or failure. Here, as always, personal ideologies and politics structure conclusions.

SOCIAL CONSTRUCTIONISM

Social constructionism has been the dominant approach in attempts to understand **Sexuality** since the 1970s. The term itself has been criticized for its harsh and mechanistic tone, and even dismissed as unfashionable and out of date (Halperin 2002: 11), as if fashion were a good ground for value or effectiveness. But the theoretical approaches embodied in the concept have been immensely influential for both the history and sociology of sexuality, and have been especially significant in thinking about the emergence and significance of sexual meanings, categories and identities. Its most contested element has been a critique of what became known as sexual **Essentialism**, the assumption that sexuality is a purely natural/ biological phenomenon to which the social has to react. Against this social constructionism has at its heart a preoccupation with the complex and multiple ways in which emotions, desires and relationships are shaped by the different cultures we inhabit. It is concerned with the historical and social organization of the erotic.

This theoretical stance has many roots. From sociological approaches such as symbolical interactionism, ethnomethodology and dramaturgy (especially Erving Goffman) came an emphasis on the importance of social interaction and language in shaping symbolic meanings and the 'social construction of reality' (Brickell 2006). From social anthropology came an awareness of the variety and relativity of **Sexual cultures**. Sex research, especially by Alfred Kinsey and his successors, revealed the huge dimensions of sexual variability and the prevalence of 'deviance'. Subsequently, post-structuralist and deconstructionist theories destabilized and problematized fixed meanings and structures. These various insights were taken up by the new social history that emerged in the 1970s, to offer a historical understanding of changing ideas of identity and the contingency of the categories we take for granted as natural. As this suggests, there are many potential constructionisms. They have cohered around a number of common assumptions. First, there is a general rejection of sex as an autonomous realm, a natural domain with specific effects, a rebellious energy that the social controls. We can no longer set 'sex' against 'society' as if they were separate domains. Second, there is a widespread recognition of the social variability of sexual forms, beliefs, ideologies, identities and behaviour, and of the existence of different sexual cultures. There are indeed sexualities rather than a single sexuality. Third, we must abandon the idea that we can fruitfully understand sexual history in terms of a dichotomy of pressure and release, repression and liberation. Sexualities are a result of diverse social practices that give meaning to human activities, of social definitions and self-definitions, of struggles between those who have power to define and regulate, and those who resist. Critics have regularly complained that social constructionists are nominal-ists, concerned with words and concepts rather than 'reality', the natural susbtratum of the erotic. Against that, constructionists would argue that we can only understand sexuality by understanding the web of meanings in which it is entwined and which shape what we think of as sexual at any particular time. 'Sexuality' is not a given, it is a product of social meanings, negotiation, struggle and human **Agency** (Weeks 2009a).

Social constructionist approaches to sexuality were initially developed in relation to **Homosexuality**. The classical starting point is widely seen as an essay on 'The Homosexual Role' by the British sociologist, Mary McIntosh (1968), whose influence can be traced in a range of historical studies from the mid-1970s (Weeks 1977; Greenberg 1988), and it has been frequently anthologized (for example, Stein 1992).What is important about the work is that it asks what was at the time a new question: not, as had been traditional from the late nineteenth century, what are the *causes* of homosexuality, but rather, why are we so concerned with seeing homo-sexuality as a condition that has causes? And in tackling that new question, McIntosh proposed an approach which opened up a new research agenda: seeing homosexuals 'as a social category, rather than a medical or psychiatric one'. Using Kinsey (Kinsey *et al.* 1948), McIntosh makes a critical distinction between homosexual behaviour and 'the homosexual role'. Homosexual behaviour is widespread; but distinctive roles have developed only in some cultures, and do not necessarily encompass all forms of homosexual activity. The creation of a specialized, despised and punished role or category of homosexual was a form of social control designed to minoritize the experience, and protect and sustain social order and traditional sexual patterns.

Another related but distinctive approach that shaped social constructionism came from the work of John Gagnon and William Simon (1974). Drawing again on the work of Kinsey, and symbolic interactionist traditions, they argued that sexuality, far from being the essence of 'the natural', was subject to socio-cultural shaping to an extraordinary degree. Sexual activities of all kinds, they suggested, were not the results of an inherent drive but of complex psychosocial processes of development, and it is only because they are embedded in **Sexual scripts** that the physical acts themselves become important. These insights suggested the possi-bility of exploring the complex processes by which individuals acquired subjective meanings in interaction with significant others, and the effects of 'sexual stigma' on these developmental processes (Plummer 1975).

By the mid-1970s it is possible to detect the clear emergence of distinctive historical and sociological accounts, with two related concerns. One focused on the social categorization of sexuality, asking questions about what historical factors shaped sexual differences, which appeared so natural, but were in fact deeply cultural. The other was primarily concerned with understanding the shaping of subjective meanings through sexual scripts and social labelling, which allowed a better understanding of the balance between individual and collective sexual meanings.

A third theoretical element now came into play, that represented by the work of Michel Foucault (1979). Foucault's essay on *The History of Sexuality* is often seen, misleadingly, as the starting point of constructionist approaches, but there can be no doubt of the subsequent impact of what was planned as a brief prolegomenon to a multi-volumed study. Like Gagnon and Simon, Foucault appeared to be arguing that 'sexuality' was a 'historical invention'. Like McIntosh, and others who had been influenced by her, he saw the emergence of the concept of a distinctive homosexual personage as a historical process, with the late nineteenth century as the key moment. The process of medicalization, in particular, was seen as a vital explanatory factor. Like McIntosh, he suggested that psychologists and psychiatrists have not been objective scientists of desire, as the sexological tradition proclaimed, but on the contrary 'diagnostic agents in the process of social labelling' (McIntosh 1968). For Foucault they were key players in the shaping of sexual discourses that created new subjectivities in the nineteenth and twentieth centuries: the hysterical woman, the sexualized child, the heterosexual couple busily controlling births, and the invert or homosexual. Each of these were axes of power-knowledge, and the focal point of new forms of biopower and forms of governmentality, regulating individuals and populations. But at the same time, his suggestion that people do not react passively to social categorization – 'where there is power, there is resistance' – left open the question of how individuals react to social definitions, how, in a phrase that now became central to the debate, **Sexual identities** are formed in the intersection of social and subjective meanings.

This proved the most controversial element of social constructionism. Many influenced by **Gay liberation** saw in the historicization of the homosexual category a way of explaining the stigma that homosexuality carried, and the possibilities of challenging it. What was made in history could be changed in history. Others, however, believed clearly that homosexuality was intrinsic to their sense of self and social identity, essential to their nature. This was at the heart of the so-called social constructionist–essentialist controversy in the 1970s and 1980s (Stein 1992). For many, a critique of essentialism could also be conceived of as an attack on the very idea of a homosexual identity, a fundamental challenge to the hard-won gains of the lesbian and gay movement, and the claim to recognition of homosexuals as a legitimate minority group. This was the source of the appeal of subsequent theories of a 'gay gene' or 'gay brain', which suggested that **Sexual orientation** was wired into the human individual.

Social constructionism, Vance (1989) noted, had initially paid little attention to the construction of **Heterosexuality**. But without a wider sense that 'the heterosexual' was also a social construction, attempts to explain the invention of 'the homosexual' made little sense. One of the early attractions of the first volume of Foucault's *The History of Sexuality* was precisely that it both offered an account of the birth of the modern homosexual, and put that into a broader historical framework: by postulating the invention of sexuality as a category in Western thought, and in delineating the shifting relationships between men and women, adults and children, the normal and the perverse, as constituent elements in this process. Foucault himself was criticized for putting insufficient emphasis on the gendered nature of this process, but this was more than compensated for by the developing feminist critique of 'the heterosexual institution', with its own complex history (MacKinnon 1987; Richardson 1996).

Central to all these debates was the perception that sexuality in general is not a domain of easy pluralism, where homosexuality and heterosexuality sit easily side by side. It is structured in dominance, with heterosexuality privileged, and that privilege is essentially male-oriented. Homosexuality is constructed as a subordinate formation within the 'heterosexual continuum', with male and female homosexuality having a different relationship to the dominant forms. In turn, once this is recognized, it becomes both possible and necessary to explore the socially constructed patterns of **Gender**.

Although the constructionist debates began within the disciplines of sociology and history, later developments, taking forward both theoretical and political (especially feminist) interventions, owed a great deal to post-structuralist and deconstructionist literary studies, and to the emergence of **Queer** studies. Whereas history and sociology have characteristically attempted to produce order and pattern out of the chaos of events, the main feature of these approaches is to show the binary conflicts reflected in literary texts. The texts are read as sites of gender and sexual contestation, and therefore of power and resistance (Sedgwick 1990). Sedgwick's work and that of the American philosopher, Judith Butler (1990), were in part attempts to move away from the essentialist/constructionist binaries by emphasizing the 'performative' nature of sex and gender (though performativity and performance were in fact already present in symbolic interactionist and dramaturgical approaches). For queer theorists, the perverse is the worm at the centre of the normal, giving rise to sexual and cultural dissidence and a transgressive ethic, which constantly works to unsettle binarism and to suggest alternatives.

Much of the debate about the homosexual/heterosexual binary divide was based on the perceived Western experience, and was located in some sense of a historical development. Yet from the beginning, comparisons with non-Western sexual patterns were central to constructionist perspectives. Foucault (1979) compared the Western 'science of sex' with the non-Western 'erotic arts'. It was the very fact of different patterns of 'institutionalized homosexuality' across cultures that formed the starting point of McIntosh's (1968) essay. So it is not surprising that constructionist approaches have led to an efflorescence of studies of sexuality in general, and homosexuality in particular, in other cultures, tribal, Islamic, southern. And this comparative framework has increasingly been deployed within contemporary Western societies to highlight the difficulty of subsuming behaviour within a confining definition of condition or fixed orientation.

Historical and social constructionism have advanced and changed rapidly since the 1970s. The 'category' that early scholars were anxious to deconstruct has become 'categories' which proliferate in contemporary societies. 'Roles', neat slots into which people could be expected to fit as a response to the bidding of the agents of social control, have become 'performances' (Butler 1990) or 'necessary fictions' (Weeks 1995), whose contingencies demand exploration. 'Identities', which once seemed categoric, are now seen as fluid, relational, hybrid: people are not quite today what they were yesterday, or will be tomorrow. Identities have come to be seen as built around personal 'narratives', **Sexual stories** people tell each other in the various interpretive communities to which they belong (Plummer 1995). Sexual orientation may, or may not, be a product of genetics, psychosocial structuring or environmental pressures. For the constructionist, however, other questions are central: not what causes the variety of sexual desires, preferences or orientations that have existed in various societies at different times, but how societies shape meanings around sexual diversity, and the effects these have on individual lives.

SPACE

Sexuality is experienced in bodies and minds, but it is played out and conducted in delimited spaces. Spaces are both metaphorical and material. There are metaphorical spaces, like the political and moral space allowed by regimes of sexuality to enact, or prevent, different types of sexuality. Here an expanding space stands for the possibilities of challenging the norms, exploring possibilities, living diversity. At times the space for experimentation might grow as the cultural climate becomes more liberal and accommodating. At other times, societies may experience a closing of space, as conservative forces signal thus far and no further, or actively attempt to turn back the clock. This was so in much of Europe in the 1930s, or the USA and Britain in the 1980s. The mental space narrows or expands as political, economic, cultural or economic circumstances change, and opportunities for active forms of erotic **Agency** are opened or foreclosed.

But however important metaphorical space is, sexuality as an ensemble of fantasies, practices, prohibitions, encouragements, values, morals, norms, pleasures and pains is largely lived, performed, celebrated, feared or articulated in material spaces: in bedrooms, homes, neighbourhoods, streets, parks, 'red-light districts', saunas, sex parties, cruising places, in cities and villages, in schools, universities, hospitals, prisons, workplaces and other sites of pleasure and potential violence, played out in Mardi Gras or LGBT Pride celebrations, fought for in protests and demonstrations or 'regain the night' marches, acted out within religious, geographical and national boundaries, and within global flows of migration, **Sex tourism**, human **Trafficking** and the every expanding sites of cyber-space (Browne *et al.* 2007). None of these spaces are neutral. They both express and constitute complex power relations, based on gendered differentiations, racial and ethnic demarcations, exclusions and possibilities, heteronormative, homophobic and transphobic practices, rituals of violence and hatred, forms of resistance, transgression, citizenship and love. Spaces mark and reinforce differences of health and poverty, youth and age, status and class, subtle and not-so-subtle distinctions of taste, fashion, style, appearance and language. Space is an arena of vigorous energy, endemic conflict and continuous contestation.

Many of the most embattled spaces are barely seen as such. Consider home and school, so evocative of resilient values, socialization, continuity, mutual support, comfort and safety, but also of hidden dangers, especially for the sexually different. For children home has historically been the space for learning about gender, sexual identities and family values, but also for the gender uncertain or the homosexually inclined young people the site of unspoken, unmarked, heteronormative assumptions that silently or sometimes violently invalidate their sexuality. As they grow up, the gender or sexually marginal may find that a new home can also represent an aspiration for a better life, or offer a bulwark against a hostile or threatening world; it is a space for building lives with others like you, for living a sense of community, and for mutual care. Home can be a haven and a jumping-off point. It can also be the site of new forms of conflict, over resources, the division of labour, and sexual desire, a site of violence and danger. Concepts of home and belonging have become crucial to the LGBT experience, but they are rarely straightforward. A home is never just a home, a private space cut off from the world. It enacts complex social relations, and is shaped by the wider world (Weeks *et al.* 2001: 77–103). Schools, similarly, can be a site of conflicting norms, sometimes a war-zone, with the playground becoming a battlefield. Gender can be reinforced by the curriculum, the attitude of teachers, demeanour, or the spatial separation of students and the furnishing of the classroom. **Homophobia** may be reinforced by the rituals of play and the verbal abuse and bullying by the those who see themselves as 'normal' of those who do not quite fit in. Schools can reinforce hierarchies, confirm prejudice, essentialize difference. They can also, of course, inculcate values of tolerance, mutual understanding, reason and justice. A school is never just a school.

It is the city that has best provided the space for **Sexual diversity** and life experiments. In the turbulence, overcrowding and vibrancy of great cities people are promiscuously thrown together in often chaotic moral confusion. The bishops of London in the Middle Ages controlled the brothels of the Borough, just across the river, which reminds us that sexual morality was for long sustained by licensed spaces of immorality, just beyond the spatial boundaries of the city. In the burgeoning cities of Western Europe or America in the nineteenth century expanding cultures and spaces of prostitution were seen by pioneering feminists and social purity campaigners as the bulwark of the double standard, yet also offered spaces for 'rescue' and re-moralization. In the city, spaces of 'gay women', that is prostitutes, overlapped with spaces of same-sex exploration – see **Gay**. The anonymity of this world of strangers casually thrown together, the promiscuous intermingling of the streets and the solidarities of the night provided the spaces for homosexual meeting places, beats and embryonic identities. These can be traced back to the Italian cities of the late Middle Ages, and by the late nineteenth century existed in all the major urban sites, from London to Berlin, Paris to New York (Higgs 1999). They existed more for men than women, which reminds us that space is highly gendered, that it was easier for men to escape the demands of home and family than women. Men were safer on the streets than unaccompanied women (who would be assumed to be prostitutes). And it was men rather than women who had the social mobility and resources to build alternative sexual ways of life. Women's space remained largely domestic, though even here alternative sexual selves could emerge – see **Lesbian**.

The urban (homo)sexual subcultures of the USA and Western Europe provided the context for the emergence of complex sexual patterns of life in the early twentieth century (Chauncey 1994), a testing ground for emerging homosexual ways of life in the 1950s and early 1960s (Houlbrooke 2005), and the site of the eruption of **Gay liberation** in the late 1960s and early 1970s. They provided the physical space of the **Closet**. Subsequently, they offered new spaces for gay sexual experimentation, for new patterns of domesticity, relationships and parenting, increasingly for women as well as men, and for a push for political power as LGBT communities achieved critical mass, mainly in North America, but also in urban gay villages in Europe (Valentine 2002).

The new visibility of lesbians and gays since the 1970s in gay spaces like New York's Greenwich Village, San Francisco's Castro, London's Soho or Manchester's gay village or Paris's Marais has had a double edge: they are sites of safety, underpinned by identity, a sense of community and new forms of gentrification and consumerism; they can play a key role in reviving a city's fortunes. But they are also sites of new demarcations and divisions, between those who have resources, and those who do not, between the assimilated and the marginalized. They also remain as potential sites of danger, subject to random violence. In a homophobic culture violence can be routine, commonplace, performed by ordinary people as part of the routine of everyday living, which is why it is so often invisible (Moran and Skeggs: 2004: 27). It readily becomes visible, however, when LGBT campaigners attempt to affirm their presence in hostile territory, as happened in post-Communist cities in Eastern Europe in the early twenty-first century when Pride events were forcefully disrupted by anti-gay demonstrators, with police and authority compliance. Even in the most gay-friendly cities space remains generally heavily hetero-sexed and heteronormative, so that any entry into the space by those deemed immoral or just different is potentially destabilizing (Hubbard 2001). The 're-territoralization' of space by LGBT people (and others on the sexual margins) through gay villages, bars, coffee shops, restaurants, festivals and the like has been a crucial stage in the evolution of safer lifestyles for LGBT people, but it is a safety that requires constant vigilance.

Spaces are governed by unspoken understandings as much as by fences and boundaries. They are policed by various authorities as well as by the discretions and self-surveillance of the inhabitants. But spaces are rarely static, and are subject to often rapid change as the meanings and practices of the erotic shift and develop, and as the sexual balance of power shifts. Spaces are sites of power, and are highly political. Sexuality is constantly being defined and redefined within their limits.

SUBJECT

Concepts of the subject, and the meanings of subjectivity, have been central to recent attempts to theorize **Gender** and **Sexuality**. The notion of the subject is closely related to cognate terms such as the self, the person, the individual, and all raise important issues about the influence of culture in shaping the human being. Each of these terms, however, has different implications for social theory. In current debates about **Individualization** ideas about the reflexive self play a key role, especially in dealing with the question of structure and **Agency**. Notions of the interactive self manipulating symbols and language to create social meanings have been central to the development of **Social constructionism**, and to the elaboration of the significance of **Sexual scripts** and **Sexual stories**. The concept of performativity which has been so central to recent developments of **Queer** theory is similar in some ways to the dramaturgical elements in interactionist theories, but also relies on notions of the individual as discursively produced in power relations. Queer theory has also been heavily influenced by selective appropriation of **Psychoanalysis**, especially the challenge to the unity of the human subject implied by the theory of the unconscious. Each of these theoretical approaches has been valuable in challenging the fixity, solidity and inevitability of received notions of gender and sexuality, and in affirming the complexities and ambivalences of subjectivity.

The notion of the subject has been particularly favoured by those who seek to displace the unitary individual as the focus of social theory. In the decades following the late 1960s this was associated with an anti-humanist approach, especially the writings of the Marxist philosopher Louis Althusser and the psychoanalyst Jacques Lacan, but also linked to the work of Michel Foucault and later post-structuralists. Both Lacan and Althusser saw their work as a recovery of the most radical elements of the work of Marx and Freud respectively, in seeing the individual as the effect of social and psychic processes. Marx famously saw the individual as an ensemble of social relations, and building on this Althusser theorized that the subject is the result of ideological 'interpellation', or 'hailing' through which the subject is constituted in the social world. Ideology is to be understood as a distortion of human beings' material circumstances, that obscures the real operations of power. Subsequent theories, rather than focusing on the determining and distorting effects of ideology, have explored the impact of different discourses in operating forms of power-knowledge, creating multiple subject positions.

For Freud the unconscious fundamentally undermines a unitary sense of self, which is only ever precariously achieved. The desiring subject is the end product of processes it is barely aware of. For Lacan, in his 'recovery' of Freud, this implied that the subject in its psychic development is positioned as a gendered and sexed being, under the sign of the Phallus, representing the law of the Father which underpins the symbolic order, the order of language and cultural meaning. The subject does not so much speak autonomously but is spoken through by discourse, law and culture, a symptom of broader psychical, libidinal and linguistic systems (Grosz 1992b: 411).

Two elements of these theoretical positions have proved especially influential in subsequent feminist and sexual theorizing. First, they see the subject as the product of wider social forces – including the structures of gender and sexuality – rather than the originator or producer of these forces. Second, they open the way to seeing the subject not only as an effect of social forces but as fundamentally divided by the host of different discourses they are subject to (the double use of subject here indicates the point made by Foucault that the word subject carries both the meaning of the focus of social action and of being subjected to wider discourses). 'Individuals are multiply constituted subjects who take up multiple subject positions within a range of discourses and social practices' (Moore 2007: 17).

This opens the way to seeing the subject as portrayed in post-structuralist theories as open, fluid, divided and subject to the multiple and complex operations of power. But the resulting subject positions are contradictory and conflicting, so that individuals construct their sense of self through a variety of possible subjectives. Discourses may work to constitute the subject, but they cannot guarantee how the subject will identify with and take up different subject positions. Both in relation to gender and sexual identities the individual subject is never wholly captured by a unitary model of who and what they are. **Desire** especially undermines a unitary vision of the self, because the self can never be regarded as complete or finished. In these multiplicities of possible identifications lies the possibility of refusing identity and the determining forces of power and discourse.

The theory of the subject, and especially the role of psychoanalysis within it, has made a major contribution to the undermining of the idea of an essential pre-given gender or sexual identity which shapes the social. It stresses in its place the variety of different social forces – historical, cultural, political, racial, gendered and sexual – that construct the individual. The challenge remains of ensuring that, in theory as well as in practice, the space of self-determination and of effective agency is recognized and promoted.

T

TOLERATION

In his ground-breaking study of the early gay movement, *Homosexual: Oppression and Liberation*, first published in 1971, Dennis Altman (1993: 59) comments that the most common form of oppression is neither outright persecution nor overt discrimination, but the patronizing tolerance of liberals, what Christopher Isherwood called 'annihilation by blandness'. This indicates a fundamental problem with the concept of toleration. It is a stance based on suspicion rather than full acceptance, on acquiescence rather than commitment. For millions across the globe still subject to various forms of sexual oppression and exploitation, tolerance might seem a glorious gift. Better the toleration that potentially demeans than the absolutism that denies or sometimes kills. Live and let live as a philosophy has offered a way of living with different, and antagonistic, moral positions for centuries, and has allowed the growth of a limited sexual pluralism. But it stops short of full recognition of the validity of different ways of life, and suffers from a basic flaw. Toleration is not seen as a good in itself, but for what it leads to. It is essentially a negative value. That stance is rooted in the history of the concept.

The roots of toleration lie in the European religious conflicts of the seventeenth century, and reflect the uneasy, and hard-won accommodation between different Christian sects who might otherwise be murdering each other. It usually reflected a reluctant acceptance by the majority or strongest group that they could not completely defeat the faiths of others, but had to find a way of living with them, as best they could (Mendus 1988). Religious toleration began hesitantly in the Netherlands and Britain, and found a home in the American colonies (which did not prevent fierce, and often intolerant moral battles being waged, even up to the present day). Toleration did not signify approval. On the contrary, it usually signalled mutual disapproval. It assumes incompatibility, and the dangers of difference and division. It is a pragmatic response to the murderous consequences of pursuing truth at all costs (Weeks 1995: 74).

The concept of toleration outlined by John Stuart Mill in the nineteenth century is less crude than this enforced pragmatism suggests. It is based on respect for the individual and his or her diverse ends. The only concept of freedom worthy of the name was that of pursuing our own good in our own way, as long as we do not try to deprive others of their own freedom (Mill 1975). But even here diversity is to be tolerated as a means to an end – intellectual advance and moral progress – rather than a good in itself. In the hands of sexual reformers who consciously adopted a Millian position it led to a cautious utilitarianism. This is apparent in the most famous elaboration of this position in relation to sexuality in the Anglo-Saxon tradition, the Wolfenden Report on prostitution and male homosexuality of 1957. Legal conservatives argued that a shared morality binds a society together. The law must therefore enforce what the majority prefer. If that involves an abhorrence of homosexuality, then the law should reflect that. Against that the liberal reformers argued that the harm done by an action must be balanced by the harm done by making it illegal. If a law was unworkable, then it should be liberalized as a marker of a necessary toleration. This proved to be a remarkably influential position that shaped a swathe of reforming legislation in England and Wales – on homosexuality, abortion, divorce, obscenity and censorship – in the years ahead. What the reforms failed to do, however, was to take any moral stance on the merits of the sexual activities themselves. There is no endorsement of sexual diversity, which tends to be seen as a problem of social order or individual responsibility rather than a potential societal good (Weeks 1995: 177).

The limitations of a traditional idea of toleration have become apparent with the post-1970s rise and rise of **Sexual diversity**. A more radical version of toleration requires doing more than leaving other people alone. As Mendus argues (1987: 14), 'it requires making opportunities for others and going out of one's way to assist them'. It involves the fostering and recognition of diversity. This suggests that all forms of sexuality, except those which use other humans as mere means, are worthy of respect and recognition. That does not mean they cannot be criticized, but that should only be done if they are granted **Recognition** first, and if the criticisms follow the rules of civilized discourse. This positive form of toleration inevitably clashes with those who claim a special relationship to the truth in their opposition, say, to **Abortion**, or **Homosexuality**, or sex education for the young. The growing recognition of sexual diversity has been accompanied by the rise of new absolutism and of various forms of **Fundamentalism**. A dialogue across difference is difficult when only one side favours talking.

That makes it all the more necessary that ideas of difference become the starting point for the advancement of wider notions of solidarity. As Bauman notes, 'tolerance as such is possible *only* in the form of solidarity: that is . . . a practical recognition of the *relevance* and *validity* of the other's difference, expressed in a willing engagement in the dialogue' (1992: xxi). This is a long way from the reluctant and patronizing toleration that Altman speaks of. In a world where clashes of conflicting truths about sexuality, and much else, still abound, it signals a challenge perhaps no less great than that faced by the first advocates of toleration in the seventeenth century.

TRAFFICKING

Human trafficking is the term widely used to describe the transnational trade in people, either for forced labour or for sexual exploitation. It is the latter which has been the most controversial issue, and has become highly contested, raising critical issues about exploitation, victimhood, the possibilities and limits of **Choice**, and the role of international agencies. Sexual trafficking is closely related to the changing forms of **Prostitution** and sex work, and generally refers to women and children, though trafficking in young men also takes place. It involves a trade in people generally from the poorest parts of the world to the richest, though many other countries are also involved as transit stops. It has become a multibillion dollar industry, and the focus of international campaigns against what has been labelled the modern form of slavery (O'Connell Davidson 2006). It has also given rise, some have argued, to an international 'rescue industry' that pathologizes the people who are engaged in the sex industry.

It is not a new phenomenon. Josephine Butler, the British feminist campaigner against the state regulation and support of prostitution founded an international organization (later known as the International Abolitionist Federation) to campaign against what became known as the 'white slave trade' in 1875. An international conference on the prevention of sexual trafficking was held in Paris as early as 1885, and the effort to control the trade became a powerful motif in feminist campaigns against sexual exploitation that has had a long resonance.

The changes associated with **Globalization** – greater ease of international travel, the breakdown of traditional structures, the disruptions caused by economic restructuring and the impact of wars – have all contributed to the massive growth of transnational movements of people, including for sexual purposes. It has generated a heightened awareness of the trade in people, and made possible a global mobilization against it. The so-called Trafficking Protocol adopted by the UN in 2000 has been signed by over 130 countries. The meanings and implications of trafficking, however, are less clear-cut than some would like to believe. There is little doubt that the global sex industry is the locus of often extreme forms of exploitation, an international 'skin trade' in Seabrook's (2001) graphic phrase. But even amongst feminists there are sharply different positions. At the centre of contemporary debates has been the question of the extent to which prostitution and sex work generally is always and inevitably exploitative of women and children, and the degree to which people who sell sex are victims or potential agents and free actors. For Kathleen Barry (1995), and the US-based Coalition Against Trafficking of Women with which she has been strongly associated, there is no doubt that prostitution is quite straightforwardly exploitation, and therefore a violation of the human right to dignity, whether a prostitute has consented or not. There can be no distinction between forced and free prostitution, only 'sex slavery'. This position has had a major impact on the attitudes of NGOs and of many governments.

On the other hand, this position has infuriated many defenders of sexual rights, including feminists, who see a sharp distinction between a child forced into prostitution and women who make a choice to enter the sex trade for economic reasons, and who see themselves as 'sex workers'. For such activists the aim is less a moral crusade against prostitution and more a struggle against legal systems and hypocritical moral codes that penalize sex workers and deny their rights (Agustin 2007). This in turn has produced international movements of sex workers. The International Committee for Prostitutes' Rights was founded in the 1970s by the US based COYOTE group (Call Off Your Old Tired Ethics) and the English Collective of Prostitutes, with the first world meeting held in Washington in 1975. At the Second World Whores' Congress held in Brussels in 1986 delegates demanded that prostitution 'should be redefined as legitimate work and the prostitutes should be redefined as legitimate citizens' (Altman 2001: 101). Defining the conditions under which the work can be legitimized has, however, proved more difficult. The Trafficking Victims Protection Act passed in the USA in 2000 gives protection to victims of trafficking (VoT) but relies heavily on a distinction between victims and 'guilty' sex workers, a distinction which has had a wide currency (O'Connell Davidson 2006: 14–15). Such distinctions do nothing to protect those deemed to be guilty, nor to support positive forms of **Agency**. Constant references to sex slavery has the effect of legitimizing stronger border protection and the surveillance of migrants, while often throwing them into the hands of criminal gangs (Schaeffer-Grabiel 2010).

The sexual exploitation of children and young people has been a particular object of international concern. An important signal of this was the emergence of the acronym 'CSEC' – the Commercial Sexual Exploitation of Children' – to bring together the varying forms of child exploitation, including child prostitution, child pornography and trafficking in children (Saunders 2005). The new definition was the result of two decades of activism, culminating in two World Congresses, in 1996 and 2001. It is based on the belief that childhood is fundamentally different from adulthood, and should be protected from commerce and sexual activity – see **Childhood sexuality**. Such a stance inevitably evokes the image of children solely as victims of exploitation, and while this has been an advance from the former stigmatizing labels, and has encouraged children to be change-agents, it produces new problems. It founders especially when faced with young people who reject the idea that they are victims, and who do not see the harm supposedly done to them, many rejecting suggestions that they have been forced into prostitution (O'Connell Davidson 2005).

The problem with many of the initiatives against trafficking is that they see those at the sharp end only as victims of exploitation and (male) violence with no effective agency. Critics have argued that a preoccupation with **Sexual violence** tends to reinforce a traditional patriarchal view of female passivity, and childhood innocence, and to reinforce a cultural essentialism about the nature of non-Western societies (Corrêa *et al.* 2008: 181). The reality is more complex, and a more nuanced view would stress the possibilities for agency and change in even the most difficult and exploitative situations.

TRANSGENDER

Transgender is a term in constant evolution. First deployed by Virginia Prince in print in 1969, it was initially used to describe people like herself who lived outside gender norms but who did not identify as transvestite or transsexual. It was thus a term that made a sharp distinction within the world of gender nonconformity. By the 1980s it had become an umbrella term for that world, and since the 1990s has become a broad radical political term that embraces a variety of challenges to gender conformity. 'Gender-fucking' had been a key element in **Gay liberation** since its stormy birth at the mythic Stonewall riots in New York in 1969, but this had always been a source of controversy, especially from feminist critics. The emergence of transgender as a central concept in sexual and gender politics marks a significant shift, a key aspect of the **Queer** moment which has challenged fixed categorization. It has given rise to new forms of activism campaigning for trans rights that are increasingly international in scope. At the same time activists have defined a specific form of hostility towards transgender, transphobia, which is analogous in many ways to **Homophobia** (Califia 1997).

Two terms, transvestism and transsexualism, dominated debates about gender nonconformity for much of the twentieth century. The first term was coined by the sexologist Magnus Hirschfeld in 1910, to describe cross-dressing, and has tended to over-write other terms which evolved at roughly the same time. (The term eonism, used by Havelock Ellis, deriving from the eighteenth-century French diplomat Chevalier d'Éon, who lived the early part of life as a man, and the latter as a woman, soon disappeared from use.) Hirschfeld saw close links between transvestism and homosexuality, but it rapidly became clear that there was no necessary relationship between the two. **Sexual orientation** and cross-dressing were different phenomena. In the same way, theorists made distinctions within transvestism, between people who felt an overwhelming emotional and psychic need to dress across **Gender** conventions, without necessarily feeling the need to change personal gender, and those whose interests in cross-dressing were more akin to a **Fetish**. Transsexualism, on the other hand, was more clearly about people feeling trapped within the wrong body, for whom a change of gender through surgery was the necessary psychic and physical solution. The term itself was invented by the American sexologist Harry Benjamin in 1954, but Hirschfeld and his colleagues had attempted what became know as gender reassignment before World War I, and there were subsequent attempts in the next few decades. Trans-sexualism received worldwide publicity in the 1950s when Christine Jorgensen, a former GI, had sex-reassignment therapy in Denmark. The clinical term Gender Dysphoria Syndrome was coined in 1974.

The subversive and transgressive emphasis of the contemporary transgender moment represents a significant shift from these earlier experiences, important as they were. Transgender has become a concept embracing all cross-living and cross-dwelling people, a whole gamut of 'gender complex' people (More and Whittle 1999). The transgender person has become an iconic figure for boundary crossing, for challenging fixity, and transgenderism has 'increasingly come to be seen as a privileged vantage point from which it is possible to observe how sexed and gendered bodies are conceived and enacted in everyday life' (Kulick 1998: 259). Cross-dressing and cross-living are practices that parody the very notion that there is an original true nature (Rubin 1999: 184).

This is not, however, quite how it is always seen or necessarily lived. Transgender contains within it both a move towards a profound unsettling of gender categories and the essentializing of traditional gender. It is the latter that has attracted the most vitriolic challenges, especially from some feminists who see both cross-dressing and transsexualism as a surrender to the most stereotyping of gender imagery (most famously Raymond 1979), an all too easy acceptance that there is a true gender that trans people want to live. It is also, ironically, a critical and necessary stance for many pre-operative trans people who have to convince the medical authorities before they can receive medical support not only that they passionately believe that they are currently living in the wrong gender, but also that they can live in the other gender. The acceptance of the idea that transsexuals can claim certain new rights, for example to medical treatment and to change their birth certificates, is based on the assumption that they have been trapped within the wrong body, and have now transitioned to a new self. The UK Gender Recognition Act of 2004 gives legal recognition to those who have taken 'decisive steps' to live fully and permanently in their 'acquired gender'. This, Morgan (1999: 234) has suggested, is the 'trans-sexual dilemma': 'They are trapped between the desire to explore the possibilities of the performative gender bending and the need to fight for basic rights . . . for which they need to present a coherent, essentialist identity without ambiguity.' The queer celebration of transgression can obliterate the ordinariness of transition, and erase crucial distinctions, for example between the butch queer lesbian and a trans person, or the specific experiences of pre- and post-operative transsexuals (Rubin 1999: 189). Prosser has spoken of transition as a journey not an event, but a journey that has its own specifications and location, rather than a postmodern celebration of mobility (1999: 91, 110).

There are many journeys, many transitions. 'Tales of transgendering', as Ekins and King (2006: xiv) remark, 'take many forms.' Drag queens, drag kings, transmen, transwomen, bigender persons, cross-dressers, gender queers, androgynes, intersex people, gender ambiguous and gender fluid – all suggest that the gender constellation is not binary but multipolar and polyvocal, and it is this diversity and multiplicity that is ultimately subversive (Halberstam 1998, 2005). It challenges the traditional monolith of gender, and breaks its imprisoning binarism. As Raewyn Connell (2010: 18) has put it: 'Transition is not a thing in itself. . . . Transition is a process of relocation in the gender order, a relocation that creates new possibilities of action. That action may be simply the making of a survivable life. . . . But it may be more; it may indeed point to historical shifts in gender relations that reach far beyond an individual life.'

V

VIAGRA

'Viagra' is the trade name for sildenafil citrate, a drug widely used in the treatment of erectile dysfunction (ED) amongst men. Originally developed for the treatment of angina, since it was launched in the USA by the Pfizer pharmaceutical company in 1998 as a cure for ED, it has become a global boom story. Sales were already $1billion by 2001, cleverly marketed by leading public personalities, including politicians and sportsmen, apparently now unafraid of confessing their little local difficulties. The little blue pill that 'changed sex in America' (Loe 2004) was soon joined by others, including Cialis (tadalfil) and Levitra (vardenafil) that compete for a multibillion dollar global market, and the search was on for 'a female viagra'.

When the British Health Secretary authorized the distribution of Viagra via the National Health Service in the late 1990s, it was supposed to be supplied only to those with serious erectile problems. Since then the criteria have been progressively loosened. The wonder pills are now available over the counter, and illicitly on a massive scale through the Web, alongside a variety of 'herbal' alternatives. A quarter of all spam at one point in the mid-noughties was allegedly linked to Viagra and similar pills. These have ceased to be simple alleviators of genuine medical problems. They have become happiness pills offering an instant fix. Governments across the world continue to fulminate against, and attempt to prohibit, illegal substances from cannabis to cocaine but they are apparently happy to license Viagra and its siblings, and to tolerate a vast grey market that has little now to do with ED as a certified male medical problem of a minority, and everything to do with enhanced performance by the majority. The mind-blowing orgasm has become a defining marker of sexual pleasure.

As science once promised to free people from reproductive inadequacy, it also now promises us freedom from sexual inadequacy. Sex may no longer be necessary to reproduction, and reproduction no longer the sole goal of sex, but this has only served to ensure that the pleasure principle has become inextricably part of the performance principle. If eros is now seen as fundamental to the successful relationship, the greatest failing is likely to be inadequate sexual performance, and increasingly this has been technologized. If the Pill was the technological fix of the 1960s, Viagra and its kin chemicals has become the fix for the early twenty-first century (Weeks 2007). In the process, there is an acute danger that anything less than a hyper performance will be pathologized. All the science is just window dressing, Tiefer (2006) argues, for an industry that wants to standardize sexual pleasures, to maximize its sales globally. In the process, new medical problems are manufactured: not so much sexual inadequacy as a result of a medical condition, but individual inadequacy because you failed to use a freely available little pill. For critics like Tiefer the most dangerous aspect of this is the invention of a wholly new medical problem for women, for which a female Viagra may be the solution: 'female sexual dysfunction' (FSD). Allegedly 43 per cent of women 'suffer' from this new condition, for which the evidence is negligible. Viagra as magical cure and as symbol of new possibilities is a more complex phenomenon than its promoters like to believe (Sexualities 2006).

In this it is like other scientific advances. The sexual liberation movements of the 1970s claimed to challenge the hegemony of science in defining the nature of the sexual. The pharmaceutical breakthroughs of recent years have suggested that applied science is more resilient than that suggests – producing unambiguous goods in combating HIV and the miserable condition of ED, and more ambivalent achievements, perhaps, in helping to redefine the new joys of sex under a blue haze of chemicals. Viagra has come to symbolize both the potentialities and dangers of medical intervention on the body and its pleasures.

REFERENCES

Adam, Barry D. (1995) *The Rise of a Lesbian and Gay Movement*, New York: Twayne.

Adam, Barry D. (1998) 'Theorizing Homophobia', *Sexualities* 1 (4), November, 387–404.

Adam, Barry D. (2006) 'Relationship Innovation in Male Couples', *Sexualities* 9 (1), February, 5–26.

Adam, Barry D., Duyvendak, Jan Willem and Krouwel, Andre (eds) (1999) *The Global Emergence of Gay and Lesbian Politics: National Imprints of a Worldwide Movement*, Philadelphia, PA: Temple University Press.

Adkins, Lisa (2002) *Revisions: Gender and Sexuality in Late Modernity*, Buckingham: Open University Press.

AFSC (American Friends Service Committee) (2002) 'AFSC Hawai'i Gay Liberation Program: Activist Materials Addressing Tourism', *GLQ: A Journal of Lesbian and Gay Studies 8* (1–2), 207–26.

Aggleton, Peter and Parker, Richard (eds) (2010) *Routledge Handbook of Sexuality, Health and Rights*, London: Routledge.

Agustin, Laura M. (2007) *Sex at the Margins: Migration, Labour Markets and the Rescue Industry*, London: Zed Books.

Alexander, M. J. (1997) 'Erotic Autonomy as a Politics of Decolonization: An Anatomy of Feminist and State Practices in the Bahamas Tourist Economy', in Alexander, M. J. and Mohanty, C. T. (eds) *Feminist Genealogies, Colonial Legacies, Democratic Futures*, New York: Routledge, 63–100.

Altman, Dennis (1993) *Homosexual: Oppression and Liberation* (first edition 1971), New York: New York University Press.

Altman, Dennis (1994) *Power and Community: Organizational and Cultural Responses to AIDS*, London and Bristol, PA: Taylor and Francis.

Altman, Dennis (2001) *Global Sex*, Chicago, IL: University of Chicago Press.

Altman, Dennis, Vance, Carol, Vicinus, Martha, Weeks, Jeffrey and others (1989) *Homosexuality, Which Homosexuality?* London: GMP Publishers.

American Psychological Association (2007) *Report of the APA Task Force on the Sexualization of Girls*, Washington, DC: American Psychological Association, www.apa. org/pi/wpo/sexualization.html, accessed 10 April 2010.

Amnesty International (1997) *Breaking the Silence: Human Rights Violations Based on Sexual Orientation*, London: Amnesty International.

Amnesty International (2001a) *Crimes of Hate, Conspiracy of Silence: Torture and Ill-treatment Based on Sexual Identity*, London: Amnesty International.

Amnesty International (2001b) *Broken Bodies, Shattered Minds: Torture and Ill-treatment of Women*, London: Amnesty International.

Amnesty International (2004) *It's in Our Hands: Stop Violence Against Women*, London: Amnesty International.

Appiah, Kwame Anthony (2006) *Cosmopolitanism: Ethics in a World of Strangers*, New York: W. W. Norton.

Archard, David (1998) *Sexual Consent*, Oxford: Westview Press.

Attwood, Feona (2009a) *porn.com: Making Sense of Online Pornography*, New York: Digital Formations/Peter Lang.

Attwood, Feona (ed.) (2009b) *Mainstreaming Sex: The Sexualization of Western Culture*, London: I. B. Tauris.

Bamforth, Nicholas (ed.) (2005) *Sex Rights*, Oxford Amnesty Lectures, Oxford: Oxford University Press.

Barker, Meg and Langdridge, Darren (eds) (2010) *Understanding Non-Monogamies*, New York: Routledge.

Barry, Kathleen (1979) *Female Sexual Slavery*, Englewood Cliffs, NJ: Prentice Hall.

Barry, Kathleen (1995) *The Prostitution of Sexuality*, New York: New York University Press.

Bates, Stephen (2004) *A Church at War: Anglicans and Homosexuality*, London: I. B. Tauris.

Bauman, Zygmunt (1989) *Legislators and Interpreters: On Modernity, Post-Modernity and Intellectuals*, Cambridge: Polity Press.

Bauman, Zygmunt (1992) *Intimations of Postmodernity*, London: Routledge.

Bauman, Zygmunt (1998) 'On Postmodern Uses of Sex', *Theory, Culture and Society* 15 (3–4), 19–33.

Bauman, Zygmunt (2003) *Liquid Love: On the Frailty of Human Bonds*, Cambridge: Polity Press.

Bauman, Zygmunt (2005) *Liquid Life*, Cambridge: Polity Press.

Bayer, Ronald (1981) *Homosexuality and American Psychiatry. The Politics of Diagnosis*, New York: Basic Books.

Bech, Henning (1999) 'After the Closet', *Sexualities* 2 (3), August, 343–6.

Beck, Ulrich (1992) *Risk Society: Towards a New Modernity*, London: Sage.

Beck, Ulrich (1994) 'The Reinvention of Politics: Towards a Theory of Reflexive Modernization', in Beck, Ulrich, Giddens, Anthony and Lash, Scott, *Reflexive Modernization: Politics, Tradition and Aesthetics in the Modern Social Order*, Cambridge: Polity Press, 1–55.

Beck, Ulrich (1999) *World Risk Society*, Cambridge: Polity Press.

Beck, Ulrich (2002) 'The Cosmopolitan Society and its Enemies', *Theory, Culture and Society* 19 (1–2), 17–44.

Beck, Ulrich (2006) *The Cosmopolitan Vision*, Cambridge: Polity Press.

Beck, Ulrich and Beck-Gernsheim, Elisabeth (1995) *The Normal Chaos of Love*, Cambridge: Polity Press.

Beck, Ulrich and Beck-Gernsheim, Elisabeth (2002) *Individualization: Institutionalized Individualism and its Social and Political Consequences*, London: Sage.

Beck, Ulrich, Giddens, Anthony and Lash, Scott (1994) *Reflexive Modernization: Politics, Tradition and Aesthetics in the Modern Social Order*, Cambridge: Polity Press.

Beckmann, Andrea (2009) The Social Construction of Sexuality and Perversion: Deconstructing Sadomasochism, London: Palgrave Macmillan.

Bell, Daniel (1996) *The Cultural Contradictions of Capitalism, Twentieth Anniversary Edition*, New York: Basic Books.

Bell, David (2006) 'Bodies, Technologies, Spaces: On "Dogging"', Sexualities 9 (4), October, 387–408.

Bell, David and Binnie, Jon (2000) *The Sexual Citizen: Queer Politics and Beyond*, Cambridge: Polity Press.

Benjamin, Jessica (1990) *The Bonds of Love: Psychoanalysis, Feminism and the Problem of Domination*, London: Virago.

Berlant, Laura (1997) *The Queen of America goes to Washington: Essays on Sex and Citizenship*, Durham, NC: Duke University Press.

Bernauer, J. and Rasmussen, D. (eds) (1988) *The Final Foucault*, Cambridge, MA: MIT Press.

Bernstein, Elizabeth (2007) *Temporarily Yours: Intimacy, Authenticity and the Commerce of Sex*, Chicago, IL: Chicago University Press.

Bernstein, Elizabeth and Schaffner, L. (eds) (2005) *Regulating Sex: The Politics of Intimacy and Identity*, New York: Routledge.

Bersani, Leo and Phillips, Adam (2008) *Intimacies*, Chicago, IL: University of Chicago Press.

Bettinger, M. (2005) 'Polyamory and Gay Men: A Family Systems Approach', *Journal of GLBT Family Studies* 1 (1), 97–116.

Bhatt, Chetan (1997) *Liberation and Purity: Race, New Religious Movements and the Ethics of Postmodernity*, London: University College London.

Binnie, Jon (2004) *The Globalization of Sexuality*, London: Sage.

Bland, Lucy and Doan, Laura (1998) *Sexology in Culture: Labelling Bodies and Desires*, Cambridge: Polity Press.

Blasius, Mark (1994) *Gay and Lesbian Politics: Sexuality and the Emergence of a New Ethics*, Philadelphia, PA: Temple University Press.

Blumstein, Philip and Schwartz, Pepper (1974) 'Lesbianism and Bisexuality', in Goode, Erich and Troiden, Richard R. (eds) *Sexual Deviance and Sexual Deviants*, New York: William Morrow.

Blumstein, Philip, and Schwartz, Pepper (1977) 'Bisexuality in Men', in Warren, Carol (ed.) *Sexuality: Encounters, Identities and Relationships*, Beverly Hills, CA: Sage Publications, 79–98.

Boswell, John (1994) *Same Sex Unions in Pre-modern Europe*, New York: Villard Books.

Bouhdiba, Abdelwahab (1985) *Sexuality in Islam*, London: Routledge and Kegan Paul.

Bourdieu, Pierre (2001) *Masculine Domination*, Cambridge: Polity Press.

Boyes, Roger (2006) 'Cannibalism is Murder – Even if the Victim Requests to be Eaten', *The Times* (London), 10 May, 3.

Brandzel, A. L. (2005) 'Queering Citizenship? Same-sex Marriage and the State', *GLQ: A Journal of Lesbian and Gay Studies* 11 (2), 171–204.

Brickell, Chris (2006) 'The Sociological Construction of Gender and Sexuality', *Sociological Review* 54 (1), 87–113.

Browne, Kath, Lim, Jason and Brown, Gavin (2007) *Geographies of Sexualities: Theory, Practices and Politics*, Aldershot and Burlington, VT: Ashgate.

Brownmiller, Susan (1974) *Against Our Will*, Harmondsworth: Penguin.

Bryant, Karl and Vidal-Ortiz, Salvador (2008) 'Introduction to Retheorizing Homophobia', *Sexualities* 11 (4), August, 387–96.

Burke, Peter (2009) *Cultural Hybridity*, Cambridge: Polity Press.

Butler, Judith (1990) *Gender Trouble: Feminism and the Subversion of Identity*, New York: Routledge.

Butler, Judith (1993) *Bodies that Matter: On the Discursive Limits of Sex*, New York and London: Routledge.

Butler, Judith (2004) *Undoing Gender*, London: Routledge.

Butler, Judith (2005) 'On Being Besides Oneself: On the Limits of Sexual Autonomy', in Bamforth, Nicholas (ed.) *Sex Rights*, Oxford Amnesty Lectures, Oxford: Oxford University Press, 48–78.

Caballero, Chamion, Edwards, Rosalind and Smith, Darren (2008) 'Cultures of Mixing: Understanding Partnerships across Ethnicity', *Twenty-first Century Society* 3 (1), 49–63.

Califia, Pat (1979) 'Unraveling the Sexual Fringe: A Secret Side of Lesbian Sexuality', *The Advocate*, 27 December.

Califia, Pat (1997) *Sex Changes: The Politics of Transgenderism*, San Francisco, CA: Cleis Press.

Callen, Michael and Berkowitz, R. (1983) *How to Have Sex in an Epidemic: One Approach*, New York: privately circulated pamphlet.

Carballo-Dieguez, A. and Bauermeister, J. (2004) '"Barebacking": Intentional Condomless Anal Sex in HIV-Risk Contexts. Reasons for and Against It', *Journal of Homosexuality* 43 (1), 1–16.

Carnes, Patrick (2001) *Out of the Shadows: Understanding Sexual Addiction*, Centre City, MN: Hazeldon Publishing.

Carsten, Janet (2004) *After Kinship*, Cambridge: Cambridge University Press.

Chaline, E. R. (2010) 'The Construction, Maintenance, and Evolution of Gay SM Sexualities and Sexual Identities: A Preliminary Description of SM Sexual Identity Practices', *Sexualities* 13 (3), June, 338–56.

Chauncey, George (1994) *Gay New York: Gender, Urban Culture, and the Making of the Gay Male World, 1890–1940*, New York: Basic Books.

Cherlin, Andrew J. (2009) *The Marriage-Go-Round: The State of Marriage and the Family in America Today*, New York: Vintage Books.

Chodorow, Nancy (1978) *The Reproduction of Mothering: Psychoanalysis and the Sociology of Gender*, Berkeley: University of California Press.

Cohen, Anthony P. (1985) *The Symbolic Construction of Community*, Chichester: Ellis Horwood/Tavistock.

Cohen, Stan (1972) *Folk Devils and Moral Panics*, London: MacGibbon and Kee.

Collins, Michael (2005) *The Likes of Us: A Biography of the White Working Class*, London: Granta.

Combahee River Collective (1982) 'A Black Feminist Statement', in Hull, G. T., Scott, P. B. and Smith, B. (eds) *All the Women are White, All the Blacks are Men, But Some of Us are Brave*, New York: The Feminist Press, 13–22.

Connell, R. W. (1993) 'The Big Picture: Masculinities in Recent World History', *Theory and Society* 22 (5), October, 597–623.

Connell, R. W. (2003) 'The Big Picture: Masculinities in Recent World History', in Weeks, Jeffrey, Holland, Janet and Waites, Matthew (eds) *Sexualities and Society: A Reader*, Cambridge: Polity Press, 46–56.

Connell, R. W. (2005) *Masculinities*, second edition, Cambridge: Polity Press.

Connell, Raewyn (2009) *Gender*, second edition, Cambridge and Malden, MA: Polity Press.

Connell, Raewyn (2010) 'Two Cans of Paint: A Transsexual Life Story, with Reflections on Gender Change and History', *Sexualities* 13 (1), February, 3–19.

Connolly, H. and White, A. (2006) 'The Different Experiences of the United Kingdom's

Ethnic and Religious Populations', in Office of National Statistics, *Population Trends 36*, London: ONS/Palgrave.

Cooper, Davina (2004) *Challenging Diversity: Rethinking Equality and the Value of Difference*, Cambridge: Cambridge University Press.

Corrêa Sonia, Petchesky, Rosalind and Parker, Richard (eds) (2008) *Sexuality, Health and Human Rights*, London: Routledge.

Crenshaw, Kimberlé W. (1989) 'Demarginalizing the Intersection of Race and Sex: A Black Feminist Critique of Antidiscrimination Doctrine, Feminist Theory, and Antiracist Politics', *University of Chicago Legal Forum 1989*, 139–67.

Crimp, Douglas (2002) *Melancholia and Moralism: Essays on Aids and Queer Politics*, Cambridge, MA: MIT Press.

Davies, William (2009) 'The Making of Neo-liberalism: Review Essay', *Renewal: A Journal of Social Democracy* 17 (4), 88–92.

Davis, M. D. M. (2005) 'Treating and Preventing HIV in the Post-crisis Situation: Perspectives from the Personal Experience Accounts of Gay Men with HIV', unpublished PhD thesis, Institute of Education, University of London.

Dawkins, Richard (1978) *The Selfish Gene*, St Albans: Granada.

Dean, Tim (2000) *Beyond Sexuality*, Chicago, IL: University of Chicago Press.

de Beauvoir, Simone (1972, originally published 1948) *The Second Sex*, Harmondsworth: Penguin.

de Lauretis, Teresa (1994) *The Practice of Love: Lesbian Sexuality and Perverse Desire*, Bloomington and Indianapolis: Indiana University Press.

Deleuze, Gilles and Guattari, Felix (1977) *Anti-Oedipus. Capitalism and Schizophrenia*, New York: Viking.

Derbyshire, Philip (2008) 'Interpellation and Intensity: Thinking Homosexuality with Psychoanalysis', *Sitegeist: A Journal of Psychoanalysis and Philosophy* 1, Spring, 77–88.

Descoutures, Virginia, Digoix, Marie, Fassin, Eric and Rault, Wilfried (eds) (2008) *Marriages et Homosexualites dans Le Monde*, Paris: Editions Autrement.

Dollimore, Jonathan (1991) *Sexual Dissidence: Augustine to Wilde, Freud to Foucault*, Oxford: Clarendon Press.

Douglas, J. D. and Atwell, F. C., with Hillebrand, J. (1988) *Love, Intimacy and Sex*, Newbury Park, CA: Sage.

Duncan, Simon and Edwards, Rosalind (1999) *Lone Mothers, Paid Work and Gendered Moral Rationalities*, Basingstoke and London: Macmillan.

Duncombe, Jean and Marsden, Dennis (2004) '"From here to Epiphany . . .": Power and Identity in the Narratives of an Affair', in Duncombe, Jean, Harrison, Kaeren, Allan, Graham and Marsden, Dennis (eds) *The State of Affairs: Explorations in Infidelity and Commitment*, Mahwah, NJ: Lawrence Erlbaum, 141–66.

Duncombe, Jean, Harrison, Kaeren, Allan, Graham and Marsden, Dennis (eds) (2004) *The State of Affairs: Explorations in Infidelity and Commitment*, Mahwah, NJ: Lawrence Erlbaum.

Dworkin, Andrea (1981) *Pornography: Men Possessing Women*, London: The Women's Press.

Dworkin, Andrea (1989) *Intercourse*, New York: The Free Press.

Dworkin, Andrea and MacKinnon, Catherine (1988) *Pornography and Civil Rights: A New Day for Women's Equality*, Minneapolis, MN: Organizing Against Pornography.

Eadie, Jo (ed.) (2004) *Sexuality: The Essential Glossary*, London: Arnold.

Eder, Franz X., Hall, Lesley and Hekma, Gert (1999a) *Sexual Cultures in Europe: National Histories*, Manchester: Manchester University Press.

Eder, Franz X., Hall, Lesley and Hekma, Gert (1999b) *Sexual Cultures in Europe: Themes in Sexuality*, Manchester: Manchester University Press.

Edwards, Rosalind (2004) 'Present and Absent in Troubling Ways: Families and Social Capital Debates', *Sociological Review* 52 (1), February, 1–21.

Edwards, Rosalind and Glover, Judith (eds) (2001) *Risk and Citizenship: Key Issues in Welfare*, London: Routledge.

Edwards, Rosalind, Hadfield, Lucy, Lucey, Helen and Mauthner, Melanie (2006) *Sibling Identity and Relationships: Sisters and Brothers*, London: Routledge.

Edwards, Rosalind, Franklin, Jane and Holland, Janet (eds) (2007) *Assessing Social Capital: Concept, Policy and Practice*, Cambridge: Cambridge Scholars Publications.

Egan, R. Danielle and Hawkes, Gail (2010) *Theorizing the Sexual Child in Modernity*, New York: Palgrave Macmillan.

Ekins, Richard and King, Dave (2006) *The Transgender Phenomenon*, London: Sage.

Elias, Norbert (2000) *The Civilizing Process: Sociogenetic and Psychogenetic Investigations*, Oxford and Malden, MA: Blackwell.

Elliott, Anthony (2002) 'Beck's Sociology of Risk: A Critical Assessment', *Sociology* 36 (2), May, 293–315.

Elliott, Anthony and Lemert, Charles (2006) *The New Individualism: The Emotional Costs of Globalization*, London: Routledge.

Ellis, Havelock (1946; first published 1933) *The Psychology of Sex*, London: Dent.

Epstein, Steven (1992) 'Gay Politics, Ethnic Identity: The Limits of Social Constructionism', in Stein, Edward (ed.) *Forms of Desire: Sexual Orientation and the Social Constructionist Controversy*, London: Routledge.

Epstein, Steven (1996) *Impure Science: AIDS, Activism and the Politics of Knowledge*, Berkeley: University of California Press.

Erel, Umut, Haritaworn, Jin, Gutiérrez Rodríguez, Encarnación and Klesse, Christian (2010) 'On the Depoliticisation of Intersectionality Talk: Conceptualising Multiple Oppressions in Critical Sexuality Studies', in Taylor, Yvette, Hines, Sally and Casey, Mark (eds) *Theorizing Intersectionality and Sexuality*, London: Palgrave.

Evans, David T. (1993) *Sexual Citizenship: The Material Construction of Sexualities*, London: Routledge.

Evans, Mary (2003) *Love: An Unromantic Discussion*, Cambridge: Polity Press.

Evans, Mary (2005) *Introducing Contemporary Feminist Thought*, Cambridge: Polity Press.

Faderman, Lillian (1981) *Surpassing the Love of Men*, London: Junction Books.

Faludi, Susan (1992) *Backlash: The Undeclared War Against Women*, London: Vintage.

Fausto-Sterling, Anne (2000) *Sexing the Body: Gender Politics and the Construction of Sexuality*, New York: Basic Books.

Ferguson, Roderick A. (2004) *Aberrations in Black: Towards a Queer of Color Critique*, Minneapolis: University of Minnesota Press.

Finch, Janet (1989) *Family Obligations and Social Change*, Cambridge: Polity Press.

Finch, Janet and Mason, Jennifer (1993) *Negotiating Family Responsibilities*, London: Routledge.

Finn, Mark (2010) 'Conditions of Freedom in Practices of Non-Monogamous Commitment', in Barker, Meg and Langdridge, Darren (eds) *Understanding Non-Monogamies*, New York: Routledge, 225–36.

Firestone, Shulamith (1971) *The Dialectic of Sex*, London: Paladin.

Foucault, Michel (1979) *The History of Sexuality, Vol. 1: An Introduction*, London: Allen Lane.

Foucault, Michel (1980) *Herculine Barbin, Being the Recently Discovered Memoirs of a Nineteenth-century French Hermaphrodite*, New York: Pantheon Books.

Foucault, Michel (1984) 'On the Genealogy of Ethics: An Overview of Work in Progress', in Rabinow, Paul (ed.) *The Foucault Reader*, New York: Pantheon Books.

Foucault, Michel (1985) *The History of Sexuality, Vol. 2: The Use of Pleasure*, London: Viking.

Foucault, Michel (1986) *The History of Sexuality, Vol. 3: The Care of the Self*, London: Viking.

Foucault, Michel (1988) 'The Ethic of Care for the Self as a Practice of Freedom', in Bernauer, J. and Rasmussen, D. (eds) *The Final Foucault*, Cambridge, MA: MIT Press.

Fraser, Nancy (1995) 'From Redistribution to Recognition? Dilemmas of Justice in a "Postsocialist" Age', *New Left Review* 212, 68–93.

Fraser, Nancy and Honneth, Axel (2003) *Redistribution or Recognition? A Political-Philosophical Exchange*, London: Verso.

Freud, Sigmund (1905) *Three Essays on the Theory of Sexuality*, in Freud 1953–74, Vol. 7.

Freud, Sigmund (1916–17) *Introductory Lectures on Psychoanalysis*, in Freud 1953–74, Vol. 16.

Freud, Sigmund (1927) 'Fetishism', in Freud 1953–74, Vol. 21.

Freud, Sigmund (1953–74) *The Standard Edition of the Complete Psychological Works of Sigmund Freud,* ed. James Strachey, London: The Hogarth Press and the Institute of Psychoanalysis.

Friedan, Betty (1992, first published 1966) *The Feminine Mystique*, Harmondsworth: Penguin.

Friedman, Richard C. (1988) *Male Homosexuality: A Contemporary Psychoanalytical Account*, New Haven, CT: Yale University Press.

Fromm, Erich (1971) *The Art of Loving*, London: Allan and Unwin.

Fukuyama, Francis (1995) *Trust: The New Foundations of Global Prosperity*, New York: The Free Press.

Fukuyama, Francis (1999) *The Great Disruption: Human Nature and the Reconstitution of Social Order*, London: Profile Books.

Furedi, Frank (2004) *Therapy Culture: Cultivating Vulnerability in an Uncertain Age*, London: Routledge.

Gagnon, John H. (1977) *Human Sexualities*, Glenview, IL: Scott, Foresman and Company.

Gagnon, John H. and Simon, William (1974) *Sexual Conduct: The Social Sources of Human Sexuality*, London: Hutchinson.

Garber, Marjorie (1995) *Vice Versa: Bisexuality and the Eroticism of Everyday Life*, New York: Routledge.

Geras, Norman (1983) 'Fetishism', in Bottomore, Tom (ed.) *A Dictionary of Marxist Thought*, Oxford: Blackwell Reference, 165–6.

Gerschick, Thomas J. (2007) 'The Body, Disability, and Sexuality', in Seidman, Steven, Fischer, Nancy and Meeks, Chet (eds) *Introducing the New Sexuality Studies: Original Essays and Interviews*, London: Routledge, 253–61.

Giddens, Anthony (1991) *Modernity and Self-Identity: Self and Society in the Late Modern Age*, Cambridge: Polity Press.

Giddens, Anthony (1992) *The Transformation of Intimacy: Sexuality, Love and Eroticism in Modern Societies,* Cambridge: Polity Press.

Giddens, Anthony (1994) 'Living in a Post-Traditional Society', in Beck, Ulrich, Giddens, Anthony and Lash, Scott, *Reflexive Modernization: Politics, Tradition and Aesthetics in the Modern Social Order*, Cambridge: Polity Press, 56–109.

Gilligan, Carol (1982) *In a Different Voice: Psychological Theory and Women's Development*, Cambridge, MA: Harvard University Press.

Gillis, John R. (1985) *For Better, For Worse: British Marriages, 1600 to the Present*, New York and Oxford: Oxford University Press.

Gilroy, Paul (2004) *After Empire: Melancholia or Convivial Culture*, Abingdon: Routledge.

Goss, E. R. (1997) 'Queering Procreative Privilege: Coming Out as Families', in Goss, E. R. and Strongheart, A. S. (eds) *Our Families, Our Values: Snapshots of Queer Kinship*, Binghampton, NJ: Harrington Park Press.

Goulbourne, Harry, Reynolds, Tracey, Solomos, John and Zontini, Elisabetta (eds) (2010) *Transnational Families: Ethnicities, Identities and Social Capital*, London: Routledge.

Greenberg, David E. (1988) *The Construction of Homosexuality*, Chicago, IL: University of Chicago Press.

Grosz, Elizabeth (1992a) 'Fetishization', in Wright, Elizabeth (ed.) *Feminism and Psychoanalysis: A Critical Dictionary*, Oxford and Cambridge, MA: Blackwell, 117–18.

Grosz, Elizabeth (1992b) 'The Subject', in Wright, Elizabeth (ed.) *Feminism and Psychoanalysis: A Critical Dictionary*, Oxford and Cambridge, MA: Blackwell, 409–16.

Grosz, Elizabeth (1994) *Volatile Bodies: Towards a Corporeal Feminism*, Bloomington: Indiana University Press.

Grosz, Elizabeth (1995) *Space, Time, and Perversions: Essays in the Politics of Bodies*, London: Routledge.

Hakim, Catherine (2010) 'Erotic Capital', *European Sociological Review*, 1–20.

Halberstam, Judith (1998) *Female Masculinity*, Durham, NC: Duke University Press.

Halberstam, Judith (2005) *In a Queer Time and Place: Transgender Bodies, Subcultural Lives*, New York: New York University Press.

Halperin, David M. (1995) *Saint Foucault: Towards a Gay Hagiography*, Oxford: Oxford University Press.

Halperin, David M. (2002) *How to Do the History of Homosexuality*, Chicago and London: University of Chicago Press.

Halperin, David M. (2007) *What Do Gay Men Want? An Essay on Sex, Risk, and Subjectivity*, Ann Arbor: University of Michigan Press.

Haraway, Donna (1991) *Simians, Cyborgs, and Women: The Reinvention of Nature*, London: Free Association Books.

Hawkes, Gail (2004) *Sex and Pleasure in Western Culture*, Cambridge: Polity Press.

Heaphy, Brian (2007) *Late Modernity and Social Change: Reconstructing Social and Personal Life*, London: Routledge.

Heaphy, Brian, Donovan, Catherine and Weeks, Jeffrey (2004) 'A Different Affair? Openness and Non-Monogamy in Same-Sex relationships', in Duncombe, Jean, Harrison, Kaeren, Allan, Graham and Marsden, Dennis (eds) *The State of Affairs: Explorations in Infidelity and Commitment*, Mahwah, NJ: Lawrence Erlbaum, 167–84.

Heath, Joseph and Potter, Andrew (2005) *The Rebel Self: How the Counterculture Became Consumer Culture*, Albany, OR: Capstone Publishing.

Held, David (1987) *Models of Democracy*, Cambridge: Polity Press.

Held, David (2000) 'Regulating Globalization?' in Held, David and McGrew, A. (eds) *The Global Transformations Reader: An Introduction to the Globalization Debate*, Cambridge: Polity Press, 420–30.

Heller, Agnes and Feher, Franc (1988) *The Postmodern Political Condition*, Cambridge: Polity Press.

Hemmings, Clare (2007) 'What's in a Name? Bisexuality, Transnational Sexuality Studies and Western Colonial Legacies', *International Journal of Human Rights* 11 (1–2), March, 13–32.

Hemmings, Clare, Gedalof, Irene and Bland, Lucy (2006) 'Sexual Moralities', *Feminist Review* 83, 1–3.

Hennessy, Rosemary (2000) *Profit and Pleasure: Sexual Identities in Late Capitalism*, New York: Routledge.

Herdt, Gilbert (ed.) (2009) *Moral Panics, Sex Panics: Fear and Fight over Sexual Rights*, New York: New York University Press.

Herek, Gregory (1986) 'On Heterosexual Masculinity', *American Behavioral Science* 29 (5), 563–77.

Higgs, David (ed.) (1999) *Queer Sites: Gay Urban Histories since 1600*, London: Routledge.

Himmelfarb, Gertrude (1995) *The De-moralization of Society: From Victorian Values to Modern Values*, London: Institute of Economic Affairs.

Hird, Myra (2004) 'Hybridity', in Eadie, Jo (ed.) *Sexuality: The Essential Glossary*, London: Arnold, 97.

Hobsbawm, Eric (1994) *Age of Extremes: The Short Twentieth Century, 1914–1991*, London: Michael Joseph.

Hochschild, Arlie R. (2003) *The Managed Heart: Commercialization of Human Feeling*, 20th Anniversary edition, Berkeley: University of California Press.

Hocquenghem, Guy (1978) *Homosexual Desire*, London: Allison and Busby.

Hoggett, Paul (2008) 'Melancholic Nation', *Soundings: A Journal of Politics and Culture*, 39, Summer, 108–16.

Holland, Janet, Weeks, Jeffrey and Gillies, Val (2003) 'Families, Intimacy and Social Capital', *Social Policy and Society* 2 (4), 339–48.

Holland, Janet, Ramazanoglu, Caroline, Sharpe, Sue and Thomson, Rachel (1998) *The Male in the Head*, London: Tufnell Press.

Holton, Robert J. (2009) *Cosmopolitanisms: New Thinking and Directions*, Basingstoke: Palgrave Macmillan.

Honneth, Axel (1995) *The Struggle for Recognition: The Moral Grammar of Social Conflicts*, Cambridge: Polity Press.

Honneth, Axel (2007) *Disrespect: The Normative Foundations of Critical Theory*, Cambridge: Polity Press.

Houlbrook, Matt (2005) *Queer London: Pleasures and Perils in the Sexual Metropolis, 1918–1957*, Chicago, IL: University of Chicago Press.

Hubbard, Phil (2001) 'Sex Zones: Intimacy, Citizenship and Public Space', *Sexualities* 4 (1), February, 51–71.

Hubbard, Phil, Matthews, Roger and Scoular, Jane (2008) 'Regulating Sex Work in the EU: Prostitute Women and the New Spaces of Exclusion', *Gender, Place and Culture* 15 (2), April, 137–52).

Humphreys, Laud (1970) *Tearoom Trade*, London: Duckworth.

Hunt, Lynn (2007) *Inventing Human Rights: A History*, New York: W. W. Norton.

Jackson, Stevi (2000) *Heterosexuality in Question*, London: Sage.

Jackson, Stevi and Scott, Sue (2004) 'The Personal *Is* Still Political: Heteronormativity, Feminism and Monogamy', *Feminism and Psychology* 14 (1), February, 151–7.

Jamieson, Lynn (1998) *Intimacy: Personal Relationships in Modern Societies*, Cambridge: Polity Press.

Jamieson, Lynn (1999) 'Intimacy Transformed: A Critical Look at the "Pure Relationship"', *Sociology* 33 (3): 447–94.

Jenkins, Roy (1970) *Essays and Speeches*, London: Collins.

Johnson, A. M., Mercer, C. H., Erens, B. *et al.* (2001) 'Sexual Behaviour in Britain: Partnerships, Practices, and HIV Risk Behaviours', *The Lancet*, 358 (9296), 1 December, 1835–42.

Johnson, Mark (1997) *Beauty and Power: Transgendering and Cultural Transformation in the Southern Philippines*, Oxford: Berg.

Johnston, Cristina (2008) 'The PACS and (Post-) Queer Citizenship in Contemporary Republican France', *Sexualities* 11 (6), December, 688–705.

Jones, Ernest (ed.) (1961) *The Letters of Sigmund Freud 1873–1939*, London: Hogarth Press.

Kandaswamy, Priya (2008) 'State Austerity and the Racial Politics of Same-Sex Marriage in the US', *Sexualities* 11 (6), December, 706–25.

Katz, Jonathan Ned (1995) *The Invention of Heterosexuality*, New York: NAL/Dutton.

Katz, Jonathan Ned (2001) *Love Stories: Sex between Men before Homosexuality*, Chicago, IL: University of Chicago Press.

Kennedy, Elizabeth and Davis, Madeline (1993) *Boots of Leather, Slippers of Gold: The History of a Lesbian Community*, New York: Routledge.

Kinsey, Alfred C., Pomeroy, Wardell B. and Martin, Clyde E. (1948) *Sexual Behavior in the Human Male*, Philadelphia, PA: W. B. Saunders.

Kinsey, Alfred C., Pomeroy, Wardell B., Martin, Clyde E. and Gebhard, Paul H. (1953) *Sexual Behavior in the Human Female*, Philadelphia, PA: W. B. Saunders.

Kippax, Susan (2010) 'Safe Sex: It's Not as Simple as ABC', in Aggleton, Peter and Parker, Richard (eds) *Routledge Handbook of Sexuality, Health and Rights*, London: Routledge, 184–92.

Klesse, Christian (2006) 'Heteronormativity, Non-monogamy and the Marriage Debate in the Bisexual Movement', *Lesbian and Gay Psychology Review* 7 (2), 162–73.

Klesse, Christian (2007) *The Spectre of Promiscuity: Gay Male and Bisexual Non-monogamies and Polyamories*, Aldershot and Burlington, VT: Ashgate.

Kollman, Kelly (2007) 'Same-Sex Unions: The Globalization of an Idea', *International Studies Quarterly* 51 (2), 329–57.

Kollman, Kelly and Waites, Matthew (2009) 'The Global Politics of Lesbian, Gay, Bisexual and Transgender Human Rights: An Introduction', *Contemporary Politics* 15 (1), 1–17.

Kristeva, Julia (1982) *Powers of Horror: An Essay on Abjection*, New York: Columbia University Press.

Kulick, Don (1998) *Travesti: Sex, Gender and Culture Among Brazilian Transgendered Prostitutes*, Chicago, IL: University of Chicago Press.

Kulick, Don (2005) 'Four Hundred Thousand Swedish Perverts', *GLQ: A Journal of Lesbian and Gay Studies* 11 (2), 205–35.

Lancaster, Roger (2003) *The Trouble with Nature: Sex in Science and Popular Culture*, Berkeley: University of California Press.

Langdridge, Darren and Barker, Meg (2007) *Safe, Sane and Consensual: Contemporary Perspectives on Sadomasochism*, London: Palgrave Macmillan.

Laplanche, J. and Pontalis, J.-B. (1980) *The Language of Psychoanalysis*, London: The Hogarth Press and the Institute of Psychoanalysis.

Laqueur, Thomas W. (1990) *Making Sex: Body and Gender from the Greeks to Freud*, Cambridge, MA: Harvard University Press.

Laqueur, Thomas W. (2003) *Solitary Sex: A Cultural History of Masturbation*, London: Zone Books.

Lasch, Christopher (1985) *The Minimal Self: Psychic Survival in Troubled Times*, New York: W. W. Norton.

Latimer, Joanna (2009) 'Introduction: Body, Knowledge, Worlds', in Latimer, Joanna and Schillmeir, Michael W. J. (eds) *Un/Knowing Bodies*, Malden, MA: Blackwell, 1–22.

Lewin, Ellen (1993), *Lesbian Mothers: Accounts of Gender in American Culture*, Ithaca, NY: Cornell University Press.

Lewin, Ellen (1998) *Recognizing Ourselves: Ceremonies of Lesbian and Gay Commitment*, New York: Columbia University Press.

Lewis, Jane (2001) *The End of Marriage? Individualism and Intimate Relations*, Cheltenham and Northampton, MA: Edward Elgar.

Loe, M. (2004) *The Rise of Viagra: How the Little Blue Pill Changed Sex in America*, New York: New York University Press.

Lupton, Deborah and Tulloch, John (2002) '"Risk is Part of Your Life": Risk Epistemologies among a Group of Australians', *Sociology* 36 (2), May, 317–34.

MacCulloch, Diarmaid (2009) *A History of Christianity*, London: Allen Lane.

McGhee, Derek (2008) *The End of Multiculturalism? Terrorism, Integration and Human Rights*, Maidenhead: Open University Press.

McGurn, William (2010) 'Our Racially Divisive Census', *Wall Street Journal*, 8 June, A17.

McIntosh, Mary (1968) 'The Homosexual Role', *Social Problems* 16 (2): 182–92.

McIntosh, Mary (1978) 'Who Needs Prostitutes? The Ideology of Male Sexual Needs', in Carol and Barry Smart (eds) *Women, Sexuality and Social Control*, London: Routledge and Kegan Paul.

MacKinnon, Catherine A. (1987) *Feminism Unmodified: Discourses on Life and Law*, Cambridge, MA: Harvard University Press.

McLaren, Angus (1999) *Twentieth-century Sexuality: A History*, Oxford: Blackwell.

McLaren, Angus (2002) *Sexual Blackmail: A Modern Story*, Boston, MA: Harvard University Press.

McNair, Brian (2002) *Striptease Culture: Sex, Media and the Democratisation of Desire*, London: Routledge.

McNay, Lois (2000) *Gender and Agency: Reconfiguring the Subject in Feminist and Social Theory*, Cambridge: Polity Press.

McNay, Lois (2008) *Against Recognition*, Cambridge: Polity Press.

Mahdavi, Pardis (2009) *Passionate Uprisings: Iran's Sexual Revolution*, Stanford, CA: Stanford University Press.

Malinowski, Bronislaw (1963) *Sex, Culture and Myth*, London: Rupert Hart-Davis.

Marcuse, Herbert (1972) *One-Dimensional Man*, London: Abacus.

Markwell, K. (2002) 'Mardi Gras Tourism and the Construction of Sydney as an International Gay and Lesbian City', *GLQ: A Journal of Lesbian and Gay Studies* 8 (1–2), 81–100.

Marshall, T. H. (1950) *Citizenship and Social Class, and Other Essays*, Cambridge: Cambridge University Press.

Mauthner, Melanie (2005) *Sistering: Power and Change in Female Relationships*, Basingstoke: Palgrave Macmillan.

Meese, Edwin (1986) *Attorney General's Commission on Pornography, Final Report of the Special Committee on Pornography and Prostitution*, Washington, DC: US Department of Justice.

Melucci, Alberto (1989) *Nomads of the Present: Social Movements and Individual Needs in Contemporary Society*, London: Radius.

Mendus, Susan (1987) 'Introduction', in Mendus, Susan and Edwards, D. (eds) *On Toleration*, Oxford: Clarendon Press.

Mendus, Susan (ed.) (1988) *Justifying Toleration: Conceptual and Historical Perspectives*, Cambridge: Cambridge University Press.

Mennell, Stephen (2008) *The American Civilizing Process*, Cambridge: Polity Press.

Micklethwait, John and Wooldridge, Adrian (2009) *God is Back: How the Global Rise of Faith is Changing the World*, London: Allen Lane.

Mill, John Stuart (1975) 'On Liberty', in *Three Essays: On Liberty, Representative Government, The Subjection of Women*, Oxford: Oxford University Press (first published 1859).

Miller, A. M. (2000) 'Sexual but Not Reproductive: Exploring the Junctions and Disjunctions of Sexual and Reproductive Rights', *Health and Human Rights* 4 (2), 68–109.

Mitchell, Juliet (1974) *Psychoanalysis and Feminism*, London: Allen Lane.

Modood, Tariq (2007) *Multiculturalism: A Civic Idea*, Cambridge: Polity Press.

Moore, Henrietta L. (2007) *The Subject of Anthropology: Gender, Symbolism and Psychoanalysis*, Cambridge: Polity Press.

Moran, Les and Skeggs, Bev (2004) *Sexuality and the Politics of Violence and Safety*, London: Routledge.

More, K. and Whittle, S. (eds) (1999) *Reclaiming Genders: Transsexual Grammars at the fin de siècle*, London: Cassell.

Morgan, David H. J. (1999) 'Risk and Family Practices: Accounting for Change and Fluidity in Family Life', in Silva, Elizabeth B. and Smart, Carol (eds) *The New Family?* London: Sage, 13–30.

Morgan, Diane (1999) 'What Does a Transsexual Want? The Encounter between Psychoanalysis and Transsexualism', in More, K. and Whittle, S. (eds) *Reclaiming Genders: Transsexual Grammars at the fin de siècle*, London: Cassell, 219–39.

Morgan, Patricia (1995) *Farewell to the Family? Public Policy and Family Breakdown in Britain and the USA*, London: Institute of Economic Affairs.

Morgan, Robin (1980) 'Theory and Practice: Porn and Rape', in Lederer, L. (ed.) *Take Back the Night: Women on Porn*, New York: Bantam Books, 125–39.

Mosse, George L. (1996) *The Image of Man: The Creation of Modern Masculinity*, Oxford: Oxford University Press.

Munson, M. and Stelboum, J. P. (eds) (1999) *The Lesbian Polyamory Reader: Non-monogamy and Casual Sex*, New York: Harrington Park Press. Published simultaneously as a special issue of *Journal of Lesbian Studies* 3 (1/2) 1999.

Nardi, Peter (1999) *Gay Men's Friendships: Invincible Communities*, Chicago, IL: Chicago University Press.

Nash, Jennifer C. (2008) 'Re-thinking Intersectionality', *Feminist Review* 89, 1–15.

Nestle, Joan, (1987) *A Restricted Country*, Ithaca, NY: Firebrand.

O'Connell Davidson, Julia (1998) *Prostitution, Power and Freedom*, Cambridge: Polity Press.

O'Connell Davidson, Julia (2001) 'The Sex Tourist, the Expatriate, his Ex-wife, and her Other: The Politics of Loss, Difference and Desire', *Sexualities* 4 (1), 6–24.

O'Connell Davidson, Julia (2005) *Children in the Global Sex Trade*, Cambridge: Polity Press.

O'Connell Davidson, Julia (2006) 'Will the Real Sex Slave Stand Up?' *Feminist Review* 83, 4–22.

O'Connell Davidson, Julia and Sanchez Taylor, Jacqueline (2005) 'Travel and Taboo: Heterosexual Sex Tourism to the Caribbean', in Bernstein, Elizabeth and Schaffner, L. (eds) *Regulating Sex: The Politics of Intimacy and Identity*, New York: Routledge, 83–100.

Oakley, Ann (1972) *Sex, Gender and Society*, London: Temple Smith.

Okin, Susan M. (2005) 'Women's Rights in the Late Twentieth Century', in Bamforth, Nicholas (ed.) *Sex Rights*, Oxford Amnesty Lectures, Oxford: Oxford University Press, 83–118.

Oosterhuis, Harry (2000) *Stepchildren of Nature: Krafft-Ebing, Psychiatry and the Making of Sexual Identity*, Chicago, IL: University of Chicago Press.

Pahl, Ray (2000) *On Friendship*, Cambridge: Polity Press.

Papadopoulos, Linda (2010) *Sexualisation of Young People Review*, London: Home Office, www.homeoffice.gov.uk/documents/sexualisation-of-young-people2835.pdf, accessed 10 April 2010.

Pateman, Carole (1988) *The Sexual Contract*, Cambridge: Polity Press.

Patton, Cindy and Sánchez Eppler, B. (eds) (2000) *Queer Diasporas*, Durham, NC: Duke University Press.

Paul, Pamela (2005) *Pornified: How Pornography Is Transforming Our Lives, Our Relationships and Our Families*, New York: Times Books.

Person, Ethel Spector (1989) *Dreams of Love and Fateful Encounters: The Power of Romantic Passion*, London: Penguin.

Petchesky, Rosalind (2000) 'Sexual Rights: Inventing a Concept, Mapping an International Practice', in Parker, R., Barbosa, R. M. and Aggleton, P. (eds) *Framing the Subject: The Politics of Gender, Sexuality and Power*, Berkeley: University of California Press, 81–103.

Petchesky, Rosalind (2003) 'Negotiating Reproductive Rights', in Weeks, Jeffrey, Holland, Janet and Waites, Matthew (eds) *Sexualities and Society: A Reader*, Cambridge: Polity Press, 226–9.

Petchesky, Rosalind and Judd, J. (eds) (1998) *Negotiating Reproductive Rights: Women's Perspectives Across Countries and Cultures*, London: Zed Books.

Phelan, Shane (2001) *Sexual Strangers: Gays, Lesbians, and Dilemmas of Citizenship*, Philadelphia, PA: Temple University Press.

Phillips, Anne (2007) *Multiculturalism without Culture*, Princeton, NJ: Princeton University Press.

Plummer, Ken (1975) *Sexual Stigma: An Interactionist Account*, London: Routledge and Kegan Paul.

Plummer, Ken (1981) 'Homosexual Categories: Some Research Problems in the Labelling Perspective of Homosexuality', in Plummer, Ken (ed.) *The Making of the Modern Homosexual*, London: Hutchinson, 53–75.

Plummer, Ken (1984) 'Sexual Diversity: A Sociological Perspective', in Howells, Kevin (ed.) *Sexual Diversity*, Oxford: Blackwell.

Plummer, Ken (ed.) (1992) *Modern Homosexualities: Fragments of Lesbian and Gay Experience*, London: Routledge.

Plummer, Ken (1995) *Telling Sexual Stories: Power, Change and Social Worlds,* London: Routledge.

Plummer, Ken (1999) 'The Lesbian and Gay Movement in Britain: Schism, Solidarities and Social Worlds', in Adam, Barry D., Duyvendak, Jan Willem and Krouwel, Andre (eds) *The Global Emergence of Gay and Lesbian Politics: National Imprints of a Worldwide Movement*, Philadelphia, PA: Temple University Press, 133–57.

REFERENCES

Plummer, Ken (2003) *Intimate Citizenship: Private Decisions and Public Dialogues*, Seattle, University of Washington Press.

Plummer, Ken (2010) 'The Social Reality of Sexual Rights', in Aggleton, Peter and Parker, Richard (eds) *Routledge Handbook of Sexuality, Health and Rights*, London: Routledge, 45–55.

Pomeroy, Wardell, B. (1972) *Dr Kinsey and the Institute for Sex Research,* New York: Harper & Row.

Ponse, Barbara (1978) *Identities in the Lesbian World: The Social Construction of Self*, Westport, CT: Greenwood.

Prosser, J. (1999) 'Exceptional Locations: Transsexual Travelogues' in More, K. and Whittle, S. (eds) *Reclaiming Genders: Transsexual Grammars at the fin de siècle*, London: Cassell, 83–114.

Putnam, Robert D. (2001) *Bowling Alone: The Collapse and Revival of American Community*, New York: Simon and Schuster.

Rajan, R. S. (2005) 'Women's Human Rights in the Third World', in Bamforth, Nicholas (ed.) *Sex Rights*, Oxford Amnesty Lectures, Oxford: Oxford University Press, 119–36.

Rajchman, J. (1991) *Truth and Eros: Foucault, Lacan and the Question of Ethics*, London: Routledge.

Raymond, Janice (1979) *The Transsexual Empire*, Boston, MA: Beacon.

Renzetti, Claire M. and Miley, Charles Harvey (eds) (1996) *Violence in Gay and Lesbian Domestic Partnerships*, New York: Harrington Park Press.

Reynolds, Robert (1999) 'Postmodernizing the Closet', *Sexualities* 2 (3), August, 346–9.

Reynolds, Tracey (2005) *Caribbean Mothers: Identity and Experience in the UK*, London: Tufnell Press.

Rich, Adrianne (1980) 'Compulsory Heterosexuality and Lesbian Existence', *Signs* 5 (4), 631–61.

Richardson, Diane (ed.) (1996) *Theorising Heterosexuality*, Buckingham: Open University Press.

Richardson, Diane (2000) *Rethinking Sexuality,* London: Sage.

Richardson, Diane (2004) 'Locating Sexualities: From Here to Normality', *Sexualities* 7 (4), 391–411.

Richardson, Diane and Seidman, Steven (eds) (2002) *Handbook of Lesbian and Gay Studies,* London: Sage.

Ridge, D. T. (2004) '"It was an Incredible Thrill": The Social Meanings and Dynamics of Younger Men's Experiences of Barebacking in Melbourne', *Sexualities* 7 (3), August, 259–79.

Riley, Denise (1983) *War in the Nursery. Theories of the Child and Mother,* London: Virago.

Riley, Denise (1988) *"Am I that Name?" Feminism and the Category of "Woman" in History*, Basingstoke: Macmillan.

Robinson, Shirleene (ed.) (2008) *Homophobia: An Australian History*, Annandale, NSW: The Federation Press.

Rose, Nickolas (1999) *Governing the Soul: The Shaping of the Private Self,* second edition, London: Free Association Books.

Roseneil, Sasha and Budgeon, S. (2004) 'Beyond the Conventional Family: Intimacy, Care and Community in the 21st Century', *Current Sociology* 52 (2), 135–59.

Roudinesco, Elisabeth (2009) *Our Dark Side: A History of Perversion*, Cambridge: Polity Press.

234

Rubin, Gayle (1974) 'The Traffic in Women: Notes on the "Political Economy" of Sex', in Reiter, Rayna R. (ed.) *Towards an Anthropology of Women*, New York: Monthly Review Press, 157–210.

Rubin, Gayle (1984) 'Thinking Sex: Notes for a Radical Theory of the Politics of Sexuality', in Vance, Carole S. (ed.) *Pleasure and Danger: Exploring Female Sexuality*, London: Routledge and Kegan Paul.

Rubin, H. S. (1999) 'Trans Studies: Between a Metaphysics of Presence and Absence', in More, K. and Whittle, S. (eds) *Reclaiming Genders: Transsexual Grammars at the fin de siècle*, London: Cassell, 174–92.

Rutherford, Jonathan (2005) 'How We Live Now', *Soundings: A Journal of Politics and Culture* 30, Summer, 9–14.

Ruthven, Malise (2004) *Fundamentalism: The Search for Meaning*, Oxford: Oxford University Press.

Saffron, Lisa (1994) *Challenging Conceptions: Planning a Family by Self-insemination*, London: Cassell.

Sahlins, Marshall (1976) *The Use and Abuse of Biology: An Anthropological Critique of Sociobiology*, London: Tavistock.

Samois (ed.) (1981) *Coming to Power: Writings and Graphics on Lesbian S/M*, Palo Alto, CA: Up Press.

Sanders, Teela (2008) *Men who Buy Sex*, Cullompton: Willan Publishing.

Saunders, P. (2005) 'Identity to Acronym: How "Child Prostitution" became "CSEC"', in Bernstein, Elizabeth and Schaffner, L. (eds) *Regulating Sex: The Politics of Intimacy and Identity*, New York: Routledge, 167–88.

Schaeffer-Grabiel, Felicity (2010) 'Sex Trafficking as the "New Slave Trade"', *Sexualities* 13 (2), April, 153–60.

Schor, Naomi (1992) 'Fetishism', in Wright, Elizabeth (ed.) *Feminism and Psychoanalysis: A Critical Dictionary*, Oxford and Cambridge, MA: Blackwell, 113–16.

Scott, Joan Wallach (1988) 'Gender as a Useful Category of Analysis', in Scott, Joan Wallach, *Gender and the Politics of History*, New York: Columbia University Press.

Scott, Joan Wallach (2007) *The Politics of the Veil*, Princeton, NJ: Princeton University Press.

Scruton, Roger (2001) *Sexual Desire: A Philosophical Investigation*, London: Phoenix Books.

Seabrook, Jeremy (2001) *Travels in the Skin Trade: Tourism and the Sex Industry*, second edition, London: Pluto Press.

Sedgwick, Eve Kosofsky (1985) *Between Men: English Literature and Male Homosexual Desire*, New York: Columbia University Press.

Sedgwick, Eve Kosofsky (1990) *Epistemology of the Closet*, Berkeley: University of California Press.

Segal, Lynne (1990) *Slow Motion: Changing Masculinities, Changing Men*, London: Virago.

Segal, Lynne (1999) *Why Feminism? Gender, Psychology, Politics*, Cambridge: Polity Press.

Segal, Lynne and McIntosh, Mary (eds) (1992) *Sex Exposed: Sexuality and the Pornography Debate*, London: Virago.

Seidman, Steven (ed.) (1996) *Queer Theory/Sociology*, Oxford, MA: Blackwell.

Seidman, Steven (2002) *Beyond the Closet: The Transformation of Gay and Lesbian Life*, London: Routledge.

Seidman, Steven, Fischer, Nancy and Meeks, Chet (eds) (2007) *Introducing the New Sexuality Studies: Original Essays and Interviews*, London: Routledge.

Sennett, Richard (1992) *The Fall of Public Man*, New York: W. W. Norton.

Sexualities (2006) 'Viagra Culture', Special issue edited by A. Potts and L. Tiefer, *Sexualities* 9 (3), July.

Sexualities (2008) 'Regulating Sexuality: Contemporary Perspectives on Lesbian and Gay Relationship Recognition', Special issue edited by Elizabeth Peel and Rosie Harding, *Sexualities* 11 (6), December.

Shakespeare, Tom (2003) '"I Haven't Seen That in the Kama Sutra": The Sexual Stories of Disabled People', in Weeks, Jeffrey, Holland, Janet and Waites, Matthew (eds) *Sexualities and Society: A Reader*, Cambridge: Polity Press, 143–52.

Shakespeare, Tom, Gillespie-Sells, Kath and Davies, Dominic (1996) *The Sexual Politics of Disability*, London: Cassell.

Shilling, Chris (2007) 'Sociology and the Body: Classical Traditions and New Agendas', in Shilling, Chris (ed.) *Embodying Sociology: Retrospect, Progress and Prospects*, Malden, MA: Blackwell, 1–18.

Shuttleworth, Russell P. (2007) 'Disability and Sexuality: Towards a Constructionist Focus on Access and the Inclusion of Disabled People in the Sexual Rights Movement', in Teunis, Niels and Herdt, Gilbert (eds) *Sexual Inequalities and Social Justice*, Berkeley: University of California Press, 174–208.

Signorile, Michelangelo (1993) *Queer in America: Sex, The Media and the Closets of Power*, New York: Random House.

Silva, Elizabeth B. and Smart, Carol (1999) *The New Family?* London: Sage.

Simon, William (2003) 'The Postmodernization of Sex', in Weeks, Jeffrey, Holland, Janet and Waites, Matthew (eds) *Sexualities and Society: A Reader*, Cambridge: Polity Press, 22–32.

Skeggs, Bev (1997) *Formations of Class and Gender: Becoming Respectable*, London: Sage.

Smart, Carol (2006) 'Children's Narratives of Post-divorce Family Life: From Individual Experience to an Ethical Disposition', *Sociological Review* 54 (1), February, 155–70.

Smart, Carol (2007) *Personal Life: New Directions in Sociological Thinking*, Cambridge: Polity Press.

Smart, Carol and Neale, Bren (1999) *Family Fragments?* Cambridge: Polity Press.

Sontag, Susan (1989) *AIDS and its Metaphors*, London: Allen Lane.

Spencer, Liz and Pahl, Ray (2006) *Rethinking Friendship: Hidden Solidarities Today*, Princeton, NJ: Princeton University Press.

Stacey, Judith (1996) *In the Name of the Family: Rethinking Family Values in the Postmodern Age,* Boston, MA: Beacon Press.

Stacey, Judith (2010) *Unhitched: Love, Sex and Family Values from West Hollywood to Western China*, New York: New York University Press.

Stallybrass, Peter and White, Allon (1986) *The Politics and Poetics of Transgression*, Ithaca, NY: Cornell University Press.

Stein, Arlene (1997) *Sex and Sensibility: Stories of a Lesbian Generation*, Berkeley: University of California Press.

Stein, Arlene (2010) 'The Incredible Shrinking Lesbian and Other Queer Conundra', *Sexualities* 13 (1), February, 21–32.

Stein, Edward (ed.) (1992) *Forms of Desire: Sexual Orientation and the Social Constructionist Controversy,* London: Routledge.

Stoler, Ann L. (1995) *Race and the Education of Desire*, Durham, NC: Duke University Press.

Stoller, Robert J. (1968) *Sex and Gender, or the Development of Masculinity and Femininity*, New York: Science Home.

Stoller, Robert J. (1977) *Perversion. The Erotic Form of Hatred*, London: Quartet.

Storr, Merl (2003) 'Postmodern Bisexuality', in Weeks, Jeffrey, Holland, Janet and Waites, Matthew (eds) *Sexualities and Society: A Reader*, Cambridge: Polity Press, 153–61.

Swiebel, Joke (2009) 'Lesbian, Gay, Bisexual and Transgender Human Rights: The Search for an International Strategy', *Contemporary Politics* 15 (1), 19–35.

Taylor, Brian (1981) 'Introduction' in Taylor, Brian (ed.) *Perspectives on Paedophilia*, London: Batsford.

Taylor, Charles (1992a) *Multiculturalism and the Politics of Recognition*, ed. Amy Gutmann, Princeton, NJ: Princeton University Press.

Taylor, Charles (1992b) *The Ethics of Authenticity*, Cambridge, MA: Harvard University Press.

Taylor, Charles (2007) *A Secular Age*, Cambridge, MA: Belknap Press.

Taylor, Yvette, Hines, Sally and Casey, Mark (eds) (2010) *Theorizing Intersectionality and Sexuality*, London: Palgrave.

Thompson, Simon (2006) *The Political Theory of Recognition: A Critical Introduction*, Cambridge: Polity Press.

Thomson, Rachel (2004) '"An Adult Thing"? Young People's Perspectives on the Heterosexual Age of Consent', *Sexualities* 7 (2), May, 133–49.

Thomson, Rachel, Bell, Robert, Holland, Janet, Henderson, Sheila, McGrellis, Sheena and Sharpe, Sue (2002) 'Critical Moments: Choice, Chance and Opportunities in Young People's Narratives of Transit', *Sociology* 36 (2), 235–54.

Tiefer, Leonore (2006) 'The Viagra Phenomenon', *Sexualities* 9 (3), July, 273–94.

Tully, James (2001) 'Introduction' in Gagnon, Alain and Tully, James (eds) *Multinational Democracies*, Cambridge: Cambridge University Press.

Turner, Bryan S. (2009) 'Review of Holton, Robert J. (2009) *Cosmopolitanisms: New Thinking and Directions*, Basingstoke: Palgrave Macmillan', *Sociological Review* 57 (4), November, 750–2.

Tyler, M. (2004) 'Managing Between the Sheets: Lifestyle Magazines and the Management of Sexuality in Everyday Life', *Sexualities* 7 (1), February, 81–106.

Valentine, Gill (2002) 'Queer Bodies and the Production of Space', in Richardson, Diane and Seidman, Steven (eds) *Handbook of Lesbian and Gay Studies*, London: Sage, 145–60.

Vance, Carol S. (ed.) (1984) *Pleasure and Danger: Exploring Female Sexuality*, London: Routledge and Kegan Paul.

Vance, Carol S. (1989) 'Social Construction Theory: Problems in the History of Sexuality', in Altman, Dennis, Vance, Carol, Vicinus, Martha, Weeks, Jeffrey and others, *Homosexuality, Which Homosexuality?* London: GMP Publishers, 13–34.

Vernon, Mark (2005) *The Philosophy of Friendship*, Basingstoke: Palgrave Macmillan.

Waaldijk, K. (2001) 'Small Change: How the Road to Same-Sex Marriage Got Paved in the Netherlands', in Wintermute, R. and Andenaes, M. (eds) *Legal Recognition of Same-Sex Partnerships: A Study of National, European and International Law*, Oxford: Hart Publishing, 437–64.

Waites, Matthew (2005) *The Age of Consent: Young People, Sexuality and Citizenship*, Basingstoke: Palgrave Macmillan.

Walkowitz, Judith R. (1980) *Prostitution and Victorian Society: Women, Class and the State*, Cambridge: Cambridge University Press.

Warner, Michael (ed.) (1993) *Fear of A Queer Planet: Queer Politics and Social Theory*, Minneapolis: University of Minnesota Press.

Warner, Michael (1999) *The Trouble with Normal: Sex, Politics and the Ethics of Queer Life*, New York: The Free Press.

Watney, Simon (1987) *Policing Desire: Pornography, AIDS and the Media*, Minneapolis: University of Minnesota Press.

Weeks, Jeffrey (1977) *Coming Out: Homosexual Politics in Britain from the Nineteenth Century to the Present*, London: Quartet Books.

Weeks, Jeffrey (1981) *Sex, Politics and Society: The Regulation of Sexuality since 1800*, Harlow: Longman.

Weeks, Jeffrey (1985) *Sexuality and its Discontents: Meanings, Myths and Modern Sexualities*, London: Routledge and Kegan Paul.

Weeks, Jeffrey (1991) *Against Nature: Essays on History, Sexuality and Identity*, London: Rivers Oram Press.

Weeks, Jeffrey (1995) *Invented Moralities: Sexual Values in an Age of Uncertainty*, Cambridge: Polity Press.

Weeks, Jeffrey (1998) 'The Sexual Citizen', *Theory, Culture and Society* 15 (3–4), 35–52.

Weeks, Jeffrey (2000a) *Making Sexual History*, Cambridge: Polity Press.

Weeks, Jeffrey (2000b) 'The Idea of a Sexual Community', in Weeks, Jeffrey, *Making Sexual History*, Cambridge: Polity Press.

Weeks, Jeffrey (2007) *The World We Have Won: The Remaking of Erotic and Intimate Life*, London: Routledge.

Weeks, Jeffrey (2009a) *Sexuality*, third edition (first published 1986), London: Routledge.

Weeks, Jeffrey (2009b) 'An "Untenable Illusion"? The Problematic Marriage of Freud and Marx', *Sitegeist: A Journal of Psychoanalysis and Philosophy*, 3, Autumn, 9–26.

Weeks, Jeffrey, Heaphy, Brian and Donovan, Catherine (2001) *Same Sex Intimacies: Families of Choice and other Life Experiments*, London: Routledge.

Weeks, Jeffrey, Holland, Janet and Waites, Matthew (eds) (2003) *Sexualities and Society: A Reader*, Cambridge: Polity Press.

Weinberg, George (1972) *Society and the Healthy Homosexual*, New York: St Martin's Press.

Weinberg, Thomas and Levi Kamel, G. W. (1983) *S and M: Studies in Sado Masochism*, Buffalo, NY: Prometheus Books.

Weininger, Otto (1906) *Sex and Character*, London: William Heinemann.

Weston, Kath (1991) *Families We Choose: Lesbians, Gays, Kinship*, New York: Columbia University Press.

White, Edmund (1988) *The Beautiful Room is Empty*, London: Picador.

Williams, Bernard (1979) *Report of the Committee on Obscenity and Film Censorship*, Cmnd 7772, London: HMSO.

Williams, Fiona (2004) *Rethinking Families*, London: Calouste Gulbenkian Foundation.

Williams, Raymond (1976) *Keywords: A Vocabulary of Culture and Society*, London: Fontana.

Wilson, Glenn and Rahman, Qazi (2005) *Born Gay: The Psychobiology of Sex Orientation*, London: Peter Owen.

Wintermute, R. and Andenaes, M. (eds) (2001) *Legal Recognition of Same-Sex Partnerships: A Study of National, European and International Law*, Oxford: Hart Publishing.

Wolfenden, John (1957) *Report of the Committee on Homosexual Offences and Prostitution*, Cmnd 247, London: HMSO.

Wouters, Cas (2004) *Sex and Manners: Female Emancipation in the West, 1890–2000*, London: Sage.

Wouters, Cas (2007) *Informalization: Manners and Emotions since 1890*, Los Angeles, CA: Sage.

Wright, Elizabeth (ed.) (1992) *Feminism and Psychoanalysis: A Critical Dictionary*, Oxford: Blackwell.

Yep, G. A., Lovanas, K. E. and Pagonis, A. V. (2002) 'The Case of "Riding Bareback": Sexual Practices and the Paradoxes of Identity in the Era of AIDS', *Journal of Homosexuality* 42 (4), 1–14.

Yuval-Davis, Nural (2005) 'Racism, Cosmopolitanism and Contemporary Politics of Belonging', *Soundings: A Journal of Politics and Culture* 30, Summer, 166–78.

INDEX

Page ranges shown in **bold** relate to main sections of the text

CPSIA information can be obtained at www.ICGtesting.com
Printed in the USA
LVOW04s1928280715

448010LV00011B/88/P

9 780415 375733